G. E. LESSING'S THEOLOGY:
A REINTERPRETATION

LEONARD P. WESSEL
University of Colorado

G. E. Lessing's Theology
A Reinterpretation

*A Study in the Problematic Nature
of the Englightenment*

MOUTON · THE HAGUE · PARIS

ISBN: 90 279 7801 8
© 1977, Mouton & Co., The Hague
Printed in the Netherlands

To Mrs. Nancy Esther Wessell
1898–1970

and

Professor Ernst Loeb
who first introduced
me to Lessing

Acknowledgments

I wish to thank the following groups for their support which made the research, typing and printing of this investigation possible:

University of California at Riverside Intramural Grants (Research)
National Endowment for the Humanities Summer Stipend (Research 1970)
Council on Research and Creative Work of the University of Colorado, Boulder (Research)
Committee on University Scholarly Publications of the University of Colorado, Boulder (Publication Subvention)

Table of contents

Lessing's '*ars dialectice cogitandi*'; D. Excursus: Lessing's concept of God.

A. Primary sources; B. General secondary sources; C. Secondary sources on Lessing.

List of abbreviations

Throughout the text of this book all citations will be taken from Gotthold Ephraim Lessing, *Gesammelte Werke,* ed. by Paul Rilla (Berlin: Aufbau Verlag, 1954—1958) in ten volumes and all references will be made in the text according to volume and page number. Abbreviations will be made in the following matter:

A.F.	Abhandlungen über die Fabel (1754, IV, 5—86)
A.—G.	Anti-Goeze. D.i. Notgedrungener Beiträge zu den 'Freiwilligen Beiträgen' des Hrn. Past. Goeze (VIII, 202—406)*
A.W.E.D.	Des Andreas Wissowatius Einwürfe wider die Dreieinigkeit (VII, 489—535)*
Axiomata	Axiomata, wenn es deren in dergleichen Dingen gibt. Wider den Herrn Pastor Goeze, in Hamburg (VIII, 164—200)* .
B.	Bibliolatrie (VIII, 482—489)*
Bemerkungen	Bemerkungen über Burkes 'Philosophische Untersuchungen über den Ursprung unserer Begriffe vom Erhabenen und Schönen' (1758 or 1759) (VII, 273—279)*
C.V.	Das Christentum der Vernunft (VII, 197—200)*
D.	Eine Duplik (VIII, 24—107)*
D.S.M.	Daß mehr als fünf Sinne für den Menschen sein können (VII, 576—579)*
E.F.	Ernst und Falk (Gespräche für Freimäurer, VIII, 547—589)*

* in *Philosophische und theologische Schriften*

Erziehung	Die Erziehung des Menschengeschlechts (VIII, 590–615)*
F.	D. Faust (Dramenfragmente, II, 553–556)
G.H.	Gegensätze des Herausgebers (VII, 812–854)*
G.M.	Gegen Friedrich Wilhelm Mascho (VIII, 143–145)*
G.ü.H.	Gedanken über die Herrnhuter (VII, 185–196)*
H.D.	Hamburgische Dramaturgie (VI, 5–534)*
J.G.L.	F. H. Jacobi über seine Gespräche mit Lessing (VIII, 616–634)*
Laokoon	Laokoon über die Grenzen der Malerei und Poesie. Anhang zum Laokoon (V, 7–346)
L.v.E.S.	Leibniz von den ewigen Strafen (VII, 454–488)*
M.P.U.	Ein Mehreres aus den Papieren des Ungenannten, die Offenbarung betreffend. 1. Fragment: Von Verschreiung der Vernunft auf den Kanzeln (by Reimarus, published by Lessing) (VII, 673–685)*
Nathan	Nathan der Weise (II, 319–482)
R.	Die Religion (1749) Delete (I, 201–209)
R.C.	Die Religion Christi (VIII, 538–539)*
R.H.C.	Rettung des Hier. Cardenus (VII, 201–228)*
S.E.	Selbstbetrachtungen und Einfälle. Unterbrechung im theologischen Kamp (VIII, 407–414)*
T.J.	Das Testament Johannis (VIII, 17–23)*
Ü.B.G.K.	Über den Beweis des Geistes und der Kraft (VIII, 9–16)*
Ü.E.G.R.	Über die Entstehung der geoffenbarten Religion (VII, 280–281)*
Ü.W.D.G.	Über die Wirklichkeit der Dinge außer Gott (VII, 305–306)*
W.R.	Womit sich die geoffenbarte Religion am meisten weiß, macht mir sie gerade am verdächtigsten (VII, 574–575)*

* in *Philosophische und theologische Schriften*

1. Methodology: Lessing as a problem

As paradoxical as it might seem, the starting point and inspiration for this investigation of Gotthold Ephraim Lessing is the reality of 'contradiction'. Despite Lessing's fame as an 'enlightenment' thinker or as a writer with a clear and precise if not logical style, twentieth-century interpreters of Lessing are far from being in accord as to what constitutes the essence of Lessing's *Weltanschauung* or, indeed, whether he had one. This disagreement, if not often an outright contradiction of opinion, is particularly evident in the various attempts to interpret Lessing as a religious thinker.[1] Did he or did he not develop a theological 'system'? If he did, is his 'system' a Christian, deistic, monistic, or Leibnizian one? Whereas there are various particular and textual reasons that cause investigators of Lessing's theological speculations to contradict each other, there is, nevertheless, in my judgment, a more basic and universal reason why Lessing's works have generated (and will continue to generate) opposing interpretations. The current quandry if not crisis concerning Lessing's theology has its roots in the general nature of Lessing's thinking *per se,* in his ars *cogitandi.* In other words, although Lessing was active in various fields of intellectual and artistic pursuits and although he could become mired in the most minute and technical problems in his historical, aesthetic, and theological investigations, there exists, nevertheless, a unifying *telos* that threads its way through the labyrinth of Lessing's writings and weaves them into a consistent tapestry. Lessing was interested in truth — in the Truth — and what such truth has to reveal to man and how man is to appropriate such truth. Lessing's ultimate interest in theology, aesthetics, and play writing was inspired by his desire to discover and communicate truth. In my judgment, the contradictions concerning Lessing's theological speculations have their origin in each investigator's explicit or even implicit interpretation of Lessing's notion of truth and of man's means for discovering it. In other words, the divergent opinions in the secondary literature on the meaning of Lessing's theology ultimately are grounded in a disagreement concerning the basic principles of Lessing's *ars cogitandi*. Investigators disagree concerning what Lessing thought — the *cogitatum* — because they disagree *first of all* concerning the dynamic nature of his thinking conceived as a cognitive movement in pursuit of truth.

Furthermore, this disagreement is not something accidental or externally related to the very nature of Lessing's ratiocinative processes. Lessing's thinking (or his thought activity) exhibits various characteristics that will inevitably cause a divergence of opinion until a heuristic key for the interpretation of them is discovered (which, indeed, will be the central task of this chapter). Lessing's creative activity, particularly in theoretical matters, is first of all *fragmentary*. This is not to say that he could not or did not write unified and developed essays. His *Erziehung des Menschengeschlechts* is just such an example. However, the work is only one hundred paragraphs long and cannot be considered an *extensively* developed treatise. Indeed, most of Lessing's theological speculations are characterized by comparable brevity. When Lessing wrote a relatively long work such as his *Laokoon* (which despite its book length remained only a fragment) or the *Hamburgische Dramaturgie* Lessing's procedure exhibited anything but systematic arrangement. Indeed, concerning the basic ideas incorporated into his *Laokoon* — Lessing writes: 'Sie sind zufälliger Weise entstanden, und mehr nach der Folge meiner Lektüre, als durch die methodische Entwicklung allgemeiner Grundsätze angewachsen. Es sind also mehr unordentliche Collectanea zu einem Buch, als ein Buch' (V, 11). The general nature of Lessing's theological as well as aesthetic speculations may also justifiably be designated as 'unordentliche Collectanea zu einem Buch'.

Moreover, Lessing uses the fragmentary and semi-impromptu style of his writings to justify the existence of the second main feature of his speculations, namely his tendency to *contradict* himself. For instance, in the *Hamburgische Dramaturgie* Lessing cautions his readers against any attempt unduly to systematize him. 'Ich erinnere hier meine Leser, daß diese Blätter nichts weniger als ein dramatisches System enthalten sollen. Ich bin also nicht verpflichtet, alle die Schwierigkeiten aufzulösen, die ich mache. Meine Gedanken mögen immer sich weniger zu verbinden, ja wohl gar sich zu widersprechen scheinen: wenn es denn nur Gedanken sind, bei welchen sie Stoff finden, selbst zu denken. Hier will ich nichts als *Fermenta cognitionis* ausstreuen' (VI, 479, § 95). One such spectacular contradiction in the realm of theology is Lessing's contention in *Die Erziehung des Menschengeschlechts* that divine revelation gives man nothing, 'worauf die menschliche Vernunft, sich selbst überlassen, nicht auch kommen würde: sondern sie gab und gibt ihm die wichtigsten dieser Dingen nur früher' (VIII, 591, § 4) and his counter-contention that religion (viz. revelation) brings man to important ideas about man and God and their interrelationship, 'auf welche die menschliche Vernunft von selbst nimmermehr gekommen wäre' (VIII, 611, § 77). Thus Lessing seems to be asserting that revelation gives man no truth he could not obtain for himself with his unaided reason and yet his reason unaided by revelation could never obtain such truth.[2]

Therefore, it is not logical consistency, but rather the generative and suggestive possibilities of an idea that interested Lessing. The purpose of an idea is to inspire further reflection. This, indeed, constitutes the third characteristic of Lessing's thinking. His theoretical speculations remained *fermenta cognitionis,* provisional hypotheses, suggestive ideas, and new approaches. He never developed a unitary system, at least in the sense that he never systematically enumerated and explicated a comprehensive set of propositions and then structurally related them together as the more specific to the more general. On the contrary, the positive content of Lessing's theoretical efforts is to be found in the ability of his speculations to suggest new ideas that might possibly lead to some future systemic comprehension of a specific subject matter.[3]

However, difficulties arise concerning the nature of the positive content of Lessing's *fermenta cognitionis.* It is at this point that investigators begin to deviate from one another. The specific conclusions an investigator derives concerning Lessing's thought depends upon his analysis of the constitutive and constructive principles of Lessing's *fermenta cognitionis,* of his *ars cogitandi,* or his concept of truth. Whatever conclusions an investigator makes, he will have to, based upon such conclusions, be able to explain and make sense of the contradictory and fragmentary nature of Lessing's thinking. Indeed, ideally he should be able to explain why Lessing's thinking is fragmentary, contradictory, and incomplete in the first place (which is something few investigators have adequately attempted). In the ensuing analysis of Lessing, I shall seek to found my position squarely upon the nature of the critical contradictions in Lessing's *ars cogitandi*.

In the remainder of this chapter I shall explicate the basic heuristic principle and assumption underlying my approach to and interpretation of Lessing. Because my interpretation of Lessing will seek to reconcile (in the German sense of the term *aufheben*) the various contradictory positions found in the secondary literature on Lessing as well as in Lessing's own writings, I will first present an exposition of the essence of previous twentieth-century scholarship on Lessing. I shall not attempt to be comprehensive as much as to outline the contradictory poles around which much twentieth-century research hovers. In particular, emphasis will be placed upon the respective interpretations of Lessing's concept of truth and the relationship of truth to theology. The reason for this is that Lessing nowhere comprehensively dealt with the problem of truth *qua* a purely epistemological problem. Indeed, even fragmentarily he only rarely focused his attention upon the nature and problem of truth *qua* the formal characteristic of truth. For the most part, Lessing was interested in the *truth* 'that saves man's soul', i.e., that mediates to man a sense of meaningfulness, of integration into some absolute order of reality. Now for Lessing such knowledge was knowledge about God and man's relationship to him. Therefore, Lessing's basic notion of truth as that which man's thinking should pursue is intimately related to his theological speculations. Indeed, the best way to approach Lessing's notion of truth, is *via* his theological speculations. Hence an investigator's analysis of Lessing's theology contains (implicitly at least) as a logical prerequisite his analysis of Lessing's *ars cogitandi*.

A. INTERPRETATIONS OF LESSING'S THEOLOGY

The central problem around which most twentieth-century interpretations of Lessing hover is whether or not Lessing, as a thinker, was a 'Systematiker' or a mere 'Gelegenheitsdenker'. In other words, is there a central unity in Lessing's thought and creativity that structures and informs his works, including his fragments? In general most interpreters have conceived Lessing as a relatively consistent if not systematic thinker. Hans Leisegang has, perhaps, stated this thesis most forceably and purely: 'Lessing hat also wirklich ein in sich geschlossenes und in allen Einzelheiten ausgedachtes "System", ein System, das schon früh fertig war . . .'[4] Leisegang is conscious, of course, of the fragmentary nature of Lessing's writings on religion. Nevertheless, Leisegang contends 'daß sich seine fragmentarischen Äußerungen als zerstreute Bruchstücke eines Sinngebildes erweisen, das sich aus ihnen erschließen läßt und das dann richtig erschlossen ist, wenn die Struktur der Teile in das Gefüge des Ganzen sinnvoll hineinpaßt'.[5] In seeking to evaluate Leisegang's contention one must be aware of the type of unity being referred to. Leisegang does not contend that Lessing created a fully developed theology such as that of St. Thomas Aquinas or a fully detailed philosophy such as that of Hegel. Given the fact (admitted by Leisegang) that Lessing's works are often fragmentary such a contention would constitute an obvious contradiction. On the contrary, the unity of Lessing's thought is not located on the level of 'systematic' theology or philosophy, rather on the level of a *Weltanschauung*. According to Leisegang, 'jede echte Welt-Anschauung entspringt aus einer besonderen Art, das Geschaute denkend zu bewältigen, aus einer besonderen Denkform und auch — und dies oft zuerst — aus einer besonderen Art der Stellungnahme zu allem, was in den Blickpunkt des persönlichen Interesses gerät oder auch nur das Interessengebiet berührt, aus einer besonderen Art des Wertens und Bewertens der Dinge, der Personen, der Ereignisse, der Gedanken'.[6] In Leisegang's opinion the 'form of thought' or 'way of looking at the world' is an *a priori* structure that a thinker brings with him as he attempts to interpret the data of his experience. Most importantly, this concept of *Weltanschauung* provides an investigator with the necessary 'regulative' (to borrow a term from Kant) principle for determining whether or not a thinker has a consistent and hence 'systematic' unity to his thought. To determine the degree of unity of an individual's thought, an investigator must ask himself: 'Hängen diese Formen miteinander zusammen? Zeigen sie alle eine einheitliche Struktur? Läßt sich in ihnen eine Grundform erkennen von bestimmten Gepräge, so daß alle anderen nur als Abwandlungen, Umbildungen, Ausgestaltungen dieser Grundform betrachtet werden können?'[7] If the answer to such questions is yes, then Lessing (or any other thinker) has a 'systematic' worldview. If the answer is no, then a thinker exhibits inconsistency and hence lacks a systematic core to his speculations.

Although I have some reservations concerning Leisegang's concept of a *Weltanschauung* (to be explicated presently), it will be accepted at this point as an adequate formulation of the formal problem of what criteria would have to be met by an interpreter if he is to interpret Lessing as a 'Systematiker'. In other words, it at least grants an investigator a preliminary standpoint from which he can formulate questions enabling him to determine the alleged unity or non-unity of Lessing's thought. At any rate, even the most divergent interpreters of Lessing have sought to establish some sort of unity in Lessing's thought by, implicitly at least, using Leisegang's concept of a *Weltanschauung*. For instance, Benno von Wiese sets it as his task, 'zu zeigen, wie in den verschiedenen Bereichen der Lessingschen Lebensleistung Dichtung, Ästhetik, Philosophie und Theologie eine einmalige Lebensanschauung sichtbar wird. . . . Es geht nicht an, Lessing den Philosophen von Lessing dem Ästhetiker und Lessing dem Dichter zu sondern. So erhalten wir immer nur ein konstruiertes Teilphänomen, das behauptet, das Ganze zu sein. Lessings Lebensanschauung ist überall gegenwärtig.'[8] Otto Mann, whose interpretation of Lessing is the contradiction of von Wiese's, maintains that man *per se* experiences a need to fulfill his being *(Sein)* and that this need 'gründet in des Menschen Teilhabe an einer höheren Seinsordnung, macht ihn zum Menschen. Das Leben ist der Güter höchstes nicht.'[9] Lessing too, according to Mann, felt this need which he tried to realize in the areas of religion, philosophy and art. 'Lessings überzeitliche Bedeutung gründet in der Echtheit, der Dringlichkeit, der Tiefe, mit der er um das Sein bekümmert ist. Nach Lage und Anlage erfüllt er dieses Bedürfnis in dessen drei Grundbereichen, der Religion, der Philosophie, der Kunst.[10] The difference between interpreters such as von Wiese and Mann is grounded not in the belief that Lessing had or did not have a unitary 'Art des Schauens, des Blickes in die Welt', but rather in what they consider to be the principle of this unity.

However, the various attempts to systematize Lessing are eventually confronted with the fragmentary, provisional, and contradictory nature of Lessing's writings, particularly in the area of theology. The result is that investigators in the twentieth century can roughly be divided into four groups depending upon how they handle the problem of these contradictions.

Until the early 1930s interpreters located the principle of unity in Lessing's *Weltanschauung* in the rationalistic or Enlightenment aspects of his thought. As von Wiese wrote: 'Lessings Lebensleistung steht . . . durchaus in der Welt der europäischen Aufklärung.'[11] Despite differences of opinion the general consensus was that Lessing conceived of reason as the only real avenue leading to truth. Truth about reality, about the objective universe in which man finds himself, about man himself, can only be *revealed* in the last analysis by reason. Rationality as the key to reality has allegedly for Lessing a subjective and an objective meaning. Subjectively, the real as the rational means that man or the essence of man's being is to *be* rational. For man to be fulfilled, his essence must be respected, i.e., before man can let himself become a part of or surrender himself to a whole greater than himself, such a totality must first legitimize itself before man's (rational) eyes, before man's very essence. This demand that man requires of any aspirant totality constitutes a manifestation of man's autonomy. Man cannot let himself be determined from without, from an *alien* source, i.e., heteronomously. Only what man can control is what man can commit himself to and it is reason — man's very subjectivity — that grants man the necessary intellectual control over reality. Objectively, the real as the rational means that truth about objective reality, particularly ultimate truth, i.e., truth about God can be no more than what reason will allow it to be. Thus God for Lessing, conceived either in a deistic or monistic manner, becomes no more than incarnated rationality. For example, von Wiese writes: '[Lessing] zerstört die allem Christentume innewohnende Paradoxie, ewiger Logos zu sein und zugleich diesen Logos durch Christi Geburt an die Zeit zu binden. Er löst den christlichen Logos aus seinem Geschichte gewordenen Mysterium und macht ihn zum vernünftigen Logos, der in der Philosophie seine eigentliche Heimat hat, nicht aber in der Erzählung vom Gottessohne Christus. Diese Auflösung des geschichtlich geoffenbarten Logos zugunsten des vernünftigen Logos vollziehet sich in der Auseinandersetzung zwischen Vernunft und Geschichte.'[12]

All truth about God, precisely because it is truth about eternal universality, is totally independent of history for its justification. Once again von Wiese: 'Die Wahrheit gehört der Sphäre reiner Innerlichkeit an. Um sie in ihrem eigengesetzlichen Wesen zu erfassen, muß man aus aller Geschichte heraustreten. Damit aber geht die Wahrheit aller Geschichte voraus. Sie läßt sich niemals aus Geschichte ableiten oder begründen. Die Wahrheit ist etwas in sich selbst, unabhängig davon, ob sie geschehen oder aufgeschrieben ist. . . . Die Idee des Wahren . . . gehört dem übergeschichtlichen Bereich der menschlichen Vernunft an. Sie ist die sinngebende Norm dieser Vernunft, die zwar stets sich am Geschichtlichen erfüllt, aber niemals durch das Geschichtliche legitimiert wird.'[13] Because history cannot be the foundation for truth, a religion of history such as Christianity cannot be accepted by Lessing. The idea of a real contingent, transcendent, and personal entrance into history by a Lord of History in the form of a supernatural revelation becomes an obvious impossibility. History *qua* historicity cannot be the mediator of the divine, of ultimate truth, of universal reason, although it is the locus, so-to-speak, where cosmic or divine (both terms are essentially equivalent) rationality actualizes itself as man comes to full consciousness of his realized rational autonomy. And such a realization is nothing other than the moral perfection of man.

This means that, when Lessing was confronted with the phenomenon of Christianity and its historically founded faith, his appropriation of it could only lead to an 'Umdeutung christlicher Gehalte in ein natürliches Weltbild der sittlichen Vernunft'.[14] 'Das Christentum ist für Lessing nur Grundlage für die Ausbildung einer philosophischen Weltanschauung. Es ist das souveräne Prinzip des Denkers, daß das Verhältnis des Menschen zur Welt bestimmt; nicht aber das im Glauben erfahrene Heil, wie es der religiösen Existenz begegnet.'[15] However much Lessing might have exhibited a positive attitude towards Christianity, however much he might have tried to save Christian doctrines, they could ultimately be for him no more than 'Vernunftwahrheiten in antiquierter Form'.[16] Therefore, the development of man's religious consciousness throughout history is not due, according to Lessing, to any transcendent activity by a God from beyond history, but to the immanent and naturalistic development of divine and/or human reason in history. Arthur von Arx makes the same essential assertion: 'So wird also die Religionsgeschichte [von Lessing] als ein allmählich fortschreitender und rein immanenter Entwicklungsprozeß betrachtet, wobei jedoch diese Entwicklung nicht etwa eine substantielle Wesensveränderung, sondern nur eine modifizierende Wandlung von etwas Ursprünglichem und Konstantem bedeutet.'[17] Similarly Ferdinand Joseph Schneider avers: 'Lessing . . . denkt sich also den intellektuellen und ethischen Aufstieg der Menschheit, wie er sich in deren geschichtlichem Werdegang darstellt, als eine spontane Entwicklung der dem menschlichen Geschlecht innewohnenden *religiösen Vernunft*. Einen außerweltlichen Gott, der irgendwie in diesen religiösen Entwicklungsgang bestimmend eingreife, gibt es für Lessing . . . nicht mehr. Mit Recht hat man darauf hingewiesen, daß solche Gedankengänge bereits vor unseren Augen die Ideenwelt Hegels auftauchen lassen.'[18] The overwhelming thrust of Lessing's *Weltanschauung* is thus seen to entail a rejection of all transcendence, of all 'Jenseitigkeit' of traditional Christianity and, instead, to entail an affirmation of an 'essentially naturalistic and immanental point of view'.[19] Thus it is not surprising that many such interpreters view Lessing as indifferent to the reality of divine being. 'But does it make any difference to [Lessing's] interpretation of man's [religious development] whether we say "God" or whether we say "human understanding" in the significant places, and whether we interpret revelation as being education by an educator or self-education or even more simply development, and thus allow the Lord of history to coincide with history itself, or alternatively with its subject, with the humanity educating, or alternatively, developing itself? It is difficult to say in what respect there is meant to be a distinction, and perhaps it is only a part of Lessing's freemason's wisdom that he did not go so far as to say openly that it really does not make any difference.'[20] '[O] ne wonders how anyone can find a real God in Lessing's picture [of the development of Christianity]. The main movement of Lessing's argument indicates that basically he is not talking about God and Reality but about the advance of rational morality. If the *Erziehung* is to show us man moving toward Reality, where is this Reality at the end of the essay? It is simply not there. The end is man's moral autonomy. A most eighteenth-century and unreligious conclusion.'[21]

When faced with the apparent contradictions between Lessing's approval and disapproval, acceptance and rejection of Christianity, investigators have followed F. Loofs' lead and distinguished between Lessing's esoteric and exoteric ways of expressing himself.[22] Lessing's esoteric thinking is allegedly derived from his philosophical and rationalistic concept of truth. However, for one reason or another (interpreters differ) Lessing was inclined to express himself in traditional Christian terminology, i.e., to express his ideas exoterically. This means that the contradictions in Lessing's theology are only apparent since his true beliefs lie in his esoteric statements whereas his apparently orthodox statements constitute only an exoteric shell or can be dismissed as not revealing Lessing's 'true' position. However, Lessing does not just treat exoteric expressions of religious truth as mere linguistic 'Spielerei'. Not only does theology (Lessing's included) make formal use of exoteric expressions, but must itself exist for a time materially as exoteric thinking. Exoteric thinking has as its object the same rational content as esoteric (i.e., pure rational) thinking. It differs only in that it appropriates such rational truth in a vague, unclear, and often emotional manner. This manner constitutes the essence of revelation. As von Wiese contends: 'Die Offenbarung steht also [bei Lessing] nicht wie bei Reimarus im supra-

naturalen Gegensatz zur vernünftigen Erkenntnis, sondern die Offenbarung unterstützt nur die Wahrheit der natürlichen Religion, das
heißt die vernünftige Wahrheit "mit einer anderen Art von Beweisen" '.[23] Exoteric and esoteric thinking exist in a developmental
relationship to each other. The *telos* of exoteric thinking is to
metamorphize eventually into esoteric thinking. Such a developmental process is nothing else but 'die Erziehung des Menschengeschlechts'.[24]

Since the late 1920s a different interpretation of Lessing has
developed. In an important article on Lessing Franz Koch sought to
focus attention upon the 'irrationalistic' aspects of Lessing's personality and thought.[25] Koch did not deny that Lessing was essentially an *Aufklärer,* he claimed only that there are certain tendencies in
Lessing's thinking that foreshadowed and later developed into the
'irrationalistic' binge that was the *Sturm und Drang* period. The
dominant principle of the *Aufklärung* was, of course, rationality. In
seeking to realize the rational, the *Aufklärer* pursued the universal,
the general, the supra-individual. Therefore, he sought to ascertain
the laws (e.g., of drama) that are to function as the normative rules
to which the human personality had to conform. Besides existing in
such a spiritual milieu, Lessing also places tremendous importance
upon the uniqueness of the individual, upon that aspect of the
human personality that seems to exist beyond the confines of lawful
and normative universality. Lessing's primary imperative, according
to Koch, is, as Lessing stated in *Das Christentum der Vernunft:*
'Handle deinen individualischen Vollkommenheiten gemäß.' This
commitment to and interest in individuality shows itself in the
various areas of Lessing's creative speculations. For instance, Lessing
emphasized strongly the importance of feeling and emotions. In
religion this is seen in his insistence that 'true' Christianity is a matter
of the 'heart'. In his dramaturgy Lessing evaluates more highly the
spontaneous, intellectually non-determinable creativity of the
genius over the consciously controlled 'making' by an artist in
accordance with *a priorily* determined rules. In his theory of tragedy,
Lessing places *Mitleid* over moral improvement as the primary effect
to be produced in tragedy. Concretely in his actual dramatic produc-
tions, Lessing achieved a degree of individualization and individuality
of characterization heretofore unobtained by other enlightenment
dramatists. In short, Lessing was highly interested in preparing the
way for 'die sich fühlende Menschheit'.

Following Koch's lead Friedrich J. Schmitz has sought to trace

Lessing's ever-increasing commitment to individualism, feeling, and subjectivity as manifested in his aesthetic, theological, and dramatic endeavors.[26] Schmitz contends: '[Lessing] bezeugt schon in seinen Erstlingswerken . . . eine wachsende Erkenntnis der Wichtigkeit seiner eigenen Individualität, deren Eigenart sich nicht durch Gesetz und Norm erfassen läßt. Diese Individualität spielt er aus gegen die ethischen und ästhetischen Gesetze der Wolff-Gottschedschen Schulphilosophie . . . Schon in seiner frühesten theologisch-philoso-phischen Abhandlung . . . dringt er zu einer Weltanschauung vor, die dem befreiten Individuum und der als notwendig erkannten und anerkannten Mannigfaltigkeit des tatsächlichen Lebens einen Sinn geben konnte, die dem Individuum als etwas Endlichem, Einmaligem, nie Wiederkehrendem einen Platz in dem ewig sich entwickelnden Weltganzen sicherte.'[27] Similarly Fritz Brüggemann, subsuming the concept of a self-feeling personality standing beyond norms of universality under the notion of 'subjectivism', sought to trace a gradual development in Lessing's thought as he sought to penetrate the shell of enlightenment objectivism to a position that would allow free scope to man's ever more problematic subjectivity.[28]

Although the theses of interpreters such as Koch, Schmitz, and Brüggemann represent a significant departure from the more 'usual' rationalistic interpretation of Lessing, none of them seriously challenged the contention that Lessing's concept of religion was immanental. For example, Koch flatly states 'daß [Lessing] die trans-zendente in eine immanente Offenbarung verwandelt'.[29] However, such interpreters have cleared the way for a more radical change in the interpretation of Lessing's 'religiöses Bewußtsein'. Insofar as it is claimed that, according to Lessing, meaningful contact with reality is had in a type of experience (e.g., feeling) that exists beyond the boundaries of universality, law, or reason, it must also be maintained that such contact in some way 'transcends' the naturalistic and intellectual nature of rational reality. If the concept of *immanence* is equated with rationality, then the actuality of the irrational or the 'beyond-the-rational' can be equated with some sort of *trans-cendence*. Questions concerning the nature, origin, and appropriation of such 'transcendent' reality can certainly be raised. In particular, Lessing's positive remarks and evaluations of Christianity may be more than a mere 'exoteric' shell concealing an 'esoteric' rationalism. In short, Lessing's 'exoteric' Christianity may well contain something more than formal significance, namely an inner substance. At any rate, this appears to be the epistemological background to three notable attempts to take Lessing's Christianity seriously, indeed, to 'save' Lessing (in Lessing's sense of the word 'Rettung') from the stain of being a 'Durchschnittsaufklärer' and show him to be perhaps even 'ein guter Lutheraner'.

In 1936 Helmut Thielicke, himself a theologian, published a study of Lessing's philosophy of religion which was revolutionary in its interpretation and which has not yet, in my judgment, been adequately dealt with.[30] Thielicke critically reviews the textual evidence that, in his opinion, indicates both an immanental and transcendent conception of revelation on Lessing's part and contends that both sets of evidence should be taken seriously. Thus the investigator, according to Thielicke, must squarely face the contradictory nature of Lessing's utterance on revelation. Thielicke also reviews previous attempts to come to terms with such contradictions and in particular subjects Loofs' thesis to a subtle and destructive analysis. In Thielicke's opinion, Loofs' attempt to mediate by means of the notion of development between Lessing's exoteric (formal) utterances and esoteric (substantial) meaning fails completely as soon as the fact is recognized that Lessing views himself as still within the historical development, not at the end of it. If Lessing thought himself already to be *fully* 'educated', then he could plausibly show how exoteric Christianity is to be reduced to esoteric rationalism. But Lessing is self-admittedly not so enlightened. Not only the form of Lessing's theological thinking, but its substantial content must hence be fully mired in exoteric thinking. Furthermore, Loofs, precisely because Lessing had not fully been educated, is not able to say much about the content of Lessing's esoteric rationale. Therefore, Loofs is ultimately left with the very same contradictoriness he had set out to explain.[31]

Thielicke goes on to elucidate the nature or style of Lessing's thinking to comprehend what Lessing theologically meant. Lessing seeks to approach truth, claims Thielicke, (1) within the terms and framework of the thinking of others. Lessing does not usually baldly state his ideas, but rather first seeks to immerse himself in the thought of others. Thielicke speaks of Lessing's 'Angleichung an den Gegner'. Such an 'Angleichung' is the source of much of the apparent contradictoriness and obtrusiveness of Lessing's theological speculations. (2) However, Lessing takes cognizance of the opinions of others, not because he wants to mold himself to these opinions as much as he seeks to find ideas in the theories of others that he can adapt to his own 'system.' (3) Based on the fact previously established that Lessing's thinking is that of a person mired in the history of a developing and hence not yet rationally self-cognizant mankind, Thielicke maintains that Lessing's 'system' does not consist of stripping off an exoteric shell in order to bring to light an esoteric kernel. 'Die exoterische Denkweise darf nicht nur als methodische *Außenseite* des Lessingschen "Systems" angesehen werden, sondern gehört in das "System" *selbst* hinein, so daß eine Untersuchung nie hinter die grundsätzliche Verwobenheit von exoterischer und esoterischer Denkweise zurückgehen darf in der Absicht, Lessings "echte", d.h. "esoterische" Überzeugung zu "isolieren". Jene "systematische" Verwobenheit ergab sich daraus, daß Lessing sich selbst noch als in der Menschheitsevolution befindlich versteht und so auch in eigener Person noch nicht vom exoterischen "Glauben" zum esoterischen "Schauen" vorgedrungen ist.'[32] Lessing's system is, then, the result of his attempt to find some way of mediating between transcendent (i.e., exoteric) and immanent (i.e., esoteric) truth. However, such mediation is not a process of progressively excluding exoteric thinking, but rather of combining it with esoteric thinking into a unity. Therefore, according to Thielicke, Lessing seriously and genuinely sought to come to terms with Christian revelation and God's act of revealing.

Through an analysis of various works of Lessing, but particularly of *Die Erziehung des Menschengeschlechts*, Thielicke seeks to show that reason conceived as an immanental power is unequal for Lessing to the task of developing itself within history to the heights of perfection. Given the epistemological weakness of man's cognitive powers, man is thrown back upon divine help, in particular upon divine revelation for guidance. This means that revelation contains a real 'Transzendenzgehalt' and is the result of an historical act of a God that exists externally to the universe conceived as a system of immanence. Man is quite literally dependent upon a "Richtungs-stoss" from God, without which he would never overcome his epistemological benightedness. Correlatively, this means that God is not an imminental principle in the sense of Spinoza's monism, but rather is a transcendent being. This, of course, means that Lessing's concept of God is essentially theistic. In short, Lessing's philosophy of religion is essentially dualistic according to Thielicke. On the one hand, the theoretical destiny of man, the ultimate *telos* of man's education is to perfect his reason, so that he might be able to grasp the universal, timeless, and rational heart of reality. On the other hand, man, not yet having achieved such a goal, is a child if not prisoner of history and hence thrown back upon history as the only vehicle of revelation if he is to obtain his religious goal. ' "Existentiell" steht der Mensch nach Lessing unter der Offenbarung, so gewiß er ja "als Mensch" Glied der Geschichte ist, die durch Offenbarung (mit) konstituiert wird; "theoretisch" steht er schon jenseits ihrer, so gewiß ihm in seiner Reflexion der Ort ihrer Relativierung bekannt ist, nämlich das Telos der Geschichte (das "reine ewige Evangelium").'[33] Nevertheless, actual historical man, no matter how much his *telos* is to obtain rational perfection, stands and stays mired in history and therefore must remain dependent upon it as a source for the development of his religious self. *On his own* man cannot progress from a state of exoteric dependence to a state of esoteric independence. Historical man, real man (Lessing) is continually faced with the irrational, the historical, revelation, or in short, transcendence as the only avenue he has to travel upon towards perfection. 'Das irrationale Geschichtsleben gewinnt aufs neue seinen teleologischen Bezug durch die "transzendente" und zielsichere Führung der menschlichen ratio — die ja, sich selbst überlassen, nur empirische ratio und insofern ir-ratio ist.'[34]

Explicitly indicating his dependence upon Thielicke, Otto Mann, in 1948, sought to Christianize Lessing even further.[35] Whereas Thielicke viewed Lessing as hovering between rationalistic and irrationalistic, immanent and transcendent, esoteric and exoteric positions, Mann subordinated more radically than Thielicke reason to revelation, immanence to transcendence in his interpretation of Lessing. The starting point of Lessing's thinking, according to Mann, is Lessing's belief, indeed, his experience of the negativity and finitude of man vis-à-vis an absolutely positive, unconditioned and infinite God. 'Der Mensch [nach Lessing] ist nicht einfach als ein Sein in ein Sein eingeordnet, sondern er ist der absolut Bedingte vor dem absolut unbedingten Gott. Hier klafft die grundsätzliche Differenz, die die Aufklärung übersehen und ausschalten möchte. Der Ansatz für die echte religiöse Frage setzt das Negativsein des Menschen voraus.'[36] Man's negativity allegedly exhibits itself in Lessing's belief that, morally and epistemologically, man is simply unable to bring himself into communion with a transcendent God who confronts him as a divine Person. Man experiences, nevertheless, the 'Anspruch einer religiösen Erfahrung, die wieder in der Negativität des Menschen und damit in der Notwendigkeit gründet, den Menschen in die Positivität Gottes zu erlösen'.[37] Within the confines of the natural and immanental system of the universe man is helpless.

He is, accordingly, dependent upon a God — a divine Person — who, in order to save man, must reveal Himself to man in a way that transcends man's normal rational powers. Man encounters this God only in the Bible. 'Diesem Menschen begegnet die Bibel als die ihn erfüllende, als die ihn erlösende Positivität. Der Mensch findet sich hier schon äußerlich weit über seine natürliche Erkenntnisfähigkeit hinaus unterrichtet, über sich selbst, über die Welt, über Gott.'[39] Therefore, only in and through the Bible does God's Word address itself to man, informs man about himself, and makes a moral response by man possible. '[Die] Offenbarung [ist] nötig, um den Menschen unter das Gebot dieser Liebe zu stellen, das er von sich selbst aus, durch seine Vernunft und Natur nie gefunden hätte. Hier ist das gegeben, was den Menschen über dieses Menschsein hinausführt . . .'[39] What is given to man is Truth and Truth is God, i.e., a God that is beyond the realm of reason. 'Nicht Gott ist an die Vernunftwahrheit gebunden, sondern Gott ist die Wahrheit schlechthin. Gottsein und Wahrsein fallen also in eins. Die Wahrheit ist zu definieren als die Wirklichkeit, wie Gott sie stiftet. Damit steht zunächst der Mensch mit seiner Endlichkeit vor dem Unendlichen der Wahrheit in Gott.'[40] In short, concerning Lessing's outlook on life Mann contends: 'Lessing begriff den Menschen im Raum des jüdisch-christlichen Theismus. Hiernach ist der letzte Seinsgrund der persönliche, der der Welt transzendente Gott. Zu diesem Gott verhält sich der Mensch als Person, und Gott verhält sich als Person zum Menschen.'[41]

More recently Willi Oelmüller has attempted to reinterpret Lessing's alleged commitment to Christianity.[42] Oelmüller has shown that Lessing lost much faith in the cognitive powers of reason and hence came to conceive of man as a prisoner of history. Because man is caught in history, history must be analyzed and comprehended as the only avenue for man open to truth. This thesis is allegedly at the basis of Lessing's interest and commitment to Christianity. Oelmüller differs, however, from Thielicke. In the expanded third edition of his work on Lessing, Thielicke had sought to compare Lessing with Kierkegaard. Indeed, Thielicke saw Lessing as a forerunner to Kierkegaard. Oelmüller feels this comparison causes a misunderstanding of Lessing. Kierkegaard, according to Oelmüller, sought religious truth in the inward, passion, faith, and decision of a subjectivity freed from all historicity. Lessing, on the other hand, sought for religious perfection within and mediated by history. 'Lessings Problem ist nicht, wie man die Subjektivität aus der Verstrickung in die Geschichte befreien kann, sondern umgekehrt, wie man sie mit der gegenwärtigen geschichtlichen Welt so vermitteln kann, daß man die Wahrheit als die für die Subjektivität gegenwärtige Wahrheit erkennen und anerkennen kann.'[43] However, Lessing was, according to Oelmüller, never able to realize such a reconciliation. 'Lessing entwickelt von der Subjektivität und Geschichte aus Denkmodelle, die Plausibles und Verbindliches für die in seiner Zeit ungelösten Spannungen zwischen dem Christentum und der Moderne entfallen sollen. Denkmodelle beanspruchen keine Totallösungen . . ., sie sind Lösungsversuche für bestimmte geschichtliche Situationen.'[44]

Since 1952 a different approach to Lessing has arisen whose representatives are J. Schneider and Georges Pons. This third position differs from the others in that it denies the existence of any 'system' in Lessing's religious thought. In conscious rejection of Leisegang's thesis (quoted above), Pons writes that 'on ne saurait parler d'un système de Lessing'.[45] Schneider himself writes: 'Die jeweiligen Aussagen in Lessings Schriften und Briefen weisen so starke Divergenzen auf, dass die Harmonisierungsversuche, zu denen sich viele Untersucher . . . haben verführen lassen, als gescheitert betrachtet werden müssen.'[46] Previous investigators, according to Schneider, have sought to understand Lessing better than Lessing did himself, i.e., they have sought to systematize his thought where no such system exists. In particular this is evident (1) in the tendency to assume that Lessing had a developed *Weltanschauung* at the time he wrote *Nathan* or the *Erziehung,* and (2) to interpret Lessing's earlier fragmentary writings as certification of the investigator's *a priori*-assumed interpretive principle. However, Schneider (and also Pons) contends that, to the contrary, Lessing was never able fully to discover a theoretical position from which to construct a systematic theology or philosophy of religion. Lessing's speculations are no more than 'Lösungsversuche'. Thus Schneider concludes: 'Lessing hatte keine Weltanschauung als Lehrmeinung. Er entwarf zwar manche weltanschaulichen Theorien, aber nur als Denkmöglichkeiten unter vielen anderen. Er suchte die überlieferten Wahrheiten des Christentums zu verstehen und ging dabei wissenschaftlich zu Werke . . . Ob er als selbständig denkender Leibnizianer spekulative Betrachtungen über Gott und Welt anstellte, ob er in den Chor der Pietisten und Neologen einstimmte und die dogmatischen Haarspaltereien einer intoleranten Orthodoxie veruteilte, ob er mit den radikalsten Deisten den Kanon kritisierte und die schnelle Verbreitung des Christentums "vernünftig" zu erklären suchte, oder ob er mit den

Orthodoxen die pietistische Konventikelfrömmelei und die Zwitter-
haltung der moralisierenden Neologie derb abkanzelte, im Grunde
war es die Frage nach dem Wesen und der Erkenntnismöglichkeit der
Religion, die sein theologisches Denken beherrschte.'[47]
To be sure, both writers reject Mann's thesis that Lessing was
essentially a Christian, and both maintain that Lessing believed in the
powers of reason. But both also note that Lessing was dissatisfied
with the previous rational 'systems' constructed by man's cognitive
powers.

The above given review of the various schools of thought concerning
the interpretation of Lessing's theology has been a *macro*analysis of
the problem. No attempt has been made to deal with the myriad of
differing opinions concerning this or that *micro*-problem in Lessing's
thought. The focal points around which the varying positions hover
and over which they conflict is (a) whether there is a 'systematic'
core to Lessing's thinking, and (b) how can the rationalistic and
irrationalistic tendencies in his speculations be integrated into the
assumed 'systematic' core. Relative to these central points it is
obvious that contradictory positions have been developed. The only
certain truth concerning Lessing's (theological) thinking is that it is
true that there is no certainty. Twentieth-century Lessing-scholarship
seems to be faced with a crisis. Since the relationship between reason
and revelation, immanence and transcendence, etc., comprehends the
fundamental and essential elements of Lessing's notion of 'truth',
and since this notion is at the basis of his ratiocinative processes,
disagreement in this level must ultimately have ramifications in
attempts to comprehend and interpret Lessing in an overall manner.
In the light of the conclusions made by Pons and especially by
Schneider the questions can be raised as to whether it might not be
presumptuous once again to attempt to find a 'systematic' core to
Lessing's theological reasonings. Must not one conclude that Lessing-
scholarship has irreversibly entered into a blind alley? However, in
the spirit of Lessing, one might also pose the counter-question: Is it
not really impossible to avoid seeking a 'systematic' core in Lessing's
thought, so much so that even, for example, Schneider's own re-
searches are grounded upon such an assumption? And if it is impossible, is there not an imperative to try a *new* approach to Lessing?
What is meant by the counter-question can be elucidated in the
following manner. Concerning his methodological position, Schneider writes: 'Wir können Lessing nur durch Lessing nahekommen.

... Was er unvollendet gelassen hat, muss unvollendet bleiben. Die Fragment gebliebenen Schriften gönnen uns einen Blick in die Werkstatt des Denkers; sie dürfen uns aber nie dazu verführen, auf ihnen irgendeine Weltanschauung Lessings aufzubauen.'[48] Manfred Durzak has perceptively commented upon this rather obscure statement of methodological principles: 'Wenn ich diesen methodischen Ansatz recht verstehe, bedeutet er eine Reproduktion von Lessings vielfältigen Denkansätzen mit allen Irr- und Abwegen, ohne daß an irgendeiner Stelle der Versuch gemacht würde, das in den zahlreichen fragmentarischen Schriften niedergelegte Denken von dessen Intention zu unterscheiden. Die Intention dieses Denkens mag durchaus indirekt erkennbar sein, auch wenn sie in den fragmentarischen Schriften nur unvollkommen realisiert wurde.'[49] Durzak's exegesis of Schneider's thesis is substantiated by other comments by Schneider. Schneider, for instance, castigates very sharply the attempt of investigators (particularly of the practitioner of 'Geistesgeschichte') to penetrate behind what Lessing explicitly states in order to get to the 'systematic' core underlying Lessing's theological ratiocinations. Schneider writes: 'Sie sind ... von einer beruhigenden und seltsamen Furcht vor erforschbarer Wirklichkeit besessen, die den einfachen Tatsachen eine geringere Bedeutung beimisst als der subjektiven Auslegung, wobei sie die Wahrheit nicht in den Dingen, sondern hinter ihnen sucht. ... Die ausschliesslich deutende Lessingforschung hat sich aber als unzulänglich erwiesen und folglich müssen wir versuchen, in Lessings Schriften selbst so viel zu finden, das wir nicht hinter ihnen zu suchen brauchen.'[50] I interpret this to mean that the investigator should remain on the 'surface' of Lessing's thinking, i.e., he should merely concern himself with what Lessing actually said, when he said it, and perhaps in what context it was said without seeking to determine any deeper structural or generative principle that could possibly integrate the statements into a meaningful whole. No wonder Guthke claimed that not only does Schneider's work produce a 'verwirrendes Bild' of Lessing's theology, but it must necessarily do so.[51] The strength of Schneider's methodology is that it strictly adheres to historical fact and chronology. The weakness is that it cannot free itself from the mere collection of such facts in order to seek (if not to find) some principle of unity.

In addition, however, if one looks closely at Schneider's actual procedure, one will find that Schneider too tried to penetrate beyond a mere 'Tatsachenforschung'. Schneider claims: '[Lessing] hofft durch unausgesetztes Suchen und Forschen das zu finden, was sein Denken befriedigt.'[52] What could this be but systematic unity? But no, Schneider goes on to conceive Lessing as '[den] nie fertigen, sensiblen Dialektiker, dem die Relativierung alles als absolut Hingestellten ein Denkbedürfnis war . . .'[53] In what sense a 'Dialektiker' cannot have a system Schneider does not explain. Thus it appears to me that Schneider, in order to explain the nature of Lessing's thought, has read an a-historical and psychological principle (a 'Denkbedürfnis') into the heart of Lessing's ratiocinative processes. How do we know that Lessing experienced such a 'Denkbedürfnis'? Schneider's answer is that Lessing continually altered and contradicted his own opinions. But why was Lessing led to contradict himself as he did? He had, of course, a 'Denkbedürfnis', etc., etc. The circularity of and hence unsatisfactoriness of Schneider's methodology is evident. The very assumption Schneider uses to explain the actual history of Lessing's theological opinions cannot itself be historically founded. What is also apparent is Schneider's inability to overcome the temptation of seeking 'die Wahrheit [über Lessing] nicht in den Dingen, sondern hinter ihnen'. It is true that Schneider acknowledges, 'Lessing weiss, dass absolute Wahrheit unerforschbar ist . . .'[54] Had Schneider been able to explicate why and how Lessing had come by such a 'truth', he might have come upon the 'systematic' core of Lessing's thought and certainly would not have to use an a-historical category in order to make some sense of the fragmentary and contradictory nature of Lessing's theological speculations. At any rate, Schneider's inadequate attempt to pin-point the generative principle underlying Lessing's thought illustrates the impossibility of not seeking to discover such a principle or, at least, to explain adequately why there is none.

It is relative to this contradictory state of affairs and to the need to discover a 'systematic' core in Lessing's thinking, that I shall seek to establish my own position. First and foremost my thinking begins with an acceptance of all three previous positions. However, such an acceptance must be qualified, if not to be misunderstood. In imitation of a similar thesis made by Leibniz, I accept what previous interpreters have basically affirmed, but not what they have denied. Insofar as any one previous position claims no more than to have cast light upon Lessing's thinking, I can accept it. Insofar as any one position claims to be 'exclusively' correct at the exclusion of the others, I must reject it. This means that, because the interpretive difference between investigators is grounded 'in der Sache', i.e., in the very nature of Lessing's theological speculations, I contend

Lessing's theological speculations (and ultimately his concept of truth) (1) are actually and factually contradictory, and (2) they hover between an immanent, naturalistic, and rationalistic concept of truth, on the one hand, and a transcendent, Christian, and irrationalistic concept of truth, on the other hand. What my paradoxical acceptance and non-acceptance of these positions *concretely* entails I will now detail.

The *first consequence* of my acceptance of the positive content of the three positions discussed is the acknowledgement that Lessing's thinking contains as *constitutive* elements an esoteric, immanent, and rationalistic tendency and an exoteric, transcendent and irrationalistic tendency. Thielicke was correct in contending that Lessing's thinking is exoteric *in substance* as well as in form. Therefore, the irrationalistic elements should not be reduced to the rationalistic ones (as Fittbogen, von Wiese, *et al.* have tried to do) nor vice versa (as Mann has attempted). A certain autonomy and actuality must be ascribed to the two sides of Lessing's thinking. The task of the current interpreters of Lessing must not be to play one tendency off against the other, but to determine how the two exist in relationship to each other. Guthke suggested (in 1962 and 1967) that such a task was one of the imperatives of current Lessing-research. Guthke writes:

'[M]an wird der Sache kaum gerecht, wenn man versucht, den "Rationalisten" Lessing gegen den "Irrationalisten" auszuspielen, den die neuere Forschung immer klarer in den Blick bekommt. Vielmehr müßte man versuchen, gerade die Art des *Miteinanders* der Ratio und ihres Widerspiels, das Lessings Lebenseinstellung und Gestalten zugrundeliegt, zu bestimmen.

'Es dürfte sich lohnen, die umstrittenen theologischen Anschauungen Lessings von diesem Gesichtspunkt aus noch einmal zu durchdenken in der Hoffnung, das seit langem anhängige Gegeneinander rationalistischer und irrationalistischer Interpretationen zu überwinden durch einen Neuansatz, der eben von dieser Fragestellung her zu gewinnen wäre; der beschriebene provisorische Charakter des Lessingschen Theologisierens dürfte dabei nicht übersehen werden.'[55]

The recognition that Lessing's thinking contains two general tendencies and that one tendency should not be played off against the other, but rather be integrated with each other constitutes the background of the fourth and most recent approach to Lessing (of which my own position must be viewed as an extension). This position conceives Lessing's 'system' to be not so much as a given, complete, and static whole as a dynamic, developing, and growing ratiocinative process. This growth is not rectilinear, rather 'dialectical'. Indeed, the hopes of the fourth approach to Lessing can be subsumed under the rubrics of 'dialectics'. Wolfgang Ritzel has summarized this position on a theoretical level. Lessing's tendency to relativize any position, to think in the terms of others, to change his own opinions, to affirm contradictory positions, in short, his intellectual movement are viewed by Ritzel as part of the systematic process of Lessing's thinking. Ritzel contends: '[N]ach Lessings Überzeugung [hat] sowohl die eine als auch die andere Position ihre guten Gründe, so daß jede der beiden im Ganzen des Denkmöglichen ihre Stelle findet.'[56] According to Ritzel, Lessing's thinking never seeks to reach an 'Entweder/Oder' conclusion. Indeed, such a conclusion brings all further thinking to a halt since of its very nature it claims to have reached final truth. Instead, Lessing's thinking remains in movement in its never ending pursuit and it does so by affirming truth as different and differing positions of a 'Sowohl/Als Auch' state of affairs. However, the various partial truths exist within the context of a whole, of a totality that does not exist over and against the parts, rather in and through them. Each individual truth *qua* its individuality differs from all others. Nevertheless, the individual truth does not exist in atomistic isolation, rather as the manifestion of the totality. The totality is, therefore, divided into continuously differing variety, and such variety is united into a continuously developing totality as a series of 'Sowohl/Als Auch' parts. The totality is 'ein gegliedertes Ganzes'.[57] The dynamic principle determining the movement of the dialectics, in short, 'der Nerv der Dialektik Lessings ist aber die Besonderheit und folglich der Unterschied der Positionen, deren keine der vollen Wahrheit angemessen ist, so daß sie verbunden werden müßen, um — mit Schlegels Worten — ihre "ganze Fülle" zu erschöpfen. . . . Sprechen wir mit Bezug auf Lessing von Dialektik, so meinen wir das Gesetz, nach dem sich die unterschiedlichen Momente zur ganzen Fülle der Wahrheit ordnen, und dem der Denker folgt, um einen jeden von ihnen und damit der Wahrheit selbst gerecht zu werden.'[58] In short, truth is for Lessing, according to Ritzel, a dynamic and continuously differentiating unity of reason and feeling, of the universal and the individual, of this and that position.

It is obvious on a methodological and heuristic level that such a 'dialectical' approach to Lessing allows the investigator to take cognizance of the many-sidedness of Lessing's thinking and affords him with an interpretive tool for relating the various sides together into some sort of meaningful whole. Indeed, for Kurt Wölfel Lessing's 'dialectics' is not just an epistemological principle but also a foundation for Lessing's very life style. 'Das dialektische Moment, das in Lessings Denken unverkennbar ist, könnte man eher ein Denk-, ja Lebensprinzip nennen als ein Erkenntnisprinzip. Es ist nicht allein Instrument und Mittel, um der Wahrheit habhaft zu werden; es ist Weg und Ziel, Mittel und Zweck zugleich. Sein Widerspruch setzt den Spruch voraus, der ihn erst ermöglicht, und Lessing weiß, daß er auf ihn angewiesen ist, von ihm denkend lebt. Indem sich der Widerspruch meldet, macht er sich seinerseits zum Spruch, der den Widerspruch auslösend das Gespräch der Geister in Gang hält, aus dem und in dem die Humanität im Grunde besteht.'[59] According to Peter Heller, Lessing conceived reality itself, including God as highest being, as dialectically structured. This dialectic becomes the very principle whereby man seeks to approach God. 'Truth [and/or God] is perfect, truth is perfection, but the human being is essentially imperfect. Thus the only approximation to truth attainable to man lies in his self-dedication to the ever inconclusive, imperfect and progressive dynamic of the dialectical process. For human beings the truth rests only in the movement.'[60] Indeed, according to Heller, the dialectical process itself becomes man's final goal for Lessing and hence becomes man's God.

For the moment I shall refrain from any analysis and criticism of the specific interpretations of Lessing deriving from a 'dialectical' premise. I accept the position insofar as it acknowledges the duality involved in Lessing's thinking and particularly insofar as it seeks an insight into Lessing *via* his cogitative processes rather than seeking to find or to construct a ready made system. Nevertheless one of the underlying premises of this dialectic methodology appears to me to be inadequate if not wrong. However, hazy, heuristically speaking, Schneider's methodology is, he has, nevertheless in my judgment, shown that Lessing's speculations contain divergent theses that *cannot* be fully harmonized with each other. This leads to the *second consequence* of my acceptance of the positive content of the first three positions discussed. The 'dialectical' approach to Lessing can take adequate cognizance of the rationalistic and irrationalistic/ Christian sides of Lessing's thinking. Therefore, it can be used as a means for reconciling, however tenuously, the Enlightenment and Christian interpretations of Lessing. It does not, however, (or has not up to now) adequately taken account of Schneider and Pons' thesis concerning the contradictory and hence systemlessness of Lessing's theology. This failure can easily be illustrated on a practical and theoretical level.

Manfred Durzak in a very subtle and stimulating essay has sought once again to rethink the relations between 'Vernunft and Offenbarung' in Lessing's theological speculations. According to Durzak these two notions constitute central elements of Lessing's theological reasonings and grant an insight into their totality. Furthermore, Durzak contends that the two concepts are related together in Lessing's thinking antithetically or dialectically. Durzak, also, in effect distinguishes between two meanings for the term 'Offenbarung'. In a narrow and strict sense 'Offenbarung' refers to 'supernatural' revelation given to man by a God who transcends nature. This, of course, is the traditional Christian position. Such revelation also transcends man's cognitive powers. In a more loose sense, 'Offenbarung' refers to any type of experience that cannot be comprehended and immediately analyzed by man's reason. This 'being-beyond-reason' means that such experience in some sense transcends rational truth and reveals something to man beyond the rational. In his analysis of 'Offenbarung und Vernunft' Durzak comes to the conclusion that the unity Lessing establishes is a unity between 'Vernunft' and 'Offenbarung' in the second sense of the term. 'Offenbarung' refers to things like Christian love, to the certainty of the heart, to practical charity, in short, to the realm of subjectivity. The two otherwise sharply distinguished realms are united according to Durzak in the *Erziehung* by means of the notion of 'Entwicklung'. The function and *telos* of 'Offenbarung' in its dialectical relationship to 'Vernunft' is to be the elementary stage of a development that ends with rational clarity. Durzak concludes: 'Die grundsätzliche Andersartigkeit, die Transzendenz der Offenbarung wird von vornherein negiert, da ihre Verstehbarkeit durch die Vernunft apodiktisch vorausgesetzt wird. Offenbarung wird also von der Vernunft her bestimmt und muß daher notwendigerweise als immanent erscheinen; Offenbarung, so kann man sagen, wird zu einem Prinzip im Erziehungsplan der Menschheit.'[61] 'Das Verhältnis zwischen den Begriffen "Vernunft" und "Offenbarung" in der *Erziehung des Menschengeschlechts* ist eindeutig zugunsten der Vernunft entschieden. Die Offenbarung ist nur eine Mode derselben Wahrheit, die sich bei der Selbstverwirklichung der Vernunft einstellt.'[62] As proof of his thesis, Durzak refers to paragraph four of the *Erziehung*.[63] This paragraph reads 'Erziehung gibt dem Menschen nichts, was er nicht auch aus sich selbst haben könnte, nur geschwinder und leichter. Also gibt auch die Offenbarung dem Menschengeschlechte nichts, worauf die menschliche Vernunft, sich selbst überlassen, nicht auch kommen würde; sondern sie gab und gibt ihm die wichtigsten dieser Dingen nur früher.' Durzak's conclusions are plausibly based upon such citations. Thielicke in his book has constructed similar arguments in favor of an immanent interpretation of 'Offenbarung'. However, mysteriously enough for an investigator committed to an antithetical interpretation of Lessing, Durzak takes *no* cognizance of paragraph 77 of the *Erziehung* in which Lessing contends that religion brings man 'auf nähere und bessere Begriffe vom göttlichen Wesen, von unserer Natur, von unsern Verhältnissen zu Gott . . ., auf welche die menschliche Vernunft von selbst nimmermehr gekommen wäre'. Thielicke has, in my judgment, convincingly shown that such a statement (and others) can only be fairly interpreted to refer to a transcendent and Christian-like activity on the part of God. By a judicious selection (or non-selection) of quotations it would be easy to imitate Thielicke and construct a plausible case in favor of the transcendent nature of 'Offenbarung' according to Lessing. Thus Durzak's attempt to construct a 'systematic' core in Lessing's religious thinking upon a dialectical basis fails precisely because it, in the long run, does not grant sufficient substance to Lessing's transcendent, irrationalistic, and Christian tendencies. To have adequately acknowledged these tendencies would have entailed a *de facto* acknowledgment of their irreducibility even in a dialectical manner to their rationalistic counterpart.

The inability of the current 'dialectical' position to acknowledge satisfactorily or even give an account of Lessing's contradictory thinking is theoretically grounded in its very heuristic principles. For instance, Ritzel contends: '[Lessing] rettet die Teilwahrheiten, indem er sie kritisch als Momente der ganzen Wahrheit betrachtet und innerhalb dieses Ganzen gewissermaßen zurechtrückt.'[64] Insofar as Ritzel conceives Lessing's disparate positions solely as 'Momente der ganzen Wahrheit', he cannot accept or treat any of them as contradictions. The very nature of a contradiction means that the opposite and opposing elements cannot be unified. Conversely, if Lessing's 'Teilwahrheiten' are truly just moments of a unity, albeit a 'dialetical' one, an investigator committed to the 'dialectical' interpretation of Lessing must inevitably either overlook, ignore, or interpret away all apparent contradictions in Lessing's thinking.

At this point the importance and paradoxical nature of my own approach to Lessing must become evident. Above I stated that I accept the positive content of the first three positions explicated, but that I also reject what they basically deny. Therefore, I can accept the fact that Lessing's thinking exhibits both Enlightenment and Christian tendencies. Hence I must reject any attempt to play one tendency off against the other or to reduce one to the other. It was for this reason that I see an advance in the fourth or 'dialectical' position, for this position recognizes both sides of Lessing. However, I cannot fully accept the dialectical approach to Lessing because it necessarily either ignores or misconstrues the contradictory nature of much of Lessing's thought. Whereas I accept Schneider's thesis that Lessing's thinking evinces truly irreconcilable contradictions, I do not accept the conclusion he draws from this fact. Schneider can find no 'systematic' core in Lessing's thought. Therefore, in effect, Lessing remains a 'Problematiker' — 'der nie fertige', sensible 'Dialektiker' for Schneider. In my judgment this is a false antithesis. The categories of 'Entweder/Oder' are not appropriate here. A thinker can be both a 'Systematiker' and a 'Problematiker' or, more precisely both 'ein systematischer Problematiker' as well as 'ein problematischer Systematiker'.

How might this be possible? One of the key notions contained in the concept of 'system' is certainly the notion of consistency. Correlatively the notion of 'contradiction' surely excluded the notion of consistency. A thesis and antithesis are contradictory precisely because they cannot be made consistent with one another. My acceptance of Schneider's thesis concerning the contradictory nature of Lessing's thinking would putatively appear to contradict my acceptance of the thesis that there is a 'systematic' core to Lessing's thinking. The resolution of this methodological contradiction will entail an analysis and exposition of my methodological principles.

B. METHODOLOGY

A key for discovering the 'systematic' core in Lessing's thinking can be found in Thomas S. Kuhn's reflections upon the nature of scientific revolutions.[65] In his *opus magnum* Kuhn is primarily concerned with the nature and structure of the thinking carried on by natural scientists, particularly by physicists, chemists, and astronomers. In my brief but *free* exposition of Kuhn's methodology I shall seek to generalize his theory as applicable not only to the domain of natural science but also to any type of 'scientific' cogitation including theology. The term 'scientific' is here being taken in the broader sense of 'knowing' a subject matter by its causes and ultimate principles. In other words, in my judgment, it is possible to abstract a formal structure from Kuhn's material analysis of natural science that is valid for other areas of systematic cognitive endeavor. It will eventually be contended that Lessing's reflective efforts only can be adequately comprehended as part of an important scientific (i.e., cognitive) revolution that took place in the eighteenth century.

In Kuhn's opinion 'scientific' knowledge does not result from an examination of an empirically given manifold. The scientific researcher does not simply gather pure though raw data — sort of atomic facts —, collate them, induce a general law conceived as a hypothesis, and then seek confirmatory corraboration by repeated empirical tests. Under such a conception of science, the researcher is ideally to approach his subject matter without any preconceived convictions, he is to allow the subject matter, so-to-speak, to speak for itself. For Kuhn the invalidity of such an interpretation of science is manifest in the problem of how the scientist approaches his material. The scientist does not pose just any question selected at random, nor does he undertake just any experiment. Also, the scientist is selective about which phenomena he considers to be 'facts'. In other words, a scientist may set up an experiment which results in numerous events from which only some will be seen to be relevant to the problem under investigation, i.e., to be 'facts' in the first place. All this suggests that the researcher approaches his material with certain analytical concepts through which he, so-to-speak, perceives his subject matter. Susan Langer has stated the reason for this. Before knowledge can be obtained, a thinker must first ask questions and develop the techniques for analyzing the object of investigation. Furthermore, 'a question is really an ambiguous proposition, the answer is its determination. There can only be a certain number of alternatives that will complete its sense. In this way, the intellectual treatment of any datum, any experience, any subject, is determined by the nature of our questions, and only carried out in the answers. . . . Therefore, a philosophy is characterized more by the *formulation* of its problems than by the solutions of them. . . . In our questions lie our principles of analysis and our answers may express whatever those principles are able to yield.'[66] Commenting upon Martin Heidegger's views on the importance of philosophical principles of analysis, Eugene T. Gendlin writes: 'Yet, [such principles] basically affect whatever we study, for depending upon which mode of approach we use, different questions and hypotheses will be formulated, different experiments set up, different illustrations cited, different arguments held to be sound, and different conclusions reached. Much in our conclusions about anything comes not from the study of things but from the philosophical decisions implicit in the way we start.'[67] The formulation and obtainment of knowledge within any specific discipline is determined by the basic concepts implicit in the investigator's questions. Kuhn calls such concepts 'paradigms'. Other writers have invented other designations. Susan Langer refers to them as 'generative ideas'.[68] Arthur O. Lovejoy (whom Kuhn acknowledges as having influenced him) calls them 'unit ideas'.[69] And T. E. Hulme calls them 'central attitudes'.[70]

A paradigm, as Kuhn notes, possesses a certain priority relative to empirical fact. This priority consists of the dependence of the manifold upon the paradigm for intelligibility. The paradigm enables a researcher, first of all, to conceptualize a problem, conceive relevant questions, invent the necessary experiments, and to interpret meaningfully the results. Indeed, as noted above, generative paradigms not only unify a given manifold of facts into an intelligible whole, but often determine what aspects of any given empirical experience will be taken to be a 'fact' or 'datum' in the first place. A paradigm, therefore, determines a theorist's approach to and expected results from his investigation. Hence, 'scientific' *thinking* is normally puzzle-solving wherein the general nature and parameters of the solution are pre-determined by the paradigm used. As Kuhn points out, it is quite possible for scientists, using differing paradigms, to diverge significantly in their analyses of essentially the same set of phenomena.

When a theorist has investigated a sufficient amount of different kinds of phenomena, has constructed whatever number of paradigms necessary to unify intelligibly such phenomena, and has determined the logical relationship between his various paradigms, he may be said to have developed a 'system' or to have carried out a 'systematic' analysis of a given subject matter. Of course, one of the primary prerequisites for a system is that the various paradigms are *consistent* with one another and are related to one another as the most general is to the most specific. A magnificient example of a 'scientific' system would be Isaac Newton's physics. Perhaps no system, before or after, has so profoundly influenced its contemporaries and inspired so much further scientific development. Newton's physics was so influential because his system of paradigms seemed to explain so much in nature and give direction to further research.

At this point, I believe, it would be worthwhile to interrupt my free exposition of Kuhn's theory and seek to show the relevance of what has been so far explained to an analysis of Lessing. Any thinker seriously interested in understanding reality, will seek to investigate more and more phenomena and thereby widen the scope of his paradigms or invent new paradigms that allow him to comprehend ever more about reality. As Stephen C. Pepper has noted: 'It thus becomes clear that, in the pursuit of reliability, structural corroboration does not stop until it reaches unlimited scope. For as long as there are outlying facts which might not corroborate the facts already organized by the structural hypothesis, so long will the reliability of the hypothesis be questionable. The ideal structural hypothesis [i.e. paradigm], therefore, is one that all facts will corroborate, a hypothesis of unlimited scope. Such a hypothesis is a world hypothesis.[71] A 'world hypothesis' is, therefore, a most general interpretation of nature and entails ideally the most unlimited paradigm (or paradigm set) beyond which there are no others and by means of which a thinker can *view* the *world*. Pepper writes: 'Ideally, through words, on the pages of a book, a world theory illuminates the world for us, and the world stands revealed to us not in imagination but in fact just as it is. For the words of the book are supposed, so to speak, to put us in gear with the world, so that all we have to do is to guide the wheel and observe how things look as the headlights bring them in view.'[72] Pepper designates world-view paradigms as 'root metaphors'.

'The method in principle seems to be this: A man desiring to understand the world looks about for a clue to its comprehension. He pitches upon some area of commonsense fact and tries if he cannot understand other areas in terms of this one. This original area becomes then his basic analogy or root metaphor. He describes as best he can the characteristics of this area, or, if you will, discriminates its structure. A list of its structural characteristics becomes his basic concepts of explanation [i.e. paradigms] and description. We call them a set of categories. In terms of these categories he proceeds to study all other areas of fact whether uncriticized or previously criticized. He undertakes to interpret all facts in terms of these categories. As a result of the impact of these other facts upon his categories, he may qualify and readjust the categories, so that a set of categories commonly changes and developes. Since the basic analogy or root metaphor normally (and probably at least in part necessarily) arises out of common sense, a great deal of development and refinement of a set of categories is required if they are to prove adequate for a hypothesis of unlimited scope.'[73]

The similarity between Pepper's notion of a world hypothesis and Hans Leisegang's definition (quoted above) of a *Weltanschauung* should be obvious. A *Weltanschauung* is, according to Leisegang, 'eine originale Art des Schauens, des Blickes in die Welt, eine besondere Art, das Geschaute denkend zu bewältigen'. What Leisegang means by 'Art des Schauens' is equivalent to Kuhn's notion of a basal paradigm or to Pepper's notion of a root metaphor. Thus Kuhn's analysis of scientific thinking can be shown to have a bearing on the problem of a *Weltanschauung*. Indeed, it constitutes a refinement of the notion. However, there is an important difference between what Leisegang meant, on the one hand, and what Pepper and Kuhn mean, on the other. Pepper and Kuhn are attempting to describe the nature of cognitive knowledge in the strict sense. Thus both writers (particularly Kuhn) make frequent reference to the ideas of scientists. A *Weltanschauung*, on the other hand, is not primarily interested in scientific cognition, be it physical or metaphysical. It is not cognition qua cognition, rather cognition that serves a certain purpose, that fulfills a special *telos* that distinguishes a *Weltanschauung* from, say, a physical cosmology. A *Weltanschauung* entails cognition of reality, but only insofar as such cognition throws light upon man's quest for meaning. It is man's need to know himself and himself as meaningfully situated into some absolute frame of reference that constitutes that which world-view cognition seeks to illuminate.[74]

In the ensuing chapters I shall be interested in the basic paradigm or root metaphor underlying the cognitive basis for Lessing's *Weltanschauung*. To borrow an idea from marxism, Lessing's concept of truth — his basic cognitive principle — is the basis upon which the superstructure of his *Weltanschauung* is built. The purpose of knowledge for Lessing is to lead man to perfection and hence cognitive knowledge is justified by the valuative self-knowledge it produces. Nevertheless, this 'saving' truth is a function of a purely cognitive conception of truth. But this leads us back to the problem of Lessing's system. I have granted that there is no objective system in Lessing's thinking analogous in the scope and systematic integrity of Newton's physics. Lessing's thinking evinces contradictions and contradictions alone exclude the possibility of a positive systematic unity. Thus far my exposition of Kuhn's theory has only cast light upon the paradigm basis of any *consistent* cognitive system. I shall now pick up the thread of my exposition and consider the most important (at least for an analysis of Lessing) point.

Although Kuhn places great importance upon the priority of a paradigm in scientific thinking, he never forgets that a paradigm is only justified because it enables a researcher to integrate and interpret a given empirical manifold. The purpose of a paradigm is to make sense of empirical experience and therefore a paradigm must be empirically corroborated. As long as a paradigm or a paradigm set can take account of new evidence, i.e., expand and adjust to new 'facts', its acceptance by a theorist is guaranteed. However, in the course of the life of most paradigms, there are times when certain events take place that run counter to what the paradigm would lead a theorist to expect. In such cases the investigator is faced with an anomaly. Normally anomalies are not immediately destructive to an established paradigm. They can be 'shelved' with the hope that they eventually will show themselves to be interpretable on the basis of the established paradigm. But should the anomaly be central enough or should there be a sufficient number of them, a break down in the acceptability of the established paradigm set will take place and eventually a scientific crisis sets in. At this point investigators seek to discover new paradigms that can explain the recalcitrant evidence. The successful replacement of one paradigm set by another constitutes a scientific revolution.

Kuhn's notion of a crisis period — that twilight zone between the old and new paradigms — will be the key heuristic principle in my interpretation of Lessing and for solving the current impasse in secondary literature concerning the 'systematic' core of Lessing's thought. The nature of a crisis period reveals more clearly the essence of paradigms. (I prefer Langer's designation of them as 'generative ideas'.) The defining characteristic of a paradigm is its generative capacity. A paradigm or paradigm set is not a system, rather it is the 'systemic' core of a theorist's thinking that enables him to construct a system. A generative paradigm is essentially a principle of activity. It enables, so-to-speak, a theorist to be in intellectual movement, i.e., cogitatively to pursue truth. In other words, a paradigm is a dynamic principle of thinking, indeed, it makes thinking possible in the first place. Thinking is a type of mental activity and a paradigm is, in Aristotelian terms, the formal cause of such activity. The final cause or *telos* of cognitive activity is, of course, the construction of an adequate system by means of which cognition is obtained. Thinking or cognitive activity can only take place, i.e., maintain itself in motion, as long as it is able continuously to expand the scope of its explanatory powers. However, when the paradigm as a generative principle is faced with an anomaly, the ratiocinative process is slowed or brought to a stand still. Psychologically such a faltering of mental activity is experienced as a time of doubt, uncertainty, and intellectual insecurity. 'Because it demands large-scale paradigm destruction and major shifts in the problems and technique of normal science, the emergence of new theories is generally preceded by a period of pronounced professional insecurity. As one might expect, that insecurity is generated by the persistent failure of the puzzles of normal science to come out as they should. Failure of existing rules is the prelude to a search for new ones.'[75] Correlative to this psychological effect upon theorists, is an obscurification of normal scientific activity. 'All crises begin with the blurring of a paradigm and the consequent loosening of the rules of normal research.'[76] In other words, during a crisis period, a researcher is aware of the inability of his established paradigms to solve all relevant problems. New evidence cannot be integrated with the previous evidence. Such new evidence leads to a blurring of the established paradigm as the researcher seeks to alter or modify his paradigm so as to be able to come to terms with the anomaly. If the anomaly remains still unsolved, the theorist must then deviate from his normal cogitative procedure and attempt new solutions which are sometimes no more than hunches or inspirations. However, in his attempt to find a new paradigm the theorist can no longer proceed with his previous consistency. Indeed, he may think up new paradigms which, while partially successful in explaining the anomaly, are, nevertheless not consistent with one another or with his previously accepted paradigm. 'During the transition period there will be a large but never complete overlap between the problems that can be solved by the old and new paradigms. But there will also be a decisive difference in the modes of solution.'[77] In short, the theorists's experimental activity will lose inner consistency and begin to show signs of randomness.

'Faced with an admittedly fundamental anomaly in theory, the scientists's first effort will often be to isolate it more precisely and to give it structure. Though now aware that they cannot be quite right, he will push the rules of normal science harder than ever to see, in the area of difficulty, just where and how far they can be made to work. Simultaneously he will seek for ways of magnifying the breakdown, of making it more striking and perhaps also more suggestive than it had been when displayed in experiments the outcome of which was thought to be known in advance. And in the latter effort, more than in any other part of the post-paradigm development of science, he will look almost like our most prevalent image of the scientist. He will, in the first place often seem a man searching at random, trying experiments just to see what will happen, looking for an effect whose nature he cannot quite guess. Simultaneously, since no experiment can be conceived without some sort of theory, the scientist in crisis will constantly try to generate speculative theories that, if successful, may disclose the road to a new paradigm and, if unsuccessful, can be surrendered with relative ease.'[78]

At this point we can formalize more explicitly the heuristic principle inherent in Kuhn's theory that will be of use in an analysis of Lessing. The *telos* of all cognitive thinking is to gain a comprehensive, structural, consistent, in short, systematic insight into any subject matter. A paradigm has generative power insofar as it enables a thinker to approach this goal. The existence of an anomaly does not alter the *telos* which thinking is pursuing. What it does, is to show that a specific paradigm cannot approach this goal any further. The theorist does not simply abandon his established paradigm, however, as it has been successful in the past. What he does, is simultaneously to modify his paradigm often resulting in a blurring of it, and to attempt new and tentative hypotheses which are often inconsistent with each other or with the established paradigm. Superficially (i.e., literally on the surface) the theorist's thinking will exhibit contradictions, randomness, and incompleteness. This does not mean that there is no inner systematic core to it or that it is purely arbitrary. This 'systematic' core *is precisely the crisis itself.* In other words, there is an inner consistency in the theorist's thinking, namely in the specific paradigm concerned, the anomalies it is faced with, and the correlative need to regain theoretical unity. From the interaction of these three factors it is possible to explain the nature of the crisis, why the thinker experiments the way he does, why his thinking is contradictory in the way it is, and the general direction in which his thinking is developing.

The concept of a scientific or cognitive crisis offers, I believe, a wealth of possibilities for coming to terms with Lessing in a manner that meets the exigencies of current scholarship (so well formulated by Guthke) and that can give proper weight to the various peculiarities of Lessing's thought. Some scholars have plausibly made a case for the rationalistic, immanent and Enlightenment elements in

Lessing's thinking, others a case for the irrationalistic, transcendent, and Christian elements, and still others for the provisional, dynamic, and contradictory nature of Lessing's speculations. Reacting to such a state of affairs Guthke has challenged Lessing scholarship to determine the reciprocal relationship of the two sides to Lessing's thinking instead of playing one side off against the other and to give adequate consideration to the tentative dynamics of Lessing's *ars cogitandi*. The 'dialectical' approach to Lessing has made great strides along these lines, but has, in my judgment, failed to grant sufficient reality to the contradictory nature of Lessing's thinking. The use of the concept of a crisis period in scientific thinking as a heuristic principle gives the investigator a means for taking account of the contradictory positions in the secondary literature and the contradictions in Lessing's thought. However, I wish to make it clear that my use of such a principle is itself a tentative and experimental attempt to solve a real crisis, namely the crisis in the secondary literature on Lessing. To test my theory adequately in the realm of Lessing's theology alone would require of an investigator that he analyze each theological writing by Lessing with the dialectical skill of a Thielicke, trace and evaluate the course of Lessing's theological speculations with the micro-analysis of a Schneider, and possess (as background knowledge) the historical erudition of an Aner. It is obvious that any work on Lessing's theology that met such criteria would be monumental in size, indeed, would in effect constitute a full-sized study of the eighteenth century. Such an undertaking is beyond the scope of this investigation and the powers of this investigator.

My intentions are much more modest. I intend merely schematically to outline, though in sufficient detail, the nature of Lessing's *ars cogitandi* as it is involved in his theological speculations. Emphasis will be placed upon Lessing's thinking as a creative and generative activity. I will, so-to-speak, seek to view Lessing from the inside out, i.e., to reveal how the generative paradigm underlying his thinking (and thereby defining his *ars cogitandi*) is active as a creative power enabling him to pursue truth in religious matters. In an exchange of letters with Mendelssohn (and Nicolai) in 1756 Lessing wrote concerning the state of his then speculations on drama: 'Ich bin es überzeugt, daß meine Worte oft meinem Sinne Schaden thun, daß ich mich nicht selten zu unbestimmt oder zu nachlässig ausdrücke. Versuchen Sie es also, liebster Freund, sich durch ein Nachdenken in den Geist meines Systems zu versetzen. Und vielleicht finden Sie es weit besser, als ich es vorstellen kann' (Letter, December 18, 1756,

IX, 99). In my analysis of Lessing I shall attempt what Mendelssohn (perhaps wisely) did not, namely to ascertain the 'Geist' of Lessing's system, not in aesthetic theory but in his general *ars cogitandi*, by *rethinking* ('Nachdenken') Lessing's ratiocinative processes as he creatively pursued truth. Of course, Lessing never created an objective and comprehensive system in any field. Nevertheless, a surprising amount of consistency in his scattered and fragmentary statements will become evident when these fragmentary judgments are viewed as plausible applications of Lessing's underlying generative paradigm. However, most importantly, the contradictory, tentative, and fragmentary nature of Lessing's *ars cogitandi* will become comprehensible once the crisis in his basal paradigm has been made explicit. No attempt will be undertaken to harmonize all of Lessing's statements. They will be left to be what they are, namely often contradictions. What will be attempted is to explain why Lessing's cogitative activity produced the kinds of contradictions it did. At no time, do I believe, did Lessing ever successfully (in his own mind too) overcome the crisis in his thinking. However, relatively ambitious attempts such as the *Erziehung* will, of course, receive special attention. The key to interpreting Lessing will be found in his concept of truth. Lessing's struggle with the problematic nature of truth constituted in effect his struggle with the crisis in the cognitive basis (or 'root metaphor') of his 'Art des Schauens, des Blickes in die Welt'. In order to situate Lessing within the historical situation in which he found himself I will first explore in the next two chapters the epistemological crisis of the eighteenth century. This will entail an analysis of the formal and material nature of truth, the anomalies encountered, and the critical and crisislike reaction to them. After having done this an analysis of Lessing's concept of truth within the context of his theological speculations (the two cannot be separated) will be undertaken.

2. The concept of truth in the Enlightenment

Whenever the eighteenth century sought to express its epistemological hopes, it could find no word more adequate to the task than the term 'reason'. Concerning this ubiquitous cognitive force Ernst Cassirer has written: 'Perhaps no other century is so completely permeated by the idea of intellectual progress as that of the Enlightenment. . . . [intellectual progress is achieved when] all the various energies of the mind are . . . held together in a common center of force. Variety and diversity of shapes are simply the full unfolding of an essentially homogeneous formative power. When the eighteenth century wants to characterize this power in a single word, it calls it "reason". "Reason" becomes the unifying and central point of this century, expressing all that it longs and strives for, and all that it achieves.'[1] In particular, the concept of 'reason' functioned as the basic paradigm for the *Weltanschauung* of the German *Aufklärung.* Furthermore, this concept, as Rudolf Unger correctly maintained, '[ist] aus der Wurzel der Rationalismus erwachsen'[2] and as such it finds its roots stretching back to Descartes. Lessing himself was aware of the epoch-making importance of Descartes for the 'modern' concept of truth. In his *Gedanken über die Herrnhuter* Lessing notes: 'Es war Zeit, daß Cartesius aufstand. Die Wahrheit schien unter seinen Händen eine neue Gestalt zu bekommen; eine desto betrüglichere, je schimmernder sie war. Er öffnete allen den Eingang ihres Tempels, welcher vorher sorgfältig durch das Ansehen jener beiden Tyrannen [Plato und Aristoteles] bewacht ward. Und das ist sein vorzügliches Verdienst' (VII, 188).

There is a certain historical similarity between the times of Lessing and of Descartes. Descartes lived in a period of philosophical crisis.

The imposing philosophico-theological systems of the Middle Ages had lost their hold on 'modern' man's intellectual allegiance. Everywhere there was philosophical disagreement. It was the age of scepticism. Descartes lived through this philosophically troubled period and, indeed, his philosophy is only comprehensible as an outgrowth of such confusing times. Descartes became, perhaps, the greatest doubter of all times. However, he did not doubt in order to destroy all possible philosophical knowledge, in order to become a sceptic, but rather in order to overcome scepticism by giving 'a critical foundation' to mathematical physics.[3] Descartes was seeking a new and reliable epistemological paradigm containing 'certain and simple rules, such that, if a man observe them accurately, he shall never assume what is false as true, and will never spend his mental efforts to no purpose, but will always gradually increase his knowledge and so arrive at a true understanding of all that does not surpass his powers'.[4]

In such a search for a reliable epistemological method one encounters the similarity between Descartes' and Lessing's times. Lessing too sought certainty. He wrote: 'Ich hungere nach Überzeugung so sehr, daß ich, wie Erysichton, alles verschlinge, was einem Nahrungsmittel nur ähnlich sieht' (*Ü.B.G.K.,* VIII, 9). Lessing too lived in a time of philosophical scepticism and crisis. Paradoxically, however, the scepticism of Lessing's time consisted of doubting the 'root metaphor' that Descartes himself had suggested. Descartes and Lessing are situated at opposite ends of the same philosophical era. From Descartes through Leibniz to Christian Wolff there existed a familial community of philosophical commitment to certain root paradigms. The critique of pure reason executed so devastatingly by Kant was only the *coup de grâce* capping off an already existing criticism. [Kant's critique was also, at the same time, the progenitor of a new philosophical vision – namely German idealism.] Kant's critique came after a period of at least thirty years of such criticism and questioning, namely between 1750 and 1781. This was also the period of Lessing's mature life and his thinking shows the scars of such an incipient philocide.

As mentioned above, Descartes' philosophical imperative was his desire to discover a procedure that would generate 'scientifically' certain knowledge. Since 'science in its entirety is true and evident cognition', Descartes rejected 'all such merely probable knowledge and [made] a rule to trust only what is completely known and incapable of being doubted'.[5] With these words Descartes exhibits

typically 'modern' characteristics: namely (1) the concern with the
problem of certainty as a prolegomenon to metaphysical speculating,
(2) the refusal to accept anything as true (at least things of foundational importance) if it is not absolutely certain, and (3) the equation
of certainty with that which cannot in any way be doubted. Descartes set himself the most arduous task of finding an epistemological
methodology which would and could guarantee *indubitable* truth.
Descartes wielded the razor edge of indubitability as a scythe with
which to lay waste to what is 'given' man by authority or by
tradition. Philosophically Descartes was a radical revolutionary who
sought to subvert the theoretical basis for the philosophical *status
quo*.

In carrying out his methodology of radical doubt Descartes also
paradoxically became the symbolic father of modern self-consciousness and in a sense of modern theological thinking. Medieval man had
felt himself at home in the universe. He was part of an objective
whole. He was being within Being. Further, his very essence as being
is to be oriented to being. He thereby habitually focused his consciousness upon such being — the being of nature, the being of God
— the creator of nature, and the being of Christ and his Church. As
Etienne Gilson contends, '[A]ll Christian and medieval philosophy
must be regarded as one in affirming the metaphysical primacy of
being . . .'[6] The self was, of course, not ignored, for it was the self
that was saved, that was at home in the universe. However, the self
qua its selfhood was not, generally speaking, the direct object of
man's reflection as a first principle for metaphysical theorizing. In a
Schillerian sense, medieval man was metaphysically naive, however
sophisticated his naivity might be.[7]

This 'realist' orientation of medieval thinking is manifested in
St. Thomas' doctrine of knowledge. Truth lies in the adequation of
the human mind to objective reality as it is in itself and is expressed
propositionally in a judgment about reality. Thomistic epistemology
does not, however, entail a 'copy' theory of knowledge. The direct
object of man's cognitive powers is not a copy of reality, but rather
reality itself. The adequation of man's judgments to reality rested on
a metaphysical foundation. Gilson writes:

'When [the medieval mind] speaks of truth it does indeed refer to
the truth of the judgment, but if the judgment is conformed to the
thing, it is only because the intellect putting forth the judgment has
first itself become conformed to the being of the thing. It is of its
very essence to be able *to become all things* in an intelligible manner.

Its affirmation, therefore, that such and such a thing is, or is this and not that, is due to the fact that the intelligible being of the thing has become its own. . . . In short, the adequation between thing and intellect set up by the judgment, always presupposes a prior adequation between concept and thing, and this, in its turn, is based upon a real adequation of the intellect and the object informing it.'[8]

In other words, the human intellect as cognizant being is consubstantial with and naturally drawn to cognizable objective being and is thereby able to abstract the intelligible essence of reality as the thought-content of its thinking. However, and this is extremely important for distinguishing the medieval 'root metaphor' from that of Descartes' (and ultimately of Lessing's), truth about reality (i.e., truth with existential purport) is only possible because reality — being — is self-manifesting to man's mind. Man grounds his first principles of reality and of thinking upon reality. The structure of the mind is not the criterion for the way reality is (or must be judged to be). Reality — real being — is the beginning and end, the *terminus ab quo* and *terminus ad quem* of man's knowing activity. Thus mental activity is formally for the medieval mind 'a conforming of the self' to extra-subjective being. The mind, to be true to itself, must be true to reality, i.e., must conform to the primacy of being. Freedom for the medieval mind is not freedom from external (i.e., extra-subjective) determination. Freedom is not the 'liberation' of the self from the non-self, rather it is the fulfillment of one's place within the objective totality of things. The 'modern' thesis that human autonomy means that it is man who is the source of good and evil would be in anathema to the medieval mind and would appear not as freedom rather as licentiousness.

In order to realize his dream of absolute cognitive certainty, Descartes resolved methodically to doubt all things and all truths until he might discover something beyond all possible doubt. The perhaps unintended result of the Cartesian doubt is to sever man from all extra-subjective being. The more Descartes was successful in doubting the ontic claims of the contents of his consciousness, the more he became aware that all he had was his consciousness and its incessant doubting and thereby the 'modern' self was begot. 'As the doubter', writes Martin Heidegger, 'Descartes forces men into doubt in this way; he led them to think of themselves, of their "I". Thus the "I", human subjectivity, came to be declared the center of thought. From here originated the I-viewpoint of modern times and its subjectivism. Philosophy itself, however, was thus brought to the insight that doubting must stand at the beginning of philosophy: reflection upon knowledge itself and its possibility. A theory of knowledge had to be erected before a theory of the world. From then on epistemology is the foundation of philosophy, and that distinguishes modern from medieval philosophy.'⁹

The Cartesian self, having become raised to the level of the direct object of consciousness, is an isolated and, so-to-speak, metaphysically naked entity. The Cartesian self pursued by a diabolic genius bent on its eternal deception resembles the Nietzschean self afloat in a tumultuous metaphysical void with no frame of reference (i.e., with no self-manifesting objective being) to guide it. If the essence of the mind is 'to conform itself to the primacy of being', then the Cartesian method has made any such conforming impossible, for in universal doubt the cognitive consubstantiality of man with being has been effectively severed. Truth for Descartes (and for thinkers until the age of the critical Kant) remained an adequation of the mind's thinking to objective reality. Descartes never doubted the existence of an object (objective being) distinct from and existing over and against the knowing self (as a *Gegen-Stand*) that must be illuminated before knowledge is to take place. Knowledge is still cognition of something else other than the self. But reality can no longer manifest itself to the human intellect. The Cartesian doubt has seen to that! The Cartesian self would seem to be caught in an impossible impasse, the impasse of modernity.

However, Descartes was supremely confident that he would not have to surrender to scepticism. The Cartesian self does not feel itself weak and helpless in its isolation, rather the very solitude of its being was to become the medium through which it could transcend the confines of the self and obtain truth about objective reality. What the self is, is a thinking being — a *res cogitans* — and thinking entails 'reason' as its generative principle. What can be said of reality, will *not* be ascertained because reality so manifests itself directly to man, rather things must be as they are for a Cartesian self because the human mind cannot think of them as being in any other way. If things (i.e., the basic ontic structure of reality) are revealed as they are because the mind must think them so, then one must conclude that things are dependent upon thought for their comprehensibility. Reality must 'conform itself to' and be revealed by the exigencies of human reason.

The epistemological starting point for Cartesian philosophizing is clear enough. The rational structure of the mind's thinking processes is to be examined for a clue to the secrets of reality. However, two basic questions suggest themselves. First of all, if universal doubt effectively severs man from an unmediated relationship to objective being and confines him to his own cogitating subjectivity, how does man know that the rationality of his thinking has any 'indubitable' reference to the ontic structure of reality? Whatever indubitableness is entailed in the interconnection of the mind's ideas, how is a philosopher to know that such ideas are valid for the essence and being of things? In examining Descartes' answer to this question, I shall also seek to exhibit the nature of the dubitable for Descartes. In other words, a full appreciation of Descartes' concept of certain knowledge requires that some attention be focused upon his concept of the dubitable. Secondly, granted that Descartes has erected a foundation principle justifying the principles of human knowledge as determinate of the structure of reality, what constitutes the essence of such principles? What is the nature of man's thinking processess? The answer, of course, is that man's cogitation is a rational cogitation. As Cassirer noted, reason is 'the homogeneous formative power' that generates the Enlightenment *Weltanschauung.* But what constitutes the essence of rationality? What makes reason rational? In attempting to answer this question I shall deal with the 'root metaphor' of the *Aufklärung.* This will entail an analysis of the formal and general material nature of rational truth for the *Aufklärung.* Once these sub-questions are answered, the meaning of the concept of rational truth for theological speculations, particularly for an evaluation of historical religions, will be examined.

B. THE EGO AS FIRST PRINCIPLE OF PHILOSOPHY

In applying his methodical doubt Descartes was not only seeking to discover the indubitable but also to locate and identify the *dubitable.*[10] One important class of the dubitable is that which is presented to human consciousness in empirical experience. For a philosopher such as St. Thomas, reality first and foremost reveals itself to the human mind as empirical experience. The path to metaphysical knowledge passes through the door of the senses. Descartes, on the contrary, contended that it is acknowledged by one and all that the mind often makes false judgments based upon the supposed evidence of the senses. Hence objective reality is not given to man according to Descartes in sensation. The human intellect cannot doubt that this or that *specific* sensation is 'given' or 'present' to the mind at any specific given 'now'. What is sensuously given, is sensuously given! Doubt is not yet possible. Doubt is possible and, indeed, unavoidable when the intellect, based upon such empirical evidence, formulates judgments about reality, i.e., asserts something concerning the way things are not only for the momentary 'now' but also for past and future 'nows'. The senses are not an indubitable pathway to the ontological structure of reality, i.e., to that which transcends, informs, and remains the same throughout time.

Borrowing terminology from Kant, one might formulate the essence of the *dubitable* for Descartes as that which is manifested to man in empirical experience. The empirical *qua* its very nature constitutes the essence of the dubitable. The material content of the dubitable is the *sensuous* and the formal structure of it is *time.* The empirical entails a manifold of distinct and discrete elements which appear as autonomous, isolated, and self-contained unities. In a Kantian sense, their interrelation can constitute no more than a synthetic *a postiori* unity, i.e., there is no more than a temporal and spatial juxtaposition of otherwise atomistically independent unities of empirical content. Thus time *qua* its very temporality entails separability, division, and distinction and hence any synthetic unity of temporally manifested contents on principle cannot be shown to be necessarily so related (since *necessity* constitutes the essence of indubitability as will be discussed presently). Therefore, time can never become the foundation for indubitable truth.

Using the tool of methodical doubt Descartes focused his 'mental vision' on the variegated contents of his consciousness and subjected them to an annihilating critique. In seeking to strip his intellect of all that comes *from without* and lays claim to ontological validity, Descartes was attempting to discover *within* the self-sufficiency of human consciousness some indubitable avenue to reality. William A. M. Luijpen writes: 'Consciousness [for Descartes] cannot manifest any sensitivity to reality [objectively given], for such a sensitivity would openly contradict the immanence of consciousness. The immanence of consciousness affirms its self-sufficiency: consciousness is closed and wrapped up in itself; it is what it is because of itself and therefore does not need anything else to be what it is. Consequently, there can be no passivity in consciousness as an essential aspect of it, for any kind of passivity would exclude the self-sufficiency of consciousness.'[11] Descartes continually turned his mind towards objectivity. This mental turning, which was called thinking, must remain in doubt relative to its content, but not, paradoxically, relative to the form of its search for truth. In other words, mental activity *qua* activity is presupposed in every act of knowledge or doubt. To doubt doubt is beyond the range of doubting. There is no doubting unless there is doubting! This sounds like a tautology, but a tautology rich in existential implications or, better, it is only because of the existence of the 'I' that there can be doubt. The Cartesian self that has *thinkingly* insolated itself from all objective being and become aware of itself as an isolated *cogito* becomes aware in the very same reflective act of itself as existing, as a *sum*. The self as an object of cognition is identical with itself as the subject of cognition and, therefore, there is no division between subject and object, between thinking and being, between seeming and reality. Absolute certainty is thereby produced.

The 'I' underlies and unites the 'thinking' activity (the *cogito*) as a cognitive pursuit of being and existing being (the *esse* of the *ego sum*) and thereby simultaneously reveals and guarantees the ontological reference of 'rational' thinking. The 'I' as a process of rational thinking posits a host of ontological principles in the very same act of positing and cognitively grasping its own reality. In other words, that which is entailed as a necessary ingredient making possible the very act of self-cognition must be granted real ontological reference since the being of the self manifests reality. That which holds formally for the reality of the self's being must by extension hold for the being of reality *per se*. Since the reality of the self's being is only revealed in and through the rationality of thinking, the principles underlying rational thinking must of necessity reveal the ontic structure of being *per se*. In short, the *cognitionis humanae principia* must contain within themselves the essential outline of the being of all possible things (*entia* or *Dinge*) and this outline can be made evident by systematically examining the content of these *principia*.[12]

Thus it is typical of a Cartesian inspired metaphysics to base its theses upon an analysis of the nature of the human faculty of reason. What can be taken as metaphysical truth becomes a function of how the mind understands itself. Whereas the *terminus ad quem* of knowledge remains objective reality for the Cartesian spirit, the *terminus ab quo* becomes the rational subjectivity of the knower. Amongst rationalists metaphysics was often defined as the science of the principles of human knowledge. For instance, Alexander Gottlieb Baumgarten, Christian Wolff's most astute disciple and a philosopher who influenced the thinking of Moses Mendelssohn and Lessing himself, defined metaphysics in the following manner: 'Metaphysica est scientia primorum in humana cognitione principiorum.'[13] Concerning this definition Heidegger has written:

'This definition of metaphysics arouses the suspicion that metaphysics is concerned with a doctrine of knowledge, thus with epistemology. But up to now metaphysics was considered as the science of what is, as such, i.e. of the being of what is. However, this metaphysics, just as the old one, is concerned with what is, as well as with being: yet the defining concept of metaphysics does not immediately say anything about that. Not immediately. . . . We must understand this definition of the concept of metaphysics in such a way that *cognitio humana* does not mean the faculty of knowledge but that which is knowable and known by the pure reason of man. That is, what is. Its "fundamental principles" will be exhibited, i.e., the fundamental determination of its essence, being. . . .

'Why are the knowable and knowledge not mentioned? Because, since Descartes, the faculty of knowledge, pure reason, has been established as that by whose guideline all definitions of what is, the thing, are to be made in rigorous proof and grounding. . . . In the development of metaphysics, it is now a question of positing out of the essence of pure rational knowledge a sketch of the being of what is, that will be decisive for everything further knowable.'[14]

Although metaphysical knowledge retains as its ideal the cognition of objective reality, it is no longer defined as the conformity of the mind's judgments to reality, rather the conformity of being to the universal principles of human knowledge. Baumgarten writes: 'Veritas metaphysica potest definiri per convenientiam entis cum principis catholicis.'[15] Thus statements or truth about that which is, about being, is not a function of self-manifesting being, but rather of the structure of the knowing self. There is no longer a primacy of self-manifesting being. The primacy lies in the cognitive structure of the knowing self.

The raising of the *ego* to the primacy and criterion of knowledge is what the noted theologian Helmut Thielicke has called the Cartesian foundation of 'modern' theologizing. 'Um dieses Einsatzes beim empfangenden Ich willen sprechen wir vom "cartesianischen Ansatz" bei jenem Denken. Es ist vornehmlich interessiert am Vorgang der Aneignung, ja noch radikaler: an der Frage nach der Möglichkeit dieser Aneignung.'[16] Illuminating this Cartesian thesis as a hermeneutic principle for theological truths, Thielicke writes:

'So ergibt sich von diesem cartesianischen Ansatz aus ein wahrer

Rattenkönig von neuen Fragestellungen. Und diese alle haben gemeinsam, daß sie auf die Situation jenes sich als mündig verstehenden Selbst zentriert sind, das zur Aneignung jener Botschaft aufgerufen ist. Deshalb rückt auch die Frage des *Verstehens* mehr und mehr in den Mittelpunkt der theologischen Thematik, bis sie schließlich dazu führt, die Hermeneutik zu einer eigenen theologischen Disziplin zu machen. Ich kann ja nur das aneignen, was ich verstehend zu durchdringen vermag. Der Anspruch verstehen zu wollen, ist geradezu der Protest gegen die nur blind-autoritäre Übernahme eines heteronomen Wahrheitsanspruchs. Und umgekehrt: Er ist die Proklamation verantwortlicher Mündigkeit.

'Indem aber das Verstehen zum Inhalt eines Anspruchs wird, entfaltet sich der cartesianische Ansatz in weiteren Fragestellungen: Wer die Frage des Verstehens aufwirft, muß nach den *Bedingungen* des Verstehens im Subjekt fragen. . . .'[17]

Furthermore, Thielicke contends, Lessing constructed 'das erste maßgebende Modell' for such a hermeneutics in the realm of theology.[18]

The act of self-knowledge is the indubitable foundation for all certain knowledge for Cartesian inspired philosophers. Descartes used such a specific instance of indubitable knowledge as a model for all reliable knowledge. In other words, the formal nature of truth can be abstracted from this one example and used as a criterion for the structure of all certain truth. Edward Caird has well summarized the essence of the Cartesian concept of truth; 'I can logically distinguish the two elements [namely the *cognito* and the sum], but I cannot separate them; whenever I clearly and distinctly conceive the one, I am forced to think the other along with it. But this gives me a rule for all judgments whatever, a principle which is related to the *cogito ergo sum* as the formal to the material principle of knowledge. Whatever we cannot separate from the clear and distinct conception of anything necessarily belongs to it in reality; and, on the other hand, whatever we can separate from the clear and distinct conception of anything does not necessarily belong to it in reality.'[19]

Inseparability or the impossibility of division of what is known (the predicate or attribute) from that about which something is known (the subject) guarantees certainty. Leibniz, who it will be recalled had resolved 'never [to] recognize as true anything but what is manifestly indubitable',[20] formulated explicitly this Cartesian first principle of truth. The only type of truth that could fulfill the criterium of indubitableness was called by Leibniz a truth of identity. Any other proposition could only be true by virtue of the fact that it could be resolved into and reduced to truths of identity. Identities are truths by virtue of the fact that the predicate of a proposition is contained in and flows from an analysis of the subject of the same proposition. 'The predicate or consequent therefore always inheres in the subject or antecedent. . . . In identities this connection and the inclusion of the predicate in the subject are explicit: in all other propositions they are implied and must be revealed through the analysis of the concepts, which constitute a demonstration *a priori.*'[21] It is easy to see why Leibniz sought to reduce all truth to identity. An identity is certain and indubitable because of the immediate and necessary relationship between the subject and predicate. A proposition of identity contains or, rather, is its own indubitable self-justification. It cannot be doubted without accepting a contradiction, i.e., a thing would be what it is (principle of identity) and not what it is (the assumption presupposed by the doubt). In short, identities are their own 'sufficient reason' for their truths. In the following section I shall seek to show how the Cartesian principle of identity becomes the 'root metaphor' both formally and materially for the Enlightenment concept of truth. In so doing, particularly concerning the material principle of truth, I shall focus attention upon eighteenth-century off-springs of Descartes such as Wolff. Whereas the spirit of Cartesianism was alive in the eighteenth century, the specific conclusions that Descartes has come to had long been rejected or revised.

C. 'MATHESIS UNIVERSALIS' AS THE FORMAL STRUCTURE OF TRUTH

The true is the indubitable and the essence of indubitability is the principle of identity. For a science to be rational it must in some way be structured around the principle of identity. But the various sciences of his day with which Descartes was acquainted contained anything but indubitable truths, i.e., all the sciences save one. Of all the subjects he had studied Descartes was most pleased with mathematics because of the certainty of its demonstrations. Because geometry and arithemetic appeared to Descartes as alone 'free from any taint of falsity or uncertainty'[22], he sought to find the key to knowledge in mathematical science. For after all, whereas there were countless schools of philosophy and theology, there was only one school of geometry. Such unanimity was a sure sign of truth for

Descartes. Thus Descartes concludes: 'Consequently if we reckon correctly, of the sciences already discovered, Arithematic and Geometry alone are left, to which the observance of this rule [for absolute certainty] reduces us.'[23] Descartes' investigation of the nature of mathematics was due to more than an interest in the rules for combining quantities. 'For I should not think much of these rules, if they had no utility save for the solution of the empty problems with which Logicians and Geometers have been wont to beguile their leisure.'[24] Descartes was, therefore, not interested in mathematics *per se.* Mathematics was to him a true and evident science. Indeed, 'the name, "Mathematics" means exactly the same as "scientific study" '.[25] What Descartes hoped for was to discover the nature of and rules of all true and evident sciences by investigating the essence of mathematical thinking. '[T]he reader who follows my drift with sufficient attention will easily see that nothing is less in my mind than ordinary Mathematics, and that I am expounding quite another science, of which these illustrations [from geometry] are rather the outer husk than the constituents. Such a science should contain the primary rudiments of human reason, and its province ought to extend to the eliciting of true results in every subject.'[26]

At this point we have come upon the 'root metaphor' of Descartes' 'world hypothesis' and ultimately of the *Aufklärung.* As Stephen Pepper has maintained, a 'root metaphor' is generated when a thinker, 'desiring to understand the world, looks about for a clue to its comprehension. He pitches upon some area of commonsense fact and tries if he cannot understand other areas in terms of this one. The original area becomes then his basic analogy or root metaphor.'[27] And the area upon which Descartes 'pitched' was nothing other than mathematics. Concerning this area Gilson has written: 'If anything can be truly said to express [Descartes'] innermost spirit, it is what I venture to call "Mathematicism", for Descartes' philosophy was nothing else than a recklessly conducted experiment to see what becomes of human knowledge when moulded into conformity with the pattern of mathematical evidence'. 'All sciences were one [for Descartes] ; all problems had to be solved by the same method, provided only they be mathematical, or could be dealt with in a mathematical way . . .'[28]

Therefore, the science that Descartes is interested in is not mathematics as a science of numbers and quantities. As general as mathematics is, it is nevertheless restricted to a specific subject matter.

Descartes' science of knowledge was to be restricted 'to no special subject matter. This I perceived, was called "Universal mathematics" *[mathesis universalis]*'.[29] Descartes' designation of his universal science as a *mathesis universalis* was an excellent idea. As Heidegger has shown, the Greek word *mathesis* means both the act of learning and the learnable. In specific, it meant for thinkers such as Plato the type of knowledge that is derived from what the knower already has. It entails making explicit what is already possessed. It is not a knowledge derived from without, rather from within the knowing self.[30] Heidegger writes: 'True learning only occurs where the taking of what one already has is a self-giving and is experienced as such.'[31] What type of knowledge could more adequately comply with the Cartesian thesis that the self is the principle of knowledge?

Mathematics in a limited sense was for Descartes an illustration or specific application of a more basic science. By abstracting from the content of specific sciences, Descartes hoped to ascertain the general and formal characteristics of scientific thinking *per se*. Although he will not be able to say in advance what the matter or content of a specific science will be, Descartes is sure that he can establish *a priori* to any empirical investigation the formal characteristics that the truth of any science will have and the general method all sciences must follow in order to arrive at indubitable truth. This is what Decartes meant, when he wrote: 'For sciences taken all together are identical with human wisdom [i.e., reason], which always remains one and the same, however applied to different subjects, and suffers no more differentiation proceeding from them than the light of the sun experiences from a variety of the things which it illuminates, there is no need for minds to be confined at all within limits; for neither does the knowing of one truth have an effect like that of the acquisition of one art and prevent us from finding out another, it rather aids us to do so.'[32]

Descartes equated his new science of relationships with the 'natural light' of human reason. The human mind is the sun that illuminates the real world. Indeed, this new science is first and foremost a science of the human mind and its rational structure. Whatever is true of reason and rational truths is true of all reality since reason as the essence of a *res cogitans* constitutes the most *general* and *formal* nature of all sciences. Therefore an analysis of reason and rational truth will reveal the nature of truth for the *rationalistic* basis of the *Aufklärung*.

In doing this, however, the point must be made that Descartes' root metaphor was essentially the same one for the rationalistic basis for the *Aufklärung*. For instance, Christian Wolff, echoing Descartes, writes: 'In philosophy we desire such complete certitude that there is no room for doubt.'[33] This is because philosophy is supposed to be a science and science is 'the habit of demonstrating propositions, i.e., the habit of inferring conclusions by legitimate sequence from certain and immutable principles'.[34] Since mathematics constitutes the model for all sciences it follows that 'the rules of philosophical method are the same as the mathematical method'.[35] Similarly Moses Mendelssohn in a prize winning essay he sent to the Berlin Academy of Sciences in 1763 wrote: 'Man hat es in unserm Jahrhunderte versucht, die Anfangsgründe der Metaphysik durch untrügliche Beweise auf einen eben so unveränderlichen Fuss zu setzen, als die Anfangsgründe der Mathematik, und man weiss, wie gross die Hoffnung war, die man anfangs von dieser Bemühung schöpfte. . . .'[36] Although Mendelssohn was very much aware of the fact that such a hope was far from fulfilled, he was nevertheless ready to make another try at it as is evidenced in his essay.

With the above discussion in mind and by abstracting from the specific subject matter of mathematics in the narrow sense, it is now possible to enunciate the formal characteristics of all rationally ascertainable truths as conceived by the *Aufklärung*.[37] The fundamental problem that rationalistic thinkers sought to solve was the problem of certitude. If reliable knowledge about the real is to be obtained, the knowing subject must be indubitably certain that his judgments are true. Conversely, all truths must of themselves be able to produce indubitable certainty in the mind of man. Certainty cannot be found where the possibility of doubt exists. Even the probable is not a sufficient source for certitude since the probable is only definable in terms of the nonprobable. If truth, or better, the enunciation of truth in the form of propositions is to be indubitable, there must be very sound and undeniable marks internal to the proposition itself immediately open to the mind's vision which lead, indeed, compel the mind to affirm or deny its truth value. All certain propositions must contain an 'inner truth' whereby it is undeniably evident that the predicate cannot be separated from the subject. In short, the 'inner truth' of mathematical thinking is logical and ontological identity. Existentially, the criterion for the certitude of knowledge for Descartes is derived from the identity of the knower and known in the *cogito, ergo sum*. Propositionally, this identity is expressed in Leibniz' thesis that truth is analytical, i.e., the predicate inseparately adheres in the subject. The impossibility of separating the predicate from the subject is equivalent to saying that they are *necessarily* related. Thus *necessity* is the primary characteristic of truths of reason (and in the last analysis all truths are theoretically reducible to such truths). A necessary truth is independent of any local, accidental, and temporal conditions. It is valid for yesterday, today, and tomorrow and is in this sense *eternal.* For instance, Mendelssohn writes: 'Ferner haben die Wahrheiten, die zu dieser Gattung gehören, das gemeinschaftliche Kennzeichen, dass sie noth- wendig und unveränderlich sind, und also von keiner Zeit abhän- gen.'[38] Since truths of reason are not limited to any contingent situation conditioned by time and space considerations, they are *universally* valid. Universal validity entails *generality,* i.e., truths of reason are applicable to whole classes of objects. That which is limited alone to a particular is, in effect, for rationalism an illusion. That which is applicable to many is the *abstract.* Furthermore, as was shown above, the empirical or temporal in itself cannot be the basis for indubitability. In other words, truths of mathematical reason are not revealed to the human mind as something sensible or imageable, but as 'that which is purely *intelligible, as being the object of the understanding alone . . .'*[39] Thus Leibniz asserts that 'we know [necessary truth] by this light [of pure reason], and not at all by the experience of the senses. For the senses can very well make known, in some sort, what is, but they cannot make known what *ought to be* or could not be otherwise.'[40] In short, rational knowledge is grounded upon a supra-sensible or intellectual intuition. Finally, since mathematical truth rests upon an intelligible 'insight' into necessary 'inner truth', it must, in order to be systematic, be axio- matic. In other words, the manifold of truths must be viewed as so many manifestations, transformations, or extensions of a principle of unity. A basic and foundational principle of unity is an axiom. An axiom is that which determines the content, form, and relationship of the elements of the manifold. Definition-wise, each unit of the manifold is only determined in its own essence by being defined by its relationship to (or as a function of) the whole. The individual unit's *to be* is to be a function of the basic axiom within the context of the totality.

Therefore, the formal characteristics of truths of reason are cer- tainty, indubitability, necessity, universality, unconditionality, eternality, generality, abstractness, intellectuality, and axiomatic unity. Whereas the dubitable is what is grounded upon the empirical and is manifest through time (i.e., limited to the peculiarities of any given 'now'), the indubitable is what is grounded upon the purely intelligible and hence is free from the effects of temporality. The temporal entails the mutable, the contingent, the eternal entails necessity, universality, and hence rationality.

D. THE MATERIAL CONTENT OF RATIONAL TRUTH

The root metaphor of Cartesian inspired rationalism — namely 'mathematicism' — served not only as a formal principle of knowledge, i.e., not only does the form of knowledge exhibit a rational structure, but the knowable itself is, so-to-speak, embodied reason. The first principle of the *Aufklärung* is that the 'real' is the 'rational' (or what can be reduced to mathematical rationality) and, conversely, the rational is the real. (This formula must, of course, not be understood in a Hegelian sense.) Johann Christoph Gottsched, one of the most influential popularizers of the *Aufklärung,* writes: 'Das Gesetz der Natur ist endlich auch einerley mit demjenigen, was einem die gesunde Vernunft giebt, oder lehret.'[41] The world has the structure of 'healthy' reason and hence reason is the judge of the structure of the world. Aspects of reality are 'real' only insofar as they participate in the intelligibility of reason.

In the ensuing analysis I shall exhibit the general ontological structure of reality according to the *Aufklärung,* i.e., the way in which the real is rational. This will entail an analysis of the problem of existence in a rationalistic metaphysics. Such a discussion will be carried out in order to cast light upon the *Weltanschauung* of the *Aufklärung.* As was noted in the first chapter, a *Weltanschauung* differs from pure epistemological concerns in that it is interested in cognitive problems only insofar as they constitute the basis for finding meaningfulness in reality. Thus the root metaphor of the *Aufklärung* was inevitably used by thinkers as, so-to-speak, a cognitive ray of light with which to illuminate meaningfully the ontological darkness in which a man finds himself. Therefore, I shall briefly and schematically discuss the Enlightenment principle of unity — namely the function of God in determining man's meaning and the manner in which man can relate himself to the source of value. In the chapters on Lessing's theology a more detailed exposition of these problems will be found.

In seeking to understand the philosophy of an Enlightenment

thinker such as Christian Wolff it is well to keep in mind that the term philosophy had a very broad meaning.[42] For Wolff the term philosophy refers more to the formal way of knowing rather than to the material content of the known. In short, philosophical knowledge is the knowledge of the causes and principles of the possibility of things insofar as such knowledge is formally of a mathematical nature. As Richard J. Blackwell has noted, Wolff's philosophizing is characterized by 'Wolff's constant procedure of developing his philosophy by drawing out new predicates by analyzing the meaning-content of a previous subject-term. In short, Wolffian philosophy progresses by an analysis of concepts rather than by an induction from experience.'[43] This, of course, is philosophizing in the Cartesian spirit.

Insofar as a thinker is seeking to philosophize about the general predicates of all reality, about being *qua* being he will be concerned with first philosophy or ontology. A comprehension of the essence of Wolff's ontology is necessary, if understanding of the Enlightenment *Weltanschauung* is to be obtained.[44] This is so because in the science of ontology a rational sketch of being will be given that determines the general nature of everything else that can be known. For instance, the very rationality that lies at the heart of being *qua* being will be found to constitute the essence and hence defining feature of man. Man's specific human destiny will be seen as a part of the rational destiny of being *per se.*

For Wolff and his followers ontology or metaphysics is the science of being and being is identified primarily with *possibility*. This is not to say that ontology excludes actuality. The actual, however, is an object of ontological knowledge only insofar as it is a manifestion of possibility, i.e., what is real, is so only because it *can* be. Therefore, knowledge of reality or of being is only possible through knowledge of possibility. The philosopher's task is to inquire into the causes of possibility.

The negative criterion of possibility is the principle of contradiction, i.e., the boundaries of possibility coincide with the limits of contradiction. What is contradictory cannot be and, conversely, what is possible cannot be contradictory. However, the principle of contradiction is only a negative determination of what possibility is. It merely indicates what possibility is not. Consubstantial with the repugnance of contradiction to possibility, is possibility's entailment of positive notes. Insofar as being can be, it must be distinguishable from non-being (or no-thing), i.e., it must have intelligible notes that make it what it is.[45] In the discussion of the formal characteristics of truths of reason it was shown that truth is obtained through an intellectual insight into the inner truth of reality. This inner truth correlatively must have an intelligible core that makes it so knowable. This intelligible core was called 'essence' by Wolff. Therefore, *essentiality* is that which constitutes possibility and thereby makes being possible. 'Essentia primum est, quod de ente concipitur, nec sine ea ens esse potest.'[46] Essence is, therefore, that which constitutes the very heart of being, of reality. This concept requires further analysis.

Essence is the principle of intelligibility. It is that through which a manifold of predicates takes on comprehensibility and by virtue of which everything can be explained. Wolff writes: 'Notio ista essentiae, quod sit primum, quod de ente concipitur, et ceterorum, cur insint, vel inesse possint, rationem contineat, est notioni philosophorum conformis. . . . [Entis essentia] rationem contineat ceterorum, quae constanter insunt, vel inesse possunt, cum alias non posset dici radix proprietatum & actionum, unde scilicet istae oriantur.'[47] Essence is literally the root metaphor of reality, i.e., 'radix proprietatum' of being. Indeed, essence constitutes being. To be is to be essential.

In the framework of Wolffianism there are three levels of essence. Insofar as an essence or a series of essential features are not further explicable in the terms of anything else and consequently serve as an axiomatic principle and insofar as they are not contradictory amongst themselves, they are called *essentialia. Essentialia* constitute the axioms of being, i.e., the *to be* of more determinate being is to be an intelligible expression of the essentialia. For instance, threeness and equal sidedness would be the essentialia of a triangle. From the essentialia there flow certain necessary predicates called *attributes.* Although attributes are inseparable from the essentialia, they are not primary because they are explained in terms of such essentialia. Finally, there is a third level of essence called modes. Modes are the ultimate and concrete properties of a being that are not logically generated by the essentialia or attributes though they are not contradictory to such higher essences. The modes are equivalent to what the Scholastics called 'accidents'. Whereas the higher essence gives a reason why the modal property can be attributed to a being, it can not serve as an axiomatic starting point from which to deduce necessarily the existence of a specific mode. Therefore the 'reason' for the presence of a mode must be looked for *external* to any specific being, namely in the being's relationship to other beings or levels of being.

It thus becomes evident that that which makes being possible, that which constitutes, so-to-speak, the ontological 'stuff' out of which being is constructed is rationality or essence. Nevertheless, the term 'being' does add a note to the concept of possibility. Being is potentiality conceived as oriented towards existence. Possibility *qua* possibility can and must remain in such a state forever. Possibility *qua* being, however, is oriented to existence. But what is existence? Is it a fourth realm of reality to be added on to the tripartite realm of essence or is it but a type of essence? Wolff is conscious of a distinction between possibility and actuality. Actuality is possibility with something else added to it. Wolff calls this something else a complement to possibility. 'Hinc Existentiam defino per complementum possibilitatis.'[48] While such a definition at least acknowledges a difference between existence and essence, reality and possibility, it does not add any information as to what this 'complement of possibility' is. At times, Wolff and his followers (e.g., Baumgarten) seek to identify existence with determinateness, i.e., a being (*ens* or *Ding*) exists in actuality when all the myriad or manifold of its possible predicates has been given to it. In other words, when a being is given with all its concrete determinations, it can be said to exist. Wolff writes: 'Quicquid existit vel actu est, id omnimode determinatum est. . . . Cum entia singularia existant, evidens est, Ens *singulare,* sive Individuum esse illud, quod omnimode determinatum est. . . . Principium individuationis est omnimoda determinatio eorum, quae enti actu insunt.'[49]

Even such a definition does not free the notion of existence from that of essence. To claim that existence coincides with determination is in Wolffian principles to make existence into a form of essence. Essence, it will be recalled, is that which explains why all the properties of a being are present. Therefore, existence as a determination of a being is constituted by essentiality. Moreover, since the essentialia and the attributes are necessary for the very possiblity of being, and since the tripart division of essence exhausts the elements of being, existence must then be a type of mode. But a mode entails only those properties of a being that cannot be explained as axiomatically deduced from the essentialia, rather that which must be explained by being *beyond* the specific being in question. Since all *finite* being, possible and actual, does not contain its own inner sufficient reason for its existence, such existence must be referred to some ontological source external to each and every finite being and specifying their modal determinations and hence ultimately their interrelationship.[50] Such an ontological principle of unity was called God by Wolff. Since existence is but the lowest or most specific determination of essence, and since essential notes must be explicable by a self-sufficient essence, God becomes the rational principle for determining the nature of the actual. God is the ontological principle or being that determines what will come into existence and how the manifold of actual existences will be structured.[51] At this point the root metaphor of Englightenment epistemology begins to become the root metaphor of the Enlightenment *Weltanschauung*. Since man is a part of the created universe, the reasons for bringing the actual universe into existence will also include an explanation of why man was created and for what purposes.

Wolff's concept of God is traditional enough. God is an infinite being distinct from the world. In rationalistic fashion, God is the only being whose very possibility entails its existence. God's essence necessarily overflows into his existence. God possesses an intellect and a will. As the source of existence God is faced with an infinite number of possibilities. Possibility has of its very nature a greater extension than actuality. Not only is there an infinite number of individual possibilities, there is also an infinite number of co-possibilities, i.e., some possibilities cannot exist with others or, conversely, can only exist simultaneously or with certain possibilities. For instance, a mountain and a valley can possibly be located in the same place, but not at the same time. The divine Mind must choose between various sets of co-possibilities. Since God is infinite reason, he must of his very nature seek to realize the most rational world. The principle of rationality conceived as a volitional principle was called 'perfection' by the Wolffians (and others). That which satisfies the divine will is perfection and hence the structure of the actual, of the existing will embody perfection. Thus Christian Wolff writes: 'In Gott ist der Grund zu finden, warum diese Welt für der andern ihre Würcklicheit erreicht. Da nun eine Welt vollkommener ist als die andere: so kann dieser Grund in nichts anderem bestehen, als daß die grössere Vollkommenheit Gott bewogen hat die eine für der anderen hervor zu bringen.'[52] In short, because perfection determines the divine will, Wolff concludes: 'So ist der Wille Gottes die Quelle der Würcklickheit der Dinge.'[53] The world must be, therefore, structured to reflect the best as only the best could 'sufficiently' determine the will. 'In my opinion', writes Leibniz, 'if there were no best possible series, God would have certainly created nothing, since he cannot act without a reason, prefer the less perfect to the more prefect.'[54] The key to reality and to man's place therein is the concept of perfection. Perfection is the principle which permits the 'best' or fullest realization of being. It can be said to be intelligibility objectified.

Insofar as God seeks to realize the 'best', this means that he seeks to create as much being as possible; that is consonant with as much order as possible. The manifold of creation must be so united so as to further the perfection of the whole and the whole so structured as to further as much as possible the perfection of the parts. In short, Gottsched writes: 'Die Vollkommenheit ist also die Übereinstimmung des Mannigfaltigen.'[55] The perfection of man as a part of the world is the perfection of a self-conscious rational being. Hence Gottsched concludes: '[Gott] hat alles Gute in diese Welt, auch unter die vernünftigen Geschöpfe gebracht, was ihnen zu ertheilen möglich gewesen. Eine grössere Güte aber können wir uns nicht aussinnen: Folglich ist denn auch die Güte Gottes unendlich, und die allervollkommenste deren ein Geist fähig ist.'[56] Since man, of all God's terrestrial creations, is capable of rational consciousness, man of all God's creatures holds a special place in God's structuring of the world. 'Ja da [Menschen] vor anderen fähig sind, [Gottes] Güte zu geniessen, und seine Gerechtigkeit in Belohnungen und Strafen zu empfinden und zu erkennen; So kan man leicht denken, daß Gott auch auf sie insbesondere acht habe.'[57] Therefore, the *telos* underlying God's creation of the world is the furtherance of man's perfection. 'Die Absicht, die Gott nach seiner Güte in der Welt hat, ... ist, die Vollkommenheit der Geschöpfe und der ganzen Welt überhaupt zu befördern. Aus der Vollkommenheit entsteht bey vernünftigen Geschöpfen Lust u. Vergnügen, und ein beständiges Vergnügen macht ihre Glückseligkeit aus. Gott will also die vernünftigen Geschöpfe glücklich machen, und richtet alles, so viel sich thun läßt, so in der Welt ein, das solches geschieht.'[58]

God creates the world in order to further human perfection. But what constitutes this perfection? Because man is a rational and conscious being, he naturally desires to enter into a union or society with other rational beings. As a rational being interested in the universal and eternal, man enters into a society with God. Gottsched avers: 'Wo zwey oder mehrere verständige Wesen eins worden, eine gemeinschaftliche Absicht zu befördern, da ist eine Gesellschaft unter ihnen. Da nun Gott mit seinen vernünftigen Geschöpfen ... in ihren Absichten eins sind: So kan man auch sagen, daß der Schöpfer mit seinen Geschöpfen in einer Gesellschaft stehe.'[59] Such a society was called by Gottsched in imitation of Leibniz and Wolff a republic in which God is the monarch. That which gives man a meaningful place in this society, that which constitutes man's meaning relative to God, is his ability to further rationally such a communion. Such a furtherance of perfection was called *morality* by Enlightenment thinkers. 'Die Tugend ist eine Fertigkeit [des Menschen] Handlungen nach dem Gesetze der Natur einzurichten. Nun gebeut uns das Gesetz der Natur nach der Vollkommenheit überhaupt zu streben, dieselbe auch bey andern zu befördern, und in allen seinen Handlungen eine Übereinstimmung zu befördern.'[60] In short, the destiny of man is to realize his rationality within rational being and such a realization manifests itself as virtue.

E. REASON AND THE CRITIQUE OF CHRISTIANITY

By founding their philosophical positions on the epistemological paradigm of mathematical reason, thinkers such as Descartes and Wolff had no intention of providing the tools to be used to destroy religion, particularly Christianity. Both men remained true to their religious heritage. But it is nevertheless obvious that the root metaphor of mathematical reason must have ominous implications for traditional Christianity. If truth can only come to man insofar as mathematical reason permits, then such truth contentwise is bound to take on rationalistic features. That such a possibility must ultimately result in a comprehensive critique and transformation of Christianity is self-evident. Indeed, the theological history of the eighteenth century in Germany is the history of just such a development. In this section I shall seek to explain the nature of this conflict. In so doing I am not trying to present a history of eighteenth-century theology. Works such as Karl Aner's have already dealt with the historical development of eighteenth-century theology.[61] What I am interested in is examining the far-reaching though plausible consequences of the Enlightenment root metaphor.[62] Some of the quotations I use will be from the theological extremists (extreme because extremely consistent). In the instance of Reimarus there is a direct connection with Lessing since Lessing viewed him as the ideal opponent to the revealed religion of Christianity. In order to comprehend Lessing's relationship to rational religion, it is first necessary to investigate it in its purity.

Moreover, in order to understand the often bitter critique of Christianity exercised by those committed to the root metaphor of the *Aufklärung,* it will be necessary briefly to analyze what rationality meant psychologically to the enlightened thinkers of the eighteenth century. Descartes and Cartesian inspired philosophy separated man from objective reality. Descartes' methodic doubt left man stranded in a metaphysical void possessing nothing but his own powers. Cartesian man was able to overcome the nihilistic implications of Cartesian doubt by the use of his own subjective powers. And what was this power? Man's faculty of reason, man's rationality! Pure reason had become the legislator of the ontological structure of reality. It also became identified with the essence of man. Man is first and foremost a rational being. Therefore, to be true to himself, the Enlightenment thinker had to be true to his own rationality. But more than that, man's rationality — man's essence — became that alone which grants him value. Moses Mendelssohn has concisely shown what rationality meant for man's self-conception. 'Der Mensch, der der edelsten Gaben des Himmels, der dem Gebrauche seiner Vernunft absagt, erniedrigt seine eigene Natur, macht sich den Sklaven des blinden Instincts, den Thieren gleich, und beleidigt den Urheber seines Daseins!'[63] Man's rationality is that which frees him from the confines of his subjectivity and places him in contact with the universal source of all value. Because of his rationality man is 'able to know the system of the universe and to imitate something of it by architectonic samples, each mind being like a little divinity in its own department'.[64] Indeed, the human soul is 'an image of the Divinity'.[65] The essence of this godlike power consists in 'discovering the sciences according to which God has regulated things, it imitates in its department and its little world, where it is permitted to exercise itself: what God does in the large world'.[66] 'Enlightenment' or *'Aufklärung'* is precisely the theoretical comprehension of 'the sciences according to which God has regulated things'. Mendelssohn, for instance, writes: 'Aufklärung ... scheint sich mehr auf das Theoretische zu beziehen. Auf vernünftige Erkenntniss (objective) und Fertigkeit (subjective) zum vernünftigen Nachdenken über Dinge des menschlichen Lebens, nach Massgabe ihrer Wichtigkeit und ihres Einflusses in die Bestimmung des Menschen.'[67]

Reason has become not only that which connects man with the universe, but is also, so-to-speak, a spark of the divine embodied in man. Therefore, in order to be true to himself, man had to become enlightened and to be enlightened meant only to accept as true that which conformed to man's rationality. The important thing is *not* the mere possession of a truth, but how man comes to possess it. Truth cannot be something mediated to man from without (viz. by authority alone) but only that which flows from and conforms to his rationality. This is 'der cartesianische Ansatz' of Enlightenment theology. Thus Karl Friedrich Bahrdt (1741–1792), a radical of reason, writes:

'Und sonach besteht das absolute Wesen der Aufklärung in einer Entschlossenheit und Gewöhnung, in wichtigen Dingen nichts für untrüglich wahr zu halten, was 1. keiner deutlichen Begriffe, 2. keiner gründlichen und eignen Überzeugung empfänglich und wo 3. keine Zusammenstimmung der Weisen vorhanden ist . . .

'Wer sich daran gewöhnt, mit fester Entschlossenheit, überall, wo seine Glückseligkeit konkurriert, den Grundsatz zu befolgen: ich muß meine Vernunft erst hören, ehe ich glaube – der ist ein aufgeklärter Mensch – gesetzt auch, daß seine Erkenntnis noch so eingeschränkt wäre und daß die ganze Summe seiner moralischen und ökonomischen Wahrheiten sich auf ein Oktavblatt schreiben ließe.'[68]

Therefore, man's subjectivity is free from any claims of objectivity unless objectivity meets the demands of the self's own rationality. Such a demand constitutes precisely man's moral autonomy. When Kant in his mature thought raised the thesis that autonomy and its manifestion in man's life constitutes the foundation and justification of morality, he was but echoing and intensifying that which the *Aufklärung* had long believed in and acted upon.

In the thinking of the *Aufklärung* man's rationality became the basis for his feeling of autonomy. To be autonomous meant that man should be free from all heteronomy. This psychological drive alone was enough to bring 'enlightened' man into conflict with Christianity, particularly with the spirit of Lutheranism. The underlying ethos of Lutheran Orthodoxy was the helplessness of man and hence his total dependence upon a source completely beyond him for salvation. Lutheran man is a man heteronomously determined. Due to the fall of Adam, man has no spiritual powers whatsoever, either to know God truly or to act in accordance with his dictates. Concerning man's spiritual incapacity the Formula of Concord states:

'Our doctrine, faith and confession are . . . that in spiritual and divine things, the intellect, heart, and will of the unregenerated man are utterly unable, by their own natural powers, to understand, believe, accept, think, will, begin, effect, do, work, or concur in working anything, but they are entirely dead to what is good, and corrupt, so that in man's nature since the Fall, before regeneration, there is not the least spark of spiritual power remaining, nor present, by which, of himself, he can prepare himself for God's grace, or accept the offered grace, not be capable of it for and of himself, etc.'[69]

By denying to man's intellect power in divine matters the Reformers did not mean to assert that man is an irrational creature. Man lives in this world and must master it by the use of his reason. Man can plan, investigate scientifically, and otherwise rationally organize his world. But beyond discovering the mere fact that God exists and that there is some sort of moral law ruling the universe, man's understanding and reason 'in spiritual things . . . are [altogether] blind, and by their own powers understand nothing'.[70]

But what is the source of man's impurity? Man tries to be pure in God's eyes, i.e., man seeks to have a worth before God based upon his *own* perfections. Man's basic perversion is to want to have just such value before God. In other words, the claim of the *Aufklärung* for autonomy and self-sufficiency is precisely what Lutheranism viewed as the essence of sin. According to Lutheranism, man possesses no righteousness of his own, but is freely given such righteousness as the undeserved gift of God. Furthermore, such righteousness is nothing else than God's designation of man as being acceptable to Him. In reality man remains a sinner, even the just man.

The world of the *Aufklärung* is a rational cosmos in which man as a rational part participates in the universal destiny of rational being, namely the obtainment of self-perfection. Such a *Weltanschauung* could not help but become the critic and enemy of traditional Christianity, particularly of Lutheranism. The basic antithesis between the *Aufklärung* and Lutheranism is nowhere more evident than in the rejection by the *Aufklärung* of the Lutheran doctrine of the spiritual death of man. The doctrine of man's spiritual death was grounded upon the doctrine of original sin. Original sin is, accordingly, for Lutheran Orthodoxy a 'hereditary evil', or 'the guilt [by which it comes to pass] that, by reason of the disobedience of Adam and Eve, we are all in God's displeasure, and by nature of wrath . . .'[71] Such a guilt totally renders man incapable of gaining any purely rational cognition of his situation and of doing anything acceptable to God. Human 'sin' is not just the actively and consciously undertaken transgression of divine law, but rather an inner and hereditary disease that corrupts man's spiritual powers at the roots.

'And first, it is true that Christians should regard and recognize as sin not only the actual transgression of God's commandments; but also that horrible, dreadful hereditary malady by which the entire nature is corrupted should above all things be regarded and recognized as sin indeed, yea, as the chief sin, which is a root and fountainhead of all actual sins. And by Dr. Luther it is called a nature-sin or person-sin, thereby to indicate that, even though a person would think, speak, or do nothing evil (which however, is impossible in this life, since the fall of our first parents), his nature and person are nevertheless sinful, that is, thoroughly and utterly infected and corrupted before God by original sin, as by a spiritual leprosy; and on account of this corruption and because of the fall of the first man, the nature or person is accused or condemned by God's Law, so that we are by nature the children of wrath, death, and damnation, unless we are delivered therefrom by the merit of Christ.'[72]

In short, original sin entails 'a deep, wicked, horrible, fathomless, inscrutable, and unspeakable corruption of the entire nature [of man's person] and all its powers, especially of the highest, principal powers of the soul in the understanding, heart, and will . . .'[73] It is obvious that such a negative interpretation of man invalidates 'der cartesianische Ansatz' of modern theologizing, i.e., the acceptance as true of only that which is manifested to the mind as clear and distinct (rational) knowledge and the attempt by man to establish a relationship with God on the basis of his moral activity.

Throughout the eighteenth century the concept of original sin was attacked not only by theologians but also by the myriad of popular weekly magazines dedicated to the moral improvement of mankind.[74] Reimarus can be taken as a representative of the general critique of original sin. In the fragment 'Von Verschreiung der Vernunft auf den Kanzeln' (which was published by Lessing and reprinted in the edition being used for Lessing's works in this book (*M.P.U.*, VII, 673–685) Reimarus interprets the mearing of the doctrine of original sin: 'Die Vernunft wird . . . als eine schwache, blinde, verdorbene und verführische Leiterin abgemalt; damit die Zuhörer, welche noch nicht einmal recht wissen, was Vernunft oder vernünftig heiße, jetzt bange werden, ihre Vernunft zur Erkenntnis göttlicher Dinge anzuwenden, weil sie dadurch leicht zu gefährlichen Irrtümern gebracht werden möchten. . . . Darum vermahnen [die Herren Prediger], als mit des Apostels Pauli Worten, daß wir unsere Vernunft gefangen nehmen sollen unter den Gehorsam des Glaubens'

(VII, 674–675). Reimarus further avers, according to the orthodox preachers: '[Der Mensch] habe, wegen der Erbsünde, keine gesunde Vernunft mehr, wenn es auf göttliche Wahrheiten ankömmt, und keine Freiheit des Willens mehr, um etwas selbst zu tun und zu üben, was gut und Gott gefällig wäre' (VII, 683). The surrender of reason to the obedience of faith constituted for Reimarus an insult to human dignity. Reimarus further contends that no such doctrine can be found in the Bible. 'Ich gestehe es, daß ich diesen Machtspruch [d.h. Gefangennehmung der Vernunft unter den Gehorsam des Glaubens], auch durch Hülfe der Konkordanz, in meiner ganzen Bibel nicht finden kann; und ich habe mich oft gewundert, wie unsre Schriftgelehrte so dreist sein können, dieses für eine göttliche Forderung an uns Menschen auszugeben' (VII, 679). Through a series of exegetical subtilities Reimarus seeks not only to demonstrate that man's reason was not considered to be 'verderbt' in the Bible, but that, insofar as Adam sinned, it was because he was not rational. '. . . [U]nsere ersten Eltern [sind] eben darum gefallen, . . . weil sie keine Vernunft gebraucht' (VII, 683). Indeed, because eighteenth-century man possesses a developed reason he is in a better position to judge about divine matters than Adam. 'Möchte doch ein jeder sich so viel ermannen, daß er mit seiner jetztigen Vernunft einen Versuch machte, ob er nicht, nach der bloß natürlichen Erkenntnis, viel richtiger von Gott, und seinem Verbot im Paradiese, zu urteilen vermögen sei, als die ersten Eltern sollen geurteilt haben' (VII, 684). Since faith, unenlightened by reason, can only result in irrational, blind, and fantastic notions about God, and since man possesses a rational faculty, Reimarus councels ministers to preach the following: 'Die Herren Prediger wären also, als wahre Seelsorger, schuldig, allen und jeden Zuhören die gesunde Vernunft und ihren Gebrauch, als eine untriegliche Richtschnur der göttlichen Erkenntnis und eines frommen Wandels zu empfehlen . . .' (VII, 683). In other words, reason alone must be granted full autonomy to determine the contents of theological belief. 'Die Vernunft kann gar nicht unter einem Gehorsam stehen, ihr Beifall ist nichts Willkürliches, ihr muß zuvor Genüge geschehen, ehe man sich mit freiem und gutem Willen entschließt, dem zu gehorchen, was die Lehre zu tun verlangt' (VII, 681). This same view concerning the reason as the final arbitrator and purifier of religious truth was echoed by the 'enlightened' minister Andreas Riem: 'Die Religion eurer Väter werdet ihr nicht verlieren; darum seid unbesorgt. Die reine Vernunft untergräbt nicht die Religion, sondern ihre Auswüchse. Ihr werdet Vorurtheile verlieren, und die Religion behalten. Sie wird, je mehr ihr sie dem Lichte der Vernunft nähert, so viel dauerhafter und fester für die Zukunft gegründet.'[75]

The ultimate reason for grounding theological knowledge upon man's intellect is the belief that human reason is qualitatively similar to God's though quantitatively weaker. Christian Wolff writes:

'Weil das Wesen Gottes eine Ähnlichkeit hat mit dem Wesen unserer Seele, die Seele aber sich selbst erkennet, und also einen Begriff von sich selbst hat; so haben wir oben dadurch zugleich einen Begriff von Gott. Denn da unser Wesen, und die in ihm gegründete Eigenschaften eingeschräncket sind, GOTT aber in allem unendlich ist; so dörffen wir nur die Einschränckungen weglassen, so bekommen wir Begriffe von dem Wesen und den Eigenschaften Gottes.'[76]

The alleged ability on man's part to penetrate into the divine mind by means of man's faculty of reason lies behind Leibniz' contention that man is 'an image of the Divinity. The *spirit* has not only a perception of the works of God, but it is even capable of producing something which resembles them, although in miniature.'[77] The primary thrust of the *Aufklärung* is to deny the Lutheran thesis of the impotency of human powers in spiritual matters.

Correlative to and derived from man's spiritual life on a theoretical level is the belief that man's perfection is a function of his rationality. 'Die Vollkommenheit der Geister', writes Gottsched, 'kommt aber auf die Vollkommenheit ihre Verstandes an, und der abervollkommenste würde also den vollkommensten Verstand besitzen.'[78] Reason as a practical guide for human perfection results in the thesis that moral activity (i.e., a rationally ordered life) is man's highest destiny. Morality is that which gives man his self-worth and upon which he can base a claim upon God, namely the right to fellowship with Him. This claim is one that is derived from the very foundation of things and to which God Himself is obligated. Summing up the importance of morality for rationally derived religious truth Riem writes: 'Die aufgeklärten Lehrer reiner Wahrheiten der Religion, und der große Mittelpunkt ihres Unterrichts, sind, daß ihre Hauptforderung in Erfüllung der Pflichten gegen seinen Nächsten mit Aufrichtigkeit, und der wahre Trost im Leben und Sterben aus dem Zeugnisse eines guten Gewissens entspringe.'[79]

The essence of a morally and rationally ordered life can be formulated briefly as: 'So sehen wir wohl', writes Gottsched, 'wozu uns die natürliche Verbindlichkeit verpflichte: Nemlich alles zu thun, was zur Vollkommenheit überhaupt gereichet, und alles zu unterlassen, was zur Unvollkommenheit des menschlichen Geschlechts gereichen könnte.'[80] However, and here is an important point, the basis of this obligation is situated not in the will of God, but in nature, i.e., in the universal, necessary and hence rational structure of being. Thus even atheists are obligated to fulfill natural law. 'Denn vorerst haben wir die Verbindlichkeit des Gesetzes der Natur nicht von dem Urheber desselben, sondern aus der Natur der Dinge hergeleitet . . .'[81] Furthermore, the laws of nature are a manifestation of man's reason. 'Das Gesetz der Natur ist endlich auch einerley mit demjenigen, was einem die gesunde Vernunft giebt, oder lehret.'[82] Therefore, even man's moral obligations and ethical destiny are but functions of man's subjectivity, i.e., of his rationality and are accordingly autonomous from anything outside of man as a self-conscious rational being. God for the *Aufklärung*, at least for the more rationalist strain, tends to become the conclusion rather than the premise of things. Beyond the fact that God must create and structure the world, he plays a very minor role since the nature of what he may create is already determined in advance by reason, namely man's.

The general picture of man and his destiny in the view of the *Aufklärung* was succinctly formulated in an article that appeared in *Der Mensch: Eine moralische Wochenschrift* (Halle, 1751–1756). 'Der Mensch ist, seiner Bestimmung nach, ein vernünftig freyes Wesen, und soll also durch sein eigenes Nachdenken, und durch einen der Natur gemäßigen Gebrauch seiner Kräfte, sich selbst, die Welt und Gott richtig kennen lernen, und nach dieser Erkenntniß handeln und dadurch seine Glückseligkeit aufs möglichste befördern.'[83] Man who is free and spiritually alive should feel himself, according to the *Aufklärung*, capable of living a perfected life without the influence of 'supernatural grace'. Friedrich Nicolai, Lessing's friend and a crusading 'enlightener', writes: 'Wir besitzen Kräfte zum Guten. Wer dies leugnen wollte, würde Gottes Schöpfung schänden, der uns so viel Vollkommenheiten hat. Ohne den Einfluß einer übernatürlichen wirkenden Gnade können wir Tugenden und edle Taten ausüben. Oder sind etwa Wohlwollen, Menschenliebe, Freundschaft, Großmut, Mitleiden, Dankbarkeit nicht Tugenden.'[84] For the 'enlightened' man of the eighteenth-century notions such as original sin were no longer possible. Karl Aner writes: 'Die Erbsündenlehre schien als erste mit dem Glauben an die Menschenwürde unvereinbar. Mögen sie sonst noch so getrennte Wege gegangen sein — in der Verurteilung des Sündenpessimissmus und dem optimistischen Glauben an die bildungsfähige Menschennatur waren alle Geister der Zeit von Goethe bis Nicolai, von Herder bis zum schlichten Dorfpfarrer einig. Die "Tugend", worunter man eine gutherzige, lautere, tätigkeitsfrohe Gesinnung verstand, war der Gegenstand der allgemeinen Begeisterung geworden . . .'[85]

F. CRITICISM OF THE BIBLE AS A MEDIUM OF REVELATION

Thus far only certain material objections to Christianity by the rationalistic *Aufklärung* have been discussed. An equally basic criticism of historical religion entails the formal nature of rational truth. It will be recalled that such truth is supposed to possess formal features such as necessity, eternality, universality, etc. Religious truth as all forms of rational truth had to be concerned with the universal good and perfection of mankind and manifested in a medium universally accessible to all men. Because of this alone, Mendelssohn could not accept any revealed or historical religion as true if it claimed exclusive possession of truth. 'Da die Menschen alle von ihrem Schöpfer zur ewigen Glückseligkeit bestimmt sein müssen, so kann eine ausschließende Religion nicht die wahre sein.'[86] However, Mendelssohn still accepted revelation for less universal needs of man. To find a more total attack upon revelation Lessing had to turn to Reimarus. Reimarus, a religious radical because radically consistent, sought to do more than to hold up specific historically grounded beliefs of Christianity to ridicule. It is true that he tried to show that historical reports, particularly of miracles, are inaccurate. But behind his attack upon specific historical truths lies a more comprehensive objection to Christianity based upon the rationalistic paradigm. According to Reimarus, God can reveal no more than what is materially and formally universal: '[Gott] hat für die leibliche und zeitliche Wohlfahrt des Menschen durch solche allgemeine Mittel, die ein jeder haben kann, in der Natur gesorget; und was nur wenige habhaft werden können, das ist auch dem Menschen zu seiner Wohlfahrt nicht nötig. Um so viel mehr muß dasjenige, was die Seele, und zwar in all Ewigkeit, so vollkommen und glücklich machen, allgemein sein: und wo es das nicht ist, wenn nur wenige dazu gelangen können: so ist es auch dem Menschen nicht nötig, und dem weisen, gütigen Gott nicht als ein notwendiges Mittel gesetzet, sondern von Menschen ersonnen' (M.P.V., VII 734). Formally, truth is the necessary and the necessary is the universal. These principles clearly underlie the contention of Reimarus just quoted. This contention coupled with Reimarus' belief in the spiritual power of man's rational faculty are at the basis of his rejection of Christian revelation. Knowledge about God derived from history is not only a non-necessity but also an impossibility.

One reason for this impossibility would be that, if truth *necessary* for man's salvation were only to be obtained or obtainable at a certain point in man's history, all the people who lived before this point would not have been able to know such necessary truth. Since God is good and accordingly must seek the welfare of the *entire* human race, such historically mediated truths of salvation constitute a contradiction. But more serious is Reimarus' attack upon the possibility of communicating through history truths about God. It is one thing for a prophet to claim that, by means of an immediate (empirical) feeling of certainty, he has access to revealed truth, and it is another thing for the people to whom the prophet related his 'revelation' to claim that they know that this or that has been revealed, particularly for people separated by thousands of years from the prophet. 'Wenn aber nur einige im Volke eine Offenbarung unmittelbar bekommen, und sie bezeugen andern Menschen, was ihnen offenbaret ist: so bekommen die andern Menschen diese Nach-richt vom Menschen. Es ist also nicht mehr eine göttliche Offen-barung, sondern ein menschliches Zeugnis von einer göttlichen Offen-barung. . . . [S]o ist dieses menschliche Zeugnis von einer göttlichen Offenbarung bei weiten so glaubwürdig nicht' (*M.P.U.*, VII, 689) The distinction between an immediate revelation and a historical report of it will be shown to play a major role in Lessing's thinking on revelation. Unfortunately; however, Reimarus at this point was not able to make fully explicit the rationalistic paradigm underlying and thereby justifying his argumentation. (We shall see in the next chapter that Lessing did accomplish such a task). Nevertheless, the inability of the historical (i.e., of historical narration) to become a reliable medium of the divine rests ultimately upon the fact that it can do no more than indicate the probable occurrence of a particular event. Since the divine is the source of the rationality of reality, the divine cannot be made manifest in the particular or in the historical, rather only as the universal and necessary truths of reason. As Spinoza wrote in his *Theologico-political Treatise*, statements about 'God always involves necessity or truth'.[87] Therefore, Spinoza concludes, truth about God 'does not depend on the truth of any historical narrative whatsoever', because historical narratives 'cannot give us the knowledge nor consequently the love of God, for love of God springs from knowledge of Him, and knowledge of Him should be derived from general ideas, in themselves certain and known [by reason] , so that the truth of a historical narrative is very far from being a necessary requisite for our attaining our highest good'.[88]

This same disdain for historically mediated truth is evident in other 'rationalists' of the time. For instance, Karl Bahrdt writes: 'Religion ist ja für alle Menschen, nicht wahr? . . . Sonach muß sie allen . . . faßlich, erkennbar und − mit der bloßen Vernunft erkennbar sind . . . Der Messias also muß . . . alles verdrängen, was nicht allgemein erkennbar, allgemein beseligend ist − muß folglich die Religion des gesunden Menschenverstandes einführen.'[89] And Fr. Röhr (1777−1848) writes: 'Beginnt nämlich der Rationalist den Bau seines christlich-religiösen Glaubenssystem damit, daß er die Idee einer unmittelbaren Offenbarung als zu unzulässig und unhaltbar ausgibt . . .'[90] Traditional Christianity is rejected formally because of its historicity. The temporal for the Cartesian inspired *Aufklärung* is not only unreliable as an epistemological medium but also as a religious mediator. In short, the temporal *qua* temporality cannot make manifest to man the necessary, unchanging, universal and hence rational core of reality. For the Cartesian spirit, the cognitive door to reality is supra-temporal and static. Such truths are supra-temporal because, although grasped in time, their justification is not affected by temporality. Reason using its own *a priori* concepts can penetrate through the unending flux of the empirical world into the ordered and unchanging essence of reality. In this sense one can speak of the rationalist's universe as static. The tendency to conceive the universe as static was almost a universal habit of the seventeenth and eighteenth centuries. Commenting upon the static nature of much eighteenth-century though Toulmin and Goodfield write:

'At first sight, a great gulf separated the Cartesians and the Deists from Protestant scientists and natural theologians. Yet those who interpreted the Order of Nature theologically, and those who refused to do so, shared a common starting-point. . . . Scientists and theologians built up a static and unhistorical system of natural philosophy, in which fixed species of living creatures and solid unbreakable atoms alike conformed to the unchanging laws and specifications appropriate to their various kinds. . . . For the moment, no one had formed any real conception of Nature as developing through time.'[91]

This anti-temporal and static concept of rationality will be shown to be a key factor in Lessing's cognitive crisis.

3. The cognitive crisis of the Enlightenment

In the preceding chapter I attempted briefly and schematically to outline the *Weltanschauung* of the *Aufklärung*. The generative idea, the basic epistemological paradigm of the *Aufklärung*, was shown to be mathematical reason or 'mathematicism' (as Gilson called it). Using such a root metaphor thinkers came to view truth as the universal, eternal, supra-temporal, and necessary. Such formal features constituted, however, only the outer shell of intelligibility surrounding an inner kernel of rational content. The ontological guarantor of the rationality of reality, the principle of rationality whose very essence generates its own existence, is God. God is not only an all-good and all-powerful being, but also an all-wise one. God's wisdom causes him to construct *actual existing reality* — the cosmos — in such a way that the rationality of being is furthered to the highest degree, i.e., he creates 'the best of all possible worlds'. Man as self-conscious rationality has as his destiny to participate in and realize the universal rationality of being, i.e., to become moral. Indeed, man is more or less the focal point around which God created the universe, in the sense that the universe is constructed so as to further the moral perfection of man. The rationalistically influenced *Aufklärung* certainly was historically one of the most ambitious attempts to interpret the world as fully transparent to the intellectual gaze of the human mind. Indeed, perhaps only Hegel claimed to have seen more and to have explained more rationally than the 'dogmatists' of the eighteenth century. Indeed, Hegel's own dialectical philosophy is a 'dialectical' descendant of the *Aufklärung* as it constitutes an all-consuming attempt to maintain and reveal the rationality of the real in the light of the criticisms of the *Aufklärung*, particularly those of Kant's critical philosophy.

However, the outline of the *Aufklärung* presented in the last chapter does not exhaust what is normally designated as Enlightenment thought in Germany (to say nothing of England and France). Max Wundt designates this positive age of constructive Wolffianism as 'das zweite Menschenalter' of the *Aufklärung* and fixes the dates as 1720 to 1750.[1] Wundt contends that there is also 'das dritte Menschenalter' of the *Aufklärung* (1750–1780) wherein the breakdown of Wolffianism is evident.[2] Ernst Cassirer for his part seems to view this age as the 'real' Enlightenment (Wolff's period of influence being more or less a hang-over from the age of seventeeth-century rationalism).[3] There is, of course, little point in quarreling over terminology so long as the referents of an investigator's vocabulary are clearly intelligible. *This third age of the Aufklärung is the age of Lessing* and was, in my judgment, an age of crisis. The fundamental philosophical basis for this crisis was the breakdown in the ability of mathematical reason to solve problems. On every level the root metaphor of the Wolffian phase of the *Aufklärung* was faced with anamolies until it itself became an anamoly. The philosophical development and crisis of the pre-critical Kant (from about 1760 onward) serves as an excellent example.[4] Hence, it is my contention that the age of Lessing can best be comprehended as an age of crisis in Kuhn's sense (as described in the first chapter). This is in direct opposition to Cassirer who has, in my judgment, interpreted the 'philosophy of the Enlightenment' as exhibiting more internal consistency and doctrinal coherence than really was the case. An excellent example of this tendency on Cassirer's part is his contention that reason was for Lessing synthetic rather than analytic as it was for Spinoza (and other dogmatists).[5] Cassirer's proto-dialectical interpretation unnecessarily Hegelianizes Lessing and leads to a misreading of Lessing's relationship to Christianity. My contention will be that Lessing's concept of reason remained essentially analytic but that this analytical reason was faced with certain anamolies it was trying to solve. In this 'trying' is contained all the ambiguous peculiarities of Lessing's *ars cogitandi* that forms the basis of his theological speculations.

A. THE ANAMOLY OF EXISTENCE AND THE RISE OF EMPIRICISM

The Cartesian spirit in the guise of triumphant Wolffianism had indeed erected an imposing edifice of rationality, but an edifice built upon a foundation of epistemological and metaphysical quicksand.

The formal essence of truth is necessity and is grounded upon the principle of identity. Descartes utilized this principle ontologically as well as logically in his contention that what is clearly and distinctly perceived as connected to something else belongs essentially to that thing and, conversely, things not necessarily connected constitute two entirely distinct and mutually exclusive realms of reality. When this principle is applied to reality as a whole or as a systematic unity, and should there be something whose being is not *to be* a deductively determined function of the totality, this something will and must be experienced as a metaphysically unwelcomed and anamolous guest. Indeed, the existence of something that cannot be viewed as an extension, transformation, and modification of a universal principle of unity will cause the world to lose its systematic intelligibility and the human mind to be faced with an atomistically given fact. As Mendelssohn wrote: 'Gesetzt, es könnte etwas ohne allen Grund vorhanden sein, so wäre das Dasein desselben eine Wahrheit, die mit keiner anderen Wahrheit verknüpft ist, eine isolierte Insel im Reiche der Wahrheiten, zu welcher auf keinerlei Weise zu gelangen ist.'[6] Now Mendelssohn, in imitation of Baumgarten, had just identified *Dasein* with the concrete *Bestimmungen* (determinations) of a thing for which it's possible to give a sufficient reason why they are predicated of a subject. For as Mendelssohn notes: 'Es ist schlechterdings unmöglich, dass eine Bestimmung wahr und unbegreiflich sein sollte.'[7]

If something should be, yet not be intelligibly united to a systematic whole, its *Dasein* would be then beyond comprehension and hence the rationality of reality to that degree would be dissolved. The metaphysical and epistemological crisis (and epistemology and ontology were just two sides of the same philosophical coin) that developed in the eighteenth century leading to Kant's 'Copernican Revolution' has its roots not so much in the fact that, if something is without a reason, its *Dasein* is unintelligible, but in the discovery that *Dasein* itself is not reasonable (i.e., is *not* an essence). Hence the very existence of things is in some sense unintelligible to the human mind. In short, the ontological anamoly of the eighteenth century developed out of the recognition that existence is a type of reality external to the class of essentiality.

A sign of the times can be found in the pre-critical Kant's work *Der einzig mögliche Beweisgrund zu einer Demonstration des Daseins Gottes* (1763).[8] The Wolffians in order to integrate existence into the rational schema of things had treated existence as a predicate that adds something as a compliment to possibility. Just what this 'compliment' was, was not at all clear. Kant for instance complains: 'Die Wolffische Erklärung des Daseins, daß es eine Ergänzung der Möglichkeit sei, ist offenbar sehr unbestimmt. Wenn man nicht schon vorher weiß, was über die Möglichkeit in einem Dinge kann gedacht werden, so wird man es durch diese Erklärung nicht lernen.'[9] Baumgarten (and Mendelssohn as just noted) had contended that the difference between existence and possibility lies in the fact that an existing object has all its determinations whereas a merely possible object is still undetermined, i.e., there are concrete predicates that have not yet received a reason for being ascribed to a subject. Kant, however, objects 'Nehmet ein Subjekt, welches ihr wollt, z.E. den Julius Cäsar. Fasset alle seine erdenkliche Prädikate, selbst die der Zeit und des Orts nicht ausgenommen, in ihm zusammen, so werdet ihr bald begreifen, daß er mit allen diesen Bestimmungen existieren oder auch nicht existieren kann.'[10] Therefore Kant concludes: 'Das Dasein ist gar kein Prädikat oder Determination von irgendeinem Dinge.'[11] Kant was not then nor, indeed, at any time quite able to specify what *Dasein* is. However, he knew what it is not. Namely it is not an essence and hence cannot be subject to the deductive manipulations to which concepts are subject. Kant used this distinction to reject the ontological proof of God's existence according to which the essence of God's very possibility is simultaneously the necessary reason for his existence. If essence and existence belong to two distinct realms and if the Cartesian principle of identity is accepted then essence cannot be used as a means to derive existence.[12] The realization of the limitations of essentiality as an all comprehensive principle of explanation could not but lead to a cognitive crisis.

 Since knowledge about the general structure of reality is derived for the Wolffians from man's pure reason, not from an immediate and unmediated self-manifestation of being to the human intellect, the placing of existence beyond the pale of essentiality was simultaneously to place reality beyond the cognitive powers of man. The Cartesian self, having confidently sought to transcend its own subjectivity by means of its own subjectivity (i.e., its rationality) was now threatened with being caught within the confines of itself, or within the circle of its own ideas. However much its own ideas (e.g., mathematical propositions) might be axiomatically deducible and hence necessarily related to each other, there was no guarantee that they are applicable to reality and correlatively if reality in itself is intelligible or not. The cognitive crisis of the eighteenth century has its roots in the inability of the root metaphor of mathematicism to deal adequately within the problem of existence.[13] This anamolous situations had ramifications in various fields and levels of scientific endeavors. Two of these in the area of philosophy will be briefly discussed. Some attention will be given to the counter-paradigm to rationalism, namely empiricism. Although the Humean extremes of empiricism seem to have had few adherents in Germany, Hume's philosophical shadow darkened the Wolffian incarnation of the Cartesian spirit throughout the eighteenth century and, after all, was it not Hume who, according to Kant, woke him from his dogmatic slumber?[14]

Although, according to rationalism, the necessary laws that govern the ontological structure of reality were supposed to be obtainable *via* pure intellectual intuition, such laws were to have, nevertheless, reference to empirical reality. The reason for the universal ac-ceptance of mathematical thinking by modern physics was its ability to explain and predict the interrelationships holding between phenomena. However, empirical phenomena could not easily be interpreted on a rationalistic basis. Leibniz, for instance, recognized the essential opaqueness of sensations when he distinguished between necessary truths of reason and contingent truths of fact. A truth of reason is one whose contradictory is impossible and hence is uni-versally and eternally valid. A contingent truth of fact (i.e., is a truth based upon sense experience) is one whose contradictory is theoreti-cally possible. However, Leibniz refused to accept the division of reality into two heterogeneous realms. According to Leibniz the apparent heterogeneity of empirical truth is due to the subjective inadequacy and incapacity of the human mind to penetrate fully into the depths of all areas of being. In other words, the opaqueness and apparent givenness of sensations is due not to anything inherent in the very nature of sensations, but rather due to the inability of the human mind to penetrate to the intelligible core underlying sensa-tions. From the divine point of view all reality is intelligible, whereas, from man's much of it is *de facto* (but not *de natura*) opaque and not open to his intellect.

Leibniz' contention that truths of fact can ultimately be reduced to necessary truths of reason rests logically upon the essentialism of his metaphysics. But once belief in essentialism is lost, i.e., once existence is acknowledged as something different from essence, the radical givenness of truths of fact and the correlative impossibility of mathematically reducing empirical experience (factuality) to a mere function of an axiomatic generative principle must be admitted. Reality becomes divided into two heterogeneous realms. The heterogeneous relationship of the existent and the conceptual, of being and thought, and of sensations and essences is the basal principle of empiricism. A derivative doctrine from this basic principle is that existence is only manifested to man in, through, and as sensate experience. However much Locke, Berkeley, and Hume theoretically accepted a realm of reality behind sensations which is supposed to cause them in the mind, practically, sensations were for them the only mediators of reality to man or, in the case of Hume, reality became *de facto* equated with sensate perceptions. In other words, if knowledge must have reference to empirical experience and if pure essence cannot legislate for such experience, then the empirical *qua* its sensuous nature must become the only source for knowledge about the real or at least the real that man can know. Furthermore, sensations are no longer viewed as merely unclearly perceived intellectual contents, rather they are irreducible atoms of consciousness. Sensations taken separately and singularly exclude conceptually all other sensations or, conversely, no necessary interconnection can be deductively shown to exist between two distinguishable empirical contents of consciousness. Nominalism is, therefore, an integral correlative to empiricism. Indeed, Hume's basic ontological principle is: 'Whatever is distinct, is distinguishable; and whatever is distinguishable, is separable by thought or imaginations. All perceptions . . . are . . . distinguishable, and separable, and may be conceived as separately existent, and may exist separately, without any contradiction or absurdity.'[15] The result of this principle is that reality is viewed as a manifold of discrete and distinct atoms of empirical content. Hume in effect used the rationalistic doctrine of identity to 'explode' the unitary world of rationalism into an empiricistic world of radical plurality.

All knowledge about reality must begin and end for empiricism with sensations. Indeed, Hume seeks to show that all so called 'intellectual' concepts of reason such as space and time are merely empirical generalizations of concrete sense experience. Thus not only was the rationalist's attempt to gain knowledge by means of pure supra-sensible concepts of reason rejected, but also the existence of such ideas was denied. In short, the web of deductive interrelationships that constituted the intelligible world of the dogmatists was dissolved into distinct, differing, and isolated atoms of empirical content. Reason can discover no principle of unity relative to 'matters of fact' that *necessarily* connects one *exisient* with another. Insofar as there is a connection between matters of a fact, this connection for Hume consists in causality. 'All reasonings concerning matters of fact seem to be founded on the relation of *Cause and Effect*. By reason of that relation alone we can go beyond the evidence of our memory and senses.'[16] However, in the empiricism of Hume, the principle of causality is reconstructed along empiricistic lines.

Hume admits that the notion of 'necessity' of 'necessary connection' is entailed by the notion of causality and, as shown in the last chapter 'necessity' is the key ingredient in the Enlightenment concept of rationality. Hume's critique of causality involves, therefore, a fundamental criticism of the root metaphor of the *Aufklärung.* Hume's critique can be seen in his explanation of why the human mind is led to 'believe' cognitively in the 'necessary connection' between empirically given objects. For the rationalists the principle of causality is grounded in the ontological essentiality of reality and is revealed as the 'inner truth' of apodictic propositions. For Hume, on the other hand, insofar as the mind does form cognitive judgments, it does *not* do so because it has obtained an intellectual insight into the 'inner truth' of a proposition. All the mind is presented with is discrete, atomistic and autonomous perceptions. The ground for 'believing' that two such perceptions are causally connected lies in the vivid manner in which they are conceived by the mind. In other words, the differences between 'true' and 'fictitious' ideas is grounded experientially rather than rationally in a quantitatively greater and more intense feeling. Hume writes: 'I conclude, by an induction which seems to me very evident, that an opinion or belief is nothing but an idea, that is different from a fiction, not in the nature, or the order of its parts, but in the manner of its being conceiv'd. But when I wou'd explain this manner, I scarce find any word that fully answers the case, but am oblig'd to have recourse to every one's feelings, in order to give him a perfect notion of this operation of the mind. An idea assented to *feels* different from a fictitious idea, that the fancy alone presents to us: And this different feeling I endeavour to explain by calling it a superior *force*, or *vivacity*, or *solidity*, or *firmness*, or *steadiness.*'[17] Insofar as Hume could discover a reason for the 'feelings' of belief in the 'causal' connection between objects, he did so in the notion of habit. In other words, the only necessity involved in man's cognitive beliefs, is 'the [mind's] determination to carry our thoughts from

one object to another'[18] and the source for such a determination is
habit based upon repeated experience. The rational world of the
rationalists was reduced accordingly to a shambles under the empiricistic hammer of Humean criticism.

B. EMPIRICISM IN GERMANY

An empiricistic development that precipitated a breakdown of the
'root metaphor' of the *Aufklärung* is evident in Germany. 'The
decisive question in the historical movement from Wolff to Kant',
writes Beck, 'turns upon the question of the relation of logical, and,
more generally, epistemological concepts and principles to ontological concepts and principles.'[19] Wolff, following the Cartesian spirit of
mathematicism, believed that the principles of human cognition (i.e.,
thinking) have unrestricted ontological validity. Since the law of
contradiction and the derivative (at least for Wolff) principle of
sufficient reason or, in short, since the principle of essentiality
structures human thinking, so too is the objective structure of reality
constituted by essentiality. Insofar as sensations were acknowledged
metaphysically by the Wolffian school, they were conceived as 'unclear' ('undeutlich') perceptions, theoretically reducible to essentiality. Christian August Crusius (1715—1755) was the most influential critic of the formalism of Wolff.[20]

Crusius begins his criticism of Wolffian philosophy by rejecting
Wolff's tendency to derive formally basic ontological principles from
supra-sensible and pure concepts of reason. On the contrary, for
Crusius metaphysics must begin with an analysis of sense experience
and abstract the universal and necessary features of reality from such
experiences. Crusius writes: 'Denn wir müssen unsere Erkenntnis von
den Sinnen anfangen, da wir also auf Begriffe kommen, die unauf-
löslich sind und die nicht mehr als die gemeine Deutlichkeit haben
können. . . . [Einige Denker] schmähen ziehmlich unbedachtsam auf
die Sinne. Sie wollen lauter Begriffe haben, die der Verstand aufgelöst haben. Wenn sie an die obersten Grenzen aller menschlichen
Erkenntnis gekommen sind, so wollen sie die einfachen Begriffe
ebenfalls durch eine fernere Auflösung definieren und deutlich
machen. Notwendig müssen sie sich aber als dann in einem Wirbel
herumdrehen und können nicht weiter kommen. Sie flechten und
wirren eins in das andere und definieren erst dieses durch jenes, und
hernach jenes durch dieses. Weil sie die rechte Methode, einfache

Begriffe deutlich zu machen, aus der Acht lassen: so verfallen sie dabei auf bloß relativische und negativische Begriffe, wobei sie aber das absolute und positive aus der Acht lassen und nicht als pure Cirkel und leere Worte übrig behalten.'[21] Concerning Crusius' method of constructing a metaphysics Randall writes: 'The goal of philosophy was no longer to be a deductive system of necessary truths, it was to be rather a critical analysis of experience and of scientific thought.'[22]

Correlative to the autonomy and reality Crusius grants to sense experience is his rejection of the equation of epistemological criteria for knowledge with ontological criteria for the real. This leads Crusius to conclude that there is a fundamental difference between a *principium cognoscendi (Grund)* and a *principium essendi (Ursache)*, i.e., between logical or mathematical necessity and real causality. In Crusius' opinion, the principle of sufficient reason (which was the logical formulation of and the onto-logical principle for, the principle of causality in Wolffian philosophy) is not derivable by logical necessity from the principle of contradiction. Crusius writes: *'[D]er Satz vom Widerspruche, weil er ein leerer Satz ist, [ist] nicht das einzige Principium der menschlichen Gewißheit. Z.E. daß* jeder *Effekt* eine *Ursache* voraussetze, läßt sich durch den Satz vom Widerspruche leicht klar machen. Es kommt aber daher, weil man unter einem Effekt die Ursache schon hineingenommen hat, welchen man daher freilich, solange man jenen setzet, nicht verneinen kann, ohne sich selbst zu widersprechen ... Das aber läßt sich aus dem Satze vom Widerspruch nicht erkennen, daß ein entstehendes *Ding* eine Ursache habe ... Gleichwohl (ist ein Geschehn ohne Ursache) etwas, welches eben so wohl als das Widersprechende von uns als schlechterdings falsch und unmöglich gedacht werden muß. Es folget also so viel daraus, daß der Satz von der zureichenden Ursache und mithin die Realität in den Begriffen der Ursache und Wirkung in unserem Verstande ursprünglich einen andern Grund als den Satz des Widerspruche habe.'*[23] The connection between events for Crusius is, if necessity is at all involved, not logical necessity. Kant later called such a non-logical yet necessary interconnection a principle of synthetic *a-priori* judgments.

The crisis in eighteenth-century metaphysics centers around the attempt to specify more clearly the nature of necessary connection (cause) that is real yet not of a logical nature and the increasing inability to do so. Correlative to the acknowledgement that causality is not a function of logical principle is the freeing of 'existence'

(Dasein) from the web of essentiality and the recognition that existence is only given in empirical experience. The problem was succinctly formulated by the pre-critical Kant (1763) who, like Crusius, distinguished between a logical foundation and a *Realgrund.* Kant found it impossible to say just what constitutes a *Realgrund* and was left asking the Humean question: 'Wie soll ich es verstehen, daß weil etwas ist, etwas anders sei?'[24] To the degree that the principle of causality came to be doubted (at least as provable), to that degree the world of the *Aufklärung* became atomized into discrete, isolated, and varied atoms of empirical existents. The *Aufklärung* was threatened with being swept into the morass of Humean scepticism.

The Cartesian revolution in philosophy began by encapsulating man epistemologically within the confines of his own self and then using the very rationality of his subjectivity (i.e., his faculty of reason) as the means for constructing an outline of the ontological structure of being. With the freeing of existence from essentiality, eighteenth-century man once again became a prisoner of his subjectivity, cut off from all objective reality. For instance, Béguelin (1714–1789), writing for the Berlin Academy, expressed his doubts concerning the possibility of proving the reality of things beyond man's mind. 'Il est donc manifeste que l'existence réelle des choses hors de nous n'est constatée par l'expérience qu'autant qu'on suppose d'avance la vérité du Principe de la raison suffisante. Par conséquent toute démonstration de ce Principe a posteriori, qui supposera l'existence réelle des choses hors de nous sera une pure pétition de principe.'[25] Similarly A. G. Kaestner plaintively notes: 'Unsere ganze Kenntnis der Natur ist doch nichts weiter, als eine Kenntnis von Erscheinungen, die uns ganz was anderes darstellen würden, wenn wir das Wirkliche in ihnen sähen.'[26] Pierre Louis Moreau de Maupertuis, who became the president of the Berlin Academy, echoes Kaestner: 'Voilà où nous en sommes: nous vivons dans un Monde où rien de ce que nous apercevons ne ressemble à ce que nous apercevons. Des êtres inconnus excitent dans notre âme tous les sentiments, toutes les perceptions qu'elle approuve; et sans ressembler à aucune des choses que nous apercevons, nous les représentent toutes.'[27] Indeed, for some, truth became no more than an association of perceptions physiologically determined. For instance, Johann Christian Lossius (1743–1813) writes concerning truth: 'Wahrheit ist . . . das angenehme Gefühl aus der Zusammenstimmung der Schwingungen der Fibern im Gehirne.'[28] Some thinkers simply placed their 'faith' in the rationality of reality. Georg Friedrich Meier writes: 'Die Natur hätte uns einen Hunger eingepflanzt und sie hätte die Nahrung desselben vergessen, und kann dieses mit der weisen Haushaltung der Natur bestehen?'[29] Finally Karl Kasimir von Creuz (1724–1770) speaks poetically of the weakness of reason.

> *Wer leuchtet mir in dieser Dunkelheit?*
> *Wo ist der Richter, der den groß Streit [um die Wahrheit]*
>   *entscheidt,*
> *Und o wie ungewiß sind sterbliche Gedanken!*
> *Ja, die Vernunft hat mir zu sehr geheuchelt,*
> *Die Wissenschaft hat mir zu viel geschmeichelt:*
> *Die Wahrheit find ich nicht, die ich gesucht!*
> *Und größre Zweifel sind des Demonstrierens Frucht.*[30]

Indeed, according to von Creuz, man is a cognitive prisoner of *time.* 'Unwissend, was wir sind, und mit unserer Vergangenheit und Künftigkeit gleich unbekannt, verlieren wir uns im dem Meere der Zeit.'[31]

Von Creuz' reference to time completes the philosophical circle and brings us back to Descartes' concept of the dubitable. The empirical constitutes the content of time and consists of isolated atoms of empirical reality. Insofar as knowledge is limited to the empirical and insofar as the empirical consists of isolated units of temporality, man cannot obtain knowledge of the universally necessary and hence rational. Indeed, for a pure empiricist such as Hume, all causal or necessary unity as the principle of rationality is nothing more than a vivid *feeling* that one event will follow another. From the necessary truths of reason to the contingent truths of feeling is the path that leads from rationalism to empiricism.

The eighteenth century thus evinces two conflicting philosophical trends. On the one hand, truth is supposedly supra-temporal and necessary because it is grounded upon an insight into the 'inner' truth' of the *mundus intelligibilis.* On the other hand, truth is grounded alone in empirical experience and is limited to the momentary, i.e., it is incapsuled within time. Truth beyond and excluding temporality versus truth solely within time and excluding all supra-temporal necessity, absolute and necessary interconnection versus atomistic pluralism, or in short pure ontological absoluteness versus empirical relativity constitute the alternative and mutually exclusive poles of much eighteenth-century European philosophy. Indeed, the paradigm of empiricism gained its influence in Germany both as a cause and result of the existential anamoly that rationalism faced. However, insight into the essence of the cognitive crisis of the *Aufklärung* has not yet been obtained.

C. THE COGNITIVE CRISIS OF THE *AUFKLÄRUNG*

However much Kant and others tended towards an empiricism, indeed, towards a Humean scepticism, such a position is not typical for the German Enlightenment nor does it give an insight into the critical nature of the age of Lessing. For instance, the empiricistic scepticism of the 1760s was not destined to be Kant's final pre-critical position or, indeed, to typify this position. In 1765 Leibniz' *New Essays on the Human Understanding* were published posthumously. Leibniz trenchantly criticized point by point the empiricism of Locke. Leibniz' critique of empiricism had a great influence upon German thinkers (including Kant).[32] The gist of Leibniz' critique is two-fold.[33] First of all, according to Leibniz, the mind (and thereby mental activity) cannot be understood as a merely passive *tabula rasa* upon which reality scribbles atomistically discrete sense impressions. Leibniz (in good rationalistic fashion) conceived the mind as a spontaneously active force. Therefore, the contents, structure, and cognitive value of man's consciousness cannot be explained without reference to the mind's formative powers. Johann Nicolas Tetens, one of the leading philosophers of the 1770s influenced by Leibniz, ascribes a creative power to the mind: 'Die *ursprünglichen Vorstellungen* sind die Materie und der Stoff aller übrigen, das ist, aller *abgeleiteten* Vorstellungen. Die Seele besitzet das Vermögen, jene auseinander zu legen, zu zertheilen, von einander abzutrennen, und die einzelnen Stücke und Bestandtheile wieder zu vermischen, zu verbinden und zusammenzusetzen. Hier zeiget sich ihr *Dichtungsvermögen*, ihre *bildende, schaffende Kraft* . . .'[34] Secondly, the formative power of the mind is most evident in the mind's development and use of relational concepts, particularly in the realm of science. Empiricists had sought to show that all man's concepts were nothing but the additive combination of discrete sensations according to spatial and temporal contiguity. Indeed, Hume sought to show that the concepts of space and time were nothing but successive or simultaneous experience of sensations. From the point of view of Leibniz and those influenced by him, the demonstrable and *a priori* certainity of geometry as the science of space could never be obtained as the result of empirical generalizations. Rather it rests upon concepts of the pure unitive power of the mind, namely the intellect and in this sense it is *a priori* to experience. Other concepts such as necessity, possibility, unity, plurality, motion, substance, force, inertia, etc. were also shown to be concepts of the pure intellect. Concerning the origin and nature of various basic concepts of physical science Tetens writes:

'Es sind ohne Zweifel Empfindungen gewesen, welche die erste Gelegenheit gegeben haben, das Gesetz zu entdecken; aber es ist ein Raisonnement hinzugekommen, eine innere Selbsttätigkeit des Verstandes, von der jene Verknüpfung der Ideen bewirket worden ist. Die Idee von einem in Bewegung gesetzten Körper, der in keinem andern wirket, und von keinem andern leidet, leitet den Verstand auf die Vorstellung, daß seine Bewegung ungeändert fortgesetzet werde; und wenn gleich auch diese letztere Idee für sich aus Empfindungen hat genommen werden müssen, sie ist doch ihre Verbindung mit jener ein Werk der Denkkraft, welche *ihrer Natur gemäß* diese Beziehung zwischen den Ideen in uns zu Stande bringet; und die durch diese ihre Operation in uns bewirkte Verbindung des Prädikats mit dem Subjekt, ist weit mehr der Grund von der Überzeugung, daß unser Urtheil ein wahres Urtheil sey, als die Ideenassociation aus Empfindungen. ... Solche allgemeine Gedanken sind wahre Gedanken, vor aller Erfahrung vorher. Wir erlernen sie aus dieser nicht durch die Abstraktion, und es hängt also auch nicht von einer mehrmals wiederholten Übung ab, daß sich solche Ideenverknüpfungen festsetzen.'[35]

Therefore, whereas knowledge may begin with sensation, it cannot be explained in the terms of sensations alone. Concerning the influence of Leibniz on the *Aufklärung* Cassirer writes:

'When the mind [according to Leibniz] becomes a mirror of reality, it is and remains a living mirror of the universe, and it is not simply a sum total of mere images but a whole composed of formative forces. The basic task of psychology and epistemology will henceforth be to elucidate these forces in their specific structure and to understand their reciprocal relations. And this task which the thinkers of the German Enlightenment now undertake and which they endeavor to accomplish by patient toil. ... The psychological formulation and defense of the spontaneity of the ego now prepare the ground for a new conception of knowledge and of art; new pathways and new goals are revealed for the advancement of both epistemology and aesthetics.'[36]

Cassirer's contention brings us to the doorstep of the cognitive crisis of the *Aufklärung*. The German Enlightenment ('das dritte Menschenalter" — 1750 to 1780 — as Wundt has called it) is dominated by the attempt to reconcile theoretically rationalistic and empiricistic root metaphors. John Herman Randall Jr. writes about this age:

'The main stream of German thought, therefore, was not prepared to see the sure foundations of its newly won freedom, its ideal of an unshakable "reason", crumble into the phenomenalism of Condillac or Hume. To it such a psychological empiricism seemed destructive, not of the defenses of its enemies, but of its own sharpest weapons. As the century advanced many Germans . . . even agreed with Locke that the truths of reason must be firmly grounded in experience. But few who had been bred in the tradition of Leibniz, few for whom his thought had been the summons to a full confidence in the powers of the human mind, could ever accept the observational and descriptive theory of science built upon by the British and French [empiricists]. Though founded on an experience of facts, knowledge for them had still to be a matter of the reasons why, reason that could not be reduced to a mere succession of sensations. The subject-matter of their critical analysis was futile if it stopped with sensations and reached no rational explanation. . . . Since knowledge has nevertheless an intelligible pattern or structure . . . and since that pattern cannot be *in* sensations or come *from* them, its source must be sought elsewhere than in sense. It must come from another organ of inward vision, from an intellectual intuition of the reality that sense cannot directly reach —, from the Platonic *Nous* that reveals the intelligible realm; or it must come from the human mind itself, from its creative activity in organizing and interpreting the bare materials of sense.'[37]

Cassirer (unlike Randall) interprets this attempted reconciliation too much as if it had been successful and had thereby obtained an inner and systematic consistency. In my judgment, the attempted reconciliation follows the pattern of what Kuhn has designated as the crisis phase of a scientific revolution (or in this case, the crisis phase of a cognitive revolution that eventually culminated in Kant's Copernican Revolution). It will be recalled that, according to Kuhn, a crisis phase arises when a paradigm previously successful, encounters an anamoly it cannot solve and a new successful one has not yet been discovered. The old paradigm cannot be rejected because of its previous success but it cannot solve recognized problems. At this point the investigator begins to search around (often with the appearance of randomness) for new ideas, new paradigms. Such a search results in a blurring of conceptual clarity and consistency and alternates between competing hypotheses. The 1760s and particularly the 1770s in Germany are characterized by the inability of thinkers to reject an a-historical, supra-sensible, and rationalistic concept of reason as the basal paradigm of truth in favor of a purely temporal, empirical, and atomistic paradigm of truth and by their inability fully to reconcile and integrate consistently and systematically apparently exclusive generative paradigms. The task of the German Enlightenment became to reconcile these two paradigm sets and, as Randall has noted, such thinkers were often 'tossed back and forth between the conflicting currents of rationalism and empiricism'.[38] In the act of being 'tossed back and forth' consists the cognitive crisis of the *Aufklärung.*

Kant of the 1770s may be taken as an ideal example of a philosopher caught in a crisis. Certainly by this period Kant had come to distinguish two sources that are integrally united in an act of cognition. Knowledge arises for Kant (1) out of empirical experience and concepts abstracted from sensations, and (2) from pure concepts of the understanding. Kant writes:

'Einige Begriffe sind von den Empfindungen abstrahiert; andere bloß von dem Gesetze des Verstandes, die abstrahierten Begriffe zu vergleichen, zu verbinden oder zu trennen. Der letzteren Ursprung ist im Verstande; der erstern in den Sinnen. Alle Begriffe von solcher Art heißen reine Verstandesbegriffe: *conceptus intellectus puri.* Zwar können wir nur bei Gelegenheit der sinnlichen Empfindungen diese Tätigkeiten des Verstandes in Bewegung setzen, und uns gewisser Begriffe von den allgemeinen Verhältnissen abstrahierter Ideen nach Gesetzen des Verstandes bewußt werden; und so gilt auch hier Lockes Regel, daß ohne sinnliche Empfindung keine Idee in uns klar wird; aber die *notiones rationales* entspringen wohl vermittelst der Empfindungen, und können nur in Applikation auf die von ihnen abstrahierten Ideen gedacht werden, aber sie liegen nicht in ihnen und sind nicht von ihnen abstrahiert; so wie wir in der Geometrie die Idee von Raume nicht von der Empfindung ausgedehnter Wesen entlehnen, ob wir diesen Begriff nur bei Gelegenheit der Empfindung körperlicher Dinge klar machen können. Daher ist die Idee des Raumes *notio intellectus puri,* welche auf die abstrahierte Idee der Berge und der Fässer kann angewandt werden.'[39]

The problem, indeed, the *critical* problem that Kant had to solve was how to justify the application of *a priori* concepts of pure reason to an empirically given manifold. In his famous letter to Marcus Herz in 1772 Kant writes:

'The pure concepts of the understanding must not be abstracted from sense-perceptions, nor express the receptivity of ideas through the senses, but must have their source in the nature of the soul, but not by being effected by the object nor by themselves creating the object. I was satisfied in the dissertation to give a merely negative expression to the nature of intellectual ideas: that they are not modifications of the soul by the object. But how an idea that referred to an object without in any way being effected by it might be possible, I passed over in silence. I had said: sensible ideas represent things as they appear, intellectual ideas, as they are. But how are these things given to us if not through the way in which they effect us, and if such intellectual ideas rest on our inner activity, whence comes the conformity they should have with objects?'[40]

Until years later when in 1781 Kant published his *Kritik der reinen Vernunft* this question remained unanswered for Kant. It is obvious from the above quotation that Kant maintains his belief in the rationalistic paradigm (i.e., the rational and conceptual source of knowledge is derived from the self's own understanding), acknowledges the validity of the empiricistic anamoly (i.e., only the senses present man with the object of knowledge) and that Kant is unable to reconcile the two positions. Thus a tension remains in Kant's thought during the 1770s. Such a tension is the tension of the cognitive crisis of the eighteenth century. Other thinkers in their own way shared in the crisis. Johann Heinrich Lambert (1728–1777) approached the same problem from a mathematician's point of view with interests in logic and Johann Nikolaus Tetens (1736–1807) approached the problem from the point of view of psychology. Some thinkers such as Mendelssohn were more conservative in that they sought to defend the Wolffian position more or less as it was. Nevertheless, the evidence of crisis is there. For instance, in his 1763 essay on the mathematical nature of metaphysical evidence Mendelssohn writes:

'Man hat es in unsern Jahrhunderte versucht, die Anfangsgründe der Metaphysik durch untrügliche Beweise auf einen eben so unveränderlichen Fuss zu setzen, als die Anfangsgründe der Mathematik, und man weiss, wie gross die Hoffnung war, die man anfangs von dieser Bemühung schöpfte; allein der Erfolg hat gezeigt, wie schwer dieses ins Werk zu reichen sei. Selbst diejenigen, welche die metaphysischen Begriffe für überzeugend und unwiderlegbar halten, müssen doch endlich gestehen, dass man ihnen noch bisher die Evidenz der mathematischen Beweise nicht gegeben hat, sonst hätten sie unmöglich einen so vielfältigen Widerspruch finden können. Die Anfangsgründe der Mathematik überzeugen einen jeden, der Menschenverstand hat, und es nur nicht an aller Aufmerksamkeit fehlen lässt. Man weiss aber, dass viele scharfsinnige Köpfe, die von ihren Fähigkeiten hinlängliche Proben abgelegt haben, gleichwohl die Anfangsgründe der Metaphysik verwerfen, und keiner andern Wissenschaft als der Mathematik die Möglichkeit an einer völligen Ueberzeugung zutrauen. Diese Gedanken scheinen eine erlauchte Akademie zu der Aufgabe veranlasst zu haben: Ob die metaphysischen Wahrheiten überhaupt einer solchen Evidenz fähig sind, als die mathematischen, u.s.w.'[41]

An interesting example of the cognitive crisis is to be found in Friedrich Eberhard von Rochow (1734—1805). Although writing sometime after Lessing's death and after the publication of Kant's first *Kritik,* von Rochow expressed clearly enough the ambiguities peculiar to a crisis period. Von Rochow did not doubt that the cosmos is structured rationally, i.e., that it exhibits a universal 'Ordnung'. Nor does he find it strange and wrong that the mind is possessed by a desire to integrate systematically its experience of the world into an intelligible whole. Indeed because of this very tendency, the human mind 'brachte die vielerlei Systeme hervor, die vorhanden sind!'[42] But no system has been able to capture *the whole* truth nor can any. Von Rochow goes on to contend: 'Das kein einziges dieser Systeme ganz wahr (d.i. fehler- und hypothesenfrei) ist, erhellt schon daher, weil es von Menschen erdachte Systeme sind, denen es in ihrem jetzigen Zustand versagt ist, in das Innere (das Wesen, Verhältnis und Absicht zum Ganzen) der Natur zu dringen. 'Wir irren also allesamt, nur jeder irrt anders.'' [43] Inadequate systems, contradictory and partial positions, the existence of hypotheses, the incapacity to obtain insight into the heart of a subject matter, all are signs of a paradigm crisis.

The crisis in the root metaphor of the *Aufklärung* described above plausibly accounts for the general outline of the thinking of the age of Lessing.[44] Max Wundt has described these features excellently.[45] In the following few paragraphs I shall focus attention upon some of the key features of this period. The reader interested in more detail is hereby referred to Wundt's masterful delineation of the period.

The age of Lessing was a period of hope despite the cognitive crisis in which it was embroiled. As Whitehead has noted, the Enlightenment was an age of reason resting on faith and this faith showed itself in the belief that the world is ultimately a manifestation of an underlying rationality and that man could and should participate in it by becoming moral. The Wolffian dogmatist had been confident that man's intellect would be able with the use of theoretical reason to show men the path to perfection. Now that the light of reason had grown a bit dim, faith that man would nevertheless find this path to the heights of 'Glückseligkeit' remained. Thinkers of the period did not despair at the inadequacies and weaknesses of theoretical reason, particularly as a prerequisite for the obtainment of practical improvement. Belief in the adequacy of practical reason remained. Indeed, if reason has as its task to discover truth that will perfect man, and should theoretical reason be unable to find its way through the maze of theoretical truths, all man has to do is to use practicality as a criterion for deciding between competing hypotheses. In other words, if truth is to improve man, then this criterion can be used for determining which alleged truth of a series of competing truths is actually 'true'.[46]

The establishment of practicality as an epistemological norm meant that man once again became self-conscious. The rationalistic systems of the Wolffians had laid stress upon the objectivity of knowledge. Knowledge is not so much one's personal opinion as that toward which man universally and necessarily tends. The age of Lessing is an age of 'Selbstdenker' as Wundt has noted, i.e., the thinker becomes acutely aware of his own subjectivity and that this subjectivity is seeking to find its way out of an epistemological blind alley. Thinkers in most fields of intellectual endeavor felt themselves obliged critically to evaluate the thinking of others in the light of their own heightened self-consciousness. Man must turn to the concrete and individual in himself in order to discover knowledge. Thus the mutability and ultimately the historicity of man and his thought was discovered. The 'Selbstdenker' became aware of themselves as temporal beings, that is as beings with a history. Correlatively, a thinker could no longer view the thought of his predecessors as expressions of truth totally independent of the historical situation in which it was spawned. The unity between different thinkers was found in their contribution historically to the development and solutions of various problems.

Above all, this period is characterized by the attention paid to the role of the self in the examination and solution of problems. Somehow the obtainment once again of the fullness of being and of certain knowledge thereof must come forth out of the very powers of the self. Wundt, for instance, writes: 'Und so sucht man den letzten Grund alles Seins und Erkennens, wo man ihm neu nachfragt, im Menschen, im Ich oder Selbst. Die einwärts gewandte Richtung hat vorläufig über die auswärts gewandte gesiegt. Damit hängt es zusammen, daß die Wahrheit, die man erstrebt, als eine Kraft des Selbst begriffen wird, als aus Freiheit vom Selbst zu vollziehen, und nicht mehr als eine Gestalt des gegebenen Seins, die als solche nur gefunden und aufgefaßt werden müßte. . . . Nicht Seinerfassung, sondern Selbstverständnis ist die Hauptsache, und nur der Selbstdenker kann sich zur Philosophie erheben.'[47] All of man's activities from theology to aesthetics, to the reflections on his own psychology[48] will find their truth and hence their being as they make manifest to man his creative self. Kant's Copernican epistemology and ethics is but a higher and more advanced stage of the promise of modernity made by the age, namely to Lessing himself.

4. The crisis in Lessing's thinking

A. THE PROBLEM OF APPROACHING LESSING

'Leibnizens Begriffe von der Wahrheit waren so beschaffen, daß er nicht vertragen konnte, wann man ihr zu enge Schranken setzte. Aus dieser Denkungsart sind viele Behauptungen geflossen, und es ist, bei dem größten Scharfsinne, oft sehr schwer, seine eigentliche Meinung zu entdecken. Eben darum halt ich ihn so wert; ich meine, wegen dieser Art zu denken; und nicht, wegen dieser oder jener Meinung, die er nur zu haben schien, oder denn auch würklich hatte' (*J.G.L.*, VIII, 623).

What Lessing had to say about Leibniz in the above quotation can, in my judgment, equally be contended of Lessing himself. First of all, as was indicated in the first chapter, it is often very difficult to determine just what Lessing's 'true' opinion was. If past scholarship on Lessing's theology has proven one thing, it is that fact. In a letter to his brother Karl, Lessing writes: 'Deine Neugierde wenigstens wird es mir verdanken, daß ich Dir hier bei eine doppelte Antwort *[Die Parabel* and *Axiomata]* gegen Goezen schicke. Es soll mir lieb sein, wenn auch diese Deinen Beifall hat. Und ich denke, sie wird ihn einigermaßen haben, wenn Du bedenkst, daß ich meine Waffen nach meinem Gegner richten muß, und daß ich nicht alles, was ich *gymnastikos* [übungsweise] schreibe, auch *dogmatikos* [dogmatisch] schreiben würde' (March 6, 1778, IX, 773). Furthermore, if one also accepts Lessing's contention concerning Leibniz's *Denkungsart* expressed in *Leibniz von den ewigen Strafen* as also applying to himself, then the difficulties entailed in trying to ascertain Lessing's precise position are all the more evident.[1] It will be recalled that Leibniz, according to Lessing, sought to find 'einen erträglichen Sinn' in the positions and opinions of thinkers in schools of thought other than his own. In doing so Leibniz was forced methodologically to speak in the language and terminology of his opponent. Leibniz's speaking in the language of an 'alien' system was designated by Lessing as Leibniz's *exoteric* manner of thinking. '[Leibniz] tat damit nichts mehr und nichts weniger, als was alle alte Philosophen in ihrem exoterischen Vortrage zu tun pflegen. Er beobachtete eine Klugheit, für die freilich unsere neuesten.Philosophen viel zu weise geworden sind. Er setzte willig sein System bei Seite; und suchte einen jeden auf demjenigen Wege zur Wahrheit zu führen, auf welchem er ihn fand' (*L.v.E.S.*, VII, 467). Insofar as it can be said that Lessing set his 'own system' to the side in order to speak within the framework of his opponent's (which included the orthodox, neologians, and rationalists) and insofar as Lessing did not always state his position 'dogmatically' but only tentatively, it becomes just that difficult to distill Lessing's allegedly true or esoteric, but alas often only implicit, position out of a mass of explicitly given exoteric statements.

The problem of finding a method to penetrate beyond the surface of Lessing's statements into his underlying substantive and informing position becomes all the more acute if one assumes that Lessing also speaks exoterically (i.e., does not openly express his 'true' and unadulterated opinions) to his friends either in conversations or in letters. For instance, some scholars, such as the Marxist Heinz Plavius, have cited various comments by Lessing written to his brother in which Lessing seems to be assuming more or less a rationalistic position vis-à-vis Christianity and Neology as proof that Lessing's theological quarrels were really 'Kämpfe, die im theologischen Gewand ausgetragen wurden' and that they had as their purpose to effect an 'allmähliche Trennung und Herauslösung der "weltlichen", d.h. philosophischen und politischen Wahrheiten aus den religiös und theologisch bestimmten Auffassungen' which were then current in German intellectual life.[2] In short, Lessing's theological interests and his apparent commitment to various theological positions were really only the masks under which he carried out his intellectual battles and the means by which he hoped to render theological discussion passé and useless. At any rate, Lessing's apparent theological positions allegedly do not constitute his true opinions.[3] The question immediately arises as to how seriously one is to take Lessing's expressed opinions to his friends, especially to his brother Karl.[4] Was Lessing speaking dogmatically or tentatively to Karl? Karl Lessing seems to have adhered precisely to the 'neumodische Theologie' that Lessing rejected. It could very well be that, in order to avoid any unnecessary quarrels with Karl, Lessing expressed himself as much as possible in a manner that would please Karl. Why assume that just because Lessing makes a derogatory evaluation of Christianity in a letter or a published work that he cannot possibly have been sincere in his positive evaluations and apparent acceptance of Christianity in other writings?

The difficulty in understanding Lessing is not just a problem for twentieth-century scholars. Lessing's own contemporaries were not always sure how literally they should interpret statements. For instance, concerning Lessing's style of argumentation Fr. Nicolai writes: 'Lessing war dogmatisch in seinen Prinzipien, aber skeptisch in seinen Untersuchungen: Eigenschaften, die er auf die edelste Weise anwandte, und die oft zu den herrlichsten Ideen leiteten, wenn er sich bloß zu verirren schien. Er ist deswegen nicht selten von Leuten, die ihn nicht recht kannten, sehr mißverstanden worden, wenn sie das, was er irgend einmal, sogar mit vieler Lebhaftigkeit und mit scharfsinnigen Gründen behauptete, für das Resultat seiner Prinzipien ansahen. Wer Lessingen nicht sehr genau kannte, konnte sich sehr an ihm irren, wenn er ihn diszeptieren hörte' (Letter, October 30, 1769, IX, 340). Nicolai further notes the following disconcerting habit of Lessing. 'Lessing ... konnte das Allzudezisive nicht wohl leiden, und pflegte in gesellschaftlichen gelehrten Unterredungen oft die Partei zu nehmen, welche die schwächere war, oder, die, wovon jemand positiv das Gegenteil behaupten wollte; zu weilen auch, umgekehrt, gerade die, wovon jemand heftig eingenommen war, der aber die Sache aus einem ihm eigenen Gesichtspunkte zu betrachten schien. ... [Lessing] war in Gesellschaften wohl Liebhaber eines Dinges, das die Engländer "Fun" nennen, und wofür unsere solennen deutschen Landsleute kein Wort haben ... Besser doch immer "Fun" zu treiben, als über die Dummköpfe ungeduldig zu werden!' (IX, 340). Lessing's good friend Moses Mendelssohn seems at times to have been disconcerted by Lessing's penchant for affirming and maintaining the weaker position. Lessing's continual shifting of positions, his tendency to contradict all allegedly established truth, even to the point of sophistry was a sign to Mendelssohn that Lessing was often more interested in mental gymnastics than in the obtainment of truth. For example, Mendelssohn writes: 'Das Neue und Auffallende galt bei ihm mehr, als Wahrheit und Einfalt.' 'Die Gymnastik des Geistes [ist für Lessing] wichtiger, als die reine Wahrheit.'[5] Unfortunately Nicolai never specified Lessing's 'dogmatically' held principles which he allegedly applied so sceptically to his investigations. Furthermore the question must always remain as to how well Nicolai really understood Lessing.

Lessing admits that he *sometimes* (note sometimes not always) does not express his own 'dogmatic' opinion but rather camouflages it. In the light of Lessing's penchant for speaking in the terminology of other systems, and in the difficulty found in comprehending Lessing by men of sound understanding from Lessing's own lifetime to the present, it borders on scholarly presumptuousness to cite a few lines from Lessing's letters (or elsewhere) that are possibly anti-Christian as irrefutable proofs of Lessing's esoteric rationalism (as Plavius has done) and then use the esoteric position as a tool with which to negate all of Lessing's apparent interests and affirmations of theological positions.[6] Even if one were to grant that there is such a thing as a rationalistic esotericism in Lessing's thinking, it is by no means an easy and evident matter to determine what this esoteric core is. But a more basic question should be raised and Thielicke has raised it. Namely, on what grounds are we to assume that Lessing's esoteric thinking is something that exists in isolation from, and must be played off against his exoteric thinking or, conversely, that Lessing's exotericism must of necessity falsify or alter his esotericism.[7] If one is to accept Lessing's own contentions as given in the *Erziehung,* then it is clear that Lessing did not conceive of himself as having yet reached the age of pure esotericism, but rather to be still mired in an exoteric age in which exoteric thinking is to a degree the only way in which man can think. Thus the truth of Lessing's thought must be sought in the exoteric as much as in the esoteric, in the Christian as much as in the rationalistic, in the irrational as much as in the rational.[8] I shall return to this point presently.

Just as Lessing found difficulty in discerning Leibniz's 'eigentliche Meinung' so too will and must Lessing scholars find it difficult to determine Lessing's true opinion. The reason why Lessing found it so difficult to interpret Leibniz was 'Leibnizens Begriffe von der Wahrheit waren so beschaffen, daß er nicht vertragen konnte, wann man ihr zu enge Schranken setzte. Aus dieser Denkungsart sind viele Behauptungen geflossen, und es ist, bei dem größten Scharfsinne, oft sehr schwer seine eigentliche Meinung zu entdecken.' Leibniz asserted hundreds of theses that 'flow' from his 'Denkungsart'. What belongs to the essence of this 'art of thinking' is that it cannot tolerate too narrow limits. But what are these limits? In my judgment, the limitations are for Lessing precisely the theses that Leibniz had made. In other words, the way in which Leibniz thought, the principles that determine his pursuit of truth entail a much broader and deeper content (i.e., paradigm commitment) than what can be expressed in any given thesis. Conversely, one cannot conclude from the content of any specific thesis that one has totally exhausted the content of Leibniz' 'Denkungsart'. There is always a gulf between this or that opinion of Leibniz and his whole manner of thinking. Thinking conceived as a mental activity and the principles that determine the way in which this activity will be carried out transcend somehow any and every specific assertion of truth. Leibniz's concept of (formal) truth is greater than any claimed (material) truth. I would suggest, that, had Lessing been asked to apply the notions of exoteric and esoteric to Leibniz in more detail, Lessing would have designated Leibniz's specific opinions of truth as the exoteric in Leibniz's thought and Leibniz's 'Denkungsart' as the esoteric inner core. In this way there is an obvious correlation between the esoteric and the exoteric, rather than an opposition.

To the degree that Lessing separated Leibniz's 'Denkungsart' from the thought content of this or that assertion of truth, to that degree the question concerning the nature of Leibniz's 'Denkungsart' and how this nature is to be discovered must arise. In other words, if Leibniz's principles of thinking transcend any given thought content, how are they to be determined? Lessing did not answer this question though he did acknowledge the difficulty in answering it. I would suggest, however paradoxical it might appear, that the way for Lessing to have penetrated the inner core of Leibniz's thinking would have been, nevertheless, *only* through what Leibniz expressly thought. Since thinking is a type of activity or movement, the only way to discover its principles of movement would be to observe just how it *actually* does move. This would not be to say that any specified type or direction of mental movement exhausts the principles of Leibniz's cogitative activity. Indeed, cogitative activity can go in other directions consonant with the parameters of its principles. It is to say, however, that, if an investigator has truly discovered the general principles that determined specific and actual movements, he will be able to predict and/or explain the formal nature of all the movements of which a specific type of 'Denkungsart' is capable or at least explain why various divergencies occur. In other words, although the material content of this or that movement cannot be deduced, the general form of all possible movements can be induced. Once this general form is established it will then be possible to determine more accurately the real meaning of this or that opinion (i.e., concrete cogitative act). The key point is to be sure that one has truly discovered the structural principles (i.e., generative paradigms) of a thinker's 'Denkungsart' based upon the limited samples at hand.

What has been said about Leibniz's 'Denkungsart' can, I contend, also be said of Lessing's. Lessing, in my judgment, admired Leibniz because he saw at least a formal similarity between himself and Leibniz, i.e., he was aware that his own 'Denkungsart' is not totally contained in what he explicitly maintained and that the very ambiguity of his asserted opinions 'flow' from his *ars cogitandi.* There is in Lessing a slightly ironic attitude towards whatever is asserted as true either by himself or by others. As Nicolai noted, that which Lessing could not endure is 'das Allzudezisive' and that when someone would maintain a position too confidently and presumptuously, Lessing would take up the cudgels of the opposite position, even if it were the weaker side. Lessing wrote to his brother Karl: 'Ich hasse all die Leute, welche Sekten stiften wollen, vom Grund meines Herzens. Denn nicht der Irrtum, sondern der sektierische Irrtum, ja sogar die sektierische Wahrheit machen das Unglück der Menschen; oder würden es machen, wenn die Wahrheit eine Sekte stiften wollte (April 30, 1774, IX, 606). Lessing even referred sceptically to his *Erziehung* as a hypothesis in a letter to Johann Reimarus: *'Die Erziehung des Menschengeschlechts* ist von einem guten Freunde, der sich gern allerlei Hypothesen und Systeme macht, um das Vergnügen zu haben, sie wieder einzureißen' (April 6, 1778, IX, 775).[9]

Any progress in interpreting Lessing, in determining his 'eigentliche Meinung' must begin with the realization that his 'System' is not simply to be found fully embodied in the various specific assertions that he made. The unity in Lessing's thought is not so much in his explicit statements (i.e., in the cognitive content of this or that specific thesis) but in the mental movement of his mind as he pursues Truth. Cognitive thinking for Lessing is essentially a mental movement in pursuit of truth and thus its principles must be of such structure as to correspond to the nature of truth (i.e., the formal structure of truth), for it is only by this correspondence that the mind can hope to approach if not to obtain truth about any aspect of reality. Since the mind seeks truth, its principles must be such that it can validly pursue truth.

Given the thesis that the unity of Lessing's thought is located in his principles of thinking, in his *ars dialectice cogitandi,* the question immediately presents itself as to how these principles are to be discovered. The only way that they can be discovered is to observe how Lessing actually does think (i.e., how he treats various intellectual problems) and to ask why he treated such and such a problem in such and such a manner rather than in a different way. In short, the *generative ideas* or *basal paradigms* of Lessing's 'Art zu denken' can only be specified by analyzing just how he did think about various problems. In doing so, this means that to a degree the distinction between Lessing's esoteric and exoteric thinking is meaningless, if it is interpreted to mean that one form of thinking is to be assumed *a priori* to be in opposition to the other. For even if one assumes that Lessing was seeking to debunk Christianity, even when he was apparently agreeing with it, one still must show just how Lessing's concrete argumentations in effect do away with Christianity. It will be, however, my contention, that an analysis of the generative principles inherent in Lessing's statements pro and contra Christianity will reveal that he did take Christianity seriously and that his defense of himself as a good Christian, particularly in *Anti-Goeze,* is not without a degree of validity. In short, I will substantiate Thielicke's contention that Lessing's exoteric language belongs as much to the heart of Lessing's though as does his esoteric language.

The decision to ascertain Lessing's 'Denkungsart' brings out once again the question of Lessing's position within the stream of eighteenth-century thought and hence the problem of paradigms. In the previous two chapters an attempt was made schematically to outline the 'cognitive crisis' of the eighteenth century. It was contended that his crisis entails (1) a breakdown of the rationalistic paradigm under the pressure of an empiricistic paradigm, (2) the inability of either paradigm to establish hegemony (at least in Germany), and (3) the resultant need to regain theoretical unity by somehow reconciling the demands of the two ontological paradigms. It will, further, be the contention of this book that the peculiarity and ambiguities of Lessing's thought are a result of the fact that the basic principles of his 'Denkungsart' were undergoing the eighteenth-century cognitive crisis and the attempt to overcome it. Lessing's basic scepticism relative to any allegedly absolute truth and his preference for 'mental gymnastics' are both an effect of and an attempt to overcome his experience of the cognitive crisis.[10] In the ensuing analysis I shall seek successively to illustrate the manifestations of the rationalistic paradigm in Lessing's theologico-philosophical speculations, then of the empiricistic paradigm, and finally of Lessing's tentative attempt to overcome the crisis in his thought. Particularly in dealing with Lessing's attempted solution(s) I shall try to ascertain (1) the *formal* structure of Lessing's ratiocinative thinking, i.e., of his *ars dialectice cogitandi,* and (2) the *material* application of this 'Denkungsart' to his speculations on Christianity. However, first I would like to stress once again that I shall not show that Lessing developed a comprehensive and contradiction free system. Lessing's theologico-philosophical speculations remained provisional, fragmentary and contradictory precisely because his response to the cognitive crisis of the eighteenth century was only tentative, inchoate, and incomplete. Or more simply, Lessing never fully overcame this crisis and hence his thinking remains scarred by it. For good or bad, right or wrong, it was Kant who overcame the cognitive crisis by enacting an epistemological revolution and thereby establishing the basis for the various systems of German Idealism. Lessing for his part remained a child (though a very precocious and advanced one) of the intellectual milieu of pre-critical Germany and hence must be understood within the terms of this period.

B. THE RATIONALISTIC PARADIGM

Lessing begins his famous answer to Director Schumann's defense of the inspiration of the Bible with the following rather revealing statement: 'Mein Herr,` Wem konnte es angelegner sein, Ihre neue Schrift sofort zu lesen, als mir? — Ich hungere nach Überzeugung so sehr, daß ich, wie Erysichthon, alles verschlinge, was einem Nahrungsmittel nur ähnlich sieht.' (*Ü.B.G.K.,* VIII, 9). The conviction about which Lessing speaks and is desirous of is, of course, conviction in religious matters. The utter importance of religious truth for Lessing, and indirectly the crisis in which he was caught, is made evident in Lessing's comparison of himself with Erysichthon. According to Ovid, Erysichthon, the son of the Thessalian king, Triopas, had felled some trees in the sacred grove of Ceres, the goddess of the earth, and was accordingly punished for his transgression by such an insatiable hunger that he ultimately consumed himself. Whereas Erysichthon was seeking physical satiation Lessing was seeking spiritual satiation. Whereas Erysichthon sought literally for food, Lessing sought for spiritual sustenance (i.e., conviction) in books for and against Christianity. In his *Bibliolatrie* Lessing reflects upon his life.

'Der bessere Teil meines Lebens ist — glücklicher oder unglücklicher Weise? — in eine Zeit gefallen, in welcher Schriften für die Wahrheit der Christlichen Religion gewissermaßen Modeschriften waren. . . . Was Wunder also, daß meine Lektüre ebenfalls darauf verfiel, und ich gar bald nicht eher ruhen konnte, bis ich jedes neue Produkt in diesem Fache habhaft werden und verschlingen konnte. Ob ich daran gut getan; auch wenn es möglich gewesen wäre, daß bei dieser Unersättlichkeit die nämlich wichtige Sache nur immer von einer Seite plädieren zu hören, die Neugierde nie enstanden wäre, endlich doch auch einmal zu erhören, was von der andern Seite gesagt wurde: will ich hier nicht entscheiden. Genug, was unmöglich ausbleiben konnte, blieb bei mir auch nicht einmal lange aus. Nicht lange; und ich suchte jede neue Schrift wider die Religion nun eben so begierig auf, und schenkte ihr eben das geduldige unparteiische Gehör, das ich sonst nur den Schriften für die Religion schuldig zu sein glaubte.' (*B.*, VIII, 488)[11]

The drive to obtain adequate certainty in religious matters for Lessing is underscored by the meaning he placed on religious or theological truth. For instance, the *Erziehung* is perhaps Lessing's most mature and systematic attempt to make manifest to his fellowman as well as to himself the content and meaning of theological truth. In the closing paragraphs Lessing toys with the notion of reincarnation. Because of his belief that man will be religiously and morally educated to ever higher degrees Lessing shows himself willing to return over and over again to this world in order to reach ever higher levels of perfection. Indeed, Lessing is apparently willing to return an eternal number of times. In paragraph 100, Lessing refers to his willingness to return over and over again in the following words: 'Ist nicht die ganze Ewigkeit mein?' (*Erziehung*, VIII, 615). By implication, the truth made known in the *Erziehung* is sufficient to fulfill man's being for an 'Ewigkeit'. Such truth must be of ultimate importance![12] Some years earlier in *Eine Duplik* Lessing rejected historical truth as the epistemological means for obtaining necessary religious knowledge. What is involved in this rejection will be examined presently. The central point now is that Lessing considers religious knowledge to be of too much importance to be grounded on the merely probable certainty that history can offer. Lessing writes: 'Wann wird man aufhören, an den Faden einer Spinne [i.e., history] nichts weniger als die ganze Ewigkeit hängen zu wollen' (*D.*, VIII, 37). In short, religion and truth about religious matters (i.e., theology) are concerned for Lessing about things of ultimate concern. Truth about man's ultimate meaning in life was for Lessing theological truth. It is for this reason that Lessing demanded and hungered after 'Überzeugung', with an intensity analogous to Erysichthon's hunger for physical satiation. The secret of man's destiny and perfection was for Lessing a matter of theological concern.

Because Lessing conceived questions about eternity and ultimate meaning to be essentially theological and because he so intensely hungered after conviction and certainty in this area, Lessing simply could not accept any alleged truth (or system of truths) that purported to have given answers to his quest for eternity without first critically testing it.[13] For instance, as a young man seeking to justify his ways to his father, the young Lessing writes: 'Die Zeit soll lehren, ob der ein beßrer Christ ist, der die Grundsätze der christlichen Lehre im Gedächtnisse, und oft, ohne sie zu verstehen, im Munde hat, in die Kirche geht, und alle Gebräuche mitmacht, weil sie gewöhnlich sind: oder der, der einmal klüglich gezweifelt hat, und durch den Weg der Untersuchung zur Überzeugung gelangt ist, oder sich wenigstens noch darzu zu gelangen bestrebet. Die christliche Religion ist kein Werk, das man von seinen Eltern auf Treue und Glaube annehmen soll' (May 30, 1749, IX, 22). In his defense of Cardanus Lessing writes: 'Was ist nötiger, als sich von seinem Glauben zu überzeugen, und was ist unmöglicher als Überzeugung, ohne vorgegangene Prüfung' (*R.H.C.*, VII, 211). And of course Saladin's request that Nathan explain the reasons for his acceptance of Judaism is also in the spirit of Lessing.

> *Ein Mann, wie du, bleibt da*
> *Nicht stehen, wo der Zufall der Geburt*
> *Ihn hingeworfen: oder wenn er bleibt,*
> *Bleibt er aus Einsicht, Gründen, Wahl des Bessern.*
> *Wohlan! so teile deine Einsicht mir*
> *Dann mit. Laß mich die Gründe hören, denen*
> *Ich selber nachzugrübeln, nicht die Zeit*
> *Gehabt. Laß mich die Wahl, die diese Gründe*
> *Bestimmt; — versteht sich, im Vertrauen — wissen,*
> *Damit ich sie zu meiner mache.*

> (*Nathan*, Act III, scene 5, II, 401.)

The demand for absolute certainty as a prerequisite for truth, the intense hungering after conviction, and the requirement that all asserted truths must be critically tested before being accepted stamp Lessing as a child of the eighteenth century and remind one of Descartes. As noted in Chapter 2, Descartes, like Lessing, lived in a period of doubt and crisis. In response to his philosophically troubled times Descartes (1) occupied himself with the problem and nature of certainty as a prerequisite to philosophical speculating, (2) refused to accept any thing as true unless it can be known with absolute certainty, and (3) located the criterion of certainty in the indubitable. The difference between Descartes and Lessing is that Descartes focused upon the formal problem of truth *qua* truth whereas Lessing concentrated primarily upon the most important type of truth, namely theological truth. Insofar as Lessing considered truth in a formal manner it was within the context of his analysis of theological problems. Nevertheless, Lessing's concern for certainty is a concern in the Cartesian spirit. Indeed, it is more than that! Lessing as a thinker stands at the end of a philosophical period begun by Descartes. In Chapter 2 it was shown that Cartesian-influenced philosophy uses the structure of the self discovered in the *cogito-sum* as the tool and criterion for unraveling the mystery of reality. The *ego* of the *cogito* is a *res cogitans,* i.e., a rational activity. Man's subjectivity, i.e., his cognitive faculty is seen as the guideline for that which is knowable, for being. Truth about reality is a function of what the essence of pure rational knowledge determines it to be. Hence, the indubitable is identified with the rational. In short, the thesis that the real is the rational (or a function thereof) lies at the heart of the 'root metaphor' of Cartesian inspired rationalism. In the ensuing analysis of Lessing's evaluation and rejection of history as a valid means for manifesting theological truth the role of the rationalistic root metaphor in his thought will be shown. But first before undertaking this analysis, the nature of the rationalistic paradigm will be briefly reviewed.

Propositionally, certainty is obtained for the rationalist when it is impossible to doubt that a given predicate inheres in a given subject. A predicate and subject are connected indubitably when they are united with necessity. *Necessity* is the primary feature of rational truth that makes it indubitable and hence certain. If a truth (or a proposition claiming truth value) is known as necessary, it is because it contains undeniable and evident marks internal to itself which compel the mind to affirm or deny its truth value. This 'being-self-contained' and yet 'self-manifesting' on a cognitive level can be called the *inner truth* of a rational and hence necessary truth. Since a rational truth is necessarily so, it cannot change and hence is not effected by the vicissitudes of time. In this sense rational truths are *immutable* and *eternal*. Furthermore, since rational truths are valid for all cases and all times, they may be said to have *universal* application. That which is revealed as universally valid is the inner ontological or *metaphysical* structure of reality. Finally such truths are knowable because they reveal themselves, so to speak, to the pure human understanding which can grasp *intellectually* the intelligible content of the inner truth of rational truths. Necessity, inner truth, universality, eternality, immutability, intellectuality, and the metaphysical constitute the formal essence of truths of reason, of 'Vernunftswahrheiten'. With this summary in mind, Lessing's evaluation of history as means or medium of revelation can now be investigated.

The Lutheran Orthodoxy of Lessing's day taught that a man named Jesus *actually* lived, was crucified, and rose from the dead. Further, Jesus claimed he was the Son of God — the Incarnation — and he sealed his claims with miracles, not the least of which was his resurrection. Finally, Jesus' death on the cross was a divine sacrifice, righting man with God. To participate in this reconciliation man has but to have faith in Christ and his salvation will be ensured. Of course orthodox Lutheranism developed these basic tenets into a sophisticated and intricate doctrinal system. Nevertheless, the basic tenets of such a system were relatively few. Also, for the most part, such tenets relative to their origin and content are based upon allegedly *real* and *actual* occurrences with time and space coordinates. In short, the basic tenets of Orthodoxy may be said either to be empirically given events or truths based upon such empirical events (e.g., Christ's claim to divinity as proven by his resurrection). These empirically given events can be known in one or both of two ways. An event is empirical precisely because it occurs at one and only one 'now', i.e., a specific empirical event is only actual once. Hence, any empirical event can either be known immediately as a given or intuited by a person who shares the same 'now' with the event or the event can be reported (verbally or written) in which case the knowledge is historical, i.e., a 'Geschichtswahrheit'. However, in a broad sense the term 'historical' or 'historisch' can be said to refer, and did refer in eighteenth-century philosophy, to any empirical event that occurs within the flow of time. In this sense, a 'Geschichtswahrheit' refers not only to the reporting of an empirical event, but to its very empirical nature as the essence of a whole class of truths. From this point of view, a historical truth has to do with empirical events both as occurring in a given present and as reported having happened. For terminological purposes I will generally refer to this dual meaning as the empirico-historical. Unfortunately Lessing does not distinguish between these two meanings of 'Geschichtswahrheit' and eventually becomes entangled in an inconsistency which will be shown to be indicative of his acceptance of both rationalistic and empiricistic paradigms and to be important for his positive evaluation of Christianity. For the moment, in my exposition of Lessing's analysis of historical truths, I shall not make the necessary distinction between the two meanings, especially since this ambiguity is an essential part of Lessing's argumentation. At the appropriate point, the distinction will be made. At any rate, the revealed truths of Christianity are first and foremost 'Geschichtswahrheiten' for Lessing, and it is his analysis thereof that shall now be examined.

Concerning the essence of historical truths as a revelatory medium of the divine, Lessing writes:

'. . . Und freilich, fügt man hinzu, könnten historische Wahrheiten nicht demonstriert werden; aber demohngeachtet müsse man sie eben so fest glauben als demonstrierte Wahrheiten.

'Hierauf nun antworte ich. *Erstlich,* wer leugnet es ich nicht, daß die Nachrichten von jenen Wundern und Weissagungen ebenso zuverlässig sind, als nur immer historische Wahrheiten sein können? — Aber nun, wenn sie *nur* ebenso zuverlässig sind, warum macht man sie bei dem Gebrauche auf einmal unendlich zuverlässiger?

'Und wodurch? — Dadurch, daß man ganz andere und mehrere Dinge auf sie bauet, als man auf historisch erwiesene Wahrheiten zu bauen befugt ist.

'Wenn keine historische Wahrheit demonstrieret werden kann, so kann auch nichts *durch* historische Wahrheiten demonstrieret werden.

'Das ist: *Zufällige Geschichtswahrheiten können der Beweis von notwendigen Vernunftswahrheiten nie werden.'* (*Ü.B.G.K.,* VIII, 12).

Lessing has explicitly rejected 'Geschichtswahrheiten' as a medium of divine revelation because they cannot be 'demonstrieret'. 'Demonstrieren' is used in the Leibniz-Wolffian philosophy of the day in a very strict and rigorous sense. It means to prove with absolute certainty the truth or falsity of a proposition with the mathematical method being an ideal model. Lessing himself defines the German derived word for 'to demonstrate', namely 'beweisen' in the fol-

lowing manner: '[A] ber *beweisen* [soll] hier heißen, was es eigentlich heißt: die Verbindung einer Wahrheit mit andern anerkannten
und ungezweifelten Wahrheiten dartun . . .' (*Axiomata,* VIII, 193).
Since only truths of reason can be demonstrated in any strict sense
and since Lessing explicitly compares disparagingly historical truths
about God with rational truths, the clear implication is, of course,
that a valid theological truth is in the same class with rational truths.
Indeed, at the end of *Ü.B.G.K.* (VIII, 15) Lessing compares religious
truths with 'eine nützliche mathematische Wahrheit' in order to
illustrate that the justification of valid theological truths are independent of their historical origin. The inevitable conclusion is that
theological truths belong to the class of rational or necessary truths
and since *eternality* is one of the prime features of necessary truth,[14]
its historical or temporal origin or nature is of no concern relative to
its validity.

But what is it about a historical truth that makes it incapable of
being demonstrated and of demonstrating valid theological truth.
Lessing refers to 'Geschichtswahrheiten' as 'zufällig' in comparison
with 'Vernunftswahrheiten' which are 'notwendig'. 'Zufällig' has a
definite meaning within the context of Leibniz-Wolffian philosophy.
That an event is 'zufällig' does not mean that it has no cause. If there
are events such as miracles, they must have a cause. Lessing, himself
is willing to admit at least verbally that the miracles of Christianity
are as historically certain as any historical event can be proven to
have happened. 'Zufällig' means that, whereas something must have a
cause, its non-existence would, nevertheless, not entail a contradiction.[15] For example, Christ's human existence may be a fact, but if it
had never occurred, it would not entail a contradiction. Indeed, it is
precisely the contention of Orthodoxy that God was in no way
necessitated to become incarnated in Christ or, in other words, Christ
and his mission have their origin in the unnecessitated freedom of
God. On the other hand, to contend that, if two things are equal to a
third, they are nevertheless not equal to each other entails a contradiction. Therefore, the truth of the proposition: 'If two things are
equal to a third, they are equal to each other' cannot but be true,
i.e., it is 'notwendig' so. It is because of his necessity that mathematical truths (such as the one just given) are rational truths. Therefore,
it follows that historical truth *qua* its very empirical content can
never be the source of immutable, eternal, and hence metaphysical
truth about God. From this point of view, it is easy to comprehend
why Lessing rejected events proven historically to have happened,

i.e., reliably reported historical events as an adequate medium for revelation. No matter how certain it is that an event has happened, this certainty can never be more than highly probable. Lessing himself writes, 'daß eine geoffenbarte Religion, die sich auf menschliche Zeugnisse gründet, unmöglich eine ungezweifelte Versicherung in irgend etwas gewähren kann . . .' (*W.R.* VII, 574). Historical reporting by its very ontological nature can never 'demonstrate' that an event happened and hence it is by its very essence 'zufällig'. At this point, Lessing should have gone on to state that not only reported events but also *immediately perceived* ones cannot be the source of valid truth about God simply because of their empirical nature. That Lessing did not do so is of importance and will be shown to be due to his inconsistent but real acceptance of the empiricistic paradigm.

Historical truths and rational truths belong to two different classes of truth and only one class can generate in the believer the necessary 'Überzeugung'. To accept historical truths as valid truths about God is, in Lessing's mind, to commit a logical fallacy. It is to ask a 'Selbstdenker' such as Lessing to predicate important metaphysical notions about God upon a cognitive source that can only generate truths that are 'zufällig' rather than 'notwendig'. This is to jump from one cognitive category to another. Lessing himself writes:

'Daß der Christus, gegen dessen Auferstehung ich nichts Historisches von Wichtigkeit einwenden kann, sich deswegen für den Sohn Gottes ausgegeben, daß ihn seine Jünger deswegen dafür gehalten, das glaube ich herzlich gern. Denn diese Wahrheiten als Wahrheiten einer und ebenderselben Klasse, folgen ganz natürlich auseinander.

'Aber nun mit jener historischen Wahrheit in eine ganz andre Klasse von Wahrheiten herüberspringen und von mir verlangen, daß ich alle meinen metaphysichen und moralischen Begriffe darnach umbilden soll, mir zumuten, weil ich der Auferstehung Christi kein glaubwürdiges Zeugnis entgegensetzen kann, all meine Grundideen von dem Wesen der Gottheit darnach abzuändern; wenn das nicht eine *metábasis eis allo génos* [Übergang in einen anderen Begriffsbereich] ist, so weiß ich nicht, was Aristotles sonst unter dieser Benennung verstanden' (*Ü.B.G.K.*, VIII, 13–14).

That Lessing should conceive truths about God as essentially metaphysical is a sign that he is thinking within the terms of the rationalistic paradigm. And because metaphysical truths are demonstrable in a strict rationalistic sense and because historical knowledge can never demonstrate anything, it constitutes a logical jump to formulate and ground one's ideas about the necessary structure of highest reality — God — on the basis of the historical.[16]

Because of Lessing's hunger for 'Überzeugung' and because of his belief that only the class of rational truths can fulfill the conditions of absolute certainty, he found it not only meaningless and futile, but actually dangerous to attempt to ground one's religious beliefs on historical evidence. Even granting the historical reality of miracles, there is still an unbridgable gulf ('der garstige breite Graben, über den ich nicht kommen kann, so oft und ernstlich ich auch den Sprung versucht habe . . .' [VIII, 14]) between the absolute certainty of metaphysical truth and the 'zufällig' certainty of historical truth. In his *Duplik* Lessing writes: 'Aber auf die historische Wahrscheinlichkeit dieser Wunder die Wahrheit der Religion gründen, wenn das richtig, wenn das auch nur klug gedacht ist! — Es sei herausgesagt! Wenn ich jemals so richtig, so klug zu denken fähig bin, so ist es um meinen Verstand geschehen. Das sagt mir mein Verstand itzt. Und habe ich jemals einen andern Verstand, so hatte ich nie einen' (*D.*, VIII, 36). In other words, Lessings *Verstand* as a rational power can only grasp the rational. The historical by its very nature excludes 'necessity' (which is the prime characteristic of rationality). Therefore, Lessing would literally lose his reason ('. . . so ist es um meinen Verstand geschehen . . .'), should he seek to ground religious truth on mere historical probability. Furthermore, since 'necessity' constitutes the definition of 'Ewigkeit' and since religious truths should reveal knowledge about eternity (and correlatively be eternal truths), any attempt to derive religious truth from mere historical truth, i.e., from 'zufällige Geschichtswahrheiten', constitutes an absurdity. Lessing counsels his readers: 'Wann wird man aufhören, an den Faden einer [historischen] Spinne nichts weniger als die ganze Ewigkeit hängen zu wollen' (VIII, 37). Similarly in *Ü.B.G.K.* Lessing queries:

'Wir alle glauben, daß ein Alexander gelebt hat, welcher in kurzer Zeit fast ganz Asien besiegte. Aber wer wollte, auf diesen Glauben hin, irgend etwas von großem dauerhaften Belange, dessen Verlust nicht zu ersetzen wäre, wagen? Wer wollte, diesem Glauben zu Folge, aller Kenntnis auf ewig abschwören, die mit diesem Glauben stritte? Ich wahrlich nicht. Ich habe itzt gegen den Alexander und seine Siege nichts einzuwenden: aber es wäre doch möglich, daß sie sich eben so wohl auf ein bloßes Gedicht des Chörlius, welcher den Alexander überall begleitete, gründeten, als die zehnjährige Belagerung von Troja sich auf weiter nichts, als auf die Gedichte des Homers gründet' (VIII, 13).

Insofar as Christian doctrines may validly effect if not determine the belief of a 'Selbstdenker', it must be due to the inner content (truth) of the doctrines themselves: 'Was verbindet mich denn dazu [i.e., to specific doctrines]? – Nichts, als diese Lehren selbst . . .' (VIII, 15). Lessing develops this theme more in his *Axiomata*. In this work Lessing is, among other things, seeking to defend the valid religious content of the Bible from the Bible's historical vulnerability. In doing so, another feature of the rationalistic paradigm becomes evident.

Lessing at one point quotes Goeze maintaining: 'Die Wahrheit der christlichen Religion beruhet allerdings auf sich selbst; sie bestehet auf ihrer Übereinstimmung mit den Eigenschaften und Willen Gottes, und auf der historischen Gewißheit der Factorum, auf welche ihre Lehrsätze sich zum Teil gründen. Allein, unsere Überzeugung von der Wahrheit der christlichen Religion beruhet doch lediglich und allein auf diesen Schriften' (*Axiomata*, VIII, 178). Lessing, because he was thinking with a rationalistic paradigm, misinterprets Goeze in his answer. For Goeze, although some rationally determined truths about God can be ascertained (e.g., his existence), the basic truths of Christianity are primarily historical in nature. The historical is the basis for learning truths that are simply not open to human reason and the content of these truths is empirical not rational. Since, however, for Lessing truth about God is ideally metaphysical (the result of the rationalistic paradigm), Goeze appeared to him as having made an illicit logical jump. Lessing writes:

'. . . Denn man überlege doch nur! Wenn die Wahrheit der christlichen Religion *teils* (dieses *teils* hat er freilich nicht buchstäblich hingeschrieben, aber sein Sinn erfordert es doch notwendig) –, wenn sie, sage ich, *teils* auf sich selbst, d.i. auf ihrer Übereinstimmung mit den Eigenschaften und dem Willen Gottes, *teils* auf der historischen Gewißheit der Factorum beruhet, auf die sich einige ihrer Lehrsätze gründen, entspringt nicht aus diesem doppelten Grunde auch eine doppelte Überzeugung? Hat nicht jeder einzelne Grund seine Überzeugung für sich? Was braucht einer von beiden die Überzeugung des andern zu entlehnen? Ist es nicht fauler Leichtsinn, dem einen die Überzeugung des andern zugute kommen zu lassen? Ist es nicht leichtsinnige Faulheit, die Überzeugung des einen auf beide erstrekken zu wollen? Warum soll ich Dinge, die ich deswegen für *wahr halten muß*, weil sie mit den Eigenschaften und dem Willen Gottes übereinstimmen, *nur* deswegen *glauben,* weil andre Dinge, die irgendeinmal Zeit und Raum mit ihnen verbunden gewesen, historisch erwiesen sind?

'Es sei immerhin wahr, daß die biblischen Bücher alle die Fakta erweisen, worauf sich die christlichen Lehrsätze zum Teil gründen; Fakta erweisen, das können Bücher, und warum sollten es diese nicht können? Genug, daß die christlichen Lehrsätze sich nicht alle auf Fakta gründen. Die übrigen gründen sich, wie zugegeben, auf ihre innere Wahrheit, und wie kann die innere Wahrheit irgendeines Satzes von dem Ansehen des Buches abhängen, in dem sie vorgetragen worden? Das ist offenbarer Widerspruch' (*Axiomata*, VIII, 179).

Whereas for Goeze essential religious truth is of its nature empirico-historical and hence only encounterable in the Bible, religious truth which is apodictic is for Lessing essentially rational and hence not dependent upon the Bible for its own justification, rather solely upon its own inner truth. 'Woher die innere Wahrheit nehmen? Aus ihr selbst. Deswegen heißt sie ja die *innere* Wahrheit, die Wahrheit, die keiner Beglaubigung von außen bedarf' (VIII, 190). Lessing goes on to illustrate what he means by referring to a geometrical theorem. 'Was müssen wir aus [den Schriften der Evangelisten und Apostel] nehmen? Die innere Wahrheit oder unsere erste historische Kenntnis dieser Wahrheit? Jenes wäre ebenso seltsam, als wenn ich ein geometrisches Theorem nicht wegen seiner Demonstration, sondern deswegen für wahr halten müßte, weil es im Euklides steht. Daß es im Euklides steht, kann gegründetes Vorurteil für seine Wahrheit sein, soviel man will. Aber ein anders ist, die Wahrheit aus Vorurteil glauben, und ein anders, sie um ihrer selbst willen glauben . . .' (VIII, 190). Lessing also refers to the 'Vernunftsmäßigkeit der christlichen Religion' (VIII, 192).

As noted above, 'inner truth' is a characteristic of the rationalistic paradigm. A rational truth manifests itself by its own inner intelligibility and is appropriated by a knower as an insight ('Einsicht') into this 'inner truth'. Lessing himself writes about the Christian, 'der sich an dem Lehrbegriffe begnügt, den man längst für ihn aus der Bibel gezogen, und diesen Lehrbegriff nicht sowohl deswegen für wahr hält, weil er aus der Bibel gezogen, sondern weil er einsieht, daß er Gott anständiger und dem menschlichen Geschlechte ersprießlicher ist als die Lehrbegriffe aller andern Religionen, weil er fühlt, daß ihn dieser christliche Lehrbegriff beruhiget' (VIII, 194). Lessing's reference to feeling in the last quotation is of interest and it will be examined later. It suffices to note that such truth does include 'insight' into the ameliorative effects of a doctrine. (It should not be forgotten that, according to the rationalistic world view, knowledge leads to man's perfection. Therefore, insight into the ameliorative content of Christian doctrine is insight into its rationality.)

Not only does religious truth possess an 'inner truth', it also is unchangeable and eternal (not necessarily eternally known, just eternally valid). The immutability of religious truth is so eternal that no one according to Lessing can arbitrarily change or invent it. Or, conversely, theological truth is not true because the apostles taught it, rather they taught it because it is true. *'Die Religion is nicht wahr, weil die Evangelisten und Apostel sie lehrten: sondern sie lehrten sie, weil sie wahr ist'* (VIII, 188). This fact is not only true of the apostles but also of God Himself. 'Auch das, was Gott lehret, ist nicht wahr, weil es Gott lehren will: sondern Gott lehrt es, weil es wahr ist' (VIII, 188). Religious truth is in no way a manifestation of arbitrariness, rather it reflects the inner and necessary structure of reality.[17]

The above exposition has shown the influence of the rationalistic paradigm upon Lessing's theological speculations. This influence can be summarized by Lessing's categorization of theological truths as 'Vernunftswahrheiten'. As far as I can ascertain, Lessing remained faithful to this paradigm (though by no means exclusively so) since, at least, *Das Christentum der Vernunft* (1754)[18] until his death. Even in his *Erziehung* the development of rational truth is viewed as the *telos* and justification of all revealed truth. '[D]ie Ausbildung ge-offenbarter Wahrheiten in Vernunftswahrheiten ist schlechterdings notwendig, wenn dem menschlichen Geschlechte damit geholfen sein soll. Als sie geoffenbaret wurden, waren sie freilich noch keine Vernunftswahrheiten; aber sie wurden geoffenbaret, um es zu wer-den' (*Erziehung*, VIII, 610, § 76). Because the heart of all religious truth is viewed (based upon the rationalistic paradigm) as rational, Lessing contends that revelation conceived as an educative influence upon man, gives man nothing other than what human reason would discover on its own. 'Erziehung gibt dem Menschen nichts, was er nicht auch aus sich selbst haben könnte: sie gibt ihm das, was er aus sich selber haben könnte, nur geschwinder und leichter. Also gibt auch die Offenbarung dem Menschengeschlechte nichts, worauf die menschliche Vernunft, sich selbst überlassen, nicht auch kommen würde: sondern sie gab und gibt ihm die wichtigsten dieser Dinge nur früher' (VIII, 591, § 4).

Based upon his belief that theological truth is a type of rational truth, it is not surprising to find Lessing at one point preferring natural or a rational religion to positive or historical religion. For example, in *Ü.E.G.R.* Lessing defines natural religion in a manner consonant with the rationalistic paradigm. 'Einen Gott erkennen, sich die würdigsten Begriffe von ihm zu machen suchen, auf diese würdigsten Begriffe bei allen unsern Handlungen und Gedanken Rücksicht nehmen: ist der vollständigste Inbegriff aller natürlichen Religion' (VII, 280). This is also to fulfill the basic commandment of the *Aufklärung,* i.e., man's destiny is rationally to cognize reality (and God as the highest Being) and to conform oneself to the rational structure of reality, (i.e., to act morally). Such a demand constitutes the essence of natural religion. 'Zu dieser natürlichen Religion, ist ein jeder Mensch, nach dem Maße seiner Kräfte, aufgelegt und verbunden' (VII, 280). But Lessing procedes to contend without giving reason why that individuals have differing capacities to live up to the dictates of natural religion. Because of man's inability to realize natural religion, positive religion arises. (The importance of this fact for the crisis in Lessing's thought will be discussed in the next section of this chapter.) Since positive religions are unavoidable, they have some inner validity or inner truth. Nevertheless, they are all equally true and equally false. 'Gleich wahr: in sofern es überall gleich notwendig gewesen ist, sich über verschiedene Dinge zu vergleichen, um Übereinstimmung und Einigkeit in der öffentlichen Religion hervorzubringen. Gleich falsch: indem nicht sowohl das, worüber man sich verglichen, neben dem Wesentlichen besteht, sondern das Wesentliche schwächt und verdrängt' (VII, 281). 'Das Wesentliche' is nothing other than the rational heart of religious truth. Lessing then concludes in an unfinished paragraph: 'Die beste geoffenbarte oder positive Religion ist die, welche die wenigsten konventionellen Zusätze zur natürlichen Religion enthält, die guten Wirkungen der natürlichen Religion am wenigsten einschränkt. . . .' (VII, 281).[19] (A possible reason for the abruptness of this paragraph will be discussed in the context of Lessing's cognitive crisis.) An extrapolated conclusion from the last quotation would be, ideally there should be no revealed or positive religion so that the essence of natural religion will not be weakened or limited in any way.

Since historical religion, particularly Christianity, cannot of its very nature generate sufficient 'Überzeugung' in a potential believer, indeed, since it constitutes a logical fallacy to confuse historical with rational knowledge, the traditional claim of Christianity to have the 'Truth' must be false. In short, Orthodoxy taken in its totality as a cohesive system is simply not true. Thus it is not surprising that Lessing compares Christianity with 'unreines Wasser' in a letter to his brother Karl (2, 1774) and then goes on to state explicitly: 'Darin sind wir einig, daß unser altes Religionsystem falsch ist . . .' (February 2, 1774, IX, 597). Indeed, from this point of view, it seems plausible to interpret Lessing's concern with theological matters (or at least Christian doctrines) as primarily a tactic to clear room for the hegemony of man's reason in theological matters. Writing to Karl, Lessing writes: '[E]s [ist] im Grunde allerdings wahr, daß es mir bei meinen theologischen — wie Du es nennen willst — Neckereien oder Stänkereien, mehr um den gesunden Menschenverstand, als um die Theologie zu tun ist . . .' (March 20, 1777, IX, 729) Indeed, at one point Lessing refers in another letter to Karl to 'das "haut-comique" der Polemik' (February 25, 1778, IX, 771) in his quarrels with orthodox theologians such as Goeze. In short, it is quite clear that Lessing could not and did not accept Christianity as conceived by the orthodoxy as true and the reason for this was his acceptance of the rationalistic paradigm as the ultimate criterion of truth.[20]

C. THE EMPIRICISTIC PARADIGM AND THE CRISIS IN LESSING'S THINKING

Based solely upon the exposition of Lessing's thought as given above, an investigator would have to conclude that Lessing's esoteric position consists in the application of the rationalistic paradigm to theological questions. Truth, particularly theological truth, must essentially be a-historical or, more accurately, entail a stepping out of and beyond history for the believer. Therefore, whatever attitude, no matter how favorable, Lessing might take towards Christianity, it entails minimally a rejection of the Christian claim that history *qua* historicity can constitute in some way the essence of divine revelation to man.[21] This is not to say that all the interpreters who accept this position do not take cognizance of the irrationalistic tendencies in Lessing's thought (i.e., tendencies that are immediately reflective of the empiricistic paradigm). It is to say, however, that such tendencies are viewed as somehow subordinated to or as a function of Lessing's rationalistic esotericism. At best, man's development from an irrationalistic exoteric consciousness to a rationalistic esoteric one is viewed allegedly by Lessing as an immanent and purely natural development of man's rational faculty. Any true influence by the divine from without is discounted and all such statements by Lessing to that effect are relegated to his exoteric language.[22]

A closer and more comprehensive examination of Lessing's writings reveals that the rationalistic paradigm was by no means the sole or exclusively dominant generative idea in Lessing's 'Denkungsart'. This can readily be illustrated in *Ü.B.G.K.* Above it was shown that Lessing rejected 'historische Wahrheiten' as a revelatory medium of the divine because they belong to the class of 'zufällig' truths, whereas a valid theological truth must possess the 'Notwendigkeit' of a 'Vernunftswahrheit'. Thus the inadequacy of historical truth is grounded upon its qualitative difference from rational truth. Logically, Lessing should not only have contended that historically proven truths (i.e., reports of empirical fact) are qualitatively incapable of mediating divine rationality, but also empirical truths experienced immediately, i.e., as happening now, are similarly incapable. The ontological ingredient of actually happening events and reports of such events is the empirical and to be empirical is to be 'zufällig'. Empirical truths can never of themselves manifest necessity. Necessity is, of course, the key ingredient out of which rationality is constituted.

At the beginning of *Ü.B.G.K.* Lessing distinguishes between immediately experienced miracles, etc., and reports of such events. 'Ein andres sind erfüllte Weissagungen, die ich selbst erlebe: ein andres erfüllte Weissagungen, von denen ich nur historisch weiß, daß sie andre wollen erlebt haben. Ein andres sind Wunder, die ich mit meinen Augen sehe, und selbst zu prüfen Gelegenheit habe: ein andres sind Wunder, von denen ich nur historisch weiß, daß sie andre wollen gesehn und geprüft haben. Das ist doch wohl unstreitig? Dagegen ist doch nichts einzuwenden?' (VIII, 10). However, although Lessing goes on to reject the reporting of historical events as a means for producing 'Überzeugung', he does not reject the immediate experience of miraculous events. Lessing writes:

'Wenn ich zu Christi Zeiten gelebt hätte, so würden mich die in seiner Person erfüllten Weissagungen allerdings auf ihn sehr aufmerksam gemacht haben. Hätte ich nun gesehen ihn Wunder tun, hätte ich keine Ursache zu zweifeln gehabt, daß es wahre Wunder gewesen, so würde ich zu einem von so lange her ausgezeichneten, wundertätigen Mann allerdings so viel Vertrauen gewonnen haben, daß ich willig meinen Verstand dem seinigen unterworfen hätte, daß ich ihm in allen Dingen geglaubt hätte, in welchen ebenso ungezweifelte Erfahrungen ihm nicht entgegen gewesen wären.

'Oder wenn ich noch itzt erlebte, daß Christum oder die christliche Religion betreffende Weissagungen, von deren Priorität ich längst gewiß gewesen, auf die unstreitigste Art in Erfüllung gingen, wenn ich noch itzt echte Wunder erkennen mußte, was könnte mich abhalten, mich diesem *Beweise des Geistes und der Kraft,* wie ihn der Apostel nennet, zu fügen?

'In dem letztern Falle war noch Origines, der sehr recht hatte, zu sagen, daß die christliche Religion an diesem Beweise des Geistes und der Kraft einen eigenen göttlichen Beweis habe, als alle griechische Dialektik gewähren können. Denn noch war zu seiner Zeit "die Kraft, wunderbare Dinge zu tun, von denen nicht gewichen", die nach Christi Vorschrift lebten; und wenn er ungezweifelte Beispiele hiervon hatte, so mußte er notwendig, wenn er nicht seine eigenen Sinne verleugnen wollte, jenen Beweis des Geistes und der Kraft anerkennen' (*Ü.B.G.K.,* VIII, 10).

Based upon his qualitative distinction between 'zufällige Geschichtswahrheiten' and 'notwendige Vernunftswahrheiten' Lessing should have, had he been consistent, rejected *immediately happening* events as well as events reported having happened because both types of historical reality belong by their empirical nature to the class of 'zufällige Wahrheiten'. The empirical *qua* its very nature is simply and constitutionally incapable of embodying rationality, i.e., necessity. Therefore, from the point of view of a consistently applied rationalistic paradigm, man should in no way restrict the rule of his reason before the cognitive claims of the empirical, e.g., as a 'real' miracle, if such empirico-historical truths run counter to the dictates of reason. Lessing's friend, Moses Mendelssohn, was a consistent 'rationalist' when, in explaining to the Prince of Braunschweig-Wolfenbüttel, why he could not accept Christian dogmas, he wrote: 'Ich kann sie [d.h. christliche Dogmen] *meiner* Ueberzeugung nach mit Dem, was mich Vernunft und Nachdenken von dem Wesen der Gottheit und ihren Eigenschaften gelehrt hat, nicht in Harmonie bringen, und bin also gezwungen, sie zu verwerfen. – Wenn ich diese Lehren im A. T. fände, so würde ich auch das A. T. verwerfen müssen, und wenn ein Wunderthäter, sie zu bewähren, vor meinen Augen alle Todten erweckte, die seit Jahrhunderten begraben worden, so würde ich sagen: der Wunderthäter hat Todte erweckt, aber seine Lehre kann ich nicht annehmen.'[23] Whereas Mendelssohn is willing to reject the empirical as given in the present, even if it were manifesting a momentous miracle, if it conflicts with the dictates of pure reason, Lessing states that, had he been an immediate witness of Christ's miracles, 'so würde ich ... so viel Vertrauen gewonnen haben, daß ich willig meinen Verstand dem seinigen unterworfen hätte, daß ich ihm in allen Dingen geglaubt hätte . . .' (VIII, 10). Lessing has, in effect, stated that the empirical as *immediately* given to man's senses *in the present* constitutes a 'Beweis des Geistes und der Kraft', i.e., is apodictic relative to valid theological truth. From this point of view, the difference between the certainty of the immediately experienced empirical and the empirical as reported as having been experienced is not a qualitative or logical difference, rather merely a quantitative one. Lessing does not claim that the reality of empirical events cannot be historically proven, rather that such a proof can never make the 'reality' of a past empirical event as real, as imposing, and as reason conquering as an immediately experienced event. Concerning the difference between experienced and reported events Lessing writes:

'Daran liegt es, daß dieser Beweis des Geistes und der Kraft itzt weder Geist noch Kraft mehr hat, sondern zu menschlichen Zeugnissen von Geist und Kraft herabgesunken ist.

'Daran liegt es, daß Nachrichten von erfüllten Weissagungen nicht erfüllte Weissagungen, daß Nachrichten von Wundern nicht Wunder sind. *Diese,* die vor meinen Augen geschehenen Wunder, wirken *unmittelbar. Jene* aber, die Nachrichten von erfüllten Weissagungen und Wundern, sollen durch ein *Medium* wirken, das ihnen alle Kraft benimmt. . . .

'Wenn nun dieser Beweis des Beweises itzt gänzlich weggefallen, wenn nun alle historische Gewißheit viel zu schwach ist, diesen weggefallenen augenscheinlichen Beweis des Beweises zu ersetzen, wie ist mir denn zuzumuten, daß ich die nämlich unbegreiflichen Wahrheiten, welche Leute vor 16 bis 18 hundert Jahren auf die kräftigste Veranlassung glaubten, auf eine unendlich mindere Veranlassung ebenso kräftig glauben soll?

'Oder ist ohne Ausnahme, was ich bei glaubwürdigen Geschichtsschreibern lese, für mich ebenso gewiß, als was ich selbst erfahre?' (*Ü.B.G.K.,* VIII, 11–12).

The difference between the two types of empirical truths is not the difference between that which is 'notwendig' and 'zufällig', rational and empirical, metaphysical and factual, etc. The difference is, in effect, the difference in the added force with which an immediately experienced event affects the experiencer over the force of a reported event. It is perhaps informative to recall that the ultimate criterion of truth for a pure empiricist such as David Hume is simply the force of vividity with which an object affects the mind. Hume writes:

'Can I be sure that in leaving all establish'd opinions I am following truth; and by what criterion shall I distinguish her, even if fortune shou'd at last guide me on her footsteps? After the most accurate and exact of my reasoning, I can give no reason why I shou'd assent to it; and feel nothing but a *strong* propensity to consider objects strongly in that view, under which they appear to me. Experience is a principle, which instructs me in the several conjunctions of objects for the past. Habit is another principle, which determines me to expect the same for the future; and both of them conspiring to operate upon the imagination, make me form certain ideas in a more intense and lively manner, than others, which are not attended with the same advantages. Without this quality, by which the mind enlivens some ideas beyond others . .,. we cou'd never assent to any argument, nor carry our view beyond those few objects, which are present to our senses.'[24]

History conceived as a reporting of events simply lacks for Lessing the quality of affecting the mind in a sufficiently 'intense and lively manner'. Thus the criterion of theological truth proposed by Lessing at this point is an empiricistic criterion.

Lessing's two-fold evaluation of historical truth introduces an inconsistency if not outright contradiction into his analysis.[25] On the one hand, he explicitly equates historical truths with 'zufällige Wahrheiten' and explicitly states that any attempt to ground valid theological truth upon such a class of truth constitutes a logical *metábasis eis allo génos* and yet he states that, had he personally witnessed a miracle, he would gladly submit his reason to its dictates. But his submission to a 'zufällige Wahrheit' that happens to be immediately experienced instead of reported constitutes, nevertheless, a *metábasis eis allo génos*.[26] This means that some of Lessing's statements analyzed above as manifestations of the rationalistic paradigm could equally be reinterpreted on the basis of the empiricistic paradigm. But if they are so reinterpreted, some questions can be raised and conclusions drawn that are not easily reconcilable with Lessing's equation of theological truth with 'Vernunftswahrheiten'. For instance, Lessing states that he like others believes that Alexander the Great had lived and conquered all of Asia. But who would want, based upon such a historical belief, to ground something of eternal value. This line of argumentation sounds as if Lessing's rejection of his belief in the historical reality of Alexander as a basis for theological belief is being used as an example of a type of truth belonging to the class of 'zufällige Wahrheiten'. Accordingly, this class of truth

by its very nature cannot generate a religious 'Überzeugung'. But
then Lessing goes on to state that, however much he believes in
Alexander's existence, Alexander still might just be the creation of a
poet such as Choerilis. This line of argumentation seems to rest upon
the empiricistic paradigm, i.e., it is not the empirical reality of
Alexander and his deeds *per se* that hinder belief in Alexander from
being a valid form of religious belief, rather it is solely the impossibility of historical reporting affecting man with the apodictic force
of immediate experience. But, and this conclusion follows with
logical necessity from the empiricistic paradigm, if Lessing had lived
during Alexander's life time and had witnessed Alexander's deeds,
Lessing would then have been willing to allow these deeds to become
the basis of his theological ideas. Of course, this is nonsense! No
orthodox believer of Lessing's time would have allowed his belief in
Alexander to be the foundation of his religious belief because
Alexander's life was not a 'religious' life. But substitute Christ for
Alexander and a different conclusion arises. For instance, let us
substitute Christ for Alexander in Lessing's statement: 'Wir alle
glauben, daß Alexander gelebt hat, welcher in kurzer Zeit fast ganze
Asien besiegte. Aber wer wollte auf diesen Glauben hin irgend etwas
von großen dauerhaften Belange, dessen Verlust nicht zu ersetzen
wäre, wagen' (*Ü.B.G.K.,* VIII, 13). Lessing's statement rewritten
would read: 'We all believe that Christ lived who claimed to be the
Son of God and sealed his claim with his actual resurrection. But
who would, based on this belief, want to venture something of great
and a lasting importance, whose loss could not be replaced?' If the
immediate experience of such an event such as the resurrection is a
valid basis for concluding truth about God and man, as Lessing's
acceptance of the empiricistic paradigm allows, then one cannot
reject belief in the theological value of such an event simply because
it is not a 'Vernunftswahrheit'. But Lessing writes:

'Wenn ich folglich historisch nichts darwider einzuwenden habe,
daß Christus einen Toten erweckt, muß ich darum für wahr halten,
daß Gott einen Sohn habe, der mit ihm gleiches Wesen sei? In
welcher Verbindung steht mein Unvermögen, gegen die Zeugnisse
von jenem etwas Erhebliches einzuwenden, mit meiner Verbindlichkeit, etwas zu glauben, wogegen sich meine Vernunft sträubt?

'Wenn ich historisch nichts darwider einzuwenden habe, daß dieser
Christus selbst von dem Tode auferstanden, muß ich darum für wahr
halten, daß ebendieser auferstandene Christus der Sohn Gottes gewesen sei?' (VIII, 13).

If Lessing had immediately experienced such an event, however, he should have been willing to submit his reason and believe precisely that, 'wogegen sich [seine] Vernunft sträubt' and conclude that Christ is God. But Lessing continues on to reject belief in Christ as God based upon the historical reality of Christ's resurrection or his miracles because such a belief would constitute a *metábasis eis allo génos* (VIII, 14), i.e., would constitute an illicit jump from one cognitive class to another. And then, Lessing immediately answers a possible objection to his rejection of Christ's divinity. 'Man sagt freilich: Aber ebender Christus, von dem du historisch mußt gelten lassen, daß er Tote erweckt, daß er selbst vom Tode erstanden, hat es selbst gesagt, daß Gott einen Sohn gleiches Wesen habe, und daß *er* dieser Sohn sei. Das wäre ganz gut, wenn nicht, daß dieses Christus gesagt, gleichfalls nicht mehr als historisch gewiß wäre' (VIII, 14). Here Lessing switches back to the empiricistic paradigm which does not require rejection of a belief in Christ as God if only it is grounded on immediate empirical experience. The confusion in Lessing's thinking is evident.

For the moment let the objection to historically based religious truth as constituting a *metábasis eis allo génos* be put aside and let Lessing's objection based upon the empiricistic paradigm remain, namely Lessing's thesis that historically reported religious events cannot generate quantitatively a sufficient 'Überzeugung'. Does it follow from all this that belief that such events 'probably' happened should have the same value and claim upon a mind, that is no claim whatsoever, as the firm belief that such events did not take place? In other words, whereas the belief in the historical reality of a religious event may not constitutionally possess apodictic certainty for the immediate present, does it follow that it can and should have no influence whatsoever upon the current 'now'? Are historical events, even miraculous ones, simply to be strung together atomistically as discrete opaque and hence totally isolated entities, as a consistent application of the empiricistic paradigm might seem to indicate they so should be? Another formulation of this question might be: Even if an empirical event that actually happened in a *past* 'now' cannot affect a mind *apodictically* in a *present* 'now', does it follow that the event and its effects were not somehow necessary religiously for that *distant* 'now' and, insofar as the past does influence the present, have some sort of necessary influence upon the *present* 'now'? Lessing's answers to these questions will be dealt with in my discussion of Lessing's positive evaluation of Christianity. But first, the nature of the cognitive crisis in Lessing's 'Denkungsart' must be investigated if Lessing's Christianity is to be comprehended.

D. THE EFFECTS OF THE EMPIRICISTIC PARADIGM ON LESSING'S ANTHROPOLOGY

The general thesis of the rationalistic influenced *Aufklärung* is three-fold: (1) reality is rational, (2) man has the epistemological capacity to discover the rationality of reality, and (3) man, grounded upon his cognition of reality, can fulfill his rational destiny, i.e., act morally. In short, man's epistemological and moral powers are sufficiently efficacious on their own to lead man along the path of perfection. Of course, in the course of the 18th century doubt arose concerning reason's ability to fathom the real.[28] The interesting thing about Lessing's early years of manhood is that they exhibit a crisis whose content is centered around the inadequacy of the general thesis of the *Aufklärung*.[29] Perhaps the most striking manifestation of this crisis is to be found in Lessing's youthful and unfinished poem *Die Religion* (1749, I, 201–209).

In this poem, Lessing sets out to further religion by revealing the inner secrets of the human self to the self. 'Man glaube nicht, daß [der Dichter] seinen Gegenstand aus den Augen läßt, wenn er sich in den Labyrinthen der Selbsterkenntnis zu verlieren scheint. Sie, die Selbsterkenntnis, war allezeit der nächste Weg zu der Religion, und ich füge hinzu, der sicherste' (*R.*, I, 201). The fact that Lessing turns to 'Selbsterkenntnis' rather than to objective metaphysical analysis is indicative of the incipient philosophico-theological crisis in eighteenth-century thinking. Lessing's methodology for ascertaining self-knowledge is essentially empirical and observational. Lessing does not, as Alexander Baumgarten did, develop a philosophical treatise concerning the ontological structure of the soul. Lessing's approach is not that of a rational psychologist. On the contrary, Lessing merely observes, i.e., he turns his 'empirical' glance inward upon the self-consciousness of man and reports what he finds. And that which he finds is vice, ignorance, confusion, and misery. 'Man schließe einen Blick in sich selbst; man setze alles, was man weiß, als wüßte man es nicht, beiseite; auf einmal ist man in einer undurch-dringlichen Nacht. Man gehe auf den ersten Tag seines Lebens zurück. Was entdeckt man? Eine mit dem Viehe gemeinschaftliche Geburt; ja, unser Stolz sage was er wolle, eine noch elendere. Ganze Jahre ohne Geist, ohne Empfindung, folgen darauf und den ersten

Beweis, daß wir Menschen sind, geben wir durch Laster, die wir in uns gelegt fanden, und mächtiger in uns gelegt fanden, als die Tugend' (I, 201–202). An empirical investigation of man according to Lessing reveals man to be caught 'in einer undurchdringlichen Nacht' which entails the existence of vices in his heart. Such a view casts Lessing into a theodicean crisis, i.e., how is such vice possible in a rational world? 'Welcher Anblick! in dem ganzen Umfange des menschlichen Herzens nichts als Laster zu finden. Und es ist von Gott? Es ist von einem allmächtigen, weisen Gott? Marternde Zweifel! ' (I, 202). If man does not seem to be able to be moral, perhaps, he has been created to know?, muses Lessing: 'Doch vielleicht ist unser Geist desto göttlicher. Vielleicht wurden wir für die Wahrheit er- schaffen, da wir es für die Tugend nicht sind. Für die Wahrheit. Wie vielfach ist sie? Jeder glaubt sie zu haben, und jeder hat sie anders. Nein, nur der Irrtum ist unser Teil, und Wahn ist unsre Wissenschaft' (I, 202). In short, man appears to be a prisoner of cognitive night.

Der ernsten erster Blick, die ich auf mich geschossen,
Hat mein erstauntes Herz mit Schwermut übergossen.
Verloren in mir selbst, sah, hört' und fühlt' ich nicht;
Ich war in lauter Nacht, und hoffte lauter Licht.
Nun zwanzig Jahre gelebt – und noch mich nicht gesehen!
Rief ich mit Schrecken aus, und blieb gleich Säulen stehen.
Was ich von mir gedacht, ist falsch, ist lächerlich;
Kaum glaub' ich, ich zu sein, so wenig kenn' ich mich.
Verdammte Schulweisheit! Ihr Grillen weiser Toren!
Bald hätt' ich mich durch euch, wie meine Zeit verloren.
Ihr habt, da Wähnen nur der Menschheit Wissen ist,
Den stolzen Sinn gelehrt, daß er mehr weiß, als schließt.
Dem Irrtum in dem Schoß, träumt er von Lehrgebäuden,
Und kann, stolz auf den Traum, kein wachsam Zweifeln
  leiden.
Das Forschen ist sein Gift, Harnäckigkeit sein Ruhm;
Wer ihn bekehren will, raubt ihm sein Eigentum;
Ihm, der stolz von der Höh.' der aufgetürmten Lügen,
Natur und Geist und Gott sieht unverhüllet liegen.
Warum? Wer? Wo bin ich? Zum Glück. Ein Mensch. Auf
  Erden.
Bescheide sonder Licht, die Kindern gnügen werden!
Was ist der Mensch? Sein Glück? Die Erde', auf der er irrt?
Erklärt mir, was ihr nennt; dann sagt auch, was er wird ...
(R., I, 203–204)

It is not that man possesses no knowledge whatsoever that bothers Lessing. Kant's epistemological crisis entails his attempt to ground Newtonian physics upon a sound and secure foundation. Lessing was not interested in epistemological questions *per se*! He was interested in knowledge that leads man to higher levels of moral perfection and hence he was interested in knowledge about God as the ground of reality and man's relationship to God. Lessing's complaint is that whatever knowledge man might have from the natural sciences or, indeed, whatever metaphysical knowledge he may think that he has, *is simply not perfective of man!* In his *G.ü.H.* Lessing writes that the fruits for man of the scientific revolution wrought by men such as Leibniz and Newton have indeed been meagre. '[Newton und Leibniz] sind unerschöpflich in Entdeckung neuer Wahrheiten. Auf dem kleinsten Raum können sie durch wenige mit Zeichen verbundene Zahlen Geheimnisse klar machen, wozu Aristoteles unerträgliche Bände gebraucht hätte. So füllen sie den Kopf, und das Herz bleibt leer. Den Geist führen sie bis in die entferntesten Himmel, unterdessen da das Gemüt durch seine Leidenschaften bis unter das Vieh heruntergesetzt wird. . . . Der Erkenntnis nach sind wir Engel, und dem Leben nach Teufel' (VII, 188–189, 193). Lessing complained in his *R.* about this same inability of apparent knowledge to affect man positively.

> *So kenn' ich Gott durch euch, ihr Israels Verwirrer,*
> *Und eure Weisheit macht den irren Geist noch irrer.*
> *Umsonst erhebt ihr mir des Willens freie Kraft!*
> *Ich will, ich will . . . Und doch bin ich nicht tugendhaft.*
> *Umsonst erhebt ihr mir des Urteils streng Entscheiden.*
> *Die Laster kenn' ich all, doch kann ich alle meiden?*
> *Hier hilft kein starker Geist, von Wissenschaft genährt,*
> *Und Schlüsse haben nie das Bös' in uns zerstört.* (I, 207)

In short, man is a puzzle for the young Lessing. 'Der Mensch? Wo ist er her? Zu schlecht für einen Gott; zu gut fürs Ungefähr' (I, 202).

The young Lessing finds man to be in a deplorable state. Besides being filled with vices that his will functioning under the guidance of his knowing mind cannot control, man's very cognitive faculty seems to be so weak that it cannot find truth or, if it does determine certain scientific truth, it nevertheless is incapable of discovering truth needed for man's perfection. Relative to questions of ultimate concern man's cognitive powers seem to be too weak to direct man to perfective knowledge. In short, the young Lessing doubts the basic underlying article of belief of the *Aufklärung*, namely that man is spiritually alive in the sense that he can cognitively discover the ultimate meaning or rationality of reality and by means of this knowledge fulfill his moral destiny.[30] Whereas Lessing, in my judgment, never doubted throughout most of his mature life that the essence of theological truth is constituted by 'Vernunftswahrheiten', he similarly appears never to have doubted that man's cognitive powers are weak and hence incapable unaided of fully grasping the rationality of reality and successfully and completely transforming man's 'practical' life into a manifestation of this basic ontological rationality. Lessing's disbelief in the cognitive and practical capacities of man was not a conclusion *a priori* deduced, from abstract metaphysical principles, rather intuitively given in empirical experience. Whatever the theoretical essence of man is, or is supposed to be, *factually* or as a *de facto* given, man is simply cognitively weak. The 'givenness' of man's cognitive weakness causes Lessing to make rather inconsistent contentions concerning man. Three such contentions in the order of their chronological occurrence will be briefly examined.

1. In *G.ü.H.* Lessing states that man's destiny is essentially practical rather than theoretical. 'Der Mensch war zum Tun und nicht zum Vernünfteln erschaffen'. (VII, 186). Lessing does not mean that man should not think at all, rather that his reflections need not be any more extensive than that which it is necessary to know for man to reach perfection. Concerning the knowledge of a wise man Lessing asserts: '[A]lle seine Ermahnungen und Lehren zielten auf das einzige, was uns ein glückliches Leben verschaffen kann, auf die Tugend. ... Erkenne die Schönheiten und Wunder der Natur nicht weiter als insoferne sie die sichersten Beweise von ihrem großen Schöpfer sind' (VII, 193–194). What bothers Lessing so deeply in his *G.ü.H.* is that the relationship between knowledge and perfection is an ideal that man cannot, seemingly constitutionally, preserve.

'Der Mensch ward zum Tun nicht zum Vernünfteln erschaffen. Aber eben deswegen, weil er nicht dazu erschaffen ward, hängt er diesem mehr als jenem nach. Seine Bosheit unternimmt allezeit das, was er nicht soll, und seine Verwegenheit allezeit das, was er nicht kann. Er, der Mensch, sollte sich Schranken setzen lassen? Glückselige Zeiten, als der Tugendhafteste der Gelehrteste war! als alle Weisheit in kurzen Lebensregeln bestand! Sie waren glückselig, als daß sie lange hätten dauern können. ...' (VII, 186).

Why could not such times last any longer (and longer than what)?

No answer! Man is simply destined to lose his pristine knowledge and become entrapped in the complications and errors of too much reflection. Lessing's break with the *Weltanschauung* of the *Aufklärung* cannot be made more evident. The hope of the *Aufklärung* was located in man's rational and cognitive powers. Man's ability to know is the one and only power he has to obtain perfection in life. Now it appears as if precisely the cognitive drive in man were the source of his downfall. Concerning Lessing's partially completed *Faust* work, now alas lost, Hauptmann von Blankenburg writes of precisely the point where Lessing located Faust's weakness. The scene is to open with a conference of devils discussing their projects.

'Denken Sie, was ein Mann, wie Lessing von diesem Stoffe zu machen weiß! — Der Letzte, welcher von den Unterteufeln erscheint, berichtet: daß er wenigstens einen Mann auf der Erde gefunden habe, welchem nun gar nicht beizukommen sei; er habe keine Leidenschaft, keine Schwachheit; in der nähren Untersuchung dieser Nachricht wird Fausts Charakter immer mehr entwickelt; und auf die Nachfragen nach allen seinen Trieben und Neigungen antwortet endlich der Geist: er hat nur einen Trieb, nur eine Neigung; einen unauslöschlichen Durst nach Wissenschaften und Kenntnis — "Ha!" ruft der Oberste der Teufel aus, "dann ist er mein, und auf immer mein, und sicherer mein, als bei jeder andern Leidenschaft!" ' (*F.*, II, 561).

This same cognitive tendency Lessing bemoans in his *G.ü.H.* as man's inclination 'zum Vernünfteln' which leads him astray from 'Truth' to lesser and irrelevant truths and ultimately to moral decay. In *R.* the truths obtained by man's reason are simply referred to as error. 'Jeder glaubt [Wahrheit] zu haben, und jeder hat sie anders. Nein, nur der Irrtum ist unser Teil, und Wahn ist unsere Wissenschaft.' Man seems, indeed, to be in a deplorable state. His irresistible drive to know only leads him astray from the truth he must know and imprisons him in 'Wahn'.

As mentioned above, Lessing does not explain why man cannot maintain the necessary harmony between his cognitive and moral powers and *must* instead debase himself in useless striving after knowledge. Of particular interest for determining the crisis nature of Lessing's thought is the question concerning the historical and anthropological status of man's cognitive weakness. Did Lessing believe that the 'first man', or men, in history really possessed moral-cognitive perfection and then lost it in the course of history or is this weakness a constitutive element of man's 'original' anthropological structure and therefore historical man never really possessed such harmony. More importantly yet is what Lessing's reasons, paradigms, were for deciding between such questions. According to Arthur O. Lovejoy, the first principle of the Enlightenment throughout Europe was the principle of 'uniformitarianism'. 'This is the first and fundamental principle of this general and pervasive philosophy of the Enlightenment. The reason, it is assumed to be evident, is identical in all men; and the life of reason therefore, it is tacitly or explicitly inferred, must admit of no diversity. Differences of opinion or taste are evidences of error. . . . The object of the effort of the religious, moral, social reformer, as of the literary critic, is therefore to standardize men and their beliefs, their likings, their activities, and their institutions.'[31] When this type of interpretation of reality and of human nature is applied to man's history, particularly to the life of the first man, or men, it results in what Lovejoy designates as 'rationalistic primitivism'. Lovejoy writes: 'The entire logic of this type of rationalism implied that the truths of "reason" or "nature", since they were universal, must have been at least *as well* known to the earliest and least sophisticated men as to any other members of the race; and, what is more, that early men were readily in a better position to apprehend such truths than men of later periods. For the minds of the men of the first ages were not corrupted by "prejudices" at all; there were no traditions and no crystallized social forms to hinder the workings of common sense in them. What is universal and uniform in man, then, but has been overlaid and obscured by historic accretions in the unhappy diversities of belief and practice of modern and civilized peoples, *must* — according to this logic — have been exemplified in the earliest age . . .'[32] All accretions to this universal and comprehensible religion of early man must constitute, accordingly, a destruction or obfuscation of the theologically necessary. The logic of 'rationalistic primitivism' rests upon an a-historical and static anthropology. Insofar as there is historical development (evolution?) it must be viewed as a degenerating process away from the universally sufficient and valid. Lessing himself seems to have shared in this paradigm of the Enlightenment when he refers to happy bygone times: 'Glückselige Zeiten, als der Tugendhafteste der Gelehrteste war! als alle Weisheit in kurzen Lebensregeln bestand!' (*G.ü.H.,* VII, 186).[33] Indeed, Lessing even avers that Adam possessed such a harmony necessary for man's perfection, — a harmony that his children and his children's children could not maintain. 'Man gehe in die ältesten Zeiten.

Wie einfach, leicht und lebendig war die Religion des Adams? Allein wie lange? Jeder von seinen Nachkommen setzte nach eignem Gutachten etwas dazu. Das Wesentliche wurde in einer Sündflut von willkürlichen Sätzen versenkt. Alle waren der Wahrheit untreu geworden, nur einige weniger als die andern . . .' (VII, 189). Thus it appears as if Lessing interprets man on the basis of an important principle of the Enlightenment. However, on the other hand, empirical man (i.e., all men except Adam) does not possess, according to Lessing, universal and perfective knowledge. This is simply a *given,* i.e., when Lessing empirically and historically looks into the heart of man he finds moral imperfection somehow integrally connected to man's inner drive to expand his cognitive horizon. This seems to be the 'primitive' state, structurally speaking, of *every* individual. If we put aside Lessing's statement that Adam as the first *historical* human possessed such a perfection of being, Lessing in effect has stated that man *as he first is,* e.g., as he matures from childhood to manhood, is cognitively and morally disoriented. Furthermore, if this view is applied consistently to man as a historical being, it should lead to the conclusion that the first men too were truly and similarly weak even as physiological adults as there were no perfected adults *then* living to teach 'primitive man' to be anything better. From this point of view Lessing's reference to Adam, if taken seriously, would constitute an inconsistency as it would imply an application of the a-historical paradigm of 'rationalistic primitivism' to human history. In his *Erziehung,* when speculatively recasting the Christian doctrine of original sin, Lessing comes close to viewing the first humans as truly 'primitive' beings. Lessing writes: 'Wie, wenn uns endlich alles überführte, daß der Mensch auf der *ersten und niedrigsten* Stufe seiner Menschheit schlechterdings so Herr seiner Handlungen nicht sei, daß er moralischen Gesetzen folgen könne?' (VIII, 609–610, § 74). The effect of Lessing's acceptance of man's cognitive weakness as a necessary aspect of his being is materially to render the Enlightenment's a-historical and static concept of human nature meaningless, however much Lessing might have formally maintained this paradigm.

However confused and confusing Lessing's acceptance of man's cognitive weakness in *G.ü.H.* is, he has, in effect, contended (1) that man is some how constitutionally necessitated to pursue an expansion of his cognitive powers, (2) that man's innate or, at least, first anthropological condition, individually and historically, is to be lost in a cognitive night, and (3) that this condition entails man's moral imperfection as an unavoidable effect. Of what this cognitive blind alley consists, how it causes man to be morally imperfect, why man must have such weakness, and how this weakness is to be overcome are not discussed nor even formulated as questions. The most interesting point of all is not even hinted at, namely, what influence, if any, will man's inescapable tendency to pursue theoretical cognition have in bringing about man's overcoming of his cognitive and moral weakness and will this tendency in any way be constitutive of man's ultimate perfection? It will be recalled that, in Lessing's *Faust* fragment, the devil thinks that he will win Faust's soul because of Faust's insatiable desire for knowledge. However, the ending was not to be tragic for Lessing, rather, as von Blankenburg noted in his letter about Lessing's development of the Faust theme, man's cognitive faculty would not be the cause of his downfall. ' "Triumphiert nicht", ruft ihnen [i.e., the devils] der Engel zu, "ihr habt nicht über Menschheit und Wissenschaft gesiegt; die Gottheit hat dem Menschen nicht den edelsten der Triebe gegeben, um ihn ewig unglücklich zu machen;..." ' (*F.*, II, 561–562).

2. In the discussion of the effect of the rationalistic paradigm upon Lessing's theological speculations it was noted that Lessing in his *Ü.E.G.R.* quite consistently expressed preference for natural religion over revealed or positive religion. Further it was shown that if one extrapolated from the last paragraph of this fragment one would have to conclude that a state in which there is no positive religion would be the best because it would be a state in which natural religion is fully realized. This indeed, seems to be the state of affairs prophecized by Lessing in the *Erziehung* for 'die Zeit eines *neuen ewigen Evangeliums*' (VIII, 612, § 86). Every individual is obliged to realize such a natural religion according to the powers he possesses. The type of knowledge entailed in natural religion seems plausibly to be of the type that Adam (*G.ü.H.*) must have possessed in his pristine wisdom, i.e., the knowledge of the type that brings about the moral perfection of man. 'Einen Gott erkennen, sich die würdigsten Begriffe von ihm zu machen suchen, auf diese würdigsten Begriffe bei allen unsern Handlungen und Gedanken Rücksicht nehmen: ist der vollständige Inbegriff aller natürlichen Religion' (*Ü.E.G.R.*, VII, 280). The paradigm of 'rationalistic primitivism' indicates that the first man (or men) should have possessed natural religion in its purity and any historical accretions to it would constitute a degeneration rather than improvement. Verbally at least, Lessing seems to have shared

this paradigm in that, according to him, Adam possessed a religious perfection in which his wisdom was his virtue and his children were not able to maintain such a pristine state as they were continually tempted to speculate, to increase their cognitive horizon. Why Adam's offspring could not preserve in tact the state of natural religion is not explained. Furthermore, if Lessing's references to Adam are left to the side, it becomes evident that Lessing has in effect contended not so much that man has fallen from a state of *already having possessed* perfective knowledge, but that he never possessed such knowledge in the first place as his natural or 'primitive' state is to be cognitively weak. A similar conception can be found in *Ü.E.G.R.*

After having stated that all men are obliged to realize natural religion Lessing notes that all men cannot accomplish this imperative and in this weakness is located the roots of positive religion. 'Da aber dieses Maß bei jedem Menschen verschieden, und sonach auch eines jeden Menschen natürliche Religion verschieden sein würde: so hat man dem Nachteile, welchen diese Verschiedenheit nicht in dem Stande der natürlichen Freiheit des Menschen, sondern in dem Stande seiner bürgerlichen Verbindung mit andern hervorbringen konnte, vorbauen zu müssen geglaubt. . . . Das ist: man mußte aus der Religion der Natur, welche einer allgemeinen gleichartigen Ausübung unter Menschen nicht fähig war, eine positive Religion bauen . . .' (*Ü.E.G.R.*, VII, 280–281). Whereas thinkers of the *Aufklärung* tended to view reason as something more or less uniformly possessed by man, Lessing simply avers (without explaining why) that man is incapable of such 'eine allgemeine gleichartige Ausübung' of his powers and that this incapacity must manifest itself as positive religion. Indeed, precisely because man is simply incapable of actualizing natural religion in a pure manner and presumably because religion is necessary for man, Lessing concludes that positive religion is 'unentbehrlich'. 'Die Unentbehrlichkeit einer positiven Religion, vermöge welcher die natürliche Religion in jedem Staate nach dessen natürlicher und zufälliger Beschaffenheit modifiziert wird, nenne ich die innere Wahrheit derselben, und diese innere Wahrheit derselben ist bei einer so groß als bei den andern' (VII, 281). Although Lessing has plausibly explained why positive religions must and do in fact arise, he has not completely revealed why their existence is 'unentbehrlich'. 'Unentbehrlich' for what? One can say that the sweating of an overheated individual is necessarily produced by his strenuous exertions and that this self-same sweating is 'unentbehrlich' if he is to remain physiologically sound. How is the origin of positive religion 'unentbehrlich' for man's religious perfection? If the highest form of man's religious existence is natural religion and if positive religion *always* entails a weakening and limiting of natural religion, how can positive religion be 'unentbehrlich' unless it is assumed that man can never realize natural religion in his actual religious life and hence positive religion is the best he can hope for? But this would be to leave man in a world that is *de facto* irrational for man. I would suggest that a possible reason why Lessing discontinued the work at this point is due to his inability at the time of writing it to solve the puzzle just described.

Not only does Lessing fail to explain fully why positive religion is 'unentbehrlich', he does not even attempt to say why man cannot constitutionally live up to the dictates of natural religion. Just as much as man's tendency to become lost in cognitive pursuits was more of a given than a proven in *G.ü.H.,* similarly man's inability to realize natural religion is simply stated as a given fact. However, what is entailed in such an imperfection is partially revealed. The commandment of rational religion is for man to know God, to construct the most worthy concepts of him, and to predicate human action upon these concepts. Since man is incapable, constitutionally, of fulfilling this imperative, it must be because he cannot construct for himself 'die würdigsten Begriffe' of God upon which to base his practical life or, conversely, man's concepts of the divine must be unclear and inadequate. What this unclarity is, is not fully given. Nevertheless, it becomes evident that the plight of man not only is caused by his inordinate drive to widen his cognitive horizons, his tendency 'zum Vernünfteln', but that it consists paradoxically in a lack of adequate cognitive awareness, i.e., man's notions about God upon which he structures his activity are somehow obscure. Since God was for the users of the rationalistic paradigm the source of the cosmos' rationality, to claim that man has inadequate concepts of God is to assert that man is not able to cognize meaningful rationality or rationality as a foundation for meaning. Insofar as positive religion weakens and limits natural religion, and insofar as positive religion is a necessary outgrowth of man's inadequate ability, it means that man's cognitive powers are weak and that his notions of the divine are limited.

Another interesting conclusion flows from Lessing's acceptance of man's inability to develop adequate concepts of God. To know, for the rationalist, is to cognize the universal. The universal is that which is valid for all times and all places. This fact is behind the tendency of thinkers of the Enlightenement to contend: 'Anything of which the intelligibility, verifiability, or actual affirmation is limited to men of a special age, race, temperament, tradition, or condition is *eo ipso* without truth or value, or at all events without importance to a reasonable man.'[34] A consistent application of this paradigm to theological matters was behind the rejection by many Enlightenment thinkers of revealed religion(s). Insofar as Lessing denies that man has the power to realize natural religion, he is also contending that man does not have the power to manifest the universal in his actual historical life. Thus for Lessing a key element of the 'Unentbehrlich-keit einer positiven Religion' is that characteristic, 'vermöge welcher die natürliche Religion in jedem Staate nach dessen natürlicher und zufälliger Beschaffenheit modifiziert wird . . .' (*Ü.E.G.R.,* VII, 281). In short, Lessing acknowledges that, with the exception of isolated individuals here and there (cf., *Erziehung*), natural religion has never actually existed for mankind as a whole. What has existed is positive religion and each such religion differs from the others, i.e., positive religions do not manifest the same uniform features, but rather different and differing characteristics. However much Lessing might have felt that the ideal for each single individual is to realize a universal humanity, the fact remains that Lessing realized that actual historical man has not fully realized such an ideal. In his famous *Gespräche für Freimäurer* Lessing has his mouthpiece Falk contend that the existence of the state is necessary if man is to live with man. However, Falk does not believe that a single superstate embodying all of mankind is possible, simply because there is something in man that causes him to differ himself (conceived as one group of men) from another group. Falk states his basic principles:

'Das ist: wenn itzt ein Deutscher einem Franzosen, ein Franzose einem Engländer, oder umgekehrt, begegnet, so begegnet nicht mehr ein bloßer Mensch [i.e., a universal man] einem *bloßen* Menschen, die vermöge ihrer gleichen Natur gegeneinander angezogen werden, sondern ein *solcher* Mensch [i.e., a being that exhibits individual rather than universal interests] begegnet einem *solchen* Menschen, die ihrer verschiedenen Tendenz sich bewußt sind, welches sie gegen-einander kalt, zurückhaltend, mißtrauisch macht, noch ehe sie für ihre einzelne Person das Geringste miteinander zu schaffen und zu teilen haben. . . .

'. . . Nicht als *bloße* Menschen gegen *bloße* Menschen; sondern alle *solche* Menschen gegen *solche* Menschen, die sich einen gewissen geistigen Vorzug streitig machen, und darauf Rechte gründen, die dem natürlichen Menschen nimmermehr einfallen könten' (*E.F.*, VIII, 559—560).

In short, Lessing's basic political paradigm is: 'So ist es. — Nun sieh da das zweite Unheil, welches die bürgerliche Gesellschaft, ganz ihrer Absicht entgegen, verursacht. Sie kann die Menschen nicht vereinigen, ohne sie zu trennen; nicht trennen, ohne Klüfte zwischen ihnen zu befestigen, ohne Scheidemauern durch sie hin zu ziehen' (VIII, 560). Just as a uniform natural religion is impossible for man, so is a uniform or universal social order impossible. The basis for this impossibility lies in man's inability to grasp cognitively the universal and to manifest it in his life. By implication this would mean that the reason why man is so immoral is because he is not able cognitively to grasp the moral universal in God and consequently is incapable of realizing such a universal in his concrete moral life. More on this point presently. For the moment it is sufficient to note that man's deviation from Adam's simple religion of nature is for Lessing a function of his cognitive incapacity to grasp the universal, i.e., divine, in reality.

3. Towards the end of his life in his *Erziehung* Lessing sought to justify his conception of revelation as an educative process in the following manner:

'Wenn auch der erste Mensch mit einem Begriffe von einem Einzigen Gott sofort ausgestattet wurde: so konnte doch dieser mitgeteilte, und nicht erworbene Begriff unmöglich lange in seiner Lauterkeit bestehen. Sobald ihn die sich selbst überlassene menschliche Vernunft zu bearbeiten anfing, zerlegte sie den Einzigen Unermeßlichen in mehrere Ermeßlichere, und gab jedem dieser Teile ein Merkzeichen.

'So entstand natürlicher Weise Vielgötterei und Abgötterei. Und wer weiß, wie viele Millionen Jahre sich die menschliche Vernunft noch in diesen Irrwegen würde herumgetrieben haben; ohnegeachtet überall und zu allen Zeiten einzelne Menschen erkannten, daß es Irrwege waren: wenn es Gott nicht gefallen hätte, ihr durch einen neuen Stoß eine bessere Richtung zu geben' (*Erziehung*, VIII, 592, §§ 6, 7).

First of all, given the fact that even the most advanced thinkers of Lessing's time thought about human history in terms of thousands of years (usually about five or six thousand) rather than in millions of years, to maintain that man would remain in the 'Irrwege' of 'Vielgötterei und Abgötterei' for 'viele Millionen Jahre' unless God interfered 'durch einen neuen Stoß', is to say, in effect, that man is *by* his very nature cognitively incapable of ascertaining important and necessary theological truth. If theological truth is essentially rational and if man's rational powers are *de facto* permanently weak, man would seem to be lost in unending darkness. Thus it is evident that the same basic cognitive problem that was facing Lessing in *R.* still was facing him at the end of his life in the *Erziehung*. Man seeks to grasp the divine, the rationality of the universe, with his rational powers and is unable to!

Of equal interest is Lessing's ambiguous use once again of the paradigm of 'rationalistic primitivism' in explaining the origin of 'Vielgötterei'. It would appear according to Lessing that the first human was immediately endowed with a concept of the unity of this divine. This contention rests, of course, upon an a-historical concept of man. But unlike the first man of the 'rationalistic primitivism' or, indeed, unlike the Adam of *G.ü.H.*, the first man of the *Erziehung* simply at no time truly possesses the true concept of the divine, i.e., he is not able intellectually to appropriate the concept. As soon as he begins to reflect upon the idea he immediately divides the indivisable and thereby obfuscates the true unity of God. Just as man must divide himself into partial and limited groups when he seeks to unite socially with other men, just as man must create limited and differing positive religions when he seeks to realize the universal imperative of natural religion, in short, just as man ends up being conscious of and interested in the particular, singular, and unique when he is seeking to penetrate to the universal, so too must his cognitive powers divide truth about God, about the unmeasurable into limited and weakened and hence degenerated partial truths. However, the question immediately rises as to how seriously Lessing believed that the first man really had been endowed with a pure concept of the divine unity. Insofar as Lessing talks in such terms he is utilizing the paradigm of rationalistic primitivism. Even if Lessing did believe in the first man's possession of pure truth (in my judgment it is impossible to decide this question definitively), he nevertheless immediately relativizes its validity in that for all practical purposes man, even the first man, could not intellectually comprehend such truth. As mentioned above, Lessing, in reinterpreting the doctrine of original sin, suggests that perhaps man 'auf der *ersten* und *niedrigsten* Stufe seiner Menschheit' was simply incapable of being master of his deeds.

Furthermore, it is plausible to conclude that man in the first stages of his humanity was morally imperfect precisely because he was also cognitively powerless to construct 'die würdigsten Begriffe' of God with which to inform his moral life. If this is so, then whether or not God had somehow made pure theological truths — truths of natural religion — manifest to man constitutes a mute question and is irrelevant to man's actual history. Man as he actually began in history was not the rationalistic primitive of Lovejoy's description, rather a true primitive in the normal sense of the word. It would seem that Lessing is inchoately breaking through the a-historical and static conceptualism of the *Aufklärung* and laying the foundations for an evolutionary interpretation of man based upon an historically constructed anthropology.

In the above given examples it was shown that man for Lessing is irresistibly inclined to pursue cognitive interests and yet paradoxically he is simultaneously *de facto* cognitively weak. Furthermore, man's moral imperfections are somehow a function of this cognitive weakness. One of the results of man's cognitive weakness is his inordinate and inescapable attachment to the unique, the singular, or the particular. What was not made fully clear was just what constitutes the 'weakness' of man's imperfect rationality. The answer to this question can be found in Lessing's early fragment *Das Christentum der Vernunft*. In this work Lessing more or less uses Leibnizian concepts to explain the genesis of the world. When God thinks his own infinitive and undivided perfections in a divided manner he simultaneously creates the world. Furthermore, God must think (create) the world in the most perfect manner, i.e., God thinks the world as an infinitive chain of ontological gradations, each grade containing more perfection than the next lower one. The entities occupying each grade of being are 'gleichsam eingeschränkte Götter' (*C.V.*, VII, 200, § 22), i.e., they all exhibit to varying degrees the perfections within God. In this 'great chain of being' there are 'Wesen, welche Vollkommenheiten haben, sich ihrer Vollkommenheiten bewußt sind, und das Vermögen besitzen, ihnen gemäß zu handeln' and such beings are called 'moralische Wesen, das ist, welche einem Gesetze folgen können' (VII, 200, § 25). Too many investigators have been content simply to identify such fully self-conscious beings with man.[35] There is little doubt, in my judgment, that Lessing considered such perfected beings to be the ideal for man. This ideal coincides perfectly with Lessing's definition of natural man in *Ü.E.G.R.* and with this ideal of virtue producing knowledge expressed in *G.ü.H.* Just as in these works it was shown that man deviates from the ideal, a similar deviation is to be found in *C.V.* In an unfinished final paragraph Lessing writes: 'Da in der Reihe der Wesen unmöglich ein Sprung statt finden kann, so müssen auch solche Wesen existieren, welche sich ihrer Vollkommenheiten nicht deutlich genug bewußt sind' (VII, 200, § 27). If Lessing had continued on with his sentence following the same line of reasoning as is evident in paragraph 25 quoted above he should have written, '...und das Vermögen *nicht völlig* besitzen, ihnen gemäß zu handeln'. Furthermore, the name that he most likely would have given to such imperfect beings would be man as he *de facto* is. At any rate, giving Lessing's repeated references to man's cognitive weakness, paragraph 27 fits this pattern.

The important point for determining the epistemological foundation of man's cognitive weakness is to be found in Lessing's use of the terms 'nicht deutlich genug'. The term 'deutlich' had a very precise meaning within the Leibniz-Wolffian epistemological tradition of the eighteenth century. For this tradition the contents of human consciousness are called 'Begriffe' or 'Vorstellungen' through which reality represents itself to man's mind. Furthermore, reality in itself as the object of truth is essentially homogeneous because it is rational. However, man's awareness of reality as a result of his limited and finite mind is not homogeneous. The contents ('Begriffe' or 'Vorstellungen') of the human mind can be divided into two basic groups. When man is conscious of rational content (e.g., of scientific truth or of 'Vernunftswahrheiten') his mind may be said to have 'deutliche Begriffe' of an object. If, however, the human mind is not rationally aware of the rationality of an object, yet is able to distinguish one object from another (e.g., without being able to specify the scientific explanation of the essence of and difference between two colors, a mind is nevertheless clearly aware of the two colors as distinct), it is said to have 'undeutliche Begriffe' of an object. A positive term for 'undeutlich' is 'sinnlich'. For instance, Alexander Baumgarten, one of the greatest of the Wolffian metaphysicians, writes: 'Eine undeutliche, das ist eine dunkele oder verworrene, Vorstellung ist sinnlich (repraesentatio sensitiva), und dergleichen sind in meiner Seele.'[36] Furthermore, the notion of 'Sinnlichkeit' entailed more than the fact that the human mind was aware of sensations. It referred also to man's volitional life. In other words, insofar as man is attracted to the 'Vollkommenheit' of an object *via* his senses, it is not because such an object directly affects the human intellect rather than the senses themselves in the form of 'sinnliche Begierden'. Baumgarten writes: 'Weil das Begehrungs- vermögen dem Erkenntnisvermögen folgt, oder durch dasselbe be- stimmt wird: so folgt es entweder dem untern oder dem obern. Jenes ist das Begehrungsvermögen (facultas appetitiva inferior). Da ich nun einige Sachen begehre und verabscheue, in so ferne ich sie mir sinnlich vorstelle: so habe ich ein solches Vermögen. Die Begierden und Verabscheuungen, welche durch dasselbe gewürkt werden, sind die sinnlichen (appetitiones et aversationes sensitivae), und sie ent- stehen aus der Kraft der Seele, wodurch sie sich die Welt nach der Lage ihres Körpers vorstellt.'[37]

Lessing was familiar with this epistemological terminology. He also had read Baumgarten certainly by 1753 if not earlier while attending the university. Indeed Baumgarten's influence upon Lessing was the greatest when Lessing wrote his *Abhandlungen über die Fabel* (1754 or a year or so after writing *C.V.*)[38] In his *Bemerkungen* (1757 or 1758), for instance, Lessing treats beauty as a type of pleasant experience and writes: 'Alle angenehmen Begriffe sind undeutliche Vorstellungen einer Vollkommenheit' (VII, 273). The use of the term 'undeutlich' to refer to sensate joy follows Baumgarten terminology. If the words 'nicht deutlich genug' are interpreted within the framework of the Leibniz-Wolffian epistemology, Lessing is contending in effect that man's lack of full self-consciousness, his 'nicht deutlich genug' awareness, is at the same time a 'sinnlich' consciousness. In short, instead of having a rational consciousness man in his first and primitive state possesses an *empirical* one.

If the epistemological interpretation of 'nicht deutlich genug' be granted, then the epistemological foundation for man's cognitive weakness and for the crisis in Lessing's theological speculations can be made evident. The common denominator implicitly underlying the examples given above is Lessing's use of the empiricistic para- digm. According to this paradigm, the object of man's cognitive pursuits can be no more than individual and unique existents as presented to man in sensations. That which is universal, eternal, and supersensate does not exist for the empiricistic paradigm in its purity. For the pure empiricist, man's consciousness is limited to empirical events, to the singular as it occurs in time. In short, the empirical is the sensuous content of any given 'now' and possesses no more apodictic certainty or necessity than the immediate undenia- bility of its existence in a given 'now'. To know the empirical content of a specific 'now' does not enable the mind to know the content of all 'nows' (as the rationalistic paradigm claims for 'Vernunftswahrheiten'). Man for Lessing is irresistibly drawn after cognition, i.e., he seeks to widen his cognitive frontiers. Further, from the point of view of Lessing's use of the rationalistic paradigm, man is accordingly seeking 'Vernunftswahrheiten', particularly about God. But *de facto* man in his first and primitive condition cannot grasp rational truth. This inability to think in 'deutliche Begriffe' implies the correlative, a thinking in 'sinnliche Vorstellungen' as the essence of an empirical consciousness.[39] Although allegedly endowed with a true transcendental (i.e., rational) concept of the divine unity, primitive man divided this concept into 'Vielgötterei' (i.e., idols). Each idol can be viewed as, so to speak, an *empirical* representation of God. For instance, Lessing contends in *Erziehung* that the ancient Jews ('das rohe Volk', cf., VIII, 593, § 11) lacked a transcendental concept of the divine unity and instead quite literally pictured Jehova as the mightiest of the gods. Although man is obliged to realize natural religion (i.e., to construct 'die würdigsten Begriffe' of God), actual man cannot and, instead, must create positive religions which weaken and limit natural religion. When man comes together socially, men are not attracted to each other as 'bloße Menschen', rather they separate into more limited groups which are related to each other somewhat antagonistically as 'solche Menschen gegen solche Menschen'. Underlying and metaphysically grounding the inevitable tendency of man's cognitive interests to focus on the particular, limited and relative instead of upon the universal, general, uniform, and necessary, is Lessing's interpretation of man's *de facto* anthropological structure on the basis of the empiricistic paradigm.

Not only is man's primitive tendency, according to Lessing, to become conscious cognitively of the empirical rather than of the rational more comprehensible when viewed in the light of the empiricistic paradigm, but so too does man's allegedly inescapable moral imperfection become more intelligible when so viewed. In *C.V.* after noting that moral beings are beings that are conscious of their own perfections, that have the power of acting according to these perfections, and hence can follow law Lessing writes: 'Dieses Gesetz ist aus ihrer eigenen Natur genommen, und kann kein anders sein, als: *handle deinen individualischen Vollkommenheiten gemäß*' (VII, 200, § 26). This imperative when applied to a being who is 'nicht deutlich genung' (i.e., 'sinnlich') conscious of himself, is bound to cause man to deviate volitionally as much from the universally valid moral law as man's empirical consciousness causes him to deviate cognitively from the true or universal concept of the unity of God. Lessing, unlike Reimarus, accepts the Christian doctrine of original sin because either as a sad fact or as an allegory it explains 'wie und warum ihre [d.h. der Menschen] Vernunft unwirksam geblieben. Mit einem Worte; die Macht unsrer sinnlichen Begierden, unsrer dunkeln Vorstellungen über alle noch so deutliche Erkenntnis ist es, welche zur kräftigsten Anschauung darin gebracht wird' (*G.H.*, VII, 818). 'Unsre sinnlichen Begierden' refers to the psychologically and empirically experienced basis for man's moral weakness and 'unsre dunkeln [d.h. nicht deutlich genung] Vorstellungen', refers to the metaphysical basis. At any rate, man is not able to predicate his moral activity upon 'deutliche Erkenntnis' (which, of course, is the imperative of natural religion) precisely because his consciousness is limited to 'dunkeln Vorstellungen'.[40] As mentioned above, if Lessing had completed paragraph 27 he would have noted that there are beings, 'welche das Vermögen nicht völlig besitzen' to act in accordance with man's own inner rationality, i.e., moral imperative. The influence of the empiricistic paradigm upon Lessing's anthropological concept of man should be evident by now.

E. THE STRUCTURE OF LESSING'S COGNITIVE CRISIS

There can be no doubt that Lessing's theological thinking remains within the parameters of the *Aufklärung*. Truth about God conceived as ultimate reality entails making manifest to human awareness the necessary, unchanging, and universal rationality of being. Pure truth about God falls within the class of 'Vernunftswahrheiten'. God as the source and highest perfection of being, is to be known as the universal *telos* of rationality informing all the ontological grades of reality. (Lessing's concept of the divine will be discussed more thoroughly in an 'excursus' at the end of the next chapter.) The experience of divine rationality is the experience of the universal informing and determining the various grades of reality. For instance, the experience of the divine in man's religious life constitutes the basis for the imperative of natural religion, i.e., to know God, to construct adequate concepts of him, and to predicate one's behavior on this knowledge. The imperative of natural religion is obligatory for man *qua* his very humanity (i.e., *qua* the universal in the anthropological grade of being), not because he is a Christian or a Jew. For instance, whereas the Jewish dietary laws are seen as being valid for the Jews alone, Lessing asserts that 'jeder Mensch' is bound to natural religion simply because he is a 'Mensch'. Insofar as natural religion is obligatory for every human being simply because of each individual's humanity, natural religion in its essence stands beyond history, i.e., it is in no way dependent upon what is temporally, historically, and socially conditioned for its validity. Natural religion manifests and embodies the universal or metaphysical structure of reality insofar as reality is comprehensible by a conscious being on the level of religious activity. For instance, Sittah in talking to Saladin in *Nathan der Weise* heaps scorn on Christians because of the exclusivity of their religious attitude and self-evaluation, i.e., they are proud first of all to be Christians, not humans. Sittah says:

> *Du kennst die Christen nicht, willst sie nicht kennen.*
> *Ihr Stolz ist: Christen sein; nicht Menschen. Denn*
> *Selbst das, was, noch von ihrem Stifter her,*
> *Mit Menschlichkeit den Aberglauben würzt*
> *Das lieben sie, nicht weil es menschlich ist;*
> *Weil's Christus lehrt; weil's Christus hat getan. –*
> *Wohl ihnen, daß er so ein guter Mensch*
> *Noch war! Wohl ihnen, daß sie seine Tugend*
> *Auf Treu' und Glaube nehmen können! Doch*
> *Was Tugend? – Seine Tugend nicht; sein Name*
> *Soll überall verbreitet werden; soll*
> *Die Namen aller guten Menschen schänden,*
> *Verschlingen. Um den Namen, um den Namen*
> *Ist ihnen nur zu tun.*
> (Act II, scene 1)

The universal manifests itself not only in man's religious life, but also in his social life, be it individual or collective. For instance, Nathan, the Jew, wins for himself the friendship of the Christian templar when he appeals to the universal humanity in each other. Nathan says:

> *. . . – Kommt,*
> *Wir müssen, müssen Freunde sein! – Verdachtet*
> *Mein Volk so sehr Ihr wollt. Wir haben beide*
> *Uns unser Volk nicht auserlesen. Sind*
> *Wir unser Volk? Was heißt denn Volk?*
> *Sind Christ und Jude eher Christ und Jude,*

Als Mensch? Ah! wenn ich einen mehr in Euch
Gefunden hätte, dem es gnügt, ein Mensch
Zu heißen!
(Act II, scene 5)[41]

In short, the universal in human relationships entails an encounter of 'ein bloßer Mensch' with 'ein bloßer Mensch'. A socio-political reflex of the universal in human affairs would be the creation of a single overriding superstate grounded upon man as a pure rational essence.

It has also been shown that, however much the rationalistic paradigm constitutes the foundation for Lessing's Enlightenment ideal, the fact remains that *de facto* man — man as he actually is — simply does not nor can he in his primitive or first condition become cognitively aware of the universal, appropriate it as his own fully comprehended concept, and inform his behavior with it. 'Natural' or rational man should be a practitioner of natural religion, actual man lives in and often fights for positive religions; 'natural' man should think only transcendental concepts about God's unity, actual man becomes a polytheist; 'natural' man should form one supernational state, actual man can only join together to form limited and mutually exclusive national states. In short, the consciousness of actual man is constitutionally limited to the concrete, individual, and empirical. It is not that reality as a whole does not constitute a *harmonia mundi*, it is just that man's mind cannot seem to become aware of the universal in the manifold of the universe. In his *Hamburgische Dramaturgie* Lessing writes: 'In der Natur ist alles mit allem verbunden; alles durchkreuzt sich, alles wechselt mit allem, alles verändert sich eines in das andere. Aber nach dieser unendlichen Mannigfaltigkeit ist sie nur ein Schauspiel für einen unendlichen Geist' (*H.D.,* VI, 358–359).

The structural features of Lessing's 'Denkungsart' are (1) that the *ideal* for human perfection according to Lessing is a function of the rationalistic paradigm, and (2) that the explanation of *actual* man's condition is a function of the empiricistic paradigm. If Lessing's *ars dialectice cogitandi* is to be comprehended, it must be clearly understood that *actual man* for Lessing *simply has not been able to grasp the universal in its purity.* Although man may be presented with a pure concept of the transcendental unity of God, simply because such a concept would not yet be his, not yet internalized, not yet self-consciously informing his being and his activity, it could not remain in its purity. As soon as man seeks actively to appropriate rationally ('erwerben') 'diesen mitgeteilten und nicht erworbenen Begriff', his cognitively weak reason cannot help but metamorphize the pure rational concept as the objectively given into 'Vielgötterei' as the subjectively possessed. Human consciousness in its *primitive* condition *can only think* by means of an empirical, imaginative, sensuous, emotional, concrete, and metaphorical language. It is for this reason that historical man has not so much been interested in the natural religion of humanity as in his own exclusive national or confessional gods.

As noted in the previous chapters, the cognitive crisis of the eighteenth century was caused by the empirically grounded anamolies that the rationalistic paradigm could not solve. Furthermore, the primary characteristic of 'das dritte Menschenalter der Aufklärung' (Wundt) is the attempt by thinkers such as Lambert, Tetens, and the pre-critical Kant to reconcile somehow the belief that the world is structurally rational with the empirical experience of the world as something beyond the realm of essentiality. It can be readily seen that Lessing in his own way participated in this cognitive crisis. The task of Lessing's speculative life particularly of the last decade or so was to reconcile the rational and the empirical, the eternal and the temporal, the metaphysical and the historical, the universal and the particular, the necessary and the mutable. Recently, Helmut Thielicke has summarized Lessing's lifetime task. 'Wie kann ich, das Vernunftswesen, mich selbst als Geschichtswesen übernehmen, ohne dabei meine Existenz zu veruntreuen.'[42]

Ernst Cassirer in his acute analysis of Lessing's theology contends that Lessing developed a new concept of reason. In place of the analytical concept of reason (i.e., of the rationalistic paradigm) Lessing allegedly developed a synthetic or dynamic concept. '[Lessing] always had been the great rationalist, and he remained so to the last; but he replaces analytical reason with synthetic reason, and static reason with dynamic reason. Reason does not exclude motion; it seeks rather to understand the immanent law of motion. It is reason itself that now plunges into the stream of becoming, not in order to be seized and carried along by its swirls but in order to find there its own security and to assert its stability and constancy. In this ideal of reason we have the dawn of a new concept of the nature and truth of history which could not achieve maturity, perfection, and confirmation in the realm of theology and metaphysics.'[43] In my judgment, Cassirer has unnecessarily Hegelianized Lessing and thereby misses the peculiarities and historical situation of Lessing's theological speculations. Lessing never fully transcended the analytical concept of reason. Such an accomplishment had to await the advent of Idealism. Lessing did not have the conceptual machinery for such a task. Lessing's concept of reason was not new, indeed, quite the reverse. Reason for Lessing was the reason of the traditional rationalistic paradigm. Even Lessing's attempted resolution of the two paradigms in *Erziehung* presupposes the validity of the rationalistic concept. Furthermore, Lessing never developed a comprehensive, contradiction free, and consistent solution that a dynamic or synthetic concept of reason would imply. His solution remained hypothetical, tentative, and contradictory. In the preface to his *Erziehung* Lessing does not claim dogmatically that he has discovered *the* solution to the theological crisis of his day, Lessing 'verlangt nicht, daß die Aussicht, die ihn entzücket, auch jedes andere Auge entzücken müsse' (VIII, 590). All Lessing claims is to have perceived a 'Fingerzeig' (VIII, 590). In a letter to Johann Albert Reimarus, Lessing refers sceptically to his *Erziehung*. 'Die *Erziehung des Menschengeschlechts* ist von einem guten Freunde, der sich gern allerlei Hypothesen und Systeme macht, um das Vergnügen zu haben, sie wieder einzureißen. Diese Hypothese nun würde freilich das Ziel gewaltig verrücken, auf welches mein Ungenannter im Anschlage gewesen. Aber was tuts? Jeder sage, was ihm Wahrheit *dünkt*, und die *Wahrheit selbst* sei Gott empfohlen!' (April 6, 1778, IX, 775–776). Indeed, there is evidence that Lessing tired of the sectarian battles in which he embroiled himself. (It will be shown that Lessing's interest in Christianity is a function of his desire to reconcile the two paradigms underlying his thought.) In a letter to Mendelssohn, Lessing refers to a Jew who wished to escape religious persecution: 'Er will von Ihnen nichts, lieber Moses, als daß Sie ihm den kürzesten und sichersten Weg nach dem europäischen Lande vorschlagen, wo es weder Christen noch Juden gibt. Ich verliere ihn ungern; aber sobald er glücklich da angelangt ist, bin ich der erste, der ihm folgt' (December 19, 1780, IX, 883).

Because of the uncertainty in his attempted solution of his cognitive crisis, Lessing's thinking can best be described in the terms of Thomas Kuhn's analysis of scientific revolutions. In specific, Lessing's thinking exhibits many of the features of what Kuhn has called the crisis phase of a scientific revolution. Such a phase is characterized by the emergence of anamolies, the correlative loss of theoretical unity based upon the established paradigm, the inability to get rid of the old paradigm because of its previous success, the need to regain theoretical unity by searching for new paradigms, and the hypothetical, fragmentary, and often inconsistent use of new ideas. Thus far the nature of Lessing's crisis has been discussed. Based upon this analysis we can now turn to his attempted solution.

5. Lessing's attempted theological synthesis

A. LESSING'S RELATIONSHIP TO CHRISTIANITY

In the previous chapter an attempt was made to analyze the crisis nature of Lessing's theological speculations. It was shown that Lessing's *ars dialectice cogitandi* evinces the influence of two contradictory philosophical paradigms. On the one hand, because rational truth is based on an insight into the 'inner truth' of the *mundus intelligiblis*, it is supra-temporal, necessary, universal, metaphysical, and unchanging. On the other hand, because truth is allegedly grounded upon empirical experience of individual events and the reporting thereof, it is encapsuled within time and is contingent, particular, factual, and historical. Truth beyond and excluding temporality versus truth solely within temporality and excluding supra-temporality; absolutely necessary connection versus contingent and atomistic juxtaposition; purely metaphysical absoluteness versus factual and historical relativity constitute the poles of much eighteenth-century philosophy including Lessing's philosophical and theological ratiocination. As long as Lessing remained within the parameters of the rationalistic and empiricistic paradigms, he was faced with momentous and insoluble problems. Both paradigm systems accepted the contention that rational truths if there be any exclude all temporality whereas empirico-historical truths because of their temporal origin exclude all necessary and hence rational content. In short, 'Geschichtswahrheiten' and 'Vernunftswahrheiten' constitute an apparent 'either-or' situation, i.e., if truth must be rational it cannot be empirico-historical and if it is empirico-historical, it cannot be rational.

If Lessing was to achieve a reconciliation between the two paradigms, if the empirico-historical and the rational were to be integrated by him, then the analytical concept of reason as the source for pure, eternal, unchanging, and universal structures had to be over-come. Reason and eternity had to be made accessible to time and uniqueness, whereas, conversely, time had to lose its atomistic opaqueness and become open to the imprint of eternal rationality. In short, time had to be able to *reveal* the divine, the historical, the metaphysical.[1] Any reconciliation between the rational and empiri-cal is possible if it can be shown *that* and *how* the temporal becomes a 'necessary' means for the realization of the eternal. Insofar as 'necessity' is the key ingredient of rationality and insofar as the temporal becomes the 'necessary' medium for the eternal, just so far does the temporal become rationalized.[2]

Given such a prerequisite for a reconciliation of the rationalistic and the empiricistic paradigms in his thought, it is easy to understand why Lessing had to turn to Christianity. Traditional Christianity with its concept of divine revelation in and through history constituted the only source open to Lessing that offered paradigms that sought to unify the divine with history, the eternal with time. Indeed, in my judgment, Lessing did not develop a philosophy of history for the simple reason that he did not possess the necessary philosophical concepts (such as those used by the Idealists). This is not to claim that Lessing made no use of philosophical concepts in his attempted reconciliation of the two paradigm sets. It is to say, however, that such concepts are often only implicit and, when explicit, are gener-ally not the object of a definitive investigation. Whereas Lessing never developed a philosophy of history, he did develop a theology of history, at least insofar as his attempt to solve the riddle of history occurs only in the context of his attempt to solve the riddle of Christianity. In a letter to Moses Mendelssohn written in his first year at Wolfenbüttel, Lessing refers to a book by Adam Ferguson which was apparently inspiring him to rethink problems he had long since thought settled. Referring to some of these truths Lessing writes: 'Wie auch solche, die ich längst für keine Wahrheiten mehr gehalten. Doch ich besorge es nicht erst seit gestern, daß, indem ich gewisse Vorurteile weggeworfen, ich ein wenig zu viel mit weggeworfen habe, was ich werde wieder holen müssen. Daß ich es zum Teil nicht schon getan, daran hat mich nur die Furcht verhindert, nach und nach den ganzen Unrat wieder in das Haus zu schleppen' (January 9, 1771, IX,406).[3] Flajole has convincingly shown that the 'lost truths' Lessing was reconsidering were Christian truths. '. . . Lessing feels obliged to take back in some way the revelation which he formerly condemned as childhood prejudice. He is taking back Christian revelation in a manner that will enable him to feel himself a Christian and to be regarded as a Christian by others.'[4] Although it is admittedly very difficult to date the changes in Lessing's theological thought, this letter can nevertheless serve as a convenient date indicating the beginnings of his attempts to reconcile the empiricistic paradigm with the rationalistic one. This reconciliation does not take place on the level of pure philosophy, but rather within the framework of Lessing's attempts to retrieve lost Christian truths. A close examination of this retrieval process will reveal the nature of Lessing's attempted resolution of his cognitive crisis.

Lessing's positive relationship to orthodox Lutheran Christianity can best be grasped by briefly contrasting him with Reimarus. Lessing was well aware that Reimarus' criticism of Christianity constituted an all out attack. In his *Eine Duplik* Lessing notes: 'Der Ungenannte, [d.h. Reimarus], so viel ich nun von seinen Papieren näher weiß, hat nichts geringers als einen Hauptsturm auf die christliche Religion unternommen. Es ist keine einzige Seite, kein einziger noch so versteckter Winkel, dem er seine Sturmleitern nicht angeworfen' (*D.*, VIII, 25) Reimarus wielded the axe of criticism first and foremost against the historical roots of Christianity. Both on a logical and on a purely historical basis Reimarus sought to prove the falsity of the Christian claim that God has historically manifested himself in and through the Christian religion. Reimarus sought to show that the Bible as the source of divine revelation was full of contradictions and hence as a historical source it was totally unreliable. Lessing acknowledged the thoroughness and cogency of Reimarus' attack. '[I]ch glaubte allerdings, daß auch in den einzeln Materien, in welche die gelieferten Fragmente schlagen, noch nicht Besseres und Gründlichers geschrieben worden, als eben diese Fragmente. Ich glaube allerdings, daß z.E. außer dem Fragmente von der Auferstehungsgeschichte noch nie und nirgends die häufigen Widersprüche der Evangelisten, die ich für wahre Widersprüche erkannte, so umständlich und geflissentlich ins Licht gesetzt worden' (VIII, 28)

Unless one is ready to assume that Lessing dissimulated, it appears evident by his own words that he was disturbed by Reimarus' attack.[5] Lessing writes in a short piece against the theologian Friedrich Wilhelm Mascho: 'Ich habe ihn [Reimarus] darum in die Welt gezogen, weil ich mit ihm nicht länger allein unter einem Dache wohnen wollte. Er lag mir unaufhörlich in den Ohren; und ich bekenne, daß ich seinen Zuraunungen nicht immer so viel entgegen

zu setzen wußte, als ich gewünscht hätte. Uns, dachte ich, muß ein
dritter entweder näher zusammen oder weiter auseinander bringen;
und dieser dritte kann niemand als das Publikum sein' (*G.M.*, VIII,
143). Hence, Lessing did not see himself as the advocate of Reimarus. On the contrary, he hoped to see Reimarus refuted. 'Ich komme
auf die Advokatur zurück und sage: der wahre eigentliche Advocat
meines Ungenannten [d.h. von Reimarus], der mit seinem Klienten
über den anhängigen Streit *ein* Herz und *eine* Seele wäre, bin ich also
nicht, kann ich also nicht sein. . . . und ich wüßte auch sonst nichts
in der Welt, was mich bewegen könne, mich lieber mit seinen
Handschriften, als mit fünfzig andern abzugeben, die mir weder so
viel Verdruß noch so viel Mühe machen würden: wenn es nicht das
Verlangen wäre, sie so bald als möglich, sie noch bei meinen Leb-
zeiten widerlegt zu sehen' (*A.–G.* VIII, 249–250). The same desire
to see Christianity proven true can be seen in Lessing's *Über den
Beweis des Geistes und der Kraft*. After making his famous statement
that 'zufällige Geschichtswahrheiten' can never be the proof of
'notwendige Vernunftswahrheiten' and after having designated such
attempts as a *metábasis eis allo génos* Lessing writes: 'Das, das ist der
garstige breite Graben, über den ich nicht kommen kann, so oft und
ernstlich ich auch den Sprung versucht habe. Kann mir jemand
hinüber helfen, der tu' es; ich bitte ihn, ich beschwöre ihn. Er
verdienet ein Gotteslohn an mir' (VIII, 14). Although within the
context of *Ü.B.G.K.*, Lessing is sceptical about the orthodox defense
of history as a revelatory medium, the above citation nevertheless
testifies to Lessing's sincerity in his attempts to accept Christianity.
Given the fact that Lessing was imploring someone to show him the
way to an acceptance of Christianity, it is no surprise that Lessing
would feel uneasy in the face of Reimarus' onslaught upon Christianity. For in Reimarus Lessing not only saw 'das Ideale eines
echten Bestreiters der [positiven] Religion' (*G.H.*, VII, 815), but he
must also have caught a glimpse of himself, i.e., of the rationalistic
paradigm underlying his own thought.

Lessing published fragments of Reimarus' work because, osten-
sibly, he hoped 'bald einen Mann zu erwecken, der dem Ideale eines
echten Verteidigers der Religion nur eben so nahe käme' (*G.H.*, VII,
815). It is clear that Lessing did not consider himself to be, nor really
want to be, such an ideal defender of Christianity. On the other
hand, it is equally clear that Lessing was totally dissatisfied with the
orthodox defenders of Christianity who responded to Reimarus'
attack. 'Ich habe es gesagt, und sage es nochmals: auch an und für

sich selbst sind die bisherigen Verteidigungen der christlichen Religion bei weitem nicht mit allen den Kenntnissen, mit aller der Wahrheitsliebe, mit allem dem Ernst geschrieben, den die Wichtigkeit und Würde des Gegenstandes erfordern!' (*Axiomata, VIII,* 165).[6] Although never claiming to be the ideal defender of Christianity, he nevertheless felt that he perhaps had something to say in its defense. 'Und nicht diesem [d.h. dem echten Verteidiger] vorzugreifen, sondern bloß urteilen zu lassen, wie viele nun er erst zu sagen haben würde, und hiernächst dem ersten panischen Schrecken zu steuern, das einen kleinmütigen Leser befallen könnte, eile ich, dem Fragmente insbesondere einige Gedanken beizufügen, die sich mir aufgedrungen haben' (*G.H.,* VII, 815). Lessing continues on to answer Reimarus' objections to Christianity while at the same time paradoxically granting the validity of many of Reimarus' contentions. Concerning his answers to Reimarus and in defense of 'his' Christianity against Goeze's accusations of infidelity, Lessing writes: 'Denn ich habe nirgend gesagt, daß ich die ganze Sache meines Ungenannten, völlig so wie sie liegt, für gut und wahr halte. Ich habe das nie gesagt: vielmehr habe ich gerade des Gegenteil gesagt. Ich habe gesagt und erwiesen, daß, wenn der Ungenannte auch noch in so viel einzeln Punkten Recht habe und Recht behalte, im Ganzen dennoch daraus nicht folge, was er daraus folgern zu wollen scheine' (*A.–G.,* VIII, 248). What Lessing claimed to have concluded from Reimarus' criticism of Christianity found its expression in his *Erziehung* (the first fifty paragraphs of which Lessing appended to his *Gegensätze des Herausgebers*). In the preface to the completed essay Lessing writes: 'Der Verfasser hat sich darin auf einen Hügel gestellt, von welchem er etwas mehr, als den vorgeschriebenen Weg seines heutigen Tages zu übersehen glaubt' (*Erziehung,* VIII, 590). And what Lessing claims to see is not something inimical to Christianity with its belief in historical revelation, though it revises somewhat the orthodox interpretations of this revelation.

In my judgment, Lessing's defense of himself against Goeze's attack upon him as an enemy of Christianity is based in part upon his belief that he had developed cogent answers to Reimarus' critique of Christianity. At any rate, Lessing did not see himself as an enemy of Christianity. 'Ich habe es nicht allein nicht ausdrücklich gesagt, daß ich der Meinung meines Ungenannten zugetan sei: ich habe auch bis auf den Zeitpunkt, da ich mich mit der Ausgabe der Fragmente befaßt, nie das geringste geschrieben, oder öffentlich behauptet, was mich dem Verdachte aussetzen könnte, ein heimlicher Feind der christlichen Religion zu sein. Wohl aber habe ich mehr als eine Kleinigkeit geschrieben, in welchen ich nicht allein die christliche Religion überhaupt nach ihren Lehren und Lehrern in dem besten Licht gezeigt, sondern auch die christlich-lutherische orthodoxe Religion insbesondere gegen Katholicken, Sozinianer und Neulinge verteidigt habe' (*A.–G.*, VIII, 248–249). Indeed, as much as possible, and in a manner yet to be explained, Lessing considered himself to be a friend of Christianity if not a genuine Christian. 'Ich habe gegen die christliche Religion nichts: ich bin vielmehr ihr Freund, und werde ihr zeitlebens hold und zugetan bleiben. Sie entspricht der Absicht einer positiven Religion, so gut wie irgend eine andere. Ich glaube sie und halte sie für wahr, so gut und so sehr man nur irgend etwas Historisches glauben und für wahr halten kann' (*S. E.,* VIII, 408–409). Whether or not Lessing was in his own mind a 'true' Christian, as opposed to an 'orthodox' Christian, is a question that cannot be definitively answered.[7] That Lessing was influenced by and open to Christianity, that he found much truth in it, that he felt attached to it, and that he believed it contained somehow a valid revelation of the divine appears to me to be undeniable. Further, I contend that Lessing's openness to Christianity is caused by his cognitive crisis and by the fact that Christianity alone offered to him a possible way to overcome this crisis by suggesting how the divine could be manifested in the historical.

It should be pointed out at this point that Lessing's defense of Christianity does not entail an unqualified acceptance of Orthodoxy. Lessing distinguished between Orthodoxy and 'true' Christianity and hence a successful attack upon one is not necessarily a refutation of the other. Although Lessing makes such a distinction between Orthodoxy and 'Christianity', it would be false to conclude that he views the two as totally disparate and opposed entities. As I shall attempt to show, Lessing seeks to develop his concept of 'true' Christianity not in isolation from Orthodoxy, rather out of it. In other words, Lessing does not unequivocally and totally reject Orthodoxy, rather he seeks to learn from it, to reform it, to reinterpret it in an acceptable manner. More importantly, Lessing tries to show that Christianity as envisioned by the Orthodoxy is a *necessary* ingredient in the ultimate perfection of man. The Hegelian use of the term 'aufheben' applies to Lessing's attitude towards Christianity, i.e., he seeks both to suppress and to preserve it. He does this because he finds something superior, truer in it than the contemporary rationalistic theology of the neologians. In a letter to his brother

Karl, who was confused by Lessing's apparent defense of Orthodoxy, Lessing writes:

'[I]ch [muß] Dir doch sagen, daß Du Dir hierin wahrlich eine ganz falsche Idee von mir machst und mein ganzes Betragen in Ansehung der Orthodoxie sehr unrecht verstehst. Ich sollte es der Welt mißgönnen, daß man sie mehr aufzuklären suche? Ich sollte es nicht von Herzen wünschen, daß ein jeder über die Religion vernünftig denken möge? Ich würde mich verabscheuen, wenn ich selbst bei meinen Sudeleien einen andern Zweck hätte, als jene große Absicht befördern zu helfen. *Laß mir aber doch nur meine eigne Art, wie ich dieses tun zu können glaube.* Und was ist simpler als diese Art? Nicht das unreine Wasser, welches längst nicht mehr zu brauchen, will ich beibehalten wissen; ich will es nur nicht eher weggossen wissen, als bis man weiß, woher reineres zu nehmen; ich will nur nicht, daß man es ohne Bedenken weggieße, und sollte man auch das Kind hernach in Mistjauche baden. Und was ist sie anders, unsere neumodische Theologie, gegen die Orthodoxie als Mistjauche gegen unreines Wasser?

'. . . Darin sind wir einig, daß unser altes Religionssystem falsch ist; aber das möchte ich nicht mit Dir sagen, daß es ein Flickwerk von Stümpern und Halbphilosophen sei. Ich weiß kein Ding in der Welt, an welchem sich der menschliche Scharfsinn mehr gezeigt und geübt hätte als an ihm. Flickwerk von Stümpern und Halbphilosophen ist das Religionssystem, welches man jetzt an die Stelle des alten setzen will, und mit weit mehr Einfluß auf Vernunft und Philosophie, als sich das alte anmaßt (February 2, 1774, IX, 596—597). (Emphasis was mine.)

The question arises as to what Lessing's 'eigne Art' is which will enlighten ('aufklären') Orthodoxy? What should be set in place of Orthodoxy, Lessing acknowledges, is of critical importance and it is that which most upsets the orthodox theologians. In another letter to Karl, Lessing notes: 'Nicht das, was man [den orthodoxen Theologen] nimmt, sondern das, was man an dessen Stelle setzen will, bringt sie auf, und das mit Recht. Denn wenn die Welt mit Unwahrheiten soll hingehalten werden, so sind die alten, bereits gangbaren, eben so gut dazu, als neue, (May 27, 1777, IX, 750). As noted above, what Lessing sought to replace Orthodoxy with is a result of his defense of Orthodoxy in the light of Reimarus' criticism of it, particularly of its concept of revelation. Lessing grants the essential validity of Reimarus' critique and for this reason Orthodoxy as a system is false. Nevertheless, the anti-Christian conclusions Reimarus draws from his premises are not valid in Lessing's view. Orthodoxy still offers truth if only it can free itself from certain theological positions so convincingly destroyed by Reimarus. In order to comprehend Lessing's conception of the valid and truly Christian in Orthodoxy, Reimarus' position must once again be examined.

Behind Reimarus' attempt to show the historical unreliability of the Bible lies his faith *in the sole sufficiency* of rational religion. Lessing himself grants the purity and honesty of Reimarus' defense of rational religion. '[O] bschon mein Ungenannter freilich all *geoffenbarte* Religion in den Winkel stellet: so ist er doch darum so wenig ein Mann ohne alle Religion, daß ich schlechterdings niemanden weiß, bei dem ich von der bloß *vernünftigen* Religion so wahre, so vollständige, so warme Begriffe gefunden hätte, als bei ihm' (*A.–G.*, VIII, 387). Reimarus' 'vernünftige Religion' is essentially the same as Lessing's concept of natural religion. Lessing writes: 'Einen Gott erkennen, sich die würdigsten Begriffe von ihm zu machen suchen, auf diese würdigsten Begriffe bei allen unsern Handlungen und Gedanken Rücksicht nehmen: ist der vollständigste Inbegriff aller natürlichen Religion' (*Ü.E.G.R.*, VII, 280). Reimarus similarly writes in one of the fragments: '[Wir vernünftigen Verehrer Gottes] bemühen uns, Gott nach einer vernünftigen Erkenntnis demütigst zu verehren, unsern Nächsten aufrichtig und tätig zu lieben, die Pflichten eines rechtschaffnen Bürgers redlich zu erfüllen, und in allen Stücken tugendhaft zu wandeln' (*M.P.U.*, VII, 654). The sufficiency of rational religion (i.e., of religion solely as a manifestation of the rationalistic paradigm) rests for Reimarus upon the strength and efficacy of human reason. Thus Reimarus asserts that preachers are obliged 'allen und jeden Zuhörern die gesunde Vernunft und ihren Gebrauch, als eine untriegliche Richtschnur der göttlichen Erkenntnis und eines frommen Wandels zu empfehlen . . .' (VII, 683). For Reimarus reason has the power to discover all *necessary* and *adequate* concepts about God, the world, and man and to inform man's activity with such concepts. It was for this reason that Reimarus rejected the Old Testament as a valid source of divine revelation because, among other things, it did not contain any doctrine of immortality, and every rationalist knows of the importance of immortality for the development of a moral life! Reimarus further rejected the Lutheran doctrine of original sin because he saw it, and correctly so, as an attack upon the autarchic sufficiency and efficacy of human reason in spiritual affairs. The idea that man's reason is spiritually dead entailed, according to Reimarus, the Christian doctrine of the 'Gefangennehmung der Vernunft' under the guidance of an historically grounded faith. This was for Reimarus an insult to the dignity of man and the source of Christian intolerance. Reimarus' attacks upon the historical reliability of the Bible were essentially an attempt on his part to invalidate the claims of the Christian's historically grounded faith, even if historical revelation should be granted as a possibility. In actuality, however, Reimarus also denied the possibility of historical revelation *as a religious necessity* for man's spiritual welfare because it could never be a universal revelation, e.g., those people who lived temporally before the date of revelation could know nothing of it. Therefore, historical revelation *qua* its very historicity must always be particular and conditioned. All such characteristics are, of course, qualities directly opposed to the universality, necessity, and unconditionality of rational truths. In short, Reimarus' 'vernünftige Religion' was more or less a pure manifestation of the rationalistic paradigm in religious matters.

The underlying premise of Reimarus' attacks upon orthodox Christianity is the unrestricted validity of the rationalistic paradigm in religious matters. But as has been shown in the last chapter, the basis for Lessing's cognitive crisis is precisely the inability of the rationalistic paradigm to answer and interpret the various anamolies of *de facto* man as he is analyzed on the basis of the empiricistic paradigm. From the point of view of the rationalistic paradigm, truth is universal in content and universally accessible to men of reason in all ages and in all lands. Concerning the meaning of reason for the *Aufklärung,* Günther Rohrmoser has written: 'Die Grundvoraussetzung der modernen, aufgeklärten, autonomen Vernunft besteht in dem Postulat, mit nichts anderem als mit sich selbst zu beginnen. Die Vernunft, die diesem Postulat nicht gehorchte, war dem Wahn oder der Autorität unterworfen, die die Vernunft bisher als faktische geschichtliche Macht daran hinderte, das zu tun, was sie wollte: mit sich anfangende Vernunft zu sein. Das bedeutet aber für eben diese Vernunft eine totale Abstraktion aus der Geschichte. . . . Aufklärung ist die Bewegung der Selbstemanzipation der Vernunft aus der Geschichte.'[8] Insofar as truth about God, that is divine revelation, exists, it is a function of rationally ascertainable truths. The only instrument of appropriation is man's unaided rational powers. It is for this reason that rational revelation can be universal for Reimarus, i.e., rational men in all times and places possess the instrument for discovering divine truth. Man possessing such cognitive strength was called 'natural man' by the rationalists. But, as has been shown, natural man was in effect never a reality for Lessing. What existed and still mostly exists is *de facto* man and *de facto* historical man was for Lessing cognitively weak. However much natural man is morally bound to natural religion, real historical man has only been able to live religiously within the framework of confessionalism. Underlying *de facto* man's imprisonment in the limited, finite, partial, or temporal, is his empirical consciousness. Historical man thinks within the terms of an emotive and metaphorical language, he is attached to the individual and to the unique. In short, the object of his consciousness is that which fills any given 'now' with sensuous content. Even when empirical man develops his rationality and begins exercising it upon his environment, he cannot, based upon the empirical content of his consciousness, construct apodictically necessary and hence certain truths. 'Zufällige Geschichtswahrheiten können der Beweis von notwendigen Vernunftswahrheiten nie werden.' The cognitive gulf between empirically grounded assertions, particularly when there are only reports of empirical events from which to draw conclusions, and rationally grounded assertions entails a logical and categorical difference. Referring to the similarity of proofs for revealed doctrines and theses of chiromancy Lessing writes: '[A]ber beide Beweise sind doch aus der nämlichen Klasse; sie gründen sich beide auf Zeugnisse und Erfahrungssätze. Und das Abstechende der stärksten Beweise dieser Art gegen Beweise, die aus der Natur der Dinge fließen, ist so auffallend, daß alle Kunst, dieses Auffallende zu vermindern, dieses Abstechende durch allerlei Schattierungen sanfter zu machen, vergebens ist' (*G.H.*, VII, 821). Thus empirico-historical cognition *qua* its very nature excludes rational, universal and certain knowledge. But according to Lessing, empirico-historical knowledge (often only in the form of metaphorical imagery) is the only knowledge *de facto* which man can comprehend.

In my judgment, the reason why Lessing was desirous to defend Orthodoxy, is because Orthodoxy with its doctrine of original sin accepts man as cognitively and morally weak and offers revelation or truth about God that an individual in such a state of imperfection can comprehend. Whereas Reimarus believed that reason alone is the 'untriegliche Richtschnur der göttlichen Erkenntnis' and accordingly rejected the doctrine of original sin, Lessing accepted it as it explained:

'wie und warum [der Menschen] Vernunft unwirksam geblieben. Mit einem Worte; die Macht unsrer sinnlichen Begierden, unsrer dunkeln Vorstellungen über alle noch so deutliche Erkenntnis ist es, welche zur kräftigsten Anschauung darin gebracht wird. Von dieser Macht berichtet die mosaische Erzählung entweder die erste traurige Erfahrung, oder erteilet das schicklichste Beispiel. Faktum oder Allegorie: in dieser Macht allein liegt die Quelle aller unserer Vergehungen, die dem Adam, des göttlichen Ebenbildes unbeschadet, eben sowohl anerschaffen war, als sie uns angeboren wird' (*G.H.*, VII, 818).

That *de facto* man cannot think in rationalistic concepts and that orthodox Christianity accepts man as he *de facto* is, constitute the basis of Lessing's attack upon the neological theology – the 'Vermittlungstheologie' – of his day. Whereas Reimarus had complained about the denigration of reason from the pulpits of the Orthodoxy, the latest theologians (ca. 1760 on) could, according to Lessing, only speak about the rationality of Christianity. Instead of attacking reason, such theologians were seeking to prove all Christian revelations as rational truths. Lessing complains:

'Die Kanzeln, anstatt von der Gefangennehmung der Vernunft unter dem Gehorsam des Glaubens zu ertönen, ertönen nun von nichts, als von dem innigen Bande zwischen Vernunft und Glauben. Glaube ist durch Wunder und Zeichen bekräftigte Vernunft, und Vernunft räsonierender Glaube geworden. Die ganze geoffenbarte Religion ist nichts, als eine erneuerte Sanktion der Religion der Vernunft. Geheimnisse gibt es entweder darin gar nicht; oder wenn es welche gibt, so ist es doch gleichviel, ob der Christ diesen oder jenen oder gar keinen Begriff damit verbindet. . . .

'Wie kitzlig hingegen ist es, mit diesen anzubinden, welche die Vernunft erheben und einschläfern, indem sie die Widersacher der Offenbarung als Widersacher des gesunden Menschenverstandes verschreien! Sie bestechen alles, was Vernunft haben will, und nicht hat' (*G.H.*, VII, 816–817). Neologians were in effect demanding and claiming that man should and could base his theological commitments upon rational insight. '[The neologians] haben seit zwanzig, dreißig Jahren in der Erkenntnis der Religion so große Schritte getan, daß, wenn ich einen ältern Dogmatiker gegen sie aufschlage, ich mich in einem ganz fremden Lande zu sein vermeine. Sie haben so viel dringende Gründe des Glaubens, so viel unumstößliche Beweise für die Wahrheit der christlichen Religion an der Hand, daß ich mich nicht genug wundern kann, wie man jemals so kurzsichtig sein können, den Glauben an diese Wahrheit für eine übernatürliche Gnadenwirkung zu halten. . . . Sie haben bewiesen, und so scharf bewiesen, daß *kein billiges Gemüt an der Gründlichkeit ihrer Beweise etwas wird auszusetzen finden'* (*A.W.E.D.*, VII, 532—533). In short, such theologians have tried 'die Vernunft zum Glauben zu zwingen' because for them 'Glaube' means nothing other than '*aus natürlichen Gründen für wahr halten'* (VII, 533).

In reducing faith to reason the neologians as much as the pure rationalists such as Reimarus were failing in Lessing's mind to address themselves to man as he *de facto* is. Historical Christianity has something to teach man precisely because the content of what it teaches somehow transcends the range of human reason. Without this 'being-beyond-reason' Christianity would never have been able to have aided man spiritually. Therefore, for Lessing there are two sources of religious knowledge, one rational and the other a-rational. For instance, in defending the genuineness of Leibniz's defense of the doctrine of the trinity (which as a doctrine is beyond man's reason) Lessing writes 'daß es [für Leibniz] zweierlei Gründe für die Wahrheit unserer Religion gebe: *menschliche* und *göttliche*, wie es die Kompendia ausdrücken; das ist, wie [Leibniz] es hernach gegen einen Franzosen ausdrückte, der unsere theologischen Kompendia ohne Zweifel nicht wie viel gelesen hatte, *erklärbare* und *unerklärbare . . .*' (VII, 533—534). 'Erklärbare Gründe' correspond to rational truths and 'unerklärbare Gründe' correspond to the type of truth necessary for the consciousness of *de facto* man. Thus it is clear that religious truths can be given to man, according to Lessing, that his reason cannot immediately establish. Concerning Leibniz's faith, which is the faith of a highly rationalistic man, not *de facto* man, Lessing writes:

'Aber was [Leibniz] denn nun sonach, aus menschlichen oder erklärbaren Gründen, nicht glaubte, hat er das darum ganz und gar nicht geglaubt? Wovon ihn seine Vernunft nicht überzeugt hatte, wovon er sogar nicht einmal verlangte, daß ihn seine Vernunft überzeugen sollte, hat ihn davon sonst nicht überzeugen können? Die von unsern Gottesgelehrten, die hierauf mit *Allerdings* antworten, die sich nicht schämen, von unerklärbaren Wahrheiten auf eine unerklärbare Art überführt zu sein, diese frage ich weiter: und woher weiß man es also, daß Leibniz die orthodoxen Lehrsätze, die er so wohl zu verteidigen wußte, selbst nicht geglaubt hat? Etwa daher, weil man vorgibt, daß er sich nach dem Äußerlichen der Religion nicht sehr bequemt habe?' (VII, 534).

Religious convictions 'aus unerklärbaren Gründen' are valid according to Lessing, and indeed are the only possible way for primitive *de facto* man.

Once the impossibility of man's immediate ability to construct for himself adequate notions about God is acknowledged as an existential fact, the doctrine of the 'Gefangennehmung der Vernunft unter den Gehorsam des Glaubens' ceases to be any longer an insult to human dignity and to the autonomy of man's reason. A cognitively weak being, be it even a rational being, has no developed autonomy precisely because it has no developed rational ability. Furthermore, precisely man's cognitive weakness and his correlative need to have knowledge that is not immediately rational constitutes the basis for the refutation of Reimarus in Lessing's mind. The orthodox theologians can and should surrender many positions to Reimarus, but there is one they cannot, Lessing writes: '[D]ie Vernunft *gibt* sich gefangen, ihre Ergebung ist nichts, als das Bekenntnis ihrer Grenzen, so bald sie von der Wirklichkeit der Offenbarung versichert ist. Dies also, dies ist der Posten, in welchem man sich schlechterdings behaupten muß...' '[Der Orthodox] braucht, wie gesagt, nur auf seinem Posten sich zu behaupten, und er kann alle die sinnreichen Einfälle entbehren, mit welchen man ihm zu Hülfe zu kommen den Schein haben will, und in der Tat ihn nur aus seiner Verschanzung heraus zu locken sucht' (*G.H.*, VII, 818–819, 828). Since man is cognitively weak and since reason cannot directly address itself to such a weakness, a non-rational way − a way 'aus unerklärbaren Gründen', is needed. In the terms of traditional Christianity, this way was called 'revelation'. Thus Lessing defends the notion that revelation contains something that transcends human reason and to which human reason must submit itself in obedience. 'Aber wenn eine [Offenbarung] sein kann, und eine sein muß, und die rechte einmal ausfündig gemacht worden: so muß es der Vernunft eher noch ein Beweis mehr für die Wahrheit derselben, als ein Einwurf dawider sein, wenn sie Dinge darin findet, die ihren Begriff übersteigen. Wer dergleichen aus seiner Religion auspolieret, hätte eben so gut gar keine. Denn, was ist eine Offenbarung, die nichts offenbaret? ... Eine *gewisse* Gefangennehmung unter den Gehorsam des Glaubens beruht also gar nicht auf dieser oder jener Schriftstelle: sondern auf dem wesentlichen Begriffe einer Offenbarung' (VII, 817). A revelation 'muß sein' precisely because man is cognitively weak. *De facto* man cannot maintain natural religion in its purity, but must fall into the confessionalism of positive religion. All positive religions constitute a weakening and limiting of natural religion and in this sense involve *error*. Nevertheless, positive religion is the only form of religion that *de facto* man can (at least up to the eighteenth century) have. Since the world is a manifestation of God and since man's religious history is the history of positive religions and their revelations, Lessing asks in his *Erziehung:* 'Warum wollen wir in allen positiven Religionen nicht lieber weiter nichts, als den Gang erblicken, nach welchen sich der menschliche Verstand jedes Orts einzig und allein entwickeln können, und noch ferner entwickeln soll; als über eine derselben entweder lächeln, oder zürnen? Diesen unsern Hohn, diesen unsern Unwillen, verdiente in der besten Welt nichts: und nur die Religionen sollten ihn verdienen? Gott hatte seine Hand bei allen im Spiele: nur bei unseren Irrtümern nicht?' (VIII, 590–591, § 2).

This last citation shows both the influence of the empiricistic paradigm, and of the rationalistic one. Positive religion is necessary for man's spiritual welfare, because it is directed to his empirical consciousness. However, the purpose of such religion is not contained within itself, rather in its ability to promote a rational consciousness in man. Traditional Christianity holds that the mysteries of revelation are and will always remain mysteries to man, because their content simply transcends the power of human reason, even in its pure state. Reason, given an eternity of time, could never deduce logically that God would become incarnate in Christ. Within the terminology of eighteenth-century metaphysics, such a truth is 'zufällig', i.e., its opposite entails no contradiction. Since reason can only make apodictic deduction based upon necessity, this incarnation of God in Christ as a type of truth belongs to a different class of truths than that of 'Vernunftswahrheiten'. For Lessing, on the other hand, the purpose of revelation based on 'unerklärbare Gründe' was to promote the development of truths known 'aus erklärbaren Gründen'. 'Als [Geheimnisse der Religion] geoffenbaret wurden, waren sie freilich noch keine Vernunftswahrheiten; aber sie wurden geoffenbaret, um es zu werden' (*Erziehung*, VIII, 610, § 76). Man's destiny is to become a practitioner of natural religion. Therefore, at the heart of every 'Offenbarung' lies a rational kernel. 'Die geoffenbarte Religion setzt im geringsten nicht eine vernünftige Religion voraus: sondern schließt sie in sich' (*G.H.*, VII, 819). The difference between revealed truths and truths of reason, between 'unerklärbare Überzeugung' and 'erklärbare Überzeugung' lies not in the ultimate *telos* of each type of truth. Though both forms belong to different categories of truth, they nevertheless have the same goal – the perfection of man's rational consciousness of his own rationality. The difference lies in the manner and mode that each class of truth reaches its goal, i.e., in the type of proof given. 'Die geoffenbarte Religion setzet im geringsten nicht eine vernünftige Religion voraus: sondern schließt sie in sich. . . . . Da sie aber dieselbe in sich schließt, da sie all Wahrheiten enthält, welche jene lehret, und sie bloß mit einer andern Art von Beweisen unterstützt: so ist es noch sehr die Frage, ob die Einförmigkeit der Beweisart, in Lehrbüchern für die Kinder und gemeine Leute, nicht bequemer und nützlicher ist, als eine genaue Absonderung der vernünftigen und geoffenbarten Lehrsätze, einen jeden aus der ihm eigentümlichen Quelle erwiesen' (*G.H.*, VII, 819–820). Although the ultimate effect of rational and revealed truths is the same, it should not be overlooked that their respective ways of proving do belong to different cognitive classes. Revealed truth is directed at *de facto* man's empirical consciousness and rational truth at a functioning human reason. How the one truth is related to the other, how one is derived from the other will reveal the principles of Lessing's reconciliation of the rationalistic and empiricistic paradigms.

B. LESSING'S PRINCIPLE OF RECONCILIATION

The problem facing Lessing was to discover some principle that would allow him to make sense out of man's empirico-historical existence. Metaphysically, the empirico-historical is limited to the contingent, non-necessary, and unique content of each and every passing 'now'. Given the empirical content of any given 'now', a thinker cannot with apodictic necessity predict the content of all other 'nows', past and future. Furthermore, the effect of reports of past 'nows' upon man's mind is quantitatively so much less vivid than the experience of the 'present' that the report of past events can never have the compelling cognitive value of the immediately experienced. In short, the problem of history is the problem of factuality, i.e., history seems to consist of discrete and distinct events which are called facts and are for the most part known through historical reports.

The question is, once again, how is man to find meaning in his factual and historical life, if meaning is conceived as a manifestation of necessary rationality. The problem facing Lessing as a 'Liebhaber der Theologie' is essentially the same question that was facing him some years earlier (at the time of the composition of the *Hamburgische Dramaturgie*) when he considered the problem of dramaturgy.[9] Indeed, in my judgment, Lessing's solution to his theological problems involves an application to theology of the same basic principles he used in the construction of his dramaturgy. Both Lessing's theology and dramaturgy are manifestations of the same *ars dialectice cogitandi.*

Drama distinguishes itself for Lessing from all other poetic genres in that its form, so-to-speak, consists of temporality, i.e., the drama presents a series of events as if they *were happening now.*[10] Of course, the drama does not make use of the *real* present. On the contrary, the drama like all forms of art has to do with the imaginary, with that which is not empirically real. However, the drama makes use of the real presence of the actor *qua* his own being in order to create the illusion of the reality, i.e., of the real presence, of some imaginary or poeticized character. Indeed, the drama influences the audience more deeply than other art genres can precisely because of the 'Lebhaftigkeit' or vividity caused by the illusion of the present. Just as in his *Ü.B.G.K.,* Lessing asserts that immediately experienced miracles effect man with such great force and vividity that he is willing to surrender his reason to the cognitive claims of the miracle worker, similarly Lessing asserts that the vivid presentation of the actions of characters on stage cause the viewer, willing or not, to sympathize with the characters, i.e., to surrender himself to the interests of the characters. '[D]ie Leidenschaften nicht beschreiben, sondern vor den Augen des Zuschauers entstehen und ohne Sprung in einer so illusorischen Stetigkeit wachsen zu lassen, daß dieser [Zuschauer] sympathisieren muß, er mag wollen oder nicht: das ist es, was dazu nötig ist; was das Genie . . . tut . . .' (*H.D.,* VI, 11–12).

The artist in general, including the dramatist, should not seek to present or represent the universal in its universality. The universal is an abstraction that exists in its purity only in the realm of ideas and concepts. That which exists in time, that which fills any given 'now' is the empirical and the empirical only exists as the reality of an individual. In his *Abhandlungen über die Fabel* Lessing writes: 'Die Wirklichkeit kömmt nur den Einzeln, dem Individuo zu; und es läßt sich keine Wirklichkeit ohne die Individualität gedanken' (*A.F.,* IV, 40). Insofar as the drama uses an illusion of the present, it can do so only by presenting individuals and their concrete actions, words, deeds, passions, etc. In short, a dramatist must make his audience aware of a series of *events in time* and space carried out by *individual* characters. Such events were called by Lessing *Fakta,* i.e., facts.

Therefore, like history, drama too is made up of facts and is concerned with the individual.

However, the drama differs from history in one important area. At the time of writing the *Hamburgische Dramaturgie* Lessing had not yet sought to reconcile the historical and the metaphysical, time and eternity. Thus his treatment of history falls within the empiricistic paradigm, i.e., 'die Geschichte geht auf das Besondere. . . . Das Besondere . . . ist, was Alcibades getan oder gelitten hat' (*H.D.*, VI, 449, § 89). In short, history is concerned with facts and their chronological order of occurrence. But facts *qua* factuality cannot alone make a drama. Indeed, if the dramatist tried to construct a drama as if he were writing a history, he would present so many individual, discrete, and isolated facts that he would confuse his audience. The dramatist must and does make use of facts (i.e., of empirical events), but he must be selective in his choice of which facts he will allow to occur upon the stage and he must have a principle that allows him to order them in the way he does. Since dramatic creation is a function of the dramatist's conscious creative activity, the dramatist must have a goal or a *telos* that he wishes to realize and which can serve as a principle of organization of facts. 'Mit Absicht handeln ist das, was den Menschen über geringere Geschöpfe erhebt: mit Absicht dichten, mit Absicht nachahmen, ist das, was das Genie von den kleinen Künstlern unterscheidet . . .' (VI, 177, § 34). The principle determining the 'Absicht' of the dramatist cannot be found in the mere factuality of facts. As a fact one event is as valid as another. The dramatist must have a purpose external to the essence of a factuality, yet which can only be realized through facts. The ultimate principle of dramatic creation Lessing locates in the ameliorative effects of the drama upon the moral life of the viewers. 'Bessern sollen uns alle Gattung der Poesie; es ist kläglich, wenn man dieses erst beweisen muß; noch kläglicher ist es, wenn es Dichter gibt, die selbst daran zweifeln' (VI, 394—395, § 77). Because the dramatist is ultimately seeking to improve morally his viewers, he is able to distinguish between facts which are relevant or not to a dramatic story, and is able to determine the order of occurrence of facts. The dramatist selects and structures a number of facts revealing the interactions of a group of characters in such a way that he interests the viewer in the action or plot of the drama which will eventually bring about an amelioration of the viewer's consciousness. The ameliorative effect of a drama constitutes its rationality or, as Lessing says: '[Die Poesie] ist philosophischer und nützlicher als die

Geschichte. Denn die Poesie geht mehr auf das Allgemeine, und die Geschichte auf das Besondere' (VI, 499, § 89). By the term 'das Allgemeine' Lessing meant ultimately that which pertains to the rationality of man, i.e., to his moral life.

A few years later in Wolfenbüttel Lessing entered into his theological controversies. When he attempted to undertake the problem of history, he was forced to reconcile the rationalistic and empiricistic paradigms. History like a drama consists of facts, i.e., of moments in time filled with empirical content. When writing the *Hamburgische Dramaturgie* Lessing had felt that in general history as a totality is not something dramatic, 'weil wir in der Geschichte doch selten das Innerste des Herzens kennen lernen' (VI, 293, § 57), i.e., seldom does one perceive the events of history as being structured around that which interests man, namely his meaning as a moral being. Indeed, history can appear to man to evince 'blindes Geschick und Grausamkeit' (VI, 402, § 79). In actuality, such 'blindes Geschick und Grausamkeit' is really a manifestation of divine 'Weisheit und Güte' (VI, 402, § 79), i.e., within the framework of the totality of creation apparent evil finds it justification before God and is seen (alas often only by God) as wisdom and goodness. Because history involves apparent examples of blind fate Lessing does not want the dramatist to copy history as it is, rather to create selectively a dramatic totality that is a manifestion *in micro* of the cosmological or divine totality *in macro*. '[D]as Ganze dieses sterblichen Schöpfers sollte ein Schattenriß von dem Ganzen des ewigen Schöpfers sein; sollte uns an dem Gedanken gewöhnen, wie sich in ihm alles zum Besten auflöse . . .' (VI, 402, § 79). By implication the universe in its totality also should be so structured so that everything ends for the best since it is the ideal analogue for the dramatic creation. By further logical extension it follows that man's history as a part of God's creation must too end for the best. It should not be forgotten that Lessing asked the following rhetorical question in the preface to the *Erziehung:* 'Gott hätte seine Hand bei allem im Spiele; nur bei unsern Irrtümern [i.e., historical and religious life] nicht?' (VIII, 591). Just as drama has as its *telos* the perfection of man, should not also history have a similar goal?[11] The belief that history must lead to man's perfection became quite literally an article of faith for Lessing. 'Geh deinen unmerklichen Schritt [in der Geschichte], ewige Vorsehung! Nur laß mich dieser Unmerklichkeit wegen an dir nicht verzweifeln. Laß mich an dir nicht verzweifeln, wenn selbst deine Schritte mir scheinen sollten, zurück zu gehen! –

Es ist nicht wahr, daß die kürzeste Linie immer die gerade ist' (VIII, 613—614, § 91). In the eighteenth century the Euclidian thesis that the shortest line between two points, is a straight line was considered to be a 'Vernunftswahrheit'. Lessing himself occasionally referred to Euclid's geometry as an example of 'Vernunftswahrheiten'. Lessing also rejected historical truth as binding in religious belief because it did not nor could it constitutionally ever possess the certainty of a 'Vernunftswahrheit'. But now he states in the *Erziehung* that even if the regressivity of history appeared to be as certain as a Euclydian theorem, he would nevertheless believe in the progressivity of history. Lessing therefore is willing to believe in the goodness of reality even if the counterthesis were apodictically certain. No quotation more aptly illustrates Alfred Whitehead's thesis that, whereas the medieval period was a time of faith based on reason, the eighteenth century was a period of reason based upon faith![12]

The concept of the progressivity of history enlightens the implicit principle underlying Lessing's reconciliation of the rationalistic and empiricistic paradigms. The concept underlying Lessing's attempted solution to his cognitive crisis is the notion of *progressive evolution.* The problem facing thinkers adhering to the rationalistic paradigm in the late eighteenth century was what to do with empirically grounded anamolies. The rationalistic paradigm underwent a crisis with the philosophical discovery that existence, individuality, the sensate, in short, the empirico-historical cannot be subsumed under the category of essentiality. Reality was rational for the rationalists as long as they were able to maintain belief in a metaphysics of essence wherein the necessary connections between the different aspects of being could be ascertained with apodictic certainty. Since the empirico-historical excludes by its very metaphysical nature all *necessity,* it would seem to exclude all rationality. One occurrence of the empirico-historical *qua* its very nature would be metaphysically and formally identical with all other empirico-historical occurrences. There is no way based on the empirico-historical alone that a thinker can deduce the structural interconnection between empirico-historical occurrences. Whereas it is universally valid and necessary that two and two is four, it is not possible to conclude with necessity that a specific belief of an individual existing in a specific time and place will with necessity be the universal belief of all men. Rationality, on the other hand, refers to that which is universally necessary or, more accurately, because it is necessary it is universally valid. This is, of course, one reason that the realm of essence is unchanging.

Thus there would seem to be no possibility of integrating the rational with the empirical.

However, if the rational is equivalent to essentiality and if there is an ontological difference between essence and existence, it means that the realm of essence, of the metaphysical does not necessarily have to possess existence or be fully actualized in each and every given 'now'. Two and two is four is conceptually true whether or not God ever created four empirically real objects or not. It is possible that the rationality of being can be realized in a progressive and hence temporal manner. This, of course, implies a teleological interpretation of rationality. Time structured according to a teleological purpose can be considered the definition of progressive evolution. In other words, from an evolutionary point of view, each moment of time with its specific empirical content can no longer be treated formally as identical, rather attention must be paid to the material differences in the contents of each 'now'. What contents will occur and the order of occurrence is a function of the manner in which each individual and unique material content of time furthers the realization of the overriding *telos*. The temporal will become rationalized insofar as the specific empirico-historical content of each successive 'now' and its order of occurrence are *necessary* steps in the realization of the rationality of the totality. Thus necessity and hence rationality will no longer lie in the unchanging but in the principle of *progressive* change.

The discussion of Lessing's principle of reconciliation has thus far been on a philosophical level. Such a discussion is bound to give the reader a false impression of Lessing's solution to his cognitive crisis. A reader will search in vain for any lengthy discussion of the concept of evolution by Lessing on a philosophical level.[13] There are a whole series of questions that Lessing would have had to answer let alone ask if he were to have constructed a dynamic philosophy of history. For instance, why does God have to bring about man's perfection over a period of time? Why not all at once? Does man's perfection through time have something to do with God's own perfection or did God arbitrarily decide to arrange things the way he has? There are some indications that Lessing toyed with a dynamic and progressive concept of God. Jacobi in his famous dialogue with Lessing reports that Lessing was bored and frightened by the idea of a static, i.e., unchanging God who has within His being all perfections realized *at once*. Furthermore, according to Lessing, 'um sich im Leben zu erhalten, müßte [Gott], von Zeit zu Zeit, sich in sich selbst gewissermaßen zurückziehen; Tod und Auferstehung, mit dem Leben, in sich vereinigen' (*J. G. L.*, VIII, 629—630). Here are perhaps the beginnings of a cosmogeny, but only the possible beginnings. How such a dynamic concept of God may be related to the notion of a progressive development of man throughout history is not even considered.

Lessing's actual discussion of the reconciliation of history and the metaphysical occurs in his *Gegensätze* to Reimarus' fragments and particularly in the *Erziehung*. In these works the concept of evolution is not as much explicit as implicit. Lessing carries out his discussion within the framework of his theological speculations and theological terminology. The explicit notion used by Lessing is that of education, i.e., he contends that the viewing of revelation as an educative process offers possibilities of overcoming the contemporary theological quandry brought about by Reimarus' attack upon Christianity. 'Ob die Erziehung aus diesem Gesichtspunkte zu betrachten in der Pädagogik Nutzen haben kann, will ich hier nicht untersuchen. Aber in der Theologie kann es gewiß sehr großen Nutzen haben, und viele Schwierigkeiten heben, wenn man sich die Offenbarung als eine Erziehung des Menschengeschlechts vorstellt' (*Erziehung*, VIII, 591, § 3). Just as the concept of amelioration constitutes the *telos* of dramatic creation, so too does the moral improvement of man constitute the *telos* of the revelatory education of man and hence can serve as the heuristic principle for comprehending man's religious history.

'Die Erziehung hat ihr Ziel; bei dem Geschlechte nicht weniger als bei dem Einzeln. Was erzogen wir, wir zu etwas erzogen. . . .'

'Nein, sie wird kommen, sie wird gewiß kommen, die Zeit der Vollendung, da der Mensch, je überzeugter sein Verstand einer immer bessern Zukunft sich fühlet, von dieser Zukunft gleichwohl Bewegungsgründe zu seinen Handlungen zu erborgen nicht nötig haben wird; da er das Gute tun wird, weil es das Gute ist, nicht weil willkürliche Belohnungen darauf gesetzt sind, die seinen flatterhaften Blick ehedem bloß heften und stärken sollten, die innern bessern Belohnungen desselben zu erkennen' (VIII, 611—612, § § 82, 85).

A good pedagogue must structure the material he wishes to teach according to the age, mental capacity, environmental background, etc. of those to be taught, so too must the divine educator of the human race order man's education in history according to the historical condition of man. 'Und so wie es der Erziehung nicht gleichgültig ist, in welcher Ordnung, die die Kräfte des Menschen entwickelt; wie sie dem Menschen nicht alles auf einmal beibringen kann; ebenso hat auch Gott bei seiner Offenbarung eine gewisse Ordnung, ein gewisses Maß halten müssen' (VIII, 591–592, § 5). In paragraph 88 Lessing refers to 'die nämliche Ökonomie des nämlichen Gottes' (VIII, 613). Therefore, the rationality of history is grounded for Lessing (1) in the fact that only through the empirico-historical can *de facto* man attain the perfection proper to his being, and (2) in the fact that man's religious and historical life is structured teleologically in analogy to the principles for educating individuals. Although the empirical existence of man in any given 'now' within the series of 'nows' that make up history is ontologically 'zufällig', the same empirical content can be seen by man as a necessary phase within the teleological context of his educational development to the level of moral self-consciousness. Therefore, the rationalistic ideal retains for Lessing its validity, but it can *only* be realized through empirical means and this *necessary* dependency of the rational on the empirical, of the metaphysical on the historical is the source for the rationality of the empirico-historical. The nature of this rationality will now be investigated.

C. THE RATIONALITY OF THE EMPIRICO-HISTORICAL LIFE OF MAN

The rationality of history is discussed by Lessing as a manifestation of revelation. It is through divine revelation that man becomes educated. Therefore, it is Lessing's interpretation of revelation that will enlighten his concept of an acceptable Christianity. However, in dealing with the concept of revelation I should like first to make a fourfold distinction that is important for a proper understanding of Lessing's theological solution to his cognitive crisis. The notion of revelation for Lessing entails four different but closely related sub-concepts. Revelation can be analyzed with regards its general content (or the formal structure of any given revelation or truth), its origin, its *telos*, i.e., that which it ultimately is to bring about, and the appropriation by man of this *telos*, i.e., the process whereby the objective content of revelation becomes subjectively internalized as belief. To a certain degree, this fourfold distinction is misleading as a complete analysis of any given sub-category requires reference to the other ones.

1. *The general content of Christian revelation.* The intelligent pedagogue educates by choosing his material and structuring its

presentation according to the limits and capacity of his students. In more general terms, that which is to be presented objectively is determined in content by its correspondence to the needs of the receiving subject. The principle of the adequation of objectivity to subjectivity when applied to the divine education of *de facto* man determines the nature and parameters of the objective content of revelation. My analysis above showed that the consciousness of *de facto* man was for Lessing limited and imperfect and that the essence of this imperfection is described in the terms of the empiricistic paradigm. *De facto* man has an empirical consciousness. Although *de facto* man has a rational faculty, this faculty exists nevertheless only in potentiality. *De facto* man in his true primitive state simply does *not* possess a functioning intellect. This is not to say that there are no differences between individual men. Within the context of history some men or even nations have, so to speak, higher historical I.Q.'s, i.e., the capacity to win for themselves rational insights. Nevertheless, the primitive state of man in general is similar to the mental state of a child. Historically this childlike mentality of *de facto* man has manifested itself in man's tendency socially and religiously to form limited and mutually exclusive groups, tribes, confessions, etc. The formal nature of any content of revelation must be of such a nature that it can educatively effect *de facto* man's primitive, childlike, and empirical consciousness.

As just mentioned, Lessing grants that individual men or individual peoples can educate themselves. 'Die meisten [der andern Völker] waren weit hinter dem [zur Erziehung] erwählten Volke zurückgeblieben: nur einige waren ihm zuvorgekommen. Und auch das geschieht bei Kindern, die man für sich aufwachsen läßt; viele bleiben ganz roh; einige bilden sich zum Erstaunen selbst' (*Erziehung*, VIII, 595, § 20). But this fact proves nothing against the utility and hence *necessity* of revelation. 'Wie aber diese glücklichen Einige nichts gegen den Nutzen und die Notwendigkeit der Erziehung beweisen: so beweisen die wenigen heidnischen Völker, die selbst in der Erkenntnis Gottes vor dem erwählten Volke noch bis itzt einen Vorsprung zu haben schienen, nichts gegen die Offenbarung' (VIII, 595, § 21). In other words, although some individual peoples seem to be able to develop some rational insights into divine reality with their own unaided rational faculties, this is no proof against the utility of the empirico-historical as a *necessary* educative means for bringing other nations and thereby mankind as a whole to a similar rational level. But Reimarus had objected that a historically grounded revelation addressed to the needs of all men is an impossibility. Christian revelation was for Reimarus necessarily always particular, never universal. But Reimarus' thought is essentially a-historical, i.e., truth about God is for him rational and hence it can be appropriated by any rational or natural man in any age and in any land. Lessing, however, did not believe in the historical reality of 'natural man', i.e., man with a fully functioning intellect. *De facto* man, historical man can in general neither possess nor immediately grasp rational truth. Therefore, although Lessing grants the validity of Reimarus' argument against the possibility of a universal revelation based on history, he does not see this as an argument against the necessity and utility of particular revelations, i.e., revelations to limited groups of men living in specific times and in specific lands. If man taken individually is generally incapable of educating himself without the use of an empirico-historical medium, then it may well be that God could select a limited number of individuals, or individual peoples, to educate in a special manner. The justification for such a particular and limited revelation would be that the specially educated would then become the educators of mankind. In other words, philosophically speaking, the particular would become the means of realizing temporally the universal.

'Führt [Reimarus] aber seine Beantwortung nicht gleich mit sich? Wenn eine *solche* Offenbarung [die alle Menschen auf eine gegründete Art glauben könnten] unmöglich ist, − nun freilich: so hat sie auch Gott nicht möglich machen können. Allein, wenn nun gleichwohl eine Offenbarung nützlich und nötig ist: sollte Gott dem ohngeachtet lieber *gar keine* erteilen, weil er keine *solche* erteilen konnte? Sollte Gott dem ganzen menschlichen Geschlechte diese Wohltat vorenthalten, weil er nicht alle Menschen zu *gleicher* Zeit, in *gleichen* Grade daran Teil nehmen lassen konnte? Wer hat das Herz, hierauf mit ja zu antworten?

'Genug, wenn die höchste Weisheit und Güte bei Erteilung der Offenbarung, die sie in jener Allgemeinheit und Allklarheit nicht gewähren konnte, nur denjenigen Weg gewählet hat, auf welchem in der *kürzesten* Zeit die *meisten* Menschen des Genusses derselben fähig wurden. Oder getraut sich jemand zu zeigen, daß dieses nicht geschehen? daß die Offenbarung, zu einer andern Zeit, einem andern Volke, in einer andern Sprache erteilet, mehrere Menschen in kurzer Zeit mit den Wahrheiten und den Bewegungsgründen zur Tugend hätte ausrüsten können, deren sich itzt die Christen, als Christen, rühmen dürfen? (*G.H.*, VII, 821−822).

Lessing repeats the same contention in the *Erziehung:* 'Da [Gott] aber einem jeden *einzeln Menschen* sich nicht mehr offenbaren konnte, noch wollte: so wählte er sich ein *einzelnes Volk* zu seiner besonderen Erziehung; und eben das geschliffenste, das verwilderste, um mit ihm ganz von vorne anfangen zu können' (VIII, 592, § 8). And these primitive, mentally underdeveloped people were Jews. Why select the Jews, why not some other people? The reason for this is that the Jews more than any other of the ancient peoples had one tendency which would enable them to further the education of mankind, namely the tendency to proselytize. 'Dieses unendlich mehr verachtete als verächtliche Volk ist doch, in der ganzen Geschichte, schlechterdings das erste und einzige, welches sich ein Geschäft daraus gemacht, seine Religion mitzuteilen und auszubreiten. Wegen des Eifers, mit welchem die Juden dieses Geschäft betrieben, bestrafte sie schon Christus, verlachte sie schon Horaz. Alle andere Völker waren mit ihren Religionen entweder zu geheim und zu neidisch, oder viel zu kalt gegen sie gesinnt, als daß sie für derselben Ausbreitung sich der geringsten Mühwaltung hätten unterziehen wollen. Die christlichen Völker, die den Juden in diesem Eifer hernach gefolgt sind, überkamen ihn bloß, in so fern sie auf den Stamm des Judentums gepfropft waren' (*G.H.*, VII, 822). In short, because of the Jewish tendency to spread and communicate their religion they were able to become the particular or empirico-historical means of educating mankind. 'Allein wozu, wird man fragen, diese Erziehung eines so rohen Volkes, eines Volkes, mit welchem Gott so ganz von vorne anfangen mußte? Ich antworte: um in der Folge der Zeit einzelne Glieder desselben so viel sicherer zu Erziehern aller übrigen Völker brauchen zu können. Er erzog in ihm die künftigen Erzieher des Menschengeschlechts. Das wurden Juden, das konnten nur Juden werden, nur Männer aus einem so erzogen Volke' (*Erziehung*, VIII, 594, § 18). And in paragraph 22 of the *Erziehung* Lessing repeats his thesis. '. . . [Gott] hatte seine Absichten damit auf das ganze jüdische Volk, auf das ganze Menschengeschlecht, die hier auf Erden vielleicht ewig dauern sollen, wenn schon jeder einzelne Jude, jeder einzelne Mensch auf immer dahinstirbt' (VIII, 596, § 22).

2. *The formal essence of 'revealed' truths.* The general content of revelation, particularly for mankind in the primitive and childlike stage of its development, is directed at people who are not able to think in abstract concepts. What then constitutes the formal nature

of revelation as an educative medium? 'Ein Volk aber, das so roh, so ungeschickt zu abgezognen Gedanken war, noch so völlig in seiner Kindheit war, was war es für einer moralischen Erziehung fähig? Keiner andern, als die dem Alter der Kindheit entspricht. Der Erziehung durch unmittelbare sinnliche Strafen und Belohnungen' (*Erziehung*, VIII, 594, § 16). It has already been shown that in *Das Christentum der Vernunft* Lessing postulates a level of consciousness that is 'nicht deutlich genug' aware of its own perfections. Such a limited consciousness would not be apt in 'abgezognen Gedanken'. As was shown, the term 'nicht deutlich' was equivalent in eighteenth-century philosophy to 'sinnlich'. Lessing suggests that the only education proper for the childlike, empirical consciousness is 'durch sinnliche Strafen und Belohnungen'. The material content of the moral education of the Jews, 'das rohe Volk', is punishment. But the metaphysical material, so to speak, out of which the punitive education of the childlike Jews is made is the sensate. The key term is 'sinnlich'. Therefore, the medium of revelation has the formal characteristic of being 'sinnlich'. Lessing's integration of the empiricistic paradigm with the rationalistic one should be obvious.

However, God does not just use anything that happens to be 'sinnlich'. For 'das Sinnliche' to become a revelatory medium it must be so structured as to produce the 'Erziehung' of childlike historical man. Perhaps, the most important function of 'sinnliche Erziehung' is to accustom childlike man to using his reason to the point that the desire to pursue rational truths independent of a 'sinnlich' medium becomes a felt need. It will be recalled that, in talking about the first man being given an adequate concept of the divine unity, Lessing maintained that 'dieser mitgeteilte, und nicht erworbene Begriff' could not remain in its purity in man's mind (VIII, 592, § 6). The important point is that man must win for himself through his won efforts ('erwerben') adequate 'Vernunftswahrheiten'. The verb 'erwerben' implies activity on the part of man's intellect. But primitive man cannot think in 'abgezognen Gedanken'. Therefore, the function of the sensate content of revelation is to activate and actualize man's intellect. Lessing uses this second formal feature of the content of revelation to refute Reimarus' charge that the Old Testament could not be a book of divine revelation.

Reimarus had contended that there is no doctrine of immortality in the Old Testament and, because immortality is necessary for a morally ordered universe, the Old Testament could not possibly be a book containing true revelation about God. Lessing not only grants the accuracy of Reimarus' exegesis of the Old Testament, but goes on to assert that there is not only no doctrine of immortality but that there is also no proper doctrine concerning the transcendental unity of God. 'Gewiß ist es wenigstens, daß die Einheit, welche das israelitische Volk seinem Gotte beilegte, gar nicht die transzendentale metaphysische Einheit war, welche itzt der Grund aller natürlichen [d.h., vernünftigen] Theologie ist. Bis zur *der* Höhe hatte sich der gemeine menschliche Verstand in so frühen Zeiten noch nicht erhoben, am wenigsten unter einem Volke erhoben, dem Künste und Wissenschaften so unangelegen waren, und das sich aller Gemeinschaft mit unterrichtetern Völkern so hartnäckig entzog' (*G.H.*, VII, 831). This fact did not prove in Lessing's opinion that the Old Testament was not divine in origin. 'Auf die Göttlichkeit der Bücher des A.T. ist aus dergleichen Dingen wenigstens gar nichts zu schließen. Denn diese muß ganz anders, als aus den darin vorkommender Wahrheiten der natürlichen Religion erwiesen werden' (*G,H.*, VII, 832—833). The absence of 'Vernunftswahrheiten' in the Old Testament was no argument against its 'Göttlichkeit' because the childlike mentality of the ancient Jews could not have grasped pure rational truth. The proof of the divine essence of the Old Testament is to be found in the fact that it brings man closer to his perfection than his unaided rational powers can. 'Diese Bücher können sogar eine seligmachende Religion enthalten; das ist, eine Religion, bei deren Befolgung sich der Mensch seiner Glückseligkeit so weit versichert halten kann, als er hinausdenkt' (VII, 834).

In the case of the Jews who had no adequate concept of the unicity of God, the absence of a doctrine of immortality is secondary. Before an individual can have a correct and functional concept of immortality he must first have a correct concept of God. Thus the function of the Old Testament was first by means of sensate or empirical concepts to accustom the Jews to thinking correctly about God, e.g., the Jewish national God is *stronger* than the gods of other peoples which leads to the idea of *one* omnipotent God.

'Diesem rohen Volke also ließ sich Gott anfangs bloß als den Gott seiner Väter ankündigen, um es nur erst mit der Idee eines auch ihm zustehenden Gottes bekannt und vertraut zu machen.

'Durch die Wunder, mit welchen er es aus Ägypten führte, und in Kanaan einsetzte, bezeugte er sich ihm gleich darauf als einen Gott, der mächtiger sei, als irgendein andrer Gott.

'Und indem er fortfuhr, sich ihm als den Mächtigsten von allen zu bezeugen, — welches doch nur *einer* sein kann, gewöhnte er es allmählnlich zu dem Begriffe des *Einigen*.

'Aber wie weit war dieser Begriff des Einigen noch unter dem wahren transzendentalen Begriffe des Einigen, welchen die Vernunft so spät erst aus dem Begriffe des Unendlichen mit Sicherheit schließen lernen!' (*Erziehung*, VIII, 593, §§ 11—14).

For a people that had such an inadequate concept of God for most its history, it is foolish to believe that a doctrine of immortality could in any way have a practical effect upon their actions. What they needed was 'unmittelbare sinnliche Strafen und Belohnungen'. 'Noch konnte Gott seinen Volke keine andere Religion, kein anders Gesetz geben, als eines, durch dessen Beobachtung oder Nichtbeobachtung es hier auf Erden glücklich oder unglücklich zu werden hoffte oder fürchtete. Denn weiter als auf dieses Leben gingen noch seine Blicke nicht. Es wußte von keiner Unsterblichkeit der Seele; es sehnte sich nach keinem künftigen Leben. Ihm aber nun schon diese Dinge zu offenbaren, welchen seine Vernunft noch so wenig gewachsen war: was würde es bei Gott anders gewesen sein, als der Fehler des eiteln Pädagogen, der sein Kind lieber übereilen und mit ihm prahlen, als gründlich unterrichten will' (VIII, 594, § 17).

But divine education like normal education is accumulative. Children who have been educated over a period of time and who have developed their minds, eventually want a higher level and more sophisticated type of education. Children who have learned to think in 'abgezognen Gedanken', eventually will wish to have less childlike and more mature material to learn. 'Der Teil des Menschengeschlechts, den Gott in *einen* Erziehungsplan hatte fassen wollen – er hatte aber nur denjenigen in einen fassen wollen, der durch Sprache, durch Handlung, durch Regierung, durch andere natürliche und politische Verhältnisse in sich bereits verbunden war – war zu den zweiten großen Schritte der Erziehung reif. . . . Das ist; dieser Teil des Menschengeschlechts war in der Ausübung seiner Vernunft so weit gekommen, daß er zu seinen moralischen Handlungen edlere, würdigere Bewegungsgründe bedurfte und brauchen konnte, als zeitliche Belohnungen und Strafen waren, die ihn bisher geleitet hatten. Das Kind wird Knabe' (VIII, 605, §§ 54, 55).

The second stage of revelation – called the New Testament – has as its educative goal to make manifest more pure and rational truths as a basis for man's moral perfection. In particular, the central truth mediated to man is the doctrine of immortality. 'Und so ward Christus der erste *zuverlässige, praktische* Lehrer der Unsterblichkeit (VIII, 605, § 58). Insofar as Lessing conceives Christ primarily as an educator, the difference between his view of Christianity and that of the orthodox is very striking. For the orthodox, Christ is a savior, a redeemer of man from his sins and only incidentally a teacher. For the orthodox, Christ is not a dispenser of wisdom, of knowledge, rather the instrument of man's salvation. This is not to say that Lessing in the *Erziehung* denied the miracles, as Reimarus did in the fragments. The New Testament is not addressed to 'adult' man, rather to man in his 'adolescence'. Therefore, although the truths of the New Testament are less 'sinnlich' than those of the Old Testament, they are nevertheless not totally free of the sensate. Thus the reliability of Christ does not stem from the fact that his followers can grasp the rational necessity of his truths and hence the reliability of his person, rather because he substantiates his doctrines with his miracles, etc. 'Der erste *zuverlässige* Lehrer. – Zuverlässig durch die Wahrsagungen, die in ihm erfüllt schienen; zuverlässig durch die Wunder, die er verrichtete; zuverlässig durch seine eigne Wiederbelebung nach einem Tode, durch den er seine Lehre versiegelt hatte' (VIII, 606, § 59). Therefore, revelation in the second phase is controlled by the same principle active in the first stage.

The principle that the medium of revelation is constituted by the sensate is also determinant for the very style in which the Bible was written. Any doctrine of revelation is to bring man closer to the consciousness of a rational content. However, this consciousness cannot be immediate or, better, non-mediated. The rational kernel can only effect man when it is, so to speak, dressed in a sensate shell. Concerning the stylistic principles of 'Einkleidung' Lessing writes: '... [D]ie Einkleidung der nicht wohl zu übergehenden abstrakten Wahrheiten in Allegorieen und lehrreiche einzelne Fälle, die als wirklich geschehen erzählet werden. Dergleichen sind die Schöpfung, unter dem Bilde des werdenden Tages; die Quelle des moralischen Bösen, in der Erzählung von verbotnem Baume; der Ursprung der mancherlei Sprachen in der Geschichte vom Turmbaue zu Babel, usw' (VIII, 603–604, § 48). The influence of Lessing's theory of the fable is evident here. Philosophy differs from art in that it directs itself to man's intellect in an effort to make man aware of the universal in its purity, whereas art forms are directed to man's heart, to his emotions and affective being. Whereas philosophy effects man's intellect and indirectly his will, art including the fable, effects man's will as its immediate object. The reason why the fable can effect the human will so forcefully is because it presents its universal in the form of an individual case, i.e., in an empirical dress. The intuition of the individual was called by Lessing in imitation of Baumgarten 'eine anschauende Erkenntnis'. 'Weil wir durch diese [anschauende Erkenntnis] einen Satz geschwinder übersehen, und so in einer kürzen Zeit mehr Bewegungsgründe in ihm entdecken können, als wenn er symbolisch [e.h. rein philosophisch] ausgedrückt ist: so hat die anschauende Erkenntnis auch einen weit größern Einfluß in den Willen, als die symbolische' (*A.F.*, IV, 42). In summary, educatively, aesthetically, and metaphysically, revelation entails the structuring of an empirical or 'sinnlich' content so as to effect the development of human consciousness.

3. *The origin of the empirical content of revelation.* The above analysis has shown that the formal structure of the content of any revelation entails a mediation of a universal kernel by means of an empirical medium. However, and this is important to remember, the rational content of revelation is not immediately apparent to the prospective believer. The ultimate purpose of the revelation is to educate the believer to the level at which he can grasp intellectually the rational kernel and make it a principle of his moral life. However, the objective content of revelation as it is first given is not rational, rather empirical, metaphorical, allegorical and emotional. The influence of Lessing's aesthetic theory upon his religious speculations is quite evident. Nevertheless the question must be asked as to what distinguishes a doctrine of revelation from, say, an Aesopian fable? Why do men fight for religious belief, but never over the meaning of a drama? A correlative question would be, what gives 'die Einkleidung der nicht wohl zu übergehenden abstrakten Wahrheiten in Allegorien' such power and control over the human mind? The answer of the orthodox was that revelations have their origin in a transcendent God's real instrusion into history. The question of the origin of revelation is the most crucial problem entailed in analyzing Lessing's relationship to Christianity. Is revelation as the divine education of man no more than an immanent though unconscious development of reason, a natural evolution of the human intellect from a primitive to a rational state, or does it entail a true entrance into history by a transcendent God?

Manfred Durzak has distinguished between two meanings for the term 'transcendent'.[14] In the most broad sense, transcendent refers to any content of a doctrine that is simply not immediately graspable by man's intellect. In short, it is that which is 'beyond' reason. From this point of view, Lessing's interpretation of revelation as a sensate datum structured to effect man's moral education must be considered as transcendent. However, there is a more narrow meaning of 'transcendent' as that which has its origins in a being external to man's, as that which has a source 'beyond' the powers of man's mind to create. In specific, transcendence in this sense refers to the orthodox conception of revelation as something objectively given to man by a God whose being is distinct from the being of the universe. The central problem to be resolved if Lessing's Christianity is to be taken as genuine is whether or not revelation was for Lessing transcendent in the second sense of the term. For if Lessing interpreted Christianity as no more than sort of a Hegelian phase in the phemenological development of the human mind in history, then, although Lessing might well have transcended the thinking of the average thinker of the *Aufklärung,* Lessing's religious opinion cannot be designated as 'Christian' in any traditional sense of the word. It appears certain to me that, when Lessing referred to 'Christianity' in his discussions with the orthodox and others, he knew that the term, if it were to have any meaning at all, had to refer to some sort of entrance into history by a Being ontologically transcending this world. Furthermore, the act of revelation is intimately bound up with the notion of the miraculous, i.e., revelation from a divine source is made known to man *via* micracles. If Lessing interpreted Christianity in a proto-Hegelian fashion, as innumerable interpreters have suggested, he was using the term in a sense that the contemporary meaning of the word in public discourse did not allow. Lessing's 'real' meaning would have, indeed, been 'esoteric'. The number of initiates would have numbered only possibly one — Lessing himself!

An insight into Lessing's position regarding the nature and origin of revelation, and the two concepts are intimately related, can be gained by examining in more detail the formal structure that revelation must possess if it is to be appropriated, or believed, by *de facto* man. In other words, the subjective conditions of the believer for accepting the 'truth' of the revelation must be analyzed.

De facto man in his primitive state is simply incapable of thinking in a purely logical or rational manner. Historical man does not wait to affirm or deny an alleged truth until he has had time critically and rationally to weigh the evidence pro and con. As noted above, Lessing maintains, 'daß es zweierlei Gründe für die Wahrheit unserer Religion gebe: *menschliche* und *göttliche . . . erklärbare* und *unerklärbare'* (*A.W.E.D.,* VII, 533—534). The 'menschliche' or 'erklärbare'

Gründe' are nothing more than 'Vernunftswahrheiten', i.e., they entail the kind of demonstration that a functioning intellect would demand as prerequisite for apodictic certainty. By 'unerklärbare Gründe' Lessing most likely meant proofs, if they may be called that, that are empirical or 'sinnlich' in essence. Revelation is grounded upon 'göttliche Gründe' not upon rational insight ('menschliche Gründe'). In other words, the 'Grund' for the belief in the truth of any given doctrine of revelation is, from a rationalistic point of view, 'unerklärbar'. But what is it that constitutes the essence of such an 'unerklärbarer Grund'? It certainly cannot be the fact alone that such proofs are 'sinnlich', for, after all, fables are empirical too, yet they do not constitute revelation. Whatever it is that constitutes an 'unerklärbarer Grund', it must be able to affect man's mind in a non-rational manner, i.e., it must be able to move man's affective being, his emotions and phantasy in such a forceful manner that the individual concerned accepts any alleged doctrine as a true datum of revelation from God.

Concerning the legitimacy of positive religion, Lessing writes: 'Diese positive Religion erhielt ihre Sanktion durch das Ansehen ihres Stifters, welcher vorgab, daß das Konventionelle derselben eben so gewiß von Gott komme, nur mittelbar durch *ihn*, als das Wesentliche [der natürlichen Religion] unmittelbar durch eines jeden Vernunft' (*Ü.E.G.R.*, VII, 281). And, of course, the 'Stifter' of a positive religion proves that his word is the word of God by performing *miracles*. Thus it is the miraculous that constitutes the essence of the 'unerklärbarer Grund' for the truth of revealed religion. For as Lessing notes, 'der menschliche Verstand [wird] nur sehr allmählich ausgebildet worden, und Wahrheiten, die gegenwärtig dem gemeinsten Manne so einleuchtend und faßlich sind, [haben] einmal sehr unbegreiflich, und daher unmittelbare Eingebungen der Gottheit geschienen [müssen] . . .' (*G.H.*, VII, 833). The same tendency of an undeveloped mind to long for the incomprehensible, for immediate inspiration from God is echoed by Lessing in his *Nathan der Weise*. Commenting upon his foster daughter's desire to believe that her being saved from a fire was due to an angel not to a human Nathan says:

Ich überdenke mir,
Was das auf einen Geist, wie Rechas, wohl
Für Eindruck machen muß. Sich so verschmäht
Von dem zu finden, den man hochzuschätzen

Sich so gezwungen fühlt; so weggestoßen,
Und doch so angezogen werden; Traun,
Da müssen Herz und Kopf sich lange zanken,
Ob Menschen Haß, ob Schwermut siegen soll.
Oft siegt auch keines; und die Phantasie,
Die in den Streit sich mengt, macht Schwärmer,
Bei welchen bald der Kopf das Herz, und bald
Das Herz den Kopf muß spielen. — Schlimmer Tausch! —
Das letztere, verkenn' ich Recha nicht,
Ist Rechas Fall: sie schwärmt.

(Act I, scene 1)

In other words, the tendency to believe in and to need the miraculous is, so to speak, built into the mentality of the pre-rational mind. In order to be able to accept a truth whose rational kernel may someday become a rational common place, the pre-rational mind of *de facto* man must feel that the said truth is somehow 'unbegreiflich' and a result of 'unmittelbare Eingebung der Gottheit'. It is only by means of the forcefulness, psychologically speaking, resulting from the belief that such and such a doctrine is directly from God that pre-rational man comes to believe in the doctrine. For, as Lessing asserts, it is only by the miracles involved in God's freeing the Jews from the Egyptian bondage that God proves to the Jews that he is the mightiest of gods and thereby begins to accustom the Jews to thinking about God as one. In the New Testament the doctrine of immortality 'wird . . . als Offenbarung *gepredigt,* nicht als Resultat menschlicher Schlüsse *gelehrt*' (*Erziehung*, VIII, 608, § 71). Christ was the first reliable preacher of the doctrine of immortality. But the legitimacy of his teaching lies not in their internal 'inner truth', rather in Christ's being 'zuverlässig'. And Christ showed himself as 'zuverlässig' through fulfilling prophecies, working miracles, and resurrecting. Indeed, it should not be forgotten that Lessing in his *Ü.B.G.K.* had stated that, had he immediately witnessed the miracles of Christ, he too would have gladly surrendered his reason to claims of Christ. Therefore, perhaps the most important characteristic of the formal structure of revelation is that the empirically embodied universal must appear as a miraculous manifestation of the divine.

The 'miraculous' is a psychological and experiential prerequisite if a pre-rational mind is to be able to believe any specific doctrine as revealed. The central question is: Did Lessing believe that the revelation received by Jews and later by Christians was grounded in the occurrence of *real* miracles and hence is *really* inspired by God, or did he believe that such revelation is either a product of pre-rational man's vivid fantasy or of the attempts of some advanced individuals to communicate their more rational insights in a manner comprehensible to their more primitive contemporaries? In short, are revelations just natural and immanental manifestations of an underdeveloped intellect as it struggles to understand reality in a semi-metaphorical semi-rational manner or are they quite literally the 'gifts' of God to man who on his own would never be able to produce for himself such 'gifts' for 'viele Millionen Jahre'? The overwhelming majority of the interpreters of Lessing's theology have concluded that revelation, however 'transcendent' it may be in content, has nevertheless formally a purely natural and immanental origin. Thielicke, Mann, and Oelmüller are notable exceptions. Manfred Durzak has, in my judgment, expressed the premise underlying the immanental interpretation of Lessing's concept of revelation. Durzak grants that the content of revelation is somehow 'transcendent' to the immediate powers of man's reason. He also noted that Lessing considered such revelation to contain a rational kernel and that it is, therefore, eventually open to rational penetration. Based on these facts, Durzak concludes: 'Die grundsätzliche Andersartigkeit, die Transzendenz der Offenbarung wird von vornherein negiert, da ihre Verstehbarkeit durch die Vernunft apodiktisch vorausgesetzt wird. Offenbarung wird also von der Vernunft her bestimmt und muß daher notwendigerweise als immanent erscheinen; Offenbarung, so kann man sagen, wird zu einem Prinzip; im Erziehungsplan der Menschheit.' 'Das Verhältnis zwischen den Begriffen "Vernunft" und "Offenbarung" in der *Erziehung des Menschengeschlechts* ist eindeutig zugunst der Vernunft entschieden. Die Offenbarung ist nur ein Modus derselben Wahrheit, die sich bei der Selbstverwirklichung der Vernunft einstellt.'[15] In other words, simply because the *telos* of revelation is for 'geoffenbarte Wahrheiten' to become 'Vernunftswahrheiten' and because man's intellect has the ability, at least in potentiality, for comprehending such rational truth, it is then concluded that 'Offenbarung' can be no more than primitive and imaginative manifestations of a reason seeking to come to itself. But does this conclusion follow from the premise given?

My own analysis fully substantiates Durzak's position regarding the ultimate *telos* of revelation. The final goal of revelation based on 'göttliche Gründe' is to become revelation based on 'menschliche

Gründe'. In this sense Durzak is perfectly correct in citing paragraph 4 as substantiation for his position: 'Erziehung gibt dem Menschen nichts, was er nicht auch aus sich selbst haben könnte: sie gibt ihm das, was er aus sich selber haben könnte, nur geschwinder und leichter. Also gibt auch die Offenbarung dem Menschengeschlecht nichts, worauf die menschliche Vernunft, sich selbst überlassen, nicht auch kommen würde: sondern sie gab und gibt ihm die wichtigsten dieser Dinger nur früher (*Erziehung*, VIII, 591, 4). Furthermore, this citation certainly shows the influence of the rationalistic paradigm on Lessing's thinking. However, this is only one side of the story. In my analysis of the influence of the empiricistic paradigm on Lessing's theological speculations it was shown that *de facto* man for Lessing is effectively weak as a cognitive being. Lessing writes, for instance, in paragraph 7: 'Und wer weiß, wie viele Millionen Jahre sich die menschliche Vernunft noch in diesen Irrwegen würde herumgetrieben haben; ohngeachtet überall und zu allen Zeiten einzelne Menschen erkannten, daß es Irrwege waren: wenn es Gott nicht gefallen hätte, ihr durch einen neuen Stoß eine bessere Richtung zu geben' (VIII, 592 § 7). To claim that man's intellect would remain in 'Irrwege' for millions of years is to assert that in effect man cannot gain for himself rational truth on a theological level. Even if Lessing's 'viele Millionen Jahre' be accepted literally, it still follows that man from the time of the ancient Jews up to Lessing's own time had not yet lived out such a length of time and that man had obviously progressed further than his *natural* and *in born* powers could effect. All this certainly implies that the 'Richtungsstoß' given to man by God is not just a natural and normal development of man's rational powers. In others words, Lessing's justification of revelation, i.e., his making it necessary and hence *rational,* is grounded upon the thesis that without it man's cognitive weakness could in effect never be overcome. 'Und warum sollten wir nicht auch durch eine Religion, mit deren historischen Wahrheit, wenn man will, es so mißlich aussieht, gleichwohl auf nähere und bessere Begriffe von göttlichen Wesen, von unsrer Natur, von unsern Verhältnissen zu Gott, geleitet werden können, auf welche die menschliche Vernunft von selbst nimmermehr gekommen wäre?' (VIII, 610—611, § 77). That Lessing should claim in paragraph 4 that education through revelation gives man nothing that he could not obtain through the use of his own unaided rational powers (this is the result of the rationalistic paradigm underlying his thought) and that in paragraph 77, with human reason being left to its own powers, man could never develop for himself better concepts of God and man's relationship to God (the result of the empiricistic paradigm) constitutes, of course, a formal contradiction — but a contradiction, nevertheless, grounded upon the crisis nature of Lessing's thinking and the tentativeness of his attempted solution and hence reflects the 'systematic kernel' underlying his religious speculations.[16] This also points out the difficulty in substantiating the position that the history of revelation is for Lessing 'nothing but' the history of the immanental and natural development of the human intellect. Other alternatives are possible.

Just because the truth of revelation has as its *telos* to become a rational truth, does it logically follow that revelation is not given to man as the result of a transcendent act by God? In the last chapter in the section on the influence of the empiricistic paradigm on Lessing's theological thinking, a question was raised and its answer deferred until my discussion of Lessing's positive evaluation of Christianity. It is therefore time to raise the question again. In *Ü.B.G.K.* it was noted that Lessing grounds his argumentation on an ambiguous premise, i.e., he unwittingly mixes the rationalistic and empiricistic paradigms together. On the one hand, a revelation having a foundation in *real* miracles can never be the basis for apodictic conclusions for an individual living in another historical era, because the very essence of a historical truth is to be 'zufällig', that is to be not necessary and hence non-rational. The attempt to ground one's beliefs upon the historical constitutes an illicit jump from one cognitive category to another. This thesis is a manifestation of the rationalistic paradigm. Based upon this premise, I asserted Lessing should have claimed, as Mendelssohn did, that even the immediately experienced empirical contents of a given 'now' could not be the basis for any theological truths, simply because the empirical can never manifest necessity. Yet Lessing does not make this logical conclusion based on the rationalistic paradigm. Lessing makes a distinction between the force and vividity of empirical events experienced by a subject in a given 'now' and historical reports of such events to a subject living in a later 'now'. This distinction is a manifestation of the empiricistic paradigm. The force and vividity of a miracle immediately experienced would be enough, Lessing grants, to cause him to surrender his intellect to the cognitive claims of the doctrines of the miracle worker. However, reports of such miracles are so much weaker and less vivid that they can never, so to speak, overcome man's intellect and take it prisoner. In other words, the empirico-historical as immediately experienced in a given 'now' can be the basis of theological judgments, but the reports of that 'now' given to someone living in a later 'now' cannot effect a person strongly enough to gain apodictic value. This, of course, constitutes another contradiction in Lessing's thought clearly manifesting the influence of the rationalistic and empiricistic paradigms. However, the contradiction also makes possible an interesting relationship between the two paradigms. Let it be granted that the empirico-historical of the past cannot ever for Lessing apodictically influence or determine the present. This is Lessing's thesis based on either of the two paradigms. Is it not possible, however, that even if an empirical event of a *past* 'now' can have no necessary cognitive value for a *present* 'now', the reality of the empirical event, e.g., of a miracle, was nevertheless necessary for the religious development of the individuals living in the *past* 'now'? In other words, if *de facto* man is in effect constitutionally weak as a cognitive being, could it not be possible that God actually manifests truths about himself in and through history *via* miracles (that do have cognitive value for those living at the time the revelation is given by a 'Stifter' of a positive religion)? Once *de facto* man accepts in a given 'now' an 'unbegreifliche Wahrheit' as true, he can later begin to reflect upon such a truth and eventually to discover its rational kernel.[17]

The relationship just suggested between revelation as a product of a transcendent act of God and revelation as a rational truth is possible based upon Lessing's simultaneous affirmation of the rationalistic and empiricistic paradigms. But the question arises, is there any evidence that Lessing did believe that the miracles reported in history *were* actually real events? First, let us ask, what it meant for Lessing to believe in the reality of historical events in the past. '[W]as heißt einen historischen Satz für wahr halten? eine historische Wahrheit glauben? Heißt es im geringsten etwas anders: als diesen Satz, diese Wahrheit gelten lassen? nichts darwider einzuwenden haben? sich gefallen lassen, daß ein andrer einen andern historischen Satz darauf bauet, eine andre historische Wahrheit daraus folgert? sich selbst vorbehalten, andere historische Dinge darnach zu schätzen? Heißt es im geringsten etwas anders? etwas mehr? Man prüfe sich genau' (*Ü.B.G.K.,* VIII, 13). Given this criterion for historical belief, then it is most probable that Lessing did believe that the miracles of Christianity were *real* ones.

'Ich habe gegen die christliche Religion nichts: ich bin vielmehr ihr Freund, und werde ihr zeitlebens hold und zugetan bleiben. Sie entspricht der Absicht einer positiven Religion, so gut wie irgend eine andere. Ich glaube sie und halte sie für wahr, so gut und so sehr man nur irgend etwas Historisches glauben und für wahr halten kann. Denn ich kann sie in ihren historischen Beweisen schlechterdings nicht widerlegen. Ich kann den Zeugnissen, die man für sie anführt, keine andere entgegen setzen: es sei nun, daß es keine andere gegeben, oder daß alle andere vertilgt oder geflissentlich entkräftet worden. . . .

'Mit dieser Erklärung, sollte ich meinen, könnten doch wenigstens diejenigen Theologen zufrieden sein, die allen christlichen Glauben auf menschlichen Beifall herabsetzen, und von keiner übernatürlichen Einwirkung des heiligen Geistes wissen wollen. Zur Beruhigung der andern, aber, die eine solche Einwirkung noch annehmen, setze ich hinzu, daß ich diese ihre Meinung allerdings für die in dem christlichen Lehrbegriffe gegründetere und von Anfang des Christentums hergebrachte Meinung halte, die durch ein bloßes philosophisches Räsonnement schwerlich zu widerlegen steht. Ich kann die Möglichkeit der unmittelbaren Einwirkung des heiligen Geistes nicht leugnen: und tue wissentlich gewiß nichts, was diese Möglichkeit zur Wirklichkeit zu gelangen hindern könnte' (*S.E.*, VIII, 408—409).

Certainly, given Lessing's own criterion concerning belief in historical events, Lessing did accept as possible the reality of the traditional interpretation of miracles and divine inspiration!

If the language and hence the 'exoteric' argument of the *Erziehung* is to be accepted as in any way directly reflecting Lessing's own views, then it is probable that Lessing believed that *real* miracles played a role in the foundation of Christianity.[18] For as has already been noted, Christ shows that he is 'zuverlässig' as a teacher of immortality through his fulfillment of prophecies, his miracles, and his resurrection. Lessing refers explicitly to the 'Wunder' that God enacted for the Jews (cf. §§ 12 ans 21). More important for the thesis that the religious development of 'das Offenbarungsvolk' is not caused by an immanent and natural development of human reason, is Lessing's contrast of the Jews with more gifted peoples. In paragraph 20 Lessing refers to the few gifted peoples who educated themselves and became more advanced than the Jews: 'Die meisten [der andern Völker] waren weit hinter dem erwählten Volke zurückgeblieben: nur einige waren ihm zuvorgekommen. Und auch das geschieht bei Kindern, die man für sich aufwachsen läßt; viele bleiben ganz roh; einige bilden sich zum Erstaunen selbst' (VIII, 595, § 20).

Relative to such naturally gifted peoples the Jews would remain undeveloped, except as 'das Offenbarungsvolk' they will overcome and perpetually outdistance the gifted peoples: 'Das Kind der Erziehung fängt mit langsam aber sichern Schritten an; es holt manches glücklicher organisierte Kind spät ein; aber es holt es doch ein, und ist als dann nie wieder von ihm einzuholen' (VIII, 595, § 21). This certainly implies that 'Offenbarung' constitutes a qualitative difference in the intellectual life of man. The gifted peoples using their own reason can develop themselves up to a certain point, but they will never be able to equal the development of 'das Kind der Erziehung'. Lessing's contrast of the Jews with other more gifted peoples certainly implies that the causative difference in their respective religious developments lies not in the normal and natural development of their rational potentialities in the course of history, rather in the fact that revelation as an educative medium is not the natural product of human reason. If revelation were for Lessing no more than a stage through which the human mind *qua* its very nature must pass in order to develop itself ('sich bilden') through its own powers to higher levels of perfection, then it would have been false for Lessing to single out the Jews and then later the Christians as the 'chosen people'. Every primitive group of people who thought in a primitive manner also would have to be said to possess 'revelation'.[19] Perhaps, their revelation would be not as good as that of the Jews (presumably because they are a less capable people), but it would belong to the class of revelation, i.e., to the class of metaphorical, imaginative, and primitive 'Einkleidungen' of rational truths. And since the Jews are not as gifted as some other peoples, then their development would most likely not be as advanced as the gifted peoples. But, of course, this line of reasoning runs counter to Lessing's explicit statements quoted above concerning the superiority of the development of the 'chosen people'.[20] Helmut Thielicke has graphically summarized the argument for the thesis that revelation was conceived as a transcendent act by God.[21]

If one goes by the clear meaning manifested by the language of the *Erziehung* then it is obvious that revelation as the educative medium of man's development is not a natural product of his mind. The question can be raised, of course, as to just how seriously and forthrightly Lessing was expressing his 'dogmatic' opinion in the language of the *Erziehung*. Could it not be that what Lessing maintained by the word is no more than an 'exoteric' shell hiding, yet also

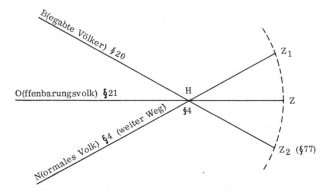

Erklärung: H = obere Grenze, bis zur der die natürliche Selbstenfaltung führen kann. Bis dahin hat jedes der drei genannten Völker — das Offenbarungsvolk (0), die normalen Völker (N), die 'glücklicheren Einzelnen', d.h. die besonders begabten Völker (B) — verschieden lange Strecken zurückzulegen. Punkt Z stellt das Ziel der Erziehung dar, das jenseits jener oberen Grenze liegt und nur von der göttlichen Offenbarungstätigkeit erreicht wird. Den Weg bis zu Punkt H beschreibt § 4. Er bildet die Grenze für die Konkurrenz von Offensbarungs- und Selbsterziehung. Die Strecke HZ (bzw. Z_1 u. Z_2) ist Offenbarungsstrecke außer Konkurrenz und weist auf die transzendente Bedeutung der Offenbarung hin. Bis zum Punkt H ist die Offenbarung von 'Nutzen' (§ 21). Von H bis Z dagegen ist sie 'notwendig' (§ 21): 'Nutzen und Notwendigkeit der Erziehung').

communicating his 'esoteric' rationalism? Perhaps the *Erziehung* is no more than a *gymnastikos* designed to mollify the orthodox? The *Erziehung* has been a very difficult work to interpret. Nevertheless the general tendency has been to assert that Lessing conceived the educative paradigm in the *Erziehung* as a natural and immanent development of the human mind (Cf. footnote § 17). One of the primary reasons given for this is the alleged monism of Lessing's conception of God. If God is monistically or immanently united with the world, then revelation in a traditional sense is impossible as it presupposes a transcendent God. I shall deal with this problem presently in the closing section of this chapter. It suffices to say that (a) I agree that in some broad sense Lessing's concept of God is monistic, and (b) that this does not exclude the possibility of revelation being the result of a transcendent act of God. This may sound like a contradiction. If it is, it is nevertheless a contradiction founded on the crisis nature of Lessing's *ars dialectice cogitandi*.

To a certain degree the argument concerning Lessing's alleged monistic concept of God is useless for an evaluation of his ideas concerning revelation. Lessing wrote very little on a *purely* philo-sophical level about God, perhaps twelve pages in all. The three pages of *Das Christentum der Vernunft*, the two pages of *Über die Wirk-lichkeit der Dinge außer Gott*, perhaps two and one half pages of *Durch Spinoza ist Leibniz nur auf die Spur der Vorherbestimmten Harmonie gekommen*, a page or so in *Die Erziehung des Menschen-geschlechts* (§§ 73–75), and perhaps a total of three or four pages of statements quoted by Jacobi in his famous dialogue with Lessing are of a pure philosophical nature. There is no doubt that Lessing carried on philosophical and theological conversations and letters with many of his friends, such as with Mendelssohn. But the content of such dialogues is not available for the Lessing interpreter. Therefore, the interpreter who sees Lessing as having developed a *philosophy* of history (the so-called 'esoteric' center of Lessing's thinking) which he expresses in Christian terminology (the so-called 'exoteric' shell of his thinking) has very little material with which he can reconstruct Lessing's purely philosophical analysis of the divine and its relation-ship to the world including human history. Quite often such investi-gators seek to interpret Lessing's philosophy in the light of the philosophical principles of others. Spinoza and particularly Leibniz are the candidates.[22] Lessing allegedly combines the monism of Spinoza with the epistemological perspectivism and incipient dynamism of Leibniz. When a philosopher from Lessing's past is not acceptable, then Lessing's beliefs are occasionally compared with Hegel's. 'Thus, we can conclude [from *Die Erziehung des Menschen-geschlechts*]', writes Henry Allison, 'that Lessing viewed the history of religion, much as Hegel viewed world history, as the result of *both* human forces and providential divine direction, and it is precisely this which provides the 'esoteric' justification for Lessing's use of the concept of revelation.'[23] But Hegel had a highly developed and dynamic concept of divine reason. Hegel wrote hundreds and hun-dreds of pages explicitly on logic, metaphysics, rational theology, and history. From these pages one can abstract Hegel's basic prin-ciples of philosophy and investigate how he applied them to human history. But one has no more than twelve pages of pure philosophical speculations from Lessing. This hardly gives the interpreter a compre-hensive source from which to explain the 'purely' philosophical basis of Lessing's theory of religious evolution. This also suggests that Lessing was a long way from having developed an 'esoteric' philos-ophy which can be contrasted with his 'exoteric' theology. It is no wonder that investigators find themselves interpreting Lessing's theology in the light of his supposed acceptance of Leibniz's or Spinoza's philosophy or of his supposed anticipation of the philosophy of thinkers such as Hegel or of Idealism in general. Once an interpreter makes this jump, he can analyze in some detail the structure of this or that philosophy and, under the assumption that his analysis represents Lessing's true philosophical position, he can then begin to (re)interpret Lessing's theological statements as so much 'exoteric' dress for his alleged 'esoteric' philosophy. This methodology entails however the danger, about which Schneider warned, namely, the construction of an *a priori* interpretation of Lessing's esoterism which is then used to 'interpret' the facts whether or not they permit such an interpretation, or, indeed, to determine what statements by Lessing will be accepted as 'facts' in the first place. That Lessing was influenced by the philosophical movements of his time, I do not deny (indeed, I have contended that the rationalistic and empiricistic paradigms have influenced his thinking). However, the identification of Lessing's philosophy with this or that one of his contemporaries, to say nothing of those who came after him, requires more knowledge than the investigator can possess. That some of his statements are 'Spinozistic', or 'Leibnizian', or even 'proto-Hegelian', I am willing to grant. They are also 'traditionally Christian'! But I believe all such statements should be treated from within the thought structure of all of Lessing's speculations, exoteric as well as esoteric ones, rather than his thought structure being interpreted from the point of view of some hidden 'esoteric' philosophy allegedly informing Lessing's thinking, but which is never explicitly stated by Lessing.

Given the absence of any explicitly detailed philosophy of immanence, given Lessing's use of Christian terminology, given his cognitive crisis (as opposed to having a consistent and functional philosophical paradigm), and given the fact that traditional Christianity does attempt to deal with the notion of the divine being manifested in and through history, it seems more probable to me that Lessing took seriously the traditional Christian position and that, therefore, his 'exotericism' is not an outer shell obscuring the pure unalloyed inner rationality, rather it is somehow intimately bound up with the origin and formal structure of revelation before it has become rational truth. And if my thesis concerning Lessing's belief in the *de facto* cognitive weakness of man is correct, then it is entirely possible that, at least on the level of a hypothesis, Lessing accepted the idea of a transcendent origin for the empirical-metaphorical content of revelation. However, the emphasis should be placed on the word 'hypothesis'. In my judgment Lessing's thought was caught in a cognitive crisis that he never fully overcame. Lessing's thinking manifests the characteristics of the crisis phase of a scientific revolution, i.e., he can not reject outright the old analytical concept of reason (the rationalistic paradigm), yet the old paradigm cannot adequately deal with anamolies (based on the empiricistic paradigm), and hence he must try out new hypotheses even at the risk of being inconsistent. This did not mean he had fully and irrevocably committed himself to a specific hypothesis. Indeed, concerning the *Erziehung* Lessing wrote in a letter: '*Die Erziehung des Menschengeschlechts* ist von einem guten Freunde, der sich gern allerlei Hypothesen und Systeme macht, um das Vernügen zu haben, sie wieder einzureißen' (April 6, 1778, IX, 775). Perhaps, it can even be maintained that in a sense Lessing was forced into a position of defending traditional Christianity. Writing to Karl, Lessing explains why he has defended 'das alte Religionssystem', (i.e., Orthodox-Lutheran Christianity) even though in its totality it is false: 'Und verdenkst Du es mir, daß ich dieses alte [Religionssystem] verteidige? Meines Nachbars Haus drohet ihm den Einsturz. Wenn es mein Nachbar abtragen will, so will ich ihm redlich helfen. Aber er will es nicht abtragen, sondern er will es, mit gänzlichem Ruin meines Hauses, stützen und unterbauen. Das soll er bleiben lassen, oder ich werde mich seines einstürzenden Hauses so annehmen, als meines eigenen' (February 2, 1774, IX, 597).[24] Did the attacks upon Lessing by the orthodox during the period of the *Fragmentenstreit* act as a stimulus on Lessing to defend the crashing structure of Orthodoxy (so violently brought about by Reimarus' critique), whether the Orthodoxy wished it or not? And if Lessing was to defend the orthodox, they would be defended in a manner acceptable to himself which, of course, in the long run might be more dangerous for the orthodox than the a-historical bludgeoning of a Reimarus as Goeze clearly saw. At any rate, in my judgment, Lessing did undertake to defend the orthodox position, but not so much for the sake of the house of the orthodox as for the sake of his own theological house. And Lessing's theological house was endangered by his cognitive crisis and thereby by the impossibility of reducing man's religious life to a function of pure rationality. If a defense of orthodoxy was to be meaningful and yet be of advantage for Lessing's own theological speculations, then the concept of the transcendent influence of God upon history (and surely this concept is so central to the orthodox position that any defense of Orthodoxy must in some way save this notion) had to be taken into account. From a Hegelian point of view with Hegel's belief in the all-sufficiency of dynamic reason, a 'synthesis' of traditional Christianity and analytic rationalism would and must appear as the heighth of philosophical nonsense. On the other hand, from the point of view of someone who has no developed concept of dynamic or synthetic reason (because he still thinks within the framework of the traditional rationalistic paradigm) and who is unable to find any rationalistic way of interpreting and overcoming man's cognitive weakness, the idea of a transcendent origin (and this constitutes the 'Rettung' of Orthodoxy) of an empirico-historical medium of education to the level of rationality might well be greeted as an acceptable hypothesis, an acceptable 'Fingerzeig' indicating a way that both explains and overcomes man's cognitive crisis.

4. *The 'telos' of revelation.* In the long run, however, i.e., from the viewpoint of an eighteenth-century thinker, not from the viewpoint of a first- or second-century Christian, the argument concerning the origin of revelation is of slight importance. The ultimate and justifying purpose of revelation is to bring man to a higher level of perfection. '[U]nd die Ausbildung geoffenbarter Wahrheiten in Vernunftswahrheiten ist schlechterdings notwendig, wenn dem menschlichen Geschlechte damit geholfen sein soll. Als sie geoffenbaret wurden, waren sie freilich noch keine Vernunftswahrheiten; aber sie wurden geoffenbaret, um es zu werden' (*Erziehung*, VIII, 610, § 76). The ultimate *telos* of revelation is to bring man to a stage of development in which he no longer needs an empirico-historical medium in order to be aware of the rationality of reality, including his own moral destiny.

'Nein. Sie wird kommen, sie wird gewiß kommen, die Zeit der Vollendung, da der Mensch, je überzeugter sein Verstand einer immer bessern Zukunft sich fühlet, von dieser Zukunft gleichwohl Bewegungsgründe zu seinen Handlungen zu erborgen, nicht nötig haben wird: da er das Gute tun wird, weil es das Gute ist, nicht weil willkürliche Belohnungen darauf gesetzt sind, die seinen flatterhaften Blick ehedem bloß heften und stärken sollten, die innern bessern Belohnungen desselben zu erkennen.'

'Sie wird gewiß kommen, die Zeit eines *neuen ewigen Evangeliums*, die uns selbst in den Elementarbüchern des Neuen Bundes versprochen wird' (VIII, 612, §§ 85–86).

The Old and New Testament are directed to an immature mankind, respectively to man as a child and man as an adolescent. Therefore, the truths presented to pre-rational man cannot be pure truths of reason because the human mind is not yet sufficiently developed to grasp such truths. Indeed, even eighteenth-century man is not so developed as to be able to function without studying the Bible. Thus Lessing gives to his contemporaries the following commandment: '—[K]ehre lieber noch einmal selbst in dieses Elementarbuch zurück, und untersuche, ob das, was du nur für Wendungen der Methode, für Lückenbüßer der Didaktik hältst, auch wohl nicht etwas Mehrers ist' (VIII, 608, § 69). Yet the time will come when man can do without the 'Elementarbuch' because his reason has matured and he is able to comprehend rationally the meaning of reality.

But as long as man has not reached the stage of 'Vollendung', he must and does think about God within the framework of the logic of revelation. Revelation before it has changed into rational truth contains a rational kernel, but one that is not immediately evident to the human mind. The underdeveloped human mind can only focus on the allegory presented in revelation. The purpose of revelation is to stimulate the human mind to reflect upon the allegory presented until its rational meaning becomes evident. E.g., the Jews in thinking about Jehova as the mightiest of gods, came gradually to conceive Jehova as the one and only God of all mankind. Lessing's rationalization of the doctrines of the trinity, original sin, and reparation (carried out in paragraphs 73—75) are other examples of how the mind can find the rational in the mysteries of revelation.[25] But does this process of reflection upon revelation require belief in the reality of the miracles that supposedly grounded its divine origin? In other words, is belief in the historical reality of Christ and his miracles necessary for someone *living in the eighteenth century* if revelation is to be able to have its ameliorative effect upon man? A more important question would be whether or not past miracles can become the basis of 18th century man's belief in revelation?

Given the fact that Lessing, either from the point of view of the rationalistic or empiricistic paradigm, always claimed that the empirico-historical content of a *past* 'now' can never be the basis for certain and hence valid cognition in a *present* 'now', it follows that the historical reality of miracles, of God's transcendent entrance into history cannot be the source for the validity and value of revelation for people living in a later historical period. In *Ü.B.G.K.*, Lessing states that, had he experienced Christ's miracles or the miracles performed by Christians in the first centuries of the founding of Christianity (miracles observed by Origines), he would have believed Christ in the same manner as does the orthodox.

'Aber ich, der ich auch nicht einmal mehr in dem Falle des Origines bin; der ich in dem 18ten Jahrhunderte lebe, in welchem es keine Wunder mehr gibt; wenn ich anstehe, noch itzt, auf den Beweis des Geistes und der Kraft, etwas zu glauben, was ich auf andere meiner Zeit angemessenere Beweise glauben kann: woran liegt es?'

'Daran liegt es: daß dieser Beweis des Geistes und der Kraft itzt weder Geist noch Kraft mehr hat; sondern zu menschlichen Zeugnissen von Geist und Kraft herabgesunken ist.'

'Daran liegt es: daß Nachrichten von erfüllten Weissagungen nicht erfüllte Weissagungen; daß Nachrichten von Wundern nicht Wunder sind. *Diese,* die vor meinen erfüllten Weissagungen, die vor meinen Augen geschehenen Wunder, wirken *unmittelbar. Jene* aber, die Nachrichten von erfüllten Weissagungen und Wundern, sollen durch ein *Medium* wirken, das ihnen alle Kraft benimmt' (VIII, 11).

In my analysis of the origin of revelation for Lessing I sought to show that, because of Lessing's belief in man's cognitive weakness, he accepted as a hypothesis the notion that ancient man (e.g., the first Christian) could only come to accept doctrines as divine truths if they are substantiated by miracles (or thought to be so proven). Indeed, in all probability Lessing held that Judaism and Christianity gained their original influence upon Western man by means of real miracles. However, at most the miraculous has only to do with *de facto* man's original acceptance of doctrine as divine. The miraculous cannot have apodictic value for a person who does not experience it as 'unmittelbar' given. Any mediation of the miraculous (and historical reporting certainly constitutes such a mediation) automatically weakens it and robs it of all its cognitive force. Therefore, whatever value the miraculous might have had at some point in the *past* in causing doctrines to be accepted as divine revelation, it cannot have that value for the (or rather Lessing's) *present.* Hence, the value of revelation for the educative improvement of the eighteenth-century man has nothing immediately to do with its immanent or transcendent origin. After stating that Christ is 'zuverlässig' as a teacher because of his miracles, Lessing writes: 'Ob wir noch itzt diese Wiederbelebung, diese Wunder beweisen können: das lass ich dahingestellt sein. So, wie ich es dahingestellt sein lasse, wer die Person dieses Christus gewesen. Alles das kann damals zur *Annehmung* seiner Lehre wichtig gewesen sein: itzt ist es zur Erkennung der Wahrheit dieser Lehre so wichtig nicht mehr' (*Erziehung*, VIII, 606, § 59). In other words, eighteenth-century man no longer needs to experience the miraculous in order to come to knowledge of the divine truth of any alleged revelation. Here a serious problem arises. It is one thing for someone who possesses in the present *full* rational insight into the inner truth of a doctrine to look back at the doctrine as first presented and in hindsight to locate its inner meaning. It is another thing for a person not yet in possession of rational insight, to be able to locate the rational core of revelation. In other words, what is the criterion of truth for someone who still does not have a fully developed intellect and yet does not experience the miraculous? The same question formulated in different terms would be: How does the *telos* of revelation become manifest to the human mind while the revelation in question is yet in a non-rational phase? To answer these questions we must once again take up the problem of the relationship of truths of reason and truths of revelation, of rational religion and revealed religion.

'Die geoffenbarte Religion setzt im geringsten nicht eine vernünftige Religion voraus: sondern schließt sie in sich. Wann sie dieselbe voraussetzte, das ist, wenn sie ohne dieselbe unverständlich wäre: so wäre der gerügte Mangel der Lehrbücher ein wahrer Mangel. Da sie aber dieselbe in sich schließt; da sie alle Wahrheiten enthält, welche jene lehret, und sie bloß mit einer andern Art von Beweisen unterstützt: so ist es noch sehr die Frage, ob die Einförmigkeit der Beweisart, in Lehrbüchern für Kinder und gemeine Leute, nicht bequemer und nützlicher ist, als eine genaue Absonderung der vernünftigen und geoffenbarten Lehrsätze, einen jeden aus der ihm eigentümlichen Quelle erwiesen' (*G.H.*, VII, 819–820).

The difference between truths of rational religion and revealed religion is paradoxically rooted in their similarity. Both forms of truth have as their ultimate *telos* the mediation to man of truth, indeed, of the same basic truth which will bring man to perfection. The difference lies in the mode of propagation, in the 'Beweisart', of such perfective truth. An analysis of the similarity and difference between the two forms of truth should reveal the criterion of truth for revealed doctrines. First the similarity.

A rational truth is a truth that is directed immediately to man's intellect. Because its formal characteristics entail necessity and universality, its very inner nature is enough to guarantee its validity. In other words, the validity of a rational truth is free from all temporal and accidental conditions. A geometric theorem is not true because Euclid taught it, rather Euclid taught it because it is true. Perhaps the most important feature of a rational truth is its freedom from the empirico-historical. Its content is *necessary* and *intellectual* not *'zufällig'* and sensate. Since eighteenth-century man cannot for Lessing believe in a doctrine as a divine because of past *miracles*, i.e., since he cannot believe in the validity of any revelation because it is legitimized by something exterior to it, e.g., a miracle, he must in effect be able to grasp a doctrine as divine, or, better, the divine in a doctrine, free from the relativizing and cognitive inadequacies of the historical. Obviously he cannot do away with the empirical and metaphorical content of revelation (should he do that it would cease being a revealed truth and have become a truth of reason). Instead, revealed truths must possess some internal marks analogous to those of rational truths, some inner truth of its own that certifies its own divine nature without reference to something beyond the revelation itself: 'Hat denn eine geoffenbarte Wahrheit gar keine innere Merkmale? Hat ihr unmittelbar göttlicher Ursprung an ihr und in ihr keine Spur zurückgelassen, als die historische Wahrheit, die sie mit so vielen Fratzen gemein hat?' . . . 'Woher die innere Wahrheit nehmen? Aus ihr selbst. Deswegen heißt sie ja die *innere* Wahrheit: die Wahrheit, die keiner Beglaubigung von außen bedarf' (*Axiomata*, VIII, 171, 190). After the second citation just given, Lessing goes on immediately to illustrate what he means concerning the 'innere Wahrheit' by referring to the acceptance of a truth of geometry because of its own inner and self-evident demonstration, not because someone taught it. However, since Christian truths of revelation are not (at least as first communicated to man) truths of reason, it is obvious that they are not doctrines that can legitimize their truths by the process of rational demonstration. Nevertheless, I think that it is fair to conclude that for Lessing truths of revelation, since they mediate the same basic inner core to man as rational truths, must possess some inner marks that somehow cause man's more advanced *pre-rational* mind to believe in them without miracles as an external source of sanction.

Now the difference!

The difference between the truths of reason and the truths of revelation is derived from the nature of the consciousness to which they are respectively directed. Rational truths are directed immediately or non-mediatedly to man's intellect. Correspondingly, man's intellect perceives the inner 'Vollkommenheit' manifested by the rational truth and, because volition is a function of knowing, he is attracted to the rational truth. The most important form of truth is 'Selbsterkenntnis'. A person who is fully conscious of the perfections of his very being, and possesses the power to act in accordance with such perfections is a moral being (cf. *C.V.*, VII, 200, § 25), and will be conscious 'daß er das Gute tut, weil es das Gute ist'. Revelation, on the other hand, is directed only mediatively to man's intellect, rather directly to his heart, i.e., his whole affective-sensuous being. In other words, revelation is directed to a person whose consciousness is 'nicht deutlich genug' aware, i.e., is 'sinnlich'. The experience of 'Vollkommenheit' on a purely empirical level was designated in eighteenth-century philosophy as 'pleasure', as 'angenehm'. Lessing himself utilizes a similar rationalistic paradigm in his discussion of the pleasure of beauty and sublimity. 'Alle angenehmen Begriffe sind undeutliche Vorstellungen einer Vollkommenheit' (*Bemerkungen*, VII, 273). The purpose of revelation is to bring man to ever higher awareness of his moral nature – of his own perfections and of his power to act lawfully in accordance with such perfections. Nevertheless, a doctrine of revelation *qua* being revelation is not experienced as a rational truth, rather as an allegorical-metaphorical-empirical datum. Revelation does not make man *immediately* rational. Instead it improves man as he is and he is a sensate being. Since the inner core of a doctrine of revelation is to mediate perfection to pre-rational or empirical man, what would be a pre-rational or sensate experience of moral perfection? Just as the 'Vollkommenheit' can be 'undeutlich' *felt* as pleasure, so, one must conclude that the perfective inner core of revelation can be *felt* as 'Seligkeit'. Lessing wrote in his *Gegensätze* and repeated in his *Axiomata* the following: 'Was gehen den Christen des Theologen Hypothesen und Erklärungen und Beweise an? Ihm ist es doch einmal da, das Christentum welches er so wahr, in welchem er sich so selig *fühlet*. Wenn der Paralytikus die wohltätigen Schläge des elektrischen Funken *erfährt*, was kümmert es ihn, ob Nollet oder ob Franklin oder ob keiner von beiden Recht hat?' (*G.H.*, VII, 812–813, and *Axiomata*, VIII, 196).

Lessing's reference to Nollet and Franklin are of some interest. Both men developed early and conflicting theories about electricity. Thomas Kuhn uses their electrical paradigms as examples of a scientific crisis in the early attempt to theorize about the phenomena of electricity. This theoretical crisis was not overcome during Lessing's lifetime. Lessing is saying in effect that the theoretical or objective paradigms underlying attempts to justify or 'prove' objectively the truths of Christianity are inconclusive, contradictory, and non-probative. Whether the reality of miracles can be proven or not, whether it is possible for the past apodictically to determine the present or not, whether revelation is of a transcendent or immanent origin, is of little importance to the empirical and affective consciousness of man the believer, of a developing pre-rational mind. The believing Christian in distinction from the learned and argumentative theologian does not apodictically know the truth of Christianity as something as certain as a demonstrated theorem in geometry. However, the believer does experience Christianity as truth and the truth of Christianity insofar as he *feels* himself to be 'selig' within his belief. Since the purpose of truth for Lessing is to make man perfected, then the 'innere Merkmal' of revelation and hence its truth is the sensate experience of perfection. Truth on the level of revelation may be defined as that which is *felt* as perfective. Whatever the objective status of Christianity might be (and, indeed, there seems to be for Lessing a crisis concerning this status), Lessing is saying, it does not really matter for the *telos* of truth is perfection and therefore the reality and genuiness of Christianity is guaranteed by the feeling of 'Seligkeit' it produces. Just how this feeling of 'Seligkeit' improves man will be discussed in the next section.

If the formal structure of revelation entails as an essential feature the ameliorative feeling of 'Seligkeit', then the purpose of religion for Lessing differs from its purpose for the orthodox. For the orthodox the purpose of revealed religion is to save man from his sins, from his spiritual death. God in Christ confronts man in history as an objective reality and man is to surrender himself in faith to this salvational being. However, man cannot surrender himself to Christ unless he knows who Christ objectively is. Therefore, *fides historica,* while not constituting the heart of faith, is nevertheless a *sine qua non* since the only way to know Christ is through history. Since the purpose of revelation for the orthodox is to relate man to an objectivity, to a transcendent God, it is incumbent upon man to know this objectivity before he relates himself to it in faith. But since the purpose of revelation for Lessing is to clarify and perfect man's own self-consciousness, to make perfect man's subjectivity, then the objective reality of revelation and of the revealer is of secondary importance. Christ may indeed have really worked miracles and these miracles may objectively have been necessary for the 'Annehmung seiner

Lehre' at that time in man's history, but they are not necessary for Lessing's present in order to bring man towards perfection. What is necessary is that the doctrines of revelation make man more perfect, which in the case of an advanced but still pre-rational man means that the believer feels himself perfected, 'selig'. Therefore, revealed religion for Lessing is not so much a 'Gabe' from God as an 'Aufgabe', i.e., it is not an objectivity whose very acceptance by human subjectivity is salvational (as the Lutheran doctrine of salvation by 'faith alone', not by works implies), rather it should function as a stimulus to the believer to develop his subjectivity on a moral level. Whereas the relationship between individuals on a purely rational level is governed by a cognitive awareness of the meaning of morality and its laws, this relationship is governed on an affective level by the feeling of love. In his short tract *Das Testament Johannis* Lessing has the 'Ich' say: 'So ist die christliche Liebe nicht die christliche Religion? . . . Aber welches von beiden möchte wohl das Schwere sein? – Die christliche Glaubenslehren annehmen und bekennen? oder die christliche Liebe ausüben?' (VIII, 21). Just as the practical effects of electrical shock remain just as beneficial irregardless of whether Franklin's, Nollet's, or anyone's theoretical interpretation is correct, so too is the practical reality of Christianity secure irregardless of whether Reimarus', Goeze's, or anyone's theories concerning the objectivity of its historical origin are correct.

The concept that the truth of religion in general and of Christianity in particular is essentially a call or 'Aufgabe' to practical improvement, to love, is manifest in the famous ring-parable of *Nathan der Weise*. Saladin asks Nathan which of the three religions – Christianity, Judaism, or Islam – is the true one:

> *Ein Mann, wie du* [Nathan] , *bleibt da*
> *Nicht stehen, wo der Zufall der Geburt*
> *Ihn hingeworfen: oder wenn er bleibt,*
> *Bleibt er aus Einsicht, Gründen, Wahl des Bessern.*
> *Wohlan! so teile deine Einsicht mir*
> *Dann mit.*
> (Act III, scene 5).

The question as posed by Saladin is essentially one based on the rationalistic paradigm. Since Truth is one, and since there are three different and differing religions each claiming to have the Truth, then logically it follows that only one of them can be true (perhaps none of them, but certainly not all of them). Since Nathan is not a person to remain where he was 'zufällig' born, and since Nathan is an intelligent man, he must have some *objective* reasons, some 'erklär-bare Gründe' why he has *consciously* chosen to remain a Jew. It is also apparent that the concept of truth underlying Saladin's question, is that truth is something objective, i.e., it manifests things as they really are.[25] Saladin is saying that, before one commits oneself to the beneficial effects (the salvation wrought) by this or that religion, one should first know if this or that religion is objectively an embodiment of the divine. Since a person must know before he consciously chooses, then the truth of religion must be something open to the intellectual powers of man, either because they contain self-evident principles or because they have been sanctioned by irrefutable demonstrations of God's intent, e.g., by miracles. Without going into the details of the parable (knowledge of which is assumed to be possessed by the reader) it will suffice to say that Lessing equated the three religions with three rings that are objectively identical. Further, an investigator has no way according to Nathan of demonstrating the inner religious power of the 'true' ring

> *vor Gott*
> *Und Menschen angenehm zu machen, wer*
> *In dieser Zuversicht ihn [the alleged original ring] trug. . . .*
> (Act III, scene 7)

Therefore, when the three brothers, each having been given a ring by their father (God?), come forth after the death of the father in order to claim their inheritance, none of them is able to prove the objective reality of his ring:

> *Umsonst; der rechte Ring war nicht*
> *Erweislich; — Fast so unerweislich, als*
> *Uns itzt der rechte Glaube.*
> (Act III, scene 7)

Saladin objects that the three religions do differ empirically, unlike the three rings. Even the food and drink of the three religions differ. Nathan's answer is yes, but not with regards the most important feature, namely their claim to be historically grounded, i.e., to have an objective and probative claim to possession of truth mediated by the medium of history:

> *Denn gründen alle sich nicht auf Geschichte?*
> *Geschrieben oder überliefert!*

retorts Nathan. Since the empirical content of a past 'now' can never become the grounds of apodictic certainty for a present 'now', then the claims of different religions to truth, whatever be the difference in the material content of their historical proofs, are immediately relativized because of the *formal* feature of being grounded in the temporal or empirico-historical.

If Lessing (and thereby his mouthpiece Nathan) had been a 'pure' rationalist, he would have had Nathan answer Saladin with the type of answer Reimarus would have given. Nathan would have contended that one should *not* be the adherent to any historical religion, rather he should be a member of the religion of reason, i.e., he should be a practitioner of natural religion. But as has been amply shown, *de facto* man for Lessing does not nor can he be a practitioner of natural religion, at least in his normal and primitive state. Instead, Nathan suggests that each person remain in the religion of his birth. Since historical religion cannot be apodictically proven and hence must be accepted on faith, who should one have more faith in than one's own ancestors, one's own traditions?[27]

> *Und*
> *Geschichte muß doch wohl allein auf Treu'*
> *Und Glauben angenommen werden? Nicht?*
> *Nun, wessen Treu' und Glauben zieh man denn*
> *Am wenigsten in Zweifel? Doch der Seinen?*
> *Doch deren Blut wir sind? doch deren, die*
> *Von Kindheit an uns Proben ihrer Liebe*
> *Gegeben? die uns nie getäuscht, als wo*
> *Getäuscht zu werden uns heilsamer war? —*
> *Wie kann ich meinen Vätern weniger*
> *Als du den deinen glauben? Oder umgekehrt?*
> (Act III, scene 7)

The question immediately arises as to what value there is in remaining in historical religion if its validity cannot be proven as objectively certain? Is not there some sort of criterion for determining the truth of historical religions? The value and criterion of truth for historical religions is for Lessing the same. The judge (who I believe represents formally man in the present 'now') suggests the following as a solution to which of the three rings (religions) is the true one.

'Wohlan!
Es eifre jeder seiner unbestochnen
Von Vorurteilen freien Liebe nach!
Es strebe von euch jeder um die Wette,
Die Kraft des Steins in seinem Ring — an Tag
Zu legen! Komme dieser Kraft mit Sanftmut,
Mit innigster Ergebenheit in Gott
Zu Hilf
                    (Act III, scene 7)

The purpose and effect of the alleged original ring (conceived as an objectivity) was to make man more perfect (pleasing to God and man). Just as the empirical nature of the ring (i.e., its objectivity consists in being empirical) cannot be the basis upon which to judge objectively concerning its inner perfective power, so too does the empirico-temporal nature of historical religion make it impossible to decide objectively which religion is the one God wants to use to perfect man. In short, the empirico-historical nature of revealed or historical religions cannot by its very essence be a medium objectively manifesting the divine to man living in a present 'now'. This does not mean that such religions are without value. Since *de facto* man does not possess a fully developed and functioning intellect, since *de facto* man on account of his empirical consciousness will inevitably form positive religions, such religions can still be the medium for manifesting God's intentions to man, but not as a content objectively given rather as a stimulus to practical perfection. Lessing *via* Nathan is saying that the adherent to a historical religion should let his feeling of 'Seligkeit' become an inspiration for love. The value and criterion of the truth of historical religion for man of the present consists in its empirically felt perfection of man's subjectivity insofar as this felt perfection leads man to do good.[28]

Although the questions Lessing was seeking to answer in *Die Erziehung des Menschengeschlechts* and in *Nathan der Weise* were different ones, the two works are nevertheless somewhat contradictory in my judgment. In the *Erziehung* Lessing was asking what sense man can make from his history, particularly of his religious history? In other words, given the fact that there are positive religions and that *de facto* man cannot possess rational truths as he should, is there some way by means of which the rational ideal can be realized through the irrational? Lessing's answer was yes, through the evolutionary idea of revelation as education. In *Nathan* Lessing is asking how a man (eighteenth century) in the present should treat historical religion since he can neither probatively prove or disprove the objective truth of such a religion?[29] Lessing's answer was that the man of the present should allow historical religion to become a spur for practical improvement. So far there is no contradiction between the two works. Nevertheless, had Nathan answered Saladin with the same evolutionary paradigm as is found in the *Erziehung,* he would have stated that the value of historical religion lies, of course, in its stimulus to practical perfection. Nevertheless, since the various religions of man are not all equally perfective (i.e., educative), Christianity is better than his (Nathan's) Judaism and Judaism is better than Saladin's Islam. Although Lessing accepts historical religion as an ingredient in man's religious life in *Nathan,* he does not make use of the notion of evolution. In the *Erziehung* historical religion is the way God seeks to bring about man's perfection, be it through immanent development or through a transcendent 'Richtungsstoß'. Indeed, the education of man is not so much something that man consciously chooses to do as it is a historical force that brings man to higher levels of perfection. In *Nathan,* on the other hand, historical religion becomes something that man consciously accepts as a stimulus to practical perfection. The lack of consistency between the two works is, in my opinion, a manifestation of the cognitive crisis that Lessing was facing. In other words, in seeking to integrate the rational and irrational, the metaphysical and empirical, Lessing was postulating 'thought models' for different though related problems concerning the nature of the reconciliation to be wrought. These 'thought models' were no more than bold hypotheses, not apodictic certainties and therefore total consistency cannot be expected.

At any rate, by locating the relevance of Christianity for the *man of the present* in the feeling of 'Seligkeit', Lessing had found a means to defend Christianity on a purely formal level against the attack of Reimarus. The believing Christian as opposed to the subtilizing theologian cannot formally be hurt by Reimarus whatever the material validity of Reimarus' arguments against Christianity is. Lessing's principle of defense, however, was also the main cause of his quarrel with the orthodox. Lessing could only defend Christianity (even perhaps including the notion of miracles) by giving up all attempts to justify it as objectively true. And since the main defense of Christianity by the orthodox rested upon the apodictic value of miracles and since the past for Lessing can never be apodictic for the present, Lessing had no other choice but to surrender objectivity to

Reimarus and defeat him with subjectivity. Whatever the origin of Christianity (and it may indeed entail real miracles), its relevancy for contemporary man is secured because *de facto* man as of yet can only have religious existence through the medium of positive religion. The cognitive weakness of man constitutes the essence of his subjectivity. Religion *per se* in order to be of value to *de facto man* must be structured in such a way that it can be addressed to man as he is. Man is cognitively weak and positive religions *alone* can address themselves to, engage, and perfect such a weak being. This Christianity does by giving man a feeling of 'Seligkeit'. Since the value of Christianity resides in its perfection of man's subjectivity, it cannot be affected by attacks upon its objective foundation. This is the reason why Lessing wanted to separate the meaning of religion from its history: 'Bei mir bleibt die christliche Religion die nämliche, nur daß ich die Religion von der Geschichte der Religion will getrennet wissen. Nur daß ich mich weigere, die historische Kenntnis von ihrer Entstehung und ihrer Fortpflanzung und eine Überzeugung von dieser Kenntnis, die schlechterdings bei keiner historischen Wahrheit sein kann, für unentbehrlich zu halten. Nur daß ich die Einwürfe, die gegen das Historische der Religion gemacht werden, für unerheblich erkläre, sie mögen beantwortet werden können oder nicht. Nur daß ich die Schwächen der Bibel nicht für Schwächen der Religion halten will' (*Axiomata*, VIII, 195—196). Lessing does not deny that the Bible contains religion. The whole argument embodied in the *Erziehung* proves this. But the Bible is only the vehicle of *religion:* 'Die historischen Worte sind das *Vehiculum* des prophetischen Wortes. Ein *Vehiculum* aber soll und darf die Kraft und der Arzenei nicht haben' (*Axiomata*, VIII, 172—173). The value of the Bible — namely, its perfective effects — is not the same as the Bible conceived as a vehicle of transmission. This vehicle is necessary for *de facto* man. Nevertheless, the religious content of the Bible is not dependent upon its historical origin for its relevancy to the needs of *present* man and hence an attack upon the Bible's historicity is not an attack upon the religion it contains.

As shown above, Lessing does not deny the real miracles might have played a role in the past in inspiring the *de facto* man of bygone times to accept various doctrines as divine. What Lessing wants is to distinguish carefully between the probable historical reality of the miraculous origins of Christianity and the *telos* that such miracles were intended to achieve. The purpose of the miracles is to 'inspire' or move man to believe in certain empirically and allegorically embodied truths. The further purpose of such truths (and hence the ultimate *telos* of miracles) is to effect the pre-rational mind in such a way that it is brought closer to a rational and hence perfected consciousness. The miracles are, therefore, no more than the 'Gerüste' upon which the 'Bau' of religion is constructed. 'Die Wunder, die Christus und seine Jünger taten, waren das Gerüste, und nicht der Bau. Das Gerüste wird abgerissen, sobald der Bau vollendet ist. Den muß der Bau wenig interessieren, der seine Vortrefflichkeit nur aus den abgerissenen Gerüste beweisen zu dürfen glaubt, weil die alten Baurechnungen vermuten lassen, daß ein eben so großer Meister zu dem Gerüste müsse gehört haben, als zu dem Baue selbst' (*D.*, VIII, 36−37). In other words, the wonderfulness of Christianity as it exists *now* may, indeed, speak for its truly miraculous origin, for its 'Gerüste'. It does not really matter, however, if the supposed origin was or was not as believed to be. The value of the 'Bau' resides in its perfection of man *now*, not in its origin. Therefore, Christianity would be of little interest to a man *now*, if the only thing that can be said for it is that its 'Gerüste' consisted of miracles that happened *in the past*.

'Allerdings ward die neue Religion auf *damalige* Überzeugung von der Auferstehung Christi gegründet, welche Überzeugung sich auf die Glaubwürdigkeit und Eintracht der Augenzeugen gründen mußte. Nun haben wir, die wir itzt leben, diese Augenzeugen nicht mehr unter uns: haben nur Geschichtsschreiber von den Aussagen dieser Augenzeugen, in welchen Geschichtsschreibern sich nur das allgemeine Resultat von Aussagen dieser Augenzeugen unverfälscht erhalten konnte: und gleichwohl soll unsere itzige Überzeugung von der Auferstehung Christi nicht gegründet genug sein, wenn sie sich bloß auf jenes Resultat der Aussagen gründet, und sich nicht zugleich auf die völlige Übereinstimmung der Geschichtsschreiber von diesen Aussagen gründen kann? − Da wären wir, die wir itzt leben, schön daran!

'Und gleichwohl möchte ich gar zu gern behaupten, daß wir, die wir itzt leben, auch in diesem Punkte besser daran sind, als die, zu deren Zeiten die Augenzeugen noch vorhanden waren. Denn der Abgang der Augenzeugen wird uns reichlich durch etwas ersetzt, was die Augenzeugen nicht haben konnten. Sie hatten nur den Grund vor sich, auf den sie, in Überzeugung seiner Sicherheit, ein großes Gebäude aufzuführen wagten. Und wir, wir haben dieses große Gebäude selbst aufgeführt vor uns. − Welcher Tor wühlet neugierig in dem Grunde sines Hauses, bloß um sich von der Güte des Grundes seines Hauses zu überzeugen? — Setzen mußte sich das Haus freilich erst, an diesem und jenem Orte. — Aber daß der Grund gut ist, weiß ich nunmehr, da das Haus so lange Zeit steht, überzeugender, als es die wissen konnten, die ihn legen sahen' (*D.*, VIII, 34—35).

The reality of Christianity is empirically given to Lessing in his experienced 'now'. Furthermore, this reality is good and marvelous. *De facto* or pre-rational man, at least Western man, cannot do without it and expect to improve religiously. But the proof of the validity of Christianity lies not in its origins but in its meaning for the perfection of present man's subjectivity. Whereas miracles might have been experienced by men of the past and whereas miracles might have been even necessary for the acceptance of revelation by men of the past, their reality can be no more than historically certain now. Historical certainty rests upon the testimony of witnesses. Witnesses assert that such and such an event objectively and actually happened or did not take place. But such probable though objective certainty can never be the source of belief in doctrines for men who live in a later 'now'. Indeed, for believers who live in this later 'now', the best proof of the reality of miracles in the past is not the inadequate testimony of men, rather *the present perfective reality* of Christianity. In other words, since the ultimate purpose of miracles is to perfect man through Christianity, the perfective effects of Christianity are more probative than that such and such events might have been miraculous occurences. Indeed, Lessing is now claiming, immediate experience of Christianity in the 18th century proves more than can be immediate experience of the miracles that allegedly grounded it. The ultimate *telos* of these miracles was to cause the construction of a means that would perfect man. Since eighteenth-century man experiences this constructed means, he knows that its origins were good, whereas the eye-witness could only know that the origin is 'miraculous' in the sense of being out of the ordinary and not that such an origin will *necessarily* produce good effects. Again Lessing is being inconsistent. In the *Ü.B.G.K.* Lessing stated that, had he witnessed the miracles of Christ, he would have surrendered his reason to Christ. In the *Duplik* Lessing contends in effect that the real test of a miracle and hence of Christ is in its effects (which takes years if not centuries to come about) and that this is a superior source of certainty for their reality. Thus it would seem that Lessing was not completely willing to surrender his reason to the cognitive claims of miraculously grounded doctrines.

5. *The act of appropriation or Lessing's 'ars dialectice cogitandi'*. It has been shown that the various elements and their interrelationship in Lessing's concept of revelation are determined by Lessing's attempt to overcome the cognitive crisis in which he found himself. Revelation is simply the manifestation of truth — of the inner rationality of reality — to a being that is *de facto* cognitively weak. The material, so to speak, of which all revelation is constituted is 'das Sinnliche'. The sensate form of all doctrines of revelation is structured so as to be able to effect *de facto* man amelioratively at specific levels of his historical development. Therefore, the ultimate *telos* of revelation is the bringing of man closer to rational consciousness. Nevertheless, revelation, before it has been transformed into truths of reason, is known to be true (or to contain truth) by being *felt* as perfective of man. Somehow, this feeling of 'Seligkeit' brings about the education of mankind. By and large revelation has been discussed thus far relative to its objective content. Just how this objective content is appropriated by man's subjectivity, i.e., just how it becomes man's own internalized principle of cognition and of action, has not been analyzed. Unfortunately Lessing never discussed this problem in any detail. Such a theory as Lessing did develop can be tentatively reconstructed and will entail admittedly more hypothesizing than was required for an analysis of the other features of Lessing's concept of revelation.

It has been noted that Lesssing's cognitive crisis is not purely epistemological as it was for philosophers such as Descartes or Kant. Both of these thinkers were interested in the *formal* problem of truth irregardless of any content. Lessing, on the other hand, was primarily interested in the highest ·content of Truth — namely in God as the source of man's meaning and destiny. Lessing's epistemological difficulties were only incidental to this quest for the Truth, i.e., they occur basically within the framework of his essentially theological ratiocination. Theological truth, however, was only one of several types of truth Lessing pursued in his lifetime. In particular, Lessing pursued aesthetic and especially dramaturgical truth. In my judgment, there is an underlying similarity in the way Lessing approached different classes of truth and the principles entailed in this similarity constitute Lessing's *ars dialectice cogitandi*. This 'Denkungsart' formally entails a broader and more comprehensive scope than the specific truth-claims made by Lessing in different fields of intellectual endeavor. Also, this way of thinking constitutes the 'systematic' or, if one will, the 'esoteric' core of Lessing's thought. In other words, that which typifies Lessing is not so much the specific conclusions about this or that that he drew, rather the principles involved in the act of investigation or the generative ideas implied in the questions he asked. An analysis of how man, according to Lessing, cognitively and volitionally appropriates the content of revelation will simultaneously reveal the nature of Lessing's *ars dialectice cogitandi* since historical or *de facto* man's cognitive problems were also Lessing's. Also an analysis of Lessing's *ars dialectice cogitandi* will provide the opportunity to summarize in a formal manner the results of the previous analysis of Lessing's concept of revelation. It can be shown, I would like to note, that this *ars dialectice cogitandi* informs also Lessing's *ars theatrice cogitandi*, i.e., his dramaturgical speculations and even the psychological structure of many of his characters in his plays. Such an exposition is, of course, beyond the formal scope of this investigation.

The first step in comprehending Lessing's *ars dialectice cogitandi* and correlatively the principle underlying man's appropriation of revelatory truth is to establish the general structure of thinking *per se* as a formal activity. In order to develop my analysis I will utilize Lessing's *Das Christentum der Vernunft*, often with speculative extrapolations of its content. Before so doing I want to make it clear that I am not treating this early work (as Leisegang has done) as an early statement of Lessing's 'philosophical system'. I am fully aware of the fragmentary and tentative nature of *C.V.* Even without the existence of this work I would suggest as a hypothesis the ensuing analysis of the nature of thinking for Lessing. The legitimacy of my use of the *C.V.* is grounded upon its ability to explain Lessing's explicit theological speculations. Up to now I have sought to enlighten the conceptual paradigm underlying the surface level of Lessing's thoughts by inducing it from this level. Now I shall attempt to penetrate a little deeper into the generative ideas, often only implicit ones, underlying not just Lessing's thought (i.e., what he explicitly stated) but his thinking activity as a generative and creative process. I find it, therefore, advantageous and corroborative that my hypothesis concerning the nature of this thinking process was more or less explicitly formulated by Lessing in some of his early speculations. I am not so much interpreting Lessing's mature thought in the light of this early work, however, as making use of this work in the light of what I take to be the *implicit* principles in Lessing's mature speculations. In short, the *C.V.* is being used more for expository rather than probative purposes.

In *C.V.* Lessing speculatively asserts that the world (i.e., finite reality as a systematic totality) is a product of God's thinking Himself and His perfections in a divided manner. 'Gott dachte seine Vollkommenheiten zerteilt, das ist, er schaffte Wesen, wovon jedes etwas von seinen Vollkommenheiten hat; denn, um es nochmals zu wiederholen, jeder Gedanke ist bei Gott eine Schöpfung. Alle diese Wesen zusammen heißen die Welt' (*C.V.*, VII, 198–199 §§ 13–14). The important thing to note for the purposes of my analysis of Lessing's 'Denkungsart' is that each finite entity, each part of divided God contains some of God's perfections. Each 'einfaches Wesen' (cf. § 19) is *in micro* an image of God as he is *in macro*. Created beings (which includes man) are, therefore, 'gleichsam eingeschränkte Götter . . ., so müssen auch ihre Vollkommenheiten den Vollkommenheiten Gottes ähnlich sein; so wie Teile dem Ganzen' (§ 22). In paragraph 23 Lessing asserts in effect that self-consciousness is 'gleichsam das Siegel seiner [d.h. Gottes] Vollkommenheiten'. In paragraph 24 Lessing suggests that one of the factors (i.e., types of perfection) that differ one created being from another is the level of development of each being's self-consciousness: 'Mit den verschiedenen Graden seiner [d.h. Gottes] Vollkommenheiten müssen also auch verschiedene Grade des Bewußtseins dieser Vollkommenheiten und der Vermögenheit, denselben gemäß zu handeln, verbunden sein' (§ 24). In other words, the difference between entities is not just due to each entity having qualitatively different perfections, but also due to their having more or less of a specific perfection (i.e., the difference is quantitative). Then in paragraph 25 Lessing contends that there are 'Wesen' (by using the plural Lessing was obviously not refering to God but to the multitude of creation) which are sufficiently self-aware and possess the power to act according to this self-consciousness, i.e., to be moral. For the moment it will suffice to state that such beings represent humans, at least as an ideal for man to attain. Since humans are 'gleichsam eingeschränkte Götter' and since man's similarity with God includes his ability to be aware of perfection and of himself, it is plausible to conclude that the structure of human consciousness for Lessing exhibits the same inner principles as does the divine mind, though, of course, in a limited manner. (The importance of this limitation will become clear presently.) In other words, an analysis of the psychology of the divine mind should cast light upon the structure of man's divine-like mind. Therefore, in effect, the activity of the divine is exemplary or paradigmatic for all lesser levels of consciousness.

(Divine) consciousness is conceived by Lessing as essentially a movement or activity in the pursuit of a material content which, because it is the final cause or *telos* of awareness, is its sufficient cause. Lessing writes: 'Das einzige vollkommenste Wesen hat sich von Ewigkeit her mit nichts als mit der Betrachtung des Vollkommensten beschäftigen können' (§ 1). God, the most perfect being, is an activity or a 'sich beschäftigen'. This mental movement is not randomly or mechanically caused. If the movement of the divine mind were merely mechanically caused, it would move blindly in any direction determined by some principle beyond its being. Instead, the mind moves in accordance with its own inner necessity, essence, and principles that determine it dynamically to pursue perfection, indeed, the highest perfection possible. Perfection or 'Vollkommenheit' in the eighteenth century was commonly defined, as Lessing himself wrote, as 'die Einheit im Mannigfaltigen' (*Bemerkungen*, VII, 273), i.e., as order. Order is another term for rationality. Hence mental activity is in its essence a drive rationally to cognize or become aware of the rational. Perfection differs from order in that it is order conceived as a principle of attraction. In other words, order is called perfection when it moves the mind (as the mind's final cause) to pursue or occupy itself with a specific type of object. In paragraph 2 Lessing identifies the activity of 'sich beschäftigen' with the concept of 'denken'. Thinking is, therefore, in this context a general term designating consciousness *per se,* its principles of activity, and the type of content or object of which it seeks to be aware.

Thinking entails two related sub-activities — namely cognition and volition. Lessing writes: 'Vorstellung, wollen und schaffen ist bei Gott eines' (§ 3). Thinking as a movement culminating in awareness of perfection can be designated as cognition. Thinking as an impulse to become aware of a certain type of content (e.g., of order as opposed to disorder) is called volition. In other words, to think is a movement of the mind to become cognitively aware of perfection and simultaneously a movement of the will to affirm or possess the same cognized perfection. Indeed, the two types of mental activity in *C.V.* are but two aspects or sides of the same mental pursuit ('sich beschäftigen') after perfection. In this sense 'Vorstellen' (i.e., the thinking of a perfection as an object of awareness) and 'Wollen' (i.e., the affirming of such a content) are 'bei Gott eines'. I suggest here the *plausible hypothesis* that thinking and wanting are also essentially one or two sides of the same mental activity in Lessing's interpretation of the human psychology. If this assumption is made, then (as will be shown) the dynamics of *de facto* man's appropriation of revelation can be rendered intelligible. At any rate, a major difference between man and God would be that God can actualize or create ('schaffen') that which He seeks to affirm and to think, whereas man, being finite, cannot create what he needs to fulfill his inner being. Man does not create, rather must make use of what is 'given' him. Man can, perhaps, transform the real world surrounding him, but he cannot create it in the first place.

Thinking *per se* is a longing for and pursuit of highest perfection. But, in the case of God at least, the highest perfection is God's own self. 'Das Vollkommenste ist [Gott] selbst; und also hat Gott von Ewigkeit her nur sich selbst denken können' (§ 2). If it be granted that the dynamics of the divine mind are paradigmatic for thinking *per se,* then it becomes evident that the *telos* informing cogitative activity, the highest perfection that attracts thinking, is none other than self-awareness. The divine mind's awareness of itself means that it is aware of itself as an activity in pursuit of perfection and that its very selfhood as perfected constitutes the essence of this perfection. Since the self is essentially a mental activity, perfection of its means consciousness of the self as acting perfectedly. Concerning the divine self Lessing asserts: 'Zu den Vollkommenheiten Gottes gehöret auch dieses, daß er sich seiner Vollkommenheit bewußt ist, und dieses, daß er seinen Vollkommerheiten gemäß handeln kann: beide sind gleichsam das Siegel seiner Vollkommenheiten' (§ 23). Self-consciousness of the self's activity in agreement with its own inner perfections is the highest perfection of selfhood and was called morality by Lessing. Although Lessing does not explicitly state it, it follows that God's deepest need is to be aware of Himself as morally perfected and thereby He must create a *real* thought-object reflecting His inner moral perfection. Since the world is but God's thinking of himself in a divided manner, then the ultimate *telos* informing the world is a moral one. *Morality is,* therefore, in effect for Lessing *self-conscious perfection or consciousness of the self as perfected.* This is the *telos* towards which all mental activity or thinking strives.

At this point Lessing's doctrine that man is 'gleichsam ein eingeschränkter Gott' becomes important. First of all, since man is a limited *divinity,* his mental activity functions similarly to God's. Just as the ultimate *telos* or highest perfection of God's "denken" is to become aware of himself as perfected, so is man's highest destiny to become conscious of himself as morally perfected, i.e., to obtain self-knowledge. Referring in effect to humans in terms similar to those used to refer to God, Lessing writes: 'Wesen, welche Voll-kommenheiten haben, sich ihrer Vollkommenheiten bewußt sind und das Vermögen besitzen, ihnen gemäß zu handeln, heißen moralische Wesen, das sind solche, welche einem Gesetze folgen können' (§ 25). Since the 'Gesetz' is derived from the structure of selfhood, it becomes an imperative for self-perfection and can be formulated as 'Handle deinen individualischen Vollkommenheiten gemäß' (§ 26). Perhaps no other thesis can demonstrate the 'modernity' of Lessing's thinking. As Etienne Gilson has noted, 'all Christian and medieval philosophy must be regarded as one in affirming the metaphysical primacy of being . . .'[30] This meant that truth and perfection is that to which man must *conform* himself. Cognitively, ethically, and religiously, man's highest destiny is to become aware of and to conform himself to that which is *beyond* and *other* than himself. Although man was created in the image of God, he is not for the Christian 'gleichsam ein eingeschränkter Gott'. God alone for the Christian can find his ultimate perfection in his own being. Man's deepest need is to become aware of the divine reality that he is not. Lessing, on the other hand, because he apparently identifies divine reality with man's being, albeit in a limited or 'eingeschränkt' manner, locates man's highest perfection not in the cognition of the reality of another being — even of God's being as distinct from his own — rather in the cognition of the perfection of man's own selfhood. In the place of the primary of Being Lessing posits the primacy of the self. In effect, Lessing raises man's moral self-aware-ness to the level of religious consciousness. In order to develop a consciousness of his self as a being which 'das Gute tun wird, weil es das Gute ist' (*Erziehung*, VIII, 612, § 85), Lessing is willing in the *Erziehung* to return to this earthly life endlessly until such a goal is realized. As Lessing writes: 'Ist nicht die ganze Ewigkeit mein?' (VIII, 615, § 100). Salvation for the Christian was the reconciliation of man with God in this life culminating in the direct vision of God, in the *visio beatifica*, in the next, not endlessly to return to this life in order to become aware of man's self as more and more perfected. In other words, the ultimate truth — the 'Ewigkeit' — that man, according to Lessing, as a thinking being seeks (to think) is not something other than himself, something objectively given and hence that which can be statically possessed. On the contrary, man seeks to become aware of himself as a perfected being or as a being becoming ever more perfect.[31] This idea that truth is more a manifestation to the self of the perfection of the self rather than a conformity of the self to and possession of objective reality is behind Lessing's famous statement in *Eine Duplik* that the total possession of truth about God (conceived as an objective content) is for God alone (presumably because in God alone is objectivity identical with subjectivity). Man's task is merely to pursue (objective) truth, for 'die aufrichtige Mühe, die [der Mensch] angewandt hat, hinter die Wahrheit zu kommen, macht den Wert des Menschen. Denn nicht durch den Besitz, sondern durch die Nachforschung der Wahrheit [i.e., through the consciously experienced subjective effort to comprehend objective truth] erweitern sich seine Kräfte, worin allein seine immer wachsende Vollkommenheit besteht' (VIII, 27). Man's perfection, therefore, consists of the consciousness of *his* expanding powers, not in the awareness of God conceived as a being *distinct from* or *other than* man.[32]

At this point, the basic ingredient in Lessing's concept of truth should be evident. Truth or, at least, perfective truth is for Lessing not the conformity of man's cognitive subjectivity (i.e., of man as a knowing self) with a cognated objectivity (i.e., being distinct from man's), rather it is in a making known of the self as perfected (i.e., of man's subjectivity) to the self. Man as 'ein eingeschränkter Gott' seeks to think *subjective truth*, i.e., to become aware of his own self becoming more and more perfect. In short, truth for Lessing coincides with 'Selbsterkenntnis'. The thesis that 'Selbsterkenntnis' is the only truth worthwhile or that makes man worthwhile is typical for Lessing's life long cogitative activity. As a young student Lessing defended his attendance of the theater (particularly his viewing of comedies) against the objections of his parents because he felt that he learned to know himself. 'Die Komödien kamen mir zu erst in die Hand. Es mag unglaublich vorkommen, wem es will, mir haben sie sehr große Dienste getan. Ich lernte daraus eine artige und gezwungne, eine grobe und natürliche Aufführung unterscheiden. Ich lernte wahre und falsche Tugenden daraus kennen, und die Laster eben so sehr wegen ihres Lächerlichen als wegen ihrer Schändlichkeit fliehen. . . . Doch bald hätte ich den vornehmsten Nutzen, den die Lustspiele bei mir gehabt haben, vergessen. Ich lernte mich selbst kennen, und seit der Zeit habe gewiß über niemanden mehr gelacht und gespottet als über mich selbst' (Letter to Lessing's mother, January 20, 1749, IX, 11). In *Gedanken über die Herrnhuter* Lessing complained that the possession of purely objective or scientific

knowledge was often correlative to man's low moral state: 'Der
Erkenntnis nach sind wir Engel, und dem Leben nuch Teufel' (*G.ü.H.*,
VII, 193). In this same work Lessing goes on to suggest the only
worthwhile type of knowledge by referring to the wisdom of
Socrates: 'Törichte Sterbliche, was über euch ist, ist nicht für euch!
Kehret den Blick in euch selbst! In euch sind die unerforschten
Tiefen, worinnen ihr euch mit Nutzen verlieren könnt. Hier unter-
sucht die geheimsten Winkel. Hier lernet die Schwäche und Stärke,
die verdeckten Gänge und den offenbaren Ausbruch eurer Leidenschaften! Hier richtet das Reich auf, wo ihr Untertan und König seid!
Hier begreifet und beherrschet das einzige, was ihr begreifen und
beherrschen sollt: euch selbst' (*G.ü.H.*, VII, 187). Years later in his
Hamburgische Dramaturgie Lessing asserts that promotion of self-
knowledge is the task of the dramatist. Referring once again to
Socrates' wisdom Lessing writes: 'Aber den Menschen, und uns selbst
kennen; auf unsere Empfindungen aufmerksam sein; in allen die
ebensten und kürzesten Wege der Natur aufforschen und lieben;
jedes Ding nach seiner Absicht beurteilen: das ist es, was wir in
seinem Umgange lernen; das ist es, was Euripides von dem Sokrates
lernte, und was ihn zu dem Ersten in seiner Kunst machte' (*H.D.*, VI,
255, § 49) And as has already been shown, the goal of the education
of mankind is to make man morally self-conscious so that self-
consciously he might do 'das Gute, weil es das Gute ist'. 'Selbsterkenntnis' was Lessing's life long imperative and gives unity to the
manifold areas of his cognitive endeavors. Throughout his life Lessing
sought to learn all sorts of objective truths. However, the ultimate
purpose underlying such a quest for objective truth, was to further
knowledge about and the perfection of his human self. As Lessing
said in his *Selbstbetrachtungen und Einfälle:* 'Ich bin nicht gelehrt –
ich habe nie die Absicht gehabt, gelehrt zu werden – ich möchte
nicht gelehrt sein, und wenn ich es im Traume werden könnte. Alles,
wornach ich ein wenig gestrebt habe, ist, im Fall der Not ein
gelehrtes Buch brauchen zu können (*S.E.*, VIII, 410).
 Lessing's idea that the *telos* of thinking is self-knowledge is a
plausible application of the rationalistic paradigm to the area of
value. The goal of man's thinking is to become aware of his inner
rationality, i.e., of his moral destiny within a moral universe. Such an
ideal certainly stamps Lessing as a child of the *Aufklärung*. But as a
child of the *Aufklärung* Lessing was also a victim of its cognitive
crisis. From the rationalist point of view man for Lessing should be
able to grasp the moral rationality of being by means of his unaided

intellect. The formal structure of such truths falls within the class of 'Vernunftswahrheiten'. In other words, the material content of the rationality of being should be cognizable formally as immutable, unconditioned, metaphysical, supra-temporal, necessary, and hence apodictically indubitable truth. Such cognition is only possible for a fully functioning rational faculty. This is precisely the beginning of Lessing's problem. 'Natural' or rational man should be a practitioner of natural religion, should feel oneness with his fellow man on a level of anthropological universality — namely as mankind, and act morally out of purely moral motivation. But actual man according to Lessing historically has only been religious in the form of positive religion, unites himself with others only on the level of tribes, nations, or confessions, and it motivated morally by extra-moral considerations. In short, actual man as a 'limited God' is cognitively weak. Instead of being open to the universal, metaphysical, rational, and intellectual man is attracted almost with compulsion to the particular, historical, emotional, and sensate. The limited consciousness of man is, in short, the original condition of *de facto* man. Whatever the material contents of the consciousness of such a cognitively weak being are, they share the formal feature of the empirico-historical. Since man's consciousness (being limited to the empirico-historical) has no more than a *childlike* development of its mental faculties, the practical impossibility of man's becoming rationally aware of the rationality of his being by his own unaided powers within the framework of Lessing's anthropological speculations becomes evident.

Whereas Lessing's ideal of truth is a manifestation of the rationalistic paradigm, his analysis of mankind's *de facto* is based upon the empiricistic paradigm. Hence Lessing's thinking was caught in a dilemma. First of all and this is highly important for an understanding of the formal principles of Lessing's thinking, man's consciousness is simply incapable in its original state of a direct, nonsensible and hence rational insight into reality. Between man's mind (his subjectivity) and the rational exists the barrier of the sensate, the emotional, the concrete and temporal. Thus the problem facing Lessing was how to discover and realize the universal in and through the particular, the eternal in and through the temporal, in short, the rational in and through the empirico-historical. It is therefore characteristic of Lessing's 'Denkungsart' that the universal (or at least the original obtainment of it) is not ascertainable by deductive and abstract reasoning. The universal exists only in the individual, the metaphysical only in the empirical. Because Lessing recognized that truth for the most part could only be obtained *via* the sensate, it is easy to understand why he was attracted by Alexander Gottlieb Baumgarten's epistemological doctrine of 'anschauende Erkenntnis'. Baumgarten, more clearly than his mentor Wolff, distinguished between rational and non-imageable knowledge and knowledge, albeit an allegedly inferior kind, that comes directly *via* and out of sensations. Influenced by Baumgarten, Lessing writes in his *Abhandlungen über die Fabel:* 'Das Allgemeine existieret nur in dem Besondern und kann nur in dem Besondern anschauend erkannt werden' (IV, 42). Ingrid Strohschneider-Kohrs has excellently summarized the principle of analysis in Lessing's critical thinking. Lessing seeks 'das Wahre, das dem Besonderen, dem Realen angemessen, – also: *sein* Maß ist'.[33] In short, the first principle of Lessing's attempted solution to man's cognitive crisis (including his own) was to recognize that *de facto* man's consciousness is and will remain in its first condition of being 'nicht deutlich genug' aware of reality. Such a state cannot be overcome inwardly by spontaneous generation of rational concepts nor exteriorily by being presented with *pure* truths of reason. Instead, the very sensuous content of such a cognitively weak and undeveloped consciousness must become the means of enlightenment.

But how does the sensate become the means of enlightenment, how can it mediate the universal to benighted man? As shown above, the universal as perfection manifests itself to an emotional and empirical consciousness as 'feeling'. The truth of ontological rationality cannot be apodictically known by a cognitively weak mind, but it can be intuited as a feeling of 'Seligkeit'. This feeling is 'das innere Merkmal' of empirical truth. Since thinking as a pursuit of knowledge is essentially a mental movement to become aware of the thinking self as perfected, the criterion of truth or, indeed, the truth of empirical cognition is a 'nicht deutlich' experience of self-perfection. *De facto* man 'feels' or 'senses' being rather than rationally cognizes it. This feeling of perfection caused by the empirico-historical content of consciousness is not dependent for its legitimacy upon the reality of historical events (and the feeling subject's knowledge thereof), i.e., it is not dependent upon anything external to it. In short, the feeling of perfection is not only 'das innere Merkmal' of revelatory truth, it is the truth of the empirico-historical.

When Lessing applied this *ars dialectice cogitandi* to the problem
of revelation given to man *via* Biblical revelation, i.e., through
history, he developed inchoately two concepts that are integral
features, of his way of analyzing cognitive problems. These two·
interrelated generative ideas are the concepts of *Geist* and *Buchstabe.*
The perfective 'feeling' of the inner truth of revelation or, in other
words, the religion contained in the Bible was called 'das innere
Zeugnis des h. Geistes' about which Lessing writes: 'Denn da dieses
Zeugnis sich doch nur bei denjenigen Büchern und Stellen der Schrift
mehr oder weniger äußern kann, welche auf unsere geistliche Besserung mehr oder weniger abzwecken, was ist billiger, als nur solcher-
lei Bücher und Stellen der Bibel den Geist zu nennen?' (*Axiomata*,
VIII, 173). The *Geist* of religious revelation is teleologically determined in content as that which aims at 'unsere geistliche Besserung'.
The Bible as history is only the *Buchstabe,* only the vehicle of
communication. However, and this is very important, the *Geist* is not
mediated to man except through the *Buchstabe* (i.e., through the
empirico-historical *per se*). The truth contained in the *Buchstabe*
(i.e., that which God wished to communicate to man) is discovered
only insofar as the *Buchstabe* is able to make man conscious (albeit
sensuously) of his own subjective truth (i.e., his being true to
himself) which is experienced as 'Seligkeit'.

However, the mere 'feeling' of perfection is not the final step in
overcoming the benightedness of the human condition. The ultimate
telos of the education of man is to develop in man a fully perfected
rational consciousness. The feeling of perfection and the correlative
interest it generates in *de facto* man in the empirical content that
stimulated such a feeling constitute only the first step in man's
education. Because man's perfection is to be 'deutlich' aware of what
he *is* and that he is acting consciously in accord with this immanent
telos of his being, Lessing writes concerning the meaning of Christianity: 'Die letzte Absicht des Christentums ist nicht unsere Seligkeit, die mag herkommen, woher sie will, sondern unsre *Seligkeit
vermittelst unsrer Erleuchtung,* welche Erleuchtung nicht bloß als
Bedingung, sondern als Ingredienz zur Seligkeit notwendig ist, in
welcher am Ende unsre ganze Seligkeit besteht' (*A.–G.,* VIII, 228).
Therefore, the mere 'feeling' of goodness or truth has as its function
to 'enlighten' man's mind.

The question arises once again as to how the feeling of perfection
can contribute to man's 'Erleuchtung'? The answer to this question
can be discovered by briefly considering Lessing's basic principle of

education. It will be recalled that 'der erste Mensch' in the *Erziehung des Menschengeschlechts* cannot preserve the adequate concept of the transcendental unity of God because it was 'ein mitgeteilter, und nicht erworbener Begriff'. *De facto* man has a childlike awareness, not because he lacks a rational faculty, rather because his intellect is .simply undeveloped. *De facto* man's reason exists, but only *in potentiality*. The educative goal is to actualize this rational faculty by stimulating it to become active, i.e., to speculate and thereby to develop adequate concepts. The secret to education lies in inspiring the student to think about or to rethink a subject matter in his own terms, not simply to present to him a completely finished objective content to be accepted all at once (which, of course, was an impossibility in Lessing's opinion). In the 11th *Literaturbrief* Lessing enunciated his basic principle of education: 'Der größte Fehler, den man bei der Erziehung zu begehen pflegt, ist dieser, daß man die Jugend nicht zum eigenen Nachdenken gewöhnet. . . . Das große Geheimnis, die menschliche Seele durch Übung vollkommen zu machen . . . bestehet einzig darin, daß man sie in steter Bemühung behalte, durch eigenes Nachdenken auf die Wahrheit zu kommen' (IV, 114). In the exchange of letters with Mendelssohn and Nicolai in 1756 concerning the nature of tragedy, Lessing asked Mendelssohn to try to make sense out of his (Lessing's) ideas by rethinking them: 'Ich bin es überzeugt, daß meine Worte oft meinem Sinne Schaden tun, daß ich mich nicht selten zu unbestimmt oder zu nachlässig ausdrücke. Versuchen Sie es also, liebster Freund, sich durch Ihr eigen Nachdenken in den Geist meines Systems zu versetzen. Und vielleicht finden Sie es weit besser, als ich es vorstellen kann' (Letter to Mendelssohn, December 18, 1756, IX, 99). Insofar as Mendelssohn can rethink Lessing's 'System' within the framework of his own ideas, Mendelssohn would be appropriating it, making it his own. Therefore, the skill of the educator is shown in his ability to structure the material to be taught in such a way that it *activates* man's rational faculty. But how is the rational faculty of *de facto* man's childlike and empirical mind to be stimulated?

Perfection is the principle determining the dynamics of the human mind and will. The mind is naturally attracted to perfection. The awareness of perfection will of necessity stimulate the human self to become conscious of it. If the assumption be granted that wanting and thinking constitute the same mental activity in Lessing's concept of man as they do in his concept of God, then the attraction of man's will to a specific content of consciousness will simultaneously act as an impetus to his cognitive powers to become fully aware of (i.e., to penetrate rationally into) what is pleasing to his will. Revelation as an educative device presents *de facto* man with an empirico-historical content which causes him to feel himself as 'selig'. Because of the unity of thinking and wanting, an improvement on man's affective life must also entail a perfective development or, more accurately, a perfective gathering together and reorientation of man's intellectual powers. In short, the experience of 'Seligkeit' inspires man's mind to penetrate speculatively the empirical content causing the experience until the rational core within the content has been made explicit, correlatively the inner rationality of revelation can only be made explicit to man's intellect, first of all by his sensuously experiencing it. This is achieved insofar as revelation inspires man's mind to speculate on the content of revelation. 'Es ist nicht wahr, daß Spekulationen über diese Dinge [d.h. über Offenbarung] jemals Unheil gestiftet, und der bürgerlichen Gesellschaft nachteilig geworden. . . . Vielmehr sind dergleichen Spekulationen − mögen sie im einzeln doch ausfallen, wie sie wollen − unstreitig die *schicklichsten* Übungen des menschlichen Verstandes überhaupt, solange das menschliche Herz überhaupt höchstens nur vermögend ist, die Tugend wegen ihrer ewigen glückseligen Folgen zu lieben' (*Erziehung*, VIII, 611, §§ 78−79). Similarly Lessing maintains that, in contradiction to the criticism of rationalists, the Bible has for seventeen hundred years helped 'de[m] menschlichen Verstand' (VIII, 607, § 66) by exercising it. But once man has had his intellectual powers stimulated by the contents of revelation in their empirical form, it becomes the reciprocal function of man's activated reason to begin to illuminate the rationality hidden in revelation, i.e., to transform 'geoffenbarte Wahrheiten' into 'Vernunftswahrheiten'. 'Die Offenbarung hatte seine [d.h. des Offenbarungsvolks] Vernunft geleitet, und nun erhellte die Vernunft auf einmal seine Offenbarung. Das war der erste wechselseitige Dienst, den beide einander leisteten . . .' (VIII, 600, §§ 36−37). In other words, the more man is inspired to exercise his reason on the *Buchstabe* of revelation in an attempt to understand its *Geist,* the more he will become aware of himself as acting 'geistig'. Since there is an identity between thinking and wanting, man is simultaneously purified as he is enlightened and enlightened as he is purified. The more man cognizes the good, the more he will want it, and the more he wants it the more he will strive to cognize it. 'Der Verstand will schlechterdings an geistigen Gegenständen geübt sein, wenn er zu seiner völligen Aufklärung gelangen, und diejenige Reinigkeit des Herzens hervorbringen soll, die uns, die Tugend um ihrer selbst willen zu lieben, fähig macht. Oder soll das menschliche Geschlecht auf diese höchste Stufen der Aufklärung und Renigkeit nie kommen? Nie?' (VIII, 611, §§ 80—81).

This concept of the perfective reciprocity between *Geist* (the rational) and *Buchstabe* (the empirico-historical) wherein the rational content of the *Buchstabe* is determined by its perfective effect on the human self and the perfective *Geist* is only mediated to man *via* the *Buchstabe* constitute the formal essence of Lessing's reconciliation of the rationalistic and empiricistic paradigms and provided him with a methodology enabling him to think speculatively about the theological (and dramaturgical, for that matter) problems facing him.[34] Lessing had faith in the ultimate rationality and hence goodness of reality. The source and cause of reality is God. Therefore, the ultimate object of Lessing's enlightened faith was, of course, God. Whereas there have been many arguments as to the nature of God according to Lessing, nevertheless there is agreement enough concerning the meaning or function of God for Lessing. Israel S. Stamm writes: 'Lessing's philosophy is a species of Natural Religion (Deism). Its focus is a God, not sharply defined, but representing in general the Providential order of the world.'[35] Whereas Stamm has failed to penetrate deeply enough Lessing's concept of God, he has nevertheless pinpointed the *Geist* of the meaning of God for Lessing. The function of God for Lessing is a guarantee that man will reach the highest stages of moral perfection, i.e., the obtainment of a self-consciousness so that the self 'das Gute tun wird, weil es das Gute ist'. The metaphysical structure of God, i.e., whether he is an immanent principle of the cosmos or a transcendent educator of man, constitutes no more than the ontological *Buchstabe*. Nevertheless the nature of this *Buchstabe* will now be briefly investigated.

D. EXCURSUS: LESSING'S CONCEPT OF GOD

As mentioned above, Lessing had faith in the ultimate meaning of reality. However much the history of man might appear to be merely a series of random events leading nowhere, or even evincing regression, Lessing did not, could not, and would not lose belief that there is an inner rationality ordering such events so as to achieve man's moral perfection. Lessing called this *telos* informing history providence. The metaphysical source for providence was, of course, designated by Lessing as God. But is Lessing's God just an immanent principle — world reason — monistically united with the world (for example, similar to Spinoza's *natura naturans* and *nature naturata*) or is God an ontologically distinct being (*vis* — the traditional Christian concept)? Equally important, what determines God's relationship to the world? Is the created world, for example, an arbitrary manifestation of the divine will or necessary expression of the divine intellect? In order to decide these questions it will be necessary first of all to determine the metaphysical relationship between God and the world for Lessing. It will be my contention that Lessing's answer to such a problem falls within the rationalistic paradigm and is, indeed, in a sense quite conservative. This can be shown in the manner in which Lessing treats the metaphysical problem of existence and essence.

It will be recalled that in Chapter 2 Christian Wolff's philosophy was treated as a metaphysics of essence and in Chapter 3 such a metaphysics was shown to have developed problems and anamolies. For Wolff and his school *being* is constituted by essence. Essence constitutes the distinction between being and non-being and is that which imparts intelligibility, 'rationem contineat ceterorum, quae constanter insunt, vel inesse possunt, cum alias non posset dici radix propietatum et actionum, unde scilicet istae oriantur'.[36] Essence is, so to speak, the 'stuff' out of which reality is constructed. To be is to be rational. However, Wolff was very much aware that the mere possibility of any given essence or essence-complex does not necessarily entail the existence of such essentiality. In some way possibility and actuality differ. Real being is possibility *plus* something extra — namely *existence.* Wolff nominally defined existence as the compliment of possibility (in German as 'die Ergänzung der Möglichkeit'.) Of what does this compliment consist? Given Wolff's analysis of being, existence is but a type of essence. In specific, existence belongs to the essential category of modes, i.e., it entails those features of essentiality which are not deducible from the *essentialia* or defining intelligibility of an entity. When pressed to clarify this concept, Wolff simply identified existence with determinateness or concreteness. An actual being is one that possesses all its possible predicates or is totally determined, whereas a merely possible being only possesses defining features but not the myriad of particular predicates that constitute the actuality of an individual. Since no possible finite being (or any possible series of such beings) contains in its essential structure the sufficient reason for possessing the predicate of existence, this reason must be sought in ontologically distinct being which in turn contains the reason for its existence. Such being was called God by Wolff. God, therefore, was the ontological source for the essential structure and existence of the Enlightenment world.

The Wolffian analysis of existence was by no means universally accepted in the course of the eighteenth century. Kant pointed out that possible beings can be just as determinate as actual ones and concluded that existence and essence belong to two different realms. Kant's distinction between essence and existence was one of the central ingredients in the crisis of his pre-critical thinking. Lessing too was aware of the Wolffian position of existence. However, unlike Kant, Lessing does not distinguish between the two categories, rather he reduces existence completely to essence and thereby established the basis for a metaphysical monism of sorts. In this sense Lessing was philosophically more conservative than Kant.

Lessing discusses the problem of existence in *Über die Wirklichkeit der Dinge außer Gott* within the context of the problem of God's relationship to the world of things. Wolffian philosophers (including Mendelssohn) had expressed the metaphysical difference between God and finite things in the statement that (finite) things exist *outside of God* (of divine being) and not 'in' Him. In other words, God and the universe of things constitute different and distinct substances. Further, the notion of existence as the compliment of possibility was the ontological basis for concluding to the 'Wirklichkeit der Dinge außer Gott'. Lessing opposed this contention with the counterthesis: '[A] lles . . . existiert in Gott' (*Ü.W.D.G.*, VII, 305). What exactly Lessing meant by the preposition 'in' is not explicitly stated. He did not mean that the world is *in* God as water is *in* a glass. This is metaphorically the Wolffian position and expresses a dualistic interpretation of the relationship between God and the World. I believe that Lessing used the preposition 'in' as applying to the ontological realm in a manner similar to its application in logic. In other words, as the conclusion (and hence rationality) of a syllogism is (contained) *in* the premises, so is the ontological reality of 'things' (contained) *in* God's very reality (i.e., in the essential rationality of His being). Just as the content of a syllogistic conclusion is constructed out of the content of the premises, similarly is the reality of things constituted in someway by the reality of God. Lessing discusses this problem in the terms of divine consciousness. Reality as a cognitive object of divine consciousness is called a 'Begriff'. The Wolffians in order to substantiate their contention must show that the 'Wirklichkeit' (or existence) of things is (or can possess) something whose reality is other than the reality of the 'Begriffe' of the divine mind. Conversely, should the reality of things be no other than the reality of the thought content of the divine mind, then things must exist *in* God. Lessing writes:

'Ich mag mir die Wirklichkeit der Dinge außer Gott erklären, wie ich will, so muß ich bekennen, daß ich mir keinen Begriff davon machen kann.

'Man nenne sie das Komplement der Möglichkeit; so frage ich: ist von diesem Komplemente der Möglichkeit in Gott ein Begriff, oder keiner? Wer wird das Letztere behaupten wollen? Ist aber ein Begriff davon in ihm; so ist die Sache selbst in ihm; so sind alle Dinge in ihm selbst wirklich.

'Aber, wird man sagen, der Begriff, welchen Gott von der Wirklichkeit eines Dinges hat, hebt die Wirklichkeit dieses Dinges außer ihm nicht auf. Nicht? So muß die Wirklichkeit außer ihm etwas haben, was sie von der Wirklichkeit in seinen Begriffe unterscheidet. Das ist: in der Wirklichkeit außer ihm muß etwas sein, wovon Gott keinen Begriff hat. Eine Ungereimtheit! Ist aber nichts dergleichen, ist in dem Begriffe, den Gott von der Wirklichkeit eines Dinges hat, alles zu finden, was in dessen Wirklichkeit ihm anzutreffen: so sind beide Wirklichkeiten eins, und alles, was außer Gott existieren soll, existiert in Gott (*Ü.W.D.G.,* VII, 305).

Thus it becomes evident that the relationship between the world and God for Lessing is similar to the relationship between a thought object ('Begriff') and the divine thinking of this object. As thought, objects are related to the 'Wirklichkeit' of God.

The Wolffians had contended however that the reality or existence of things was identical with their being totally determined. Lessing does not deny this, only he does not see where such a contention can be the basis for the proof of the reality of things outside of God:

'Oder man sage: *die Wirklichkeit eines Dinges sei der Inbegriff aller möglichen Bestimmungen, die ihm zukommen können.* Muß nicht dieser Inbegriff auch in der Idee Gottes sein? Welche Bestimmung hat das Wirkliche außer ihm, wenn nicht auch das Urbild in Gott zu finden wäre? Folglich ist dieses Urbild das Ding selbst, und sagen, daß das Ding auch außer diesem Urbild existiere, heißt, dessen Urbild auf eine eben so unötige als ungereimte Weise verdoppeln' (VII, 305–306).

What is the purpose for contending that things exist outside of God? The reason for this, Lessing notes, is that thinkers want to be able to distinguish between God and the world. 'Ich glaube zwar, die Philosophen sagen, von einem Dinge die Wirklichkeit außer Gott bejahen, heiße weiter nichts, als dieses Ding bloß von Gott unterscheiden, und dessen Wirklichkeit von einer andern Art zu sein erklären, als die notwendige Wirklichkeit Gottes ist' (VII, 306). The essence of rationality is necessity and that which constitutes God in his reality is 'Notwendigkeit' or the 'notwendige Wirklichkeit Gottes'. Traditional theism (of which Wolff's theology is representative) conceives of reality (divine and finite) as dualistically divideable, i.e., God and the world constitute at least two different and separate substances. Concerning the theological thinking of traditional theism, Charles Hawthorne and William L. Reese write: 'The method here is this: taking each pair of ultimate contraries, such as one and many, permanence and change, being and becoming, necessity and contingency, the self-sufficient or nonrelative versus the dependent or relative, the actual versus the potential, one decides in each case which member of the pair is good or admirable and then attributes it (in some supremely excellent or transcendent form) to deity, while wholly denying the contrasting term [to the world]. What we propose to call "classical theism" is, in the West, the chief product of this method . . . [Classical] theism admits the reality of plurality, potentiality, becoming-as a secondary form of existence "outside" God, in no way constitute of his reality . . .'[37] Lessing for his part is willing to grant that the metaphysical contingency or 'Zufälligkeit' constitutes the essence of 'things', but he does not see why this should lead a thinker to conclude that such things are 'außer Gott'. The 'Wirklichkeit' of 'Zufälligkeit' as a mode of existence too must be identical with the reality of God's 'Begriffe' and therefore contingency must also be 'in' God.

'Wenn [Philosophen] bloß dieses wollen, warum sollen nicht die Begriffe, die Gott von den wirklichen Dingen hat, diese wirklichen Dinge selbst sein? Sie sind von Gott noch immer genugsam unterschieden, und ihre Wirklichkeit wird darum noch nichts weniger als notwendig, weil sie in ihm wirklich sind. Denn müßte nicht der Zufälligkeit, die sie außer ihm haben sollte, auch in seiner Idee ein Bild entsprechen? Und dieses Bild ist nur ihre Zufälligkeit selbst. Was außer Gott zufällig ist, wird auch in Gott zufällig sein, oder Gott müßte von dem Zufälligen außer ihm keinen Begriff haben. —Ich brauche dieses *außer ihm*, so wie man es gemeiniglich zu brauchen pflegt, um aus der Anwendung zu zeigen, daß man es nicht brauchen sollte.

'Aber, wird man schreien: Zufälligkeiten in dem unveränderlichen Wesen Gottes annehmen! —Nun? Bin ich es allein, der dieses tut? Ihr selbst, die ihr Gott Begriffe von zufälligen Dingen beilegen müßt, ist euch nie beigefallen, daß Begriffe von zufälligen Dingen zufällige Begriffe sind?' (*Ü.W.D.G.,* VII, 306).

Lessing's opinion here is anything but definitely expressed and philosophically clear. However, so much seems certain: Lessing, in contradiction to Spinoza, is contending that the reality of contingency, mutability, finiteness, time, becoming, and particularity or, in short, the reality of the empirico-historical is in someway existent *in* God. Lessing is willing to distinguish between the world and God, but not to the degree that he is willing to allow for the reality of things outside of God. In some sense, it is valid, in my judgment, to conclude that Lessing conceived of God in a pan*en*theistic manner.[38] Whether this panentheism excludes the possibility of a transcendent revelation or not will be discussed presently.

The reality of the world is *in* God or identical with God's 'Begriffe'. But what is the nature of the relationship between God's 'Begriffe' and his own cognizing being. Lessing did not analyze this relationship in *Über die Wirklichkeit.* Given the terminology Lessing was using, I contend that it is plausible to conclude that the ontological matter, so to speak, out of which God's 'Begriffe' are made, is none other than God's very own reality. For instance, Lessing makes statements such as: 'Zufälligkeiten *in dem unveränderlichen Wesen Gottes* annehmen!' and 'Muß nicht dieser Inbegriff *auch in der Idee Gottes sein?*' Phrases such as *in dem unveränderlichen Wesen Gottes* and *in der Idee Gottes sein* certainly suggest that the reality of 'Begriffe' is in some sense the reality of God as thinking being. This contention is substantiated by Jacobi's report of his conversation with Lessing wherein Lessing stated: 'Die orthodoxen Begriffe von der Gottheit sind nicht mehr für mich; ich kann sie nicht genießen. *Hen kai pan!* Ich weiß nichts anders' (*J.G.L.,* VIII, 618).[39] Further light can be cast upon Lessing's meaning by referring to paragraph 73 of the *Erziehung* and in particular to *Das Christentum der Vernunft.* Before doing so, I should like to give some speculative background to my interpretation of these statements.

It will be recalled that in Chapter 2 Descartes' grounding of the rationalistic paradigm was discussed. Because Descartes had by means of his universal doubt cut himself off from any self-manifesting (objective) being, he had to ground the source of all apodicity upon his famous *cogito, ergo sum.* The principle of all apodictic knowledge was for Descartes contained in this indubitable intuition. The mind can doubt an objective content, but it cannot doubt the reality of itself. Descartes encountered reality when he discovered his *sum*. But what constitutes the *esse* (i.e., 'existence') as the ontological as well as grammatical root of the *sum*. Descartes' self is an undeniably existing *res cogitans*. However, the question must be raised concerning how the Cartesian self's existence differs from its essence or how its *real* being differs from its *essential* being? The answer is by no means easy to ascertain. As Etienne Gilson has pointed out, Descartes treats existence as a primitive notion about which speculation is not very helpful.[40] Descartes could not see (nor would his implicit principle of identity allow him to see) any *real* distinction between existence and essence. At the most they are only modes of the same ontological unity. 'In quo manifestum mihi videtur essentiam et existentiam nullo modo distingui.'[41] Indeed, since the predicate *sum* is only given in and through the subject *cogito*, it is hard to avoid the conclusion that *existential* being for Descartes is but a determination of *essential* being, i.e., a type of essence. Briefly I should like to suggest what I think is implicit in Descartes' principle of identity when applied to the *cogito, ergo sum* foundation of his metaphysics. What is to be suggested is admittedly speculative.

Descartes is seeking reality. His mind continually focuses itself on this or that allegedly objective truth and doubts it. At this stage in the cognitive process there is no self-consciousness and no encountering reality. But in the repeated mental acts of doubting, an awareness of the thinking activity is slowly developed in the mind, i.e., the acting self becomes present to itself as acting (via doubting). This presence entails logically first an awareness of thinking, i.e., the underlying activity of *cogitare* is made explicitly known. This specific type of activity constitutes the essence of the Cartesian self. Now mental activity *qua* a species of change always entails a *terminus ab quo* and a *terminus ad quem*. The *terminus ad quem* of mental activity is reality or real essence. The *terminus ab quo* − 'the mental movement towards reality' or the 'tendency to become aware of being' − is what is meant grammatically by the first person or metaphysically by the self. When the *cogitare* is, so to speak, conjugated by consciousness as the *(ego cogit-o*, i.e., when the *cogitare*-movement becomes reflectively aware of itself as a *terminus ad quem*, it simultaneously becomes aware of itself as a *terminus ab quo* or, more simply, self-consciousness is generated since the *ad quem* and *ab quo* are identical. This very self-consciousness sees itself as the *necessary* condition for the activity of doubting any allegedly objective *terminus ad quem*. And this self-seeing is precisely what is meant by the *sum*. In other words, the 'exist' of 'I exist' (*sum*) is identical with the content of reflective awareness. The *sum* differs *modally* from the thinking process in that the *cogitare*-activity does not necessarily require an explicit or conscious recognition of itself. The *sum* does not differ really from the *cogitare*-activity in that it is a constituitive though implicit ingredient of the activity and can be made explicitly known in an act of self-reflection. Grammatically speaking, when the *cogitare* is conjugated to become the *cogito*, the *ego* becomes self-aware or, indeed, in a sense, it is generated and this self-awareness constitutes precisely its *sum*. This interpretation is admittedly idealistic. But in my judgment not only is a *sum* contained in Decartes' *cogito*, but also a *Hegelius est*.

Before utilizing the above interpretation of Descartes to illuminate Lessing's own speculations, it must be noted that Descartes' *cogito, ergo sum* was applied by him basically to the isolated individual. He did not use it to illucidate the nature of God. Indeed, Descartes' concept of God is quite traditional. Whether this traditional notion is logically consistent with his metaphysical premises, is a different problem and one that will not be discussed here. Suffice it to note that Spinoza thought that it was not. However, such a line of reasoning can be applied to an analysis of God and His relationship to the world. The important point is that essence and existence are in effect for this line of reasoning two aspects of the same basic unity. The common element linking the two concepts is mentality, ideality, or subjectivity. Concerning the central message of Descartes' philosophy M. Kronenberg writes: 'Hierin also liegt die große Entdeckung Descartes', in der Einsicht: alles Sein ist gegründet auf das Bewußt-Sein, der stete Punkt aller "Wirklichkeit" ist nicht das Objektive, sondern die reine Subjektivität, der Ausgangspunkt aller Erkenntnis ist nicht die Natur, sondern das Ich. . . . [D]er ganze deutsche Idealismus, kann man sagen, zu dessen Entwicklung Descartes hier den ersten Anstoß gegeben, ist eine forschreitende Enthüllung des Wesens der intellektuellen Anschauung [here self-intuition] und des Ich, und eine forschreitende Unterwerfung des Objektiven unter das reine Ich, unter die, intuitiv erfaßte, reine Subjektivät.'[42] And for Kronenberg, Lessing is one step in this philosophical development from Descartes to German Idealism. At any rate, *Sein* as a function of *Bewußt-Sein* is the central legacy of Descartes' to subsequent philosophy. Existence denotes a 'being cognized' or a 'being thought' or, simply, 'being the object of awareness'. In other words, essence as possibility becomes actual when it is *being* thought or being the object of consciousness. Therefore, that which distinguishes real from the possible being is the mental activity of the Ego as it posits ('vorstellen') a possible thought content as an actual object of awareness. This line of thinking is certainly implied in Lessing's identification of the 'Wirklichkeit der Dinge' with the 'Wirklichkeit' of the 'Begriffe' as they are *in* God, i.e., as they are in the thought-objects of His mind. This implies that the 'reality' of the universe of things is constituted by being the thought content of the divine mind. All that needs to be added in order to have a theory of cosmogenesis or of 'creation' is the notion that the *cogito, ergo sum*-thesis is first and foremost valid for the divine self. In other words, God's own reality or existence is generated in and by an act of self-reflection and since the reality of the world is identical with the reality of the thought-content (the 'Begriffe') of God's mind, God simultaneously generates the reality of the world by thinking Himself in some manner. God is, in short, self-conscious rationality and hence the world as objectified divine subjectivity is rationality incarnated. Such an application of the rationalistic paradigm to the problem of cosmosgenesis is evident in Lessing's *Das Christentum der Vernunft.*

In the section on Lessing's *ars dialectice cogitandi* I discussed in some detail the nature of divine psychology as developed in *C.V.* It was shown that God for Lessing is essentially a mental movement to become aware of the rationality of itself, i.e., of itself as acting perfectly. This movement towards self-awareness, towards the manifestation of subjectivity to subjectivity, was called God the Father by Lessing and as an impulse it underlies both the 'creation' of the world and the generation of God the Son as the thought contents of divine thinking. The key metaphysical assumption grounding Lessing's conclusion is the doctrine of the identity of thinking, wanting, and creating. 'Vorstellen, wollen und schaffen ist bei Gott eines. Man kann also sagen, alles, was sich Gott vorstellet, alles das schafft er auch' (*C.V.*, VII, 197, § 3). Thielicke has sought to disarm the monistic implications of such a statement by pointing out that the notion of creation is totally absent in and foreign to the monistic pantheism of Spinoza.[43] This is absolutely true. Lessing was not a Spinozist in any strict sense. When Jacobi said: 'Aber in Spinoza steht mein Credo nicht', Lessing answered: 'Ich will hoffen, es steht in keinem Buch' (*J.G.L.*, VIII, 621). Certainly Lessing's

Credo is not to be identified *in toto* with Spinoza's or anybody's. If 'schaffen' or creation by God be defined in part as God's imparting of 'Wirklichkeit' to the universe of things (and I do not see what objection Thielicke could have to such a definition) and if the 'Wirklichkeit der Dinge' is identical for Lessing with the thought content (the 'Begriffe') of God's mind, then creating is for Lessing no more than the very act of thinking whereby the 'Begriffe' of things are thought(-objects). In other words, the concept of creation (i.e., the making actual of existence) receives for Lessing its intelligibility from the notion of thinking. Correlatively, if thinking is creating for God, then a thought as a 'Vorstellung' of thinking is creation, for as Lessing says, 'um es nochmals zu wiederholen, jeder Gedanke ist bei Gott eine Schöpfung' (*C.V.*, VII, 198, § 13).

'Vorstellen' or 'schaffen' is not an arbitrary or random activity of the divine mind. The divine mind is structured so as to pursue highest rationality and rationality as a principle of volition is called 'Vollkommenheit'. Furthermore, since the infinite perfection is divine rationality, then the divine self must of necessity think itself. This the divine can and does actually do in two possible ways. 'Gott kann sich nur auf zweierlei Art denken; entweder er denkt alle seine Vollkommenheiten auf einmal, und sich als den Inbegriff derselben; oder er denkt seine Vollkommenheiten zerteilt, eine von der andern abgesondert, und jede von sich selbst nach Graden abgeteilt' (VII, 197, § 4). Insofar as God thinks his infinite perfection in an undivided manner he in effect 'creates' God the Son as a thought-object. 'Gott dachte sich von Ewigkeit her in aller seiner Vollkommenheit; das ist, Gott schuf sich von Ewigkeit her ein Wesen, welchem keine Vollkommenheit mangelte, die er selbst besaß. Dieses Wesen nennt die Schrift den *Sohn Gottes,* oder welches noch besser sein würde, den *Sohn Gott.* Einen *Gott,* weil ihm keine von den Eigenschaften fehlt, die Gott zukommen. Einen *Sohn*, weil unserm Begriffe nach dasjenige, was sich etwas vorstellt, vor der Vorstellung eine gewisse Priorität zu haben scheint' (VII, 197, §§ 5–6). Whereas Thielicke has noted that Spinoza never uses the term 'creation' to refer to the relationship between God and the world as proof of a possible theistic meaning of the term 'schaffen' for Lessing, he neglects to note that Christianity traditionally would never apply the term 'creation' to the Second Person of the Trinity, all of which certainly implies a deviation on Lessing's part from traditional Christianity. The only way in which the term 'creation' applied to God the Son would have any meaning for Lessing, given the fact that God the Son is identical with God the Father, is to interpret the term to denote self-thought. Also, it should be noted that Lessing does not refer to the Son of God as Christ — the God-Man. Even in paragraph 73 of the *Erziehung*, the term 'Son of God' is explicitly used as a metaphorical name for the special type of duality contained within the transcendental unity of God. Lessing is careful never unequivocably to deny the divinity of Christ as the Son of God. He simply brackets this thesis as a possibility or as something irrelevant to the point he wants to make and proceeds to treat Christ as a *human* teacher (cf. *G.ü.H.*, VII, 190; *Erziehung*, VIII, 606, § 59; and *R.C.*, VIII, 538, § 1). Lessing does not treat the doctrine of the trinity as a permanent revealed mystery about God, but as a 'vorgespiegelte Vernunftswahrheit' (cf. *Erziehung*, VIII, 608, § 72), i.e., as a speculative truth derived through reflecting upon a metaphorically expressed doctrine. I shall not investigate Lessing's trinitarian doctrine any further. What is of importance for Lessing's concept of the relationship between the world and God is Lessing's thesis that God the Son is God the Father's 'vollständige Vorstellung [d.h. Gedanke] von sich selbst . . ., d.i. eine Vorstellung, in der sich alles befindet, was in ihm selbst ist' (*Erziehung*, VIII, 609, § 73). In short, God the Son is but a thought-object of God the Father's *thinking* of Himself.

God can also think his infinite perfection in a divided manner and hence Himself as divided in the universe of things. 'Gott dachte seine Vollkommenheiten zerteilt, das ist, er schaffte Wesen, wovon jedes etwas von seinen Vollkommenheiten hat; denn, um es nochmals zu wiederholen, jeder Gedanke ist bei Gott eine Schöpfung. Alle diese [gedachten] Wesen zusammen heißen die Welt?' (*Axiomata*, VIII, 198–199, §§ 13–14. Although Lessing does not state it explicitly, he should have also called the world of things God the Son. God the Son as undivided infinity is but God the Father's infinite perfection as a thought-object. Since the universe is God the Father's divided infinity as a thought-object, the world has equal logical claim to being God the Son *qua* being a thought-object. Of course, there is a difference between God the Son and the World, namely the difference of being undivided and divided. But both are metaphysically identical in being 'Vorstellungen' of God's subjective being to Himself as objective being. In paragraph 6 Lessing states that the term 'Sohn' can be applied to undivided God as a thought object simply because this content of consciousness has been 'vorgestellt'. However, being 'vorgestellt' is equally true of the world of things and hence this world must in some sense be the 'Sohn Gottes' or a 'Gott

Sohn'. Lessing should have stated that God the Father has two 'God the *Sons*'.

The above analysis has shown that at least from the time of *Das Christentum der Vernunft* to the time of *Gespräche mit Jacobi* Lessing's concept of the relationship of God to the World was in some sense monistic. In my judgment, the term 'pan*en*theistic' would perhaps be the most accurate one to describe Lessing's philosophical theology. In the light of this analysis, Lessing's statements to Jacobi that the orthodox conception of God was no longer acceptable to him and that he knew only the doctrine of *Hen kai pan* must be taken seriously. Lessing consistently rejected the orthodox conception of God in at least three respects. First of all, the orthodox contended that God created the world *ex nihilo*, not *ex deo*. The universe of things is not, for traditional Christianity metaphysically identical with God's own self-thought. The world is not divided divinity and it is accordingly false to call created beings 'gleichsam eingeschränkte Götter'. The universe and particularly man was, of course for the orthodox, created *in the image* of God. But this doctrine implied no ontological identity between finite and infinite being. For Lessing finite being is somehow limited infinite being in that creation is *ex deo*. For Christianity the finite being is the finite and hence radically other than infinite being. The idea (implicit in Lessing's *C.V.*) that the world is the Son of God or God the Son and therefore equal in value and total perfection to the Second Person of the Trinity is blasphemy for the orthodox. This thesis leads to the second major difference in Lessing's concept of God from that of the orthodox. For the orthodox, because finite reality is ontologically other or distinct from God, God is in no way *necessitated* to create it. 'Creation' is for Christianity a free and gracious gift of God. God could have *not* created the world and have remained perfected within the fullness of his inifinite Being. For Lessing, on the other hand, the universe as divine being must be thought and hence created by God. Lessing's God must of necessity penetrate the rationality of Himself in a divided manner, i.e., as the world. There is no freedom involved in God's creation of the world for Lessing, just perfective necessity, i.e., rationality. A third deviation from the orthodox concept of God flowing from the notion of the identity of man's reality with the reality of God's self-thought is Lessing's concept of the ultimate perfection of man. For traditional Christianity man's highest perfection is the contemplation after death of the undivided, infinite, and immutable perfection that is God. God as the ontological 'other' is the direct object of perfection. On the other hand, man as 'gleichsam ein eingeschränkter Gott' has for Lessing as the direct object of his ultimate perfection the awareness of himself. Just as God for Lessing seeks to become aware of Himself, so too does Lessing's mankind seek moral self-consciousness as the *eschaton* of his existence.

The overwhelming evidence is that Lessing's concept of God is monistic and a manifestation of the rationalistic paradigm. Does this concept exclude the possibility of transcendent activity by God, particular in the form of historical revelation? The gist of my analysis of Lessing's concept of revelation is that transcendent revelation is accepted by Lessing as a possibility. Certainly the line of argument in the *Erziehung* is that God in some way imparts to man an educative 'Richtungsstoß' to achieve higher levels of perfection than man would otherwise be able to by means of his own unaided powers. Whereas Lessing's theology has shown itself metaphysically to be monistic, it nevertheless deviates from monism (at least of the Spinozian variety) in two important respects.

The first major difference from monism such as Spinoza's lies in Lessing's notion of individuality. Lessing was aware that the reason for the thesis concerning 'die Wirklichkeit der Dinge außer Gott' being posited lies in the desire of philosophers to be able to distinguish between God and the world, Lessing at no time wanted to erase this distinction and he obviously felt that his theological position in no way did this. If Lessing had been a strict Spinozian monist, he would have talked about finite entities as modes of the divine being. This he does not do. Instead, Lessing uses the Leibnizian concept of finite entities or 'einfache Wesen' (cf. *C.V.*, VII, 199, § 20, and *D.S.M.*, VII, 576, § 1). Therefore, despite being 'gleichsam eingeschränkter Gott', man is also 'ein einfaches Wesen' distinct and differing from all other such simple beings. Lessing's universe is not just *one* ontological substance as it was for Spinoza, but a universe of multitudes of distinct substances as it was for Leibniz. By implication, then, God should be a simple though albeit infinite being. If this is so, then God is distinct from or transcends the world and hence theoretically at least can be the source of transcendent revelation.

The separateness of God from the world can also be gleaned from Lessing's trinitarian doctrine. For a strict panentheism (as for German Idealism), reality as a totality is bi-polar. Infinitude and finitude, eternity and time, being and becoming, or, in short, God and the World are two aspects of one overriding unity. From this point of view, the World is the *only* begotten Son of God. In other words, the trinitarian structure is seen as applicable to God, the World, and their interrelationship as a single totality. There can be for this view no undivided God the Son. God the Father is infinite unity and God the Son (the World) is infinite diversity and both constitute only one totality. Since God and the World are ontological correlatives constituting one substantial unity, the metaphysical possibility for transcendent revelation is rendered null. There can be no revelation from a source transcendent to the world, because there is no such divine source. This type of concept is implicit in Lessing's notion that the world is God divided infinitely. The world would be just the correlative and necessary compliment of God the Father. However, Lessing also posits God the Son as a reality distinct from the world and making a totality with God the Father.[44] In other words, Lessing's theology retains or conserves the traditional Christian position that God is a complete trinity of three persons, though at the same time it affirms an immanental and monistic position that God and the World are ontological correlatives. There is some evidence that Lessing might have been moving towards a purer monistic position at the end of his life. In his conversation with Jacobi Lessing apparently expressed dislike for the concept of an immutable and infinitely perfected God. Jacobi writes: 'Mit der Idee eines persönlichen schlechterdings unendlichen Wesens, in dem unveränderlichen Genusse seiner allerhöchsten Vollkommenheit, konnte sich Lessing nicht vertragen. Er verknüpfte mit derselben eine solche Vorstellung von *unendlicher Langerweile*, daß ihm angst und weh dabei wurde' (*J.G.L.*, VIII, 630). Such a God as Lessing now disdains fits perfectly the description of a God who thinks and contemplates his infinite but *undivided* perfections in one all-embracing and unending intuition 'von Ewigkeit her'. In other words, God the Son of both the *C.V.* and the *Erziehung* corresponds to the 'Idee eines persönlichen schlechterdings unendlichen Wesens, in dem unveränderlichen Genusse seiner allerhöchsten Vollkommenheit'. Perhaps, if Lessing had lived longer he would have developed a dynamic panentheism similar to Herder's. Nevertheless, as long as God was conceived by Lessing as somehow constituting a unity as undivided perfection in contradistinction to the divided nature of the world, the metaphysical basis for transcendent activity by God is grounded.

6. Summary and conclusions

The examination of Lessing's philosophical interpretation of God has revealed still further inconsistencies in Lessing's theology. Those who accept the monistic implications in Lessing's conversation with Jacobi, in his *Christentum der Vernunft* and in his *Über die Wirklichkeit der Dinge außer Gott* as the true 'esoteric' core of Lessing's thought must and do seek to reduce to a mere 'esoteric' shell the myriads of Lessing's statements wherein he seems to accept the possibility if not actuality of transcendent activity by God. However, as just has been shown, even a monistic interpretation of Lessing's strictly philosophical statements about God and the world, does not exclude the metaphysical possiblity of God being transcendent.

This is, perhaps, a contradiction, but nevertheless part of Lessing's theological reflections. On the other hand, those who accept Lessing's apparently sincere interest in Christianity and his equally apparent acceptance of some kind of transcendent influence of God *via* revelation must and do seek to deny or interpret away the monistic statements made by Lessing. Both lines of reasoning rest upon the assumption that Lessing's thinking (at least in his final years) was consistent and relatively systematic. It is my contention that Lessing's philosophy and theological speculations were never fully consistent. Lessing's thinking was caught on the horns of a cognitive crisis. The *Geist* of Lessing's thinking is derived from a practical application of the rationalistic paradigm, i.e., man's destiny for Lessing is to become aware of himself as morally perfected. Insofar as man develops a moral self-consciousness, he becomes aware of the rationality of his being. Such a self-consciousness is only possible if man's intellect is fully developed and functioning, i.e., only if man can cognize the rationality of being, can he begin to become aware of his moral destiny as a manifestation of the rationality of being. This is also the beginning of Lessing's problems. *De facto* man is cognitively weak. The rationality of reality is, objectively speaking, only a fully intelligible spectacle to the infinite mind of God. *De facto* man's intellect is 'nicht deutlich genug' aware and hence his consciousness is 'sinnlich'. How is such a being to know the truth that perfects and, indeed, what is this truth? These were the two central questions of Lessing's life. In my judgment, Lessing was never fully able to solve his cognitive problems and hence he was never fully able to ascertain apodictically the Truth (or all of the Truth). What Lessing knew with certainty, i.e., what he knew with the certainty of his faith in the rationality of reality, was that truth must perfect man. Given this premise, Lessing speculated, constructed hypothesies, developed new thought-models, anything to overcome his cognitive crisis. Lessing was willing to examine and find some acceptable truth in most diverse and contradictory generative paradigms for reconciling eternity and time, or the metaphysical and the historical. At the same time, Lessing could not relinquish the rationalistic paradigm and hence tried to transform 'geoffenbarte Wahrheiten' into 'Vernunfswahrheiten'. The result was *not* a consistent philosophy or theology. Lessing conceived God both as an immanent principle and as a transcendent reality. This is a fundamental contradiction. There is no way, in my judgment, to reconcile fully Lessing's sincere interest in and partial acceptance of Christianity and his sincere interest in and partial acceptance of rationalistic philosophy. The unity of Lessing's thought lies in his attempt to discover truth perfective of man in each paradigmatic position. Such positions are no more than the *Buchstabe* (the term is here taken in the broadest sense as a means for an end) of Lessing's thought. The *Geist* and hence value of each position is the perfective truth each reveals to man, i.e., its ability to develop in man the awareness of the rationality and hence truth of his own being. Insofar as man becomes morally improved through his belief in the objective content of any position, that position has proved its truth to that degree.[1] This is not to claim that Lessing did not seek to combine the 'acceptable truths' in each position into a consistent theory. The very nature of thinking is to seek systematic unity. It is just that Lessing did not possess adequate generative ideas to accomplish this task. The result is that Lessing's speculations show the unity that is characteristic of the crisis phase of a scientific (cognitive) revolution. Lessing's hypotheses are brilliant and imaginative, but fragmentary, tentative, and contradictory. He is, indeed, a forerunner to Idealism, but also to Existentialism. He is an ancestor to Neo-Protestantism and of extreme interest to twentieth-century Christians. Lessing is all things to thinkers of all persuasions, because he was open to any position so long as it contributed something to the 'Aufklärung' and education of mankind.

Notes

CHAPTER 1: METHODOLOGY: LESSING AS A PROBLEM

1. For a discussion of the secondary material on the subject of Lessing's theology see Karl S. Guthke, *Der Stand der Lessing Forschung: Ein Bericht über die Literatur von 1932–1962* (1965), pp. 88–95. According to Guthke, 'Die klaffensten Widersprüche der Lessing-Deutung sind in der Interpretation der theologischen Schriften zu beobachten' (p. 88).
2. This 'contradiction' will be discussed in Chapter 4 and relevant secondary sources will be given there. For a brief but sober discussion of the problem which also mentions a few secondary sources see F. Andrew Brown, *Gotthold Ephraim Lessing* (1971), pp. 144–145.
3. The 'hypothetical' nature of Lessing's theological speculations has been most forcefully and exhaustively presented by Willi Oelmüller. Indeed, Oelmüller contends that Lessing's major statements on religion are but so many 'Denkmodelle' tentatively suggested as solutions to his theological problems. See his *Unbefriedigte Aufklärung: Beiträge zu einer Theorie der Moderne von Lessing, Kant und Hegel* (1969), pp. 35–102.

A. Interpretations of Lessing's theology

4. Hans Leisegang, *Lessings Weltanschauung* (1931), p. 97.
   In opposition to this interpretation stands Leopold Zscharnack's contention: 'Lessing war kein Systematiker; er was als Theologe wie als Philosoph ein Fragmentist und Gelegenheitsdenker . . .' ('Einleitung des Herausgebers', in *Lessings Werke*, Band XX, p. 24).
5. Leisegang, *Lessings Weltanschauung*, p. 6.
6. Ibid., pp. 6–7.
7. Ibid., p. 7.
8. Von Wiese, *Lessing: Dichtung, Ästhetik, Philosophie* (1931), p. vii.
9. Mann, *Lessing: Sein und Leistung*, 2nd ed. (1961), p. 54.
10. Ibid.
11. *Lessing*, p. 151.
    For other similar interpretations see: Karl Aner, *Die Theologie der Lessing-*

zeit (1929), pp. 343–361; Gottfried Fittbogen, *Die Religion Lessings* (1923); Martin Haug, *Entwicklung und Offenbarung bei Lessing* (1928); and Karl Barth, 'Lessing', in *Protestant Thought from Rousseau to Ritschl* (1959), pp. 118–149.
Since the 1930s similar attempts to comprehend Lessing as a non-Christian in a traditional sense and as a child of the Enlightenment have been published. See Henry Allison, *Lessing and the Enlightenment* (1966); Arthus von Arx, *Lessing und die geschichtliche Welt* (1944); Lewis White Beck, *Early German Philosophy: Kant and His Predecessors* (1969), pp. 340–360; Henry Chadwick, 'Introduction', in *Lessing's Theological Writings* (1957), pp. 9–49; Paul Hazard, *European Thought in the Eighteenth Century* (1954), pp. 440–459; Friedrich Wilhelm Katzenbach, *Protestantisches Christentum im Zeitalter der Aufklärung* (1965), pp. 148–165; Leonard de Moor, 'The Problem of Revelation in Eighteenth-Century Germany: With Particular Reference to Lessing', *Evangelical Quarterly*, 39 (1967), pp. 66–74, 139–151, 205–215; and Wilm Pelters, *Lessings Standort: Sinndeutung der Geschichte als Kern seines Denkens* (1972), pp. 28–77.

12. *Lessing*, p. 138.
13. Ibid., pp. 138–139.
14. Ibid., p. 144.
15. Ibid., p. 147.
16. Aner, *Theologie der Lessingzeit*, p. 348.
17. Cf. Arx, *Lessing und die geschichtliche Welt*, p. 125.
18. Cf. Schneider, *Lessing und die monistische Weltanschauung*, p. 13.
19. Stamm, 'Lessing and Religion', *Germanic Review*, 43 (1968), 240.
20. Barth, *Protestant Thought*, p. 148.
21. Stamm, 'Lessing and Religion', pp. 246–247.
22. Loofs, 'Lessings Stellung zum Christentum', *Theologische Studien und Kritiken* (1913), pp. 31–64. For a detailed discussion of the problem of contradictions in Lessing's theological speculations and in his attempts to deal with the problem see Helmut Thielicke, *Offenbarung, Vernunft und Existenz: Studien zur Religionsphilosophie Lessings*, 3rd ed. (1957), pp. 15–57.
23. Von Wiese, *Lessing: Dichtung, Ästhetik, Philosophie*, p. 142.
24. Martin Haug has systematically used the concept of 'development' as a heuristic means to determine the relationship between Lessing's 'esoteric' and 'exoteric' thinking; cf. *Entwicklung und Offenbarung bei Lessing*, pp. 17–47. Haug comes to the following conclusion concerning the relationship between reason and revelation: '*Denn Offenbarung ist werdende, sich-entwickelnde Vernunft. Und Vernunft ist entwickelte Offenbarung.* . . . Die Wahrheiten der Religion sind in Wirklichkeit ihrem Ursprung wie ihrem Inhalt nach rein vernünftig. Sie *erscheinen* nur als Offenbarung, solange und sofern sie noch nicht von der Vernunft begriffen sind' (p. 79).
25. Koch, 'Lessing und der Irrationalismus', *Deutsche Vierteljahrsschrift für Literaturwissenschaft und Geistesgeschichte*, 6 (1928), pp. 114–143. Cf. also Arnold E. Berger, *Lessings geistesgeschichtliche Stellung* (1929).
26. Schmitz, *Lessings Stellung in der Entfaltung des Individualismus* (1941).

27. Ibid., p. 143.
28. Brüggemann, 'Lessings Bürgerdramen und der Subjektivismus als Problem', *Jahrbuch des Freien Deutschen Hochstifts* (1936), pp. 69—110.
29. Koch, 'Lessing und der Irrationalismus', p. 129.
30. Thielicke, *Offenbarung, Vernunft und Existenz*.
31. Ibid., pp. 32—36.
32. Ibid., p. 55.
33. Ibid., p. 129.
34. Ibid., p. 139.
35. In *Lessing: Sein und Leistung* (1948). Otto Mann explicitly writes: 'Lessing steht grundsätzlich auf der Seite des orthodoxen Luthertums' (p. 335). Unless otherwise noted all quotations will be taken from the second edition cited above in note 9.
36. Ibid., p. 60.
37. Ibid., p. 62.
38. Ibid., p. 318.
39. Ibid., p. 329.
40. Ibid., p. 319.
41. Ibid., pp. 7—8.
42. Oelmüller, *Die unbefriedigte Aufklärung*, pp. 35—102.
43. Ibid., p. 100.
44. Ibid., pp. 101—102.
45. Pons, *Gotthold Ephraim Lessing et le Christianisme*, p. 487.
46. Schneider, *Lessings Stellung zur Theologie vor der Herausgabe der Wolfenbüttler Fragmente*, p. 227.
47. Ibid., pp. 227—228.
48. Ibid., p. 11.
49. Durzak, 'Vernunft und Offenbarung im Denken Lessings', in *Poesie und Ratio: Vier Lessing-Studien*, pp. 106—107.
50. Schneider, *Lessings Stellung*, p. 15.
51. Guthke, *Der Stand der Lessing Forschung*, p. 95.
52. Schneider, *Lessings Stellung*, p. 13.
53. Ibid., p. 227.
54. Ibid., p. 13.
55. Guthke, *Der Stand der Lessing Forschung*, p. 99.
    Willi Oelmüller is the only non-marxist investigator, I am aware of who explicitly rejects Guthke's contention that Lessing is contradictory; cf. *Die unbefriedigte Aufklärung*, p. 297, footnote 54. Nevertheless, Oelmüller's interpretation of Lessing's thinking as an attempt to mediate between subjectivity and history substantiates, in my judgment, Guthke's thesis.
56. Ritzel, *Gotthold Ephraim Lessing*, p. 144.
57. Ibid., p. 143.
58. Ibid., pp. 154—155.
59. Wölfel, Einleitung', in *Lessings Werke*, Band II, p. 675.
60. Heller, *Dialectics and Nihilism: Essays on Lessing, Nietzsche, Mann and Kafka*, pp. 46—47.
61. Durzak, 'Vernunft und Offenbarung', p. 130.
62. Ibid., p. 133.

63. Ibid., pp. 127—128.
64. *Lessing*, p. 145.

B. *Methodology*

65. Kuhn, *The Structure of Scientific Revolutions*, 2nd ed. (1970).
66. Langer, *Philosophy in a New Key: A Study in the Symbolism of Reason, Rite, and Art* (1961), pp. 15—16. Cf. also Felix Cohn, 'What is a Question?', *The Mind* 39 (1929), 350—364.
67. 'Analysis', in Martin Heidegger, *What is a Thing* (1967), pp. 248—249.
68. In *Philosophy in a New Key* Langer writes: 'Most new discoveries are suddenly-seen things that were always there. A new idea is a light that illuminates presences which simply had no form for us before the light fell on them. . . . Such ideas as identity of matter and change of form, or as value, validity, virtue, or as outer world and inner consciousness, are not theories; they are the terms in which theories are conceived; they give rise to specific questions, and are articulated only in the form of these questions. Therefore one can call them generative ideas in the history of thought' (p. 19).
69. Lovejoy, *The Great Chain of Being: A Study of the History of an Idea* (1960), pp. 3—23.
70. In 'Humanism and the Religious Attitude' Hulme writes: 'It is possible to trace, in every man's mind, then, trains [of thought] leading in various directions, from his detailed ethical political opinions back to a few of these central attitudes. . . . These abstract categories . . . *limit* our thinking; our thought is compelled to move inside certain limits. . . . We do not [usually] see [a central attitude], but other things *through it;* and, consequently, take what we see for facts, and not for what they are — opinions based on a particular abstract valuation' (pp. 65, 66, 69).
71. Pepper, *World Hypotheses: A Study in Evidence* (1961), p. 77.
72. Ibid., p. 80.
73. Ibid., p. 91.
74. Pitirim A. Sorokin has designated the synthetic principle of unity which generates and structures a *Weltanschauung* as 'the logico-meaningful principle of integration.' Sorokin writes: The ordering element is not uniformity of relationship between the fragmentary variables, but *identity of meaning* or logical coalescense. Hidden behind the empirically different, seemingly unrelated fragments of the cultural complex lies an identity of meaning, which brings them together into consistent *styles, typical* forms, and significant *patterns.* If, therefore, *uniformity of relationship is the common denominator of causally united phenomena, in the logico-meaningful union it is identity of central meaning or idea.'* Cf. *Social and Cultural Dynamics.* Vol. 1: *Fluctuation of Forms of Art*, p. 23.
75. Kuhn, *The Structure*, pp. 67—68.
76. Ibid., p. 84.
77. Ibid., p. 85.
78. Ibid., pp. 86—87

CHAPTER 2: THE CONCEPT OF TRUTH IN THE ENLIGHTENMENT

A. The problem of certainty

1. Cassirer, *The Philosophy of the Enlightenment* (trans. 1951), p. 5.
2. Unger, *Hamann und die Aufklärung*, 2nd ed. (1925), Band I, 41.
3. Cf. John Herman Randall, Jr., *The Career of Philosophy*. Vol. 1: *From the Middle Ages to the Enlightenment* (1970), p. 382.
4. Descartes, *Rules for the Direction of the Mind'* (1628), in *The Philosophical Works of Descartes* (1968), Vol. 1, Rule IV. The secondary literature on Descartes is vast. The following are a few studies of value: E. A., Burtt, *The Metaphysical Foundations of Modern Science* (1955), pp. 105—124; Frederick Coplestone, S. J., *A History of Philosophy*, Vol. 4: *Modern Philosophy: Descartes to Leibniz* (1963), 76—160; Etienne Gilson, *The Unity of Philosophical Experience* (1937), pp. 125—220; Robert Heiss, *Der Gang des Geistes: Eine Geschichte des neuzeitlichen Denkens* (1959), pp. 30—76; John Herman Randall, Jr., *The Career of Philosophy*, Vol. 1, pp. 371—395; and Wolfgang Röd, *Descartes: Die innere Genesis des cartesianischen Systems* (1964).
5. Descartes, *'Rules for the Direction'*, Vol. I, p. 3, Rule II.
6. Gilson, *The Spirit of Medieval Philosophy* (1940), p. 61.
7. Although the nature of truth was discussed in medieval philosophy, epistemological studies, particularly as a prolegomenon to metaphysical speculation, were not developed. Indeed, for a modern Thomist such as Frederick D. Wilhelmsen, epistemology is a study of the metaphysics of knowledge rather than a study of the problem of knowing as a preliminary to constructing a metaphysics, cf. his *Man's Knowledge of Reality: An Introduction to Thomistic Epistemology* (1958), pp. 3—7.
8. Gilson, *The Spirit of Medieval Philosophy*, p. 236.
9. Heidegger, *What is a Thing?* (trans. 1967), p. 99.

B. The ego as first principle of philosophy

10. For a discussion of Descartes' rejection of sensation as an avenue to reality see Norman Kemp Smith, *New Studies in the Philosophy of Descartes* (1952), pp. 63—83, 163—188, 221—260.
11. W. A. M. Luijpen, *Existential Phenomenology* (1965), p. 81.
12. For an analysis of the function of the 'I' as the first principle of Cartesian inspired metaphysics see Heidegger, *What is a Thing?*, pp. 98—108. Moses Mendelssohn, Lessing's closest friend, writes concerning the self and knowledge: 'Lasset uns sehen, wie wir zur Idee des Wirklichen gelangen, und mit welchem Grunde wir von manchen Dingen überführt sind, oder überführt zu sein glauben, dass sie Wirklichkeit haben. Der Mensch ist sich selbst die erste Quelle seines Wissens; er muss also von sich selbst ausgehen, wenn er sich von dem, was er weiss, und was er nicht weiss, Rechenschaft geben will' ('Morgenstunden', in *Schriften,* Band I, p. 306).
    Indeed, Mendelssohn goes so far as to use Descartes' *cogito, ergo sum*

argument. Mendelssohn writes: 'Auf diesem Grundsatze [Ich denke, also bin ich] muss sich das ganze philosophische Lehrgebäude aufführen lassen, ohne sich irgend auf ein anderes Zeugniss der äussern Sinne zu stützen. Denn was die Sinne von den äussern Dingen wahrnehmen ist verdächtig; nur diese einzige innerliche Empfindung: Ich denke, hat das Vorrecht, dass man mit völliger Gewissheit von ihr sagen kann, sie sei keine blosse Erscheinung, sondern eine wahre Realität, wie ich solches in der Folge zeigen werde' ('Über die Evidenz', in *Schriften*, Band I, pp. 69—70).

13. Baumgarten, *Metaphysica*, p. 1, § 1. Similarly Johann Christoph Gottsched writes: 'Die Grundlehre *[ontologia]* ist eine Wissenschaft von den ersten Gründen unseres Erkenntnisses' (*Erste Gründe: Erster, Theoretischer Theil*, Band I, p. 115, § 209).

14. *What is a Thing?*, p. 116. Heidegger apparently used a different edition of Baumgarten's *Metaphysica* (for which he gave no source). According to Heidegger the first paragraph reads: 'Metaphysica est scientia prima cognitionis humanae principia contenens'. There is obviously no difference in meaning.

15. Baumgarten, *Metaphysica*, pp. 92—93, § 92.

16. Thielicke, *Der Evangelische Glaube: Grundzüge der Dogmatik*. Band I: *Prolegomena*, p. 23.

17. Ibid., p. 25.

18. Ibid., p. 29.

19. Caird, *Essay on Literature and Philosophy*, Vol. II, pp. 278—279.

20. *On Wisdom in Leibniz: Selections* (ed. by Philip P. Wiener), p. 77.

21. *First Truths in Leibniz: Philosophical Papers and Letters* (ed. by Leroy E. Loemker), Vol. I, p. 412.

C. 'Mathesis universalis' as the formal structure of truth

22. Descartes, *'Rules for the Direction'*, Vol. I, p. 4, Rule II.

23. Ibid., pp. 3—4.

24. Ibid., p. 10, Rule IV.

25. Ibid., p. 13.

26. Ibid., p. 11. The importance in distinguishing between the term *mathesis* meaning the study of numbers, figures, etc., and a study of the formal characteristics of rational truths cannot be overstressed and the failure to do so has recently led to an inadequate comprehension of the *Aufklärung*. In a recent book Eberhard Reichmann has sought to place the locus of unity in the *Aufklärung* in the attempts to analyse various subjects within the framework of mathematics (i.e., numbers): 'Das heißt, wenn in der wissenschaftlichen Praxis vom rationalen Geist der Aufklärung gesprochen wird, begnügt man sich im allgemeinen damit, das Rationale als das Vernünftige, Verstandesmäßige, Logische zu begreifen, ohne auf das Quantitative als weiteres Wesenselement einzugehen. Der rationale Geist, aber, in seinen reinsten wie in seinen trivialsten Verkörperungen, will in letzter Instanz die Reduktion aller Phänomene auf die ihnen innewohnende pythagoräische Essenz, die Zahl' (*Die Herrschaft der Zahl*, pp. 7—8). Reichmann is correct

in noting that insufficient attention has been paid to the use of quantity in the thinking of the *Aufklärer*. Lessing's treatment of the doctrine of satisfaction in the *Erziehung* is an example of such thinking. Nevertheless, 'mathematical thinking' entailed more than the material application of quantity to problems. It also involved the abstraction of the formal characteristic of 'das Vernünftige' *per se* and thereby the logical dimension assumes primary importance. Indeed, the epistemological crisis of the eighteenth century as exemplified by Kant deals not with the application of quantity to specific problems, but with the general validity and justification of such a procedure. Thus the problem (as described by Heidegger) is the problem of mathematical thinking in the broadest sense.

27. Pepper, *World Hypotheses*, p. 91.
28. Gilson, *The Unity of Philosophical Experience*, pp. 133, 137.
29. Descartes, *Directions*, Vol. I, p. 13, Rule IV.
30. Cf. Heidegger, *What is a Thing?*, pp. 69–76.
31. Ibid., p. 73.
32. *Directions*, Vol. I, pp. 1–2, Rule I.
33. Wolff, *Preliminary Discourse on Philosophy in General* (1728), (trans. 1963), p. 62.
34. Ibid., p. 17.
35. Ibid., p. 76.
36. Mendelssohn, *Über die Evidenz*, Band I, p. 47.
37. Hermann Samuel Reimarus recommends the study of mathematics (as a science of numbers, figures, etc.) as a formal model for the development of rational thinking *per se*. '[Die mathematische Erkenntnis] ist nun also zwar die höchste [Stufe der Erkenntnis] ; aber wegen ihrer Gewißheit und Lehr-Art sollte sie billig in der Ordnung unsers Lernens nicht die letzte seyn, sondern der Weltweisheit vorgeschoben werden; damit sich der Verstand an ein ordentliches Denken gewöhne, und von der unwiderstreblichen Klarheit und Deutlichkeit des Zusammenhangs der Wahrheiten, welche uns eine volle Gewißheit zu geben vermögen ist; selbst die innere Erfahrung und einen Maßstab bekomme' (*Die Vernunftslehre*, p. 15, § VIII).
38. Mendelssohn, 'Morgenstunden', in *Schriften*, Band I, p. 305.
39. Leibniz, *On the Supersensible Element in Knowledge and the Immaterial in Nature* (1702), in *Selections*, p. 358.
40. Ibid., p. 361.

D. The material content of rational truth

41. Gottsched, *Erste Gründe: Anderer, Practischer Theil*, Band II, p. 25, § 35.
42. Concerning Wolff's concept of philosophy see Richard J. Blackwell, 'The Structure of Wolffian Philosophy', *The Modern Schoolman*, 37 (1961), pp. 203–218, and Hans Lüthje, 'Christian Wolffs Philosophiebegriff', *Kant Studien*, 30 (1925), pp. 39–66.
   For general treatments of Wolff's philosophy see Lewis White Beck, *Early German Philosophy: Kant and His Predecessors* (1969), pp. 247–256; John Hermann Randall, Jr. *The Career of Philosophy*, Vol. 2: *From the En-*

lightenment to the Age of Darwin (1970), pp. 55—61, and Eduard Zeller, *Geschichte der deutschen Philosophie seit Leibniz* (1873), pp. 211—272. Also of some value is Richard J. Blackwell's 'Christian Wolff's Doctrine of the Soul', *Journal of the History of Ideas,* 22 (1961), pp. 339—354.

43. Blackwell, 'The Structure of Wolffian Philosophy', p. 217.
44. For an incisive analysis of the basic principles of Wolff's ontology see Etienne Gilson, *Being and Some Philosophers,* 2nd ed. (1952), pp. 112—121.
45. Cf. Baumgarten's argumentation seeking to establish the principle of contradiction and the principle of sufficient reason. *Metaphysica,* pp. 3—6, §§ 7—18.
46. Wolff, *Philosophia prima,* p. 121, § 141.
47. Ibid., pp. 137—138, §169.
48. Ibid., p. 143, § 174.
49. Ibid., pp. 187, 188, 189, §§ 226, 227, 229. Cf. also Mendelssohn, 'Über die Evidenz', in *Schriften,* Band I, pp. 76—77.
50. Wolff designated as contingent all being that does not contain its sufficient reason for existence in its own essence. 'Cum contingens sit, quod necessarium non est; *Ens contigens* est, quod existentiae rationem sufficientem in essentia sua non habeat, seu, quod rationem existentiae suae extra se in ente alio, aut in ente a se diverso habet' (Ibid., p. 245, § 310). Mendelssohn maintained essentially the same position; cf. 'Morgenstunden', in *Schriften,* Band I, p. 385.
51. Concerning Wolff's conception of God see Anton Bissinger, *Die Struktur der Gotteserkenntnis: Studien zur Philosophie Christian Wolffs* (1970), and James Collins, *God in Modern Philosophy* (1969), pp. 133—143. Bissinger's study is a comprehensive analysis of Wolff's proofs for God's existence, structure of divine being and God's relationship to the world within the framework of Wolff's metaphysics.
52. Wolff, *Vernünftige Gedanken,* p. 588, § 951; cf. also p. 604, § 981. Mendelssohn writes: 'Vielmehr wird also [die] Abhängigkeit [eines zufälligen Dings] vom nothwendigen Wesen darin zu suchen sein, dass es ein Gegenstand des Billigungsvermögens geworden. Vermöge seiner innern Güte und Vollkommenheit muss er unter gewissen Umständen *irgendwo* und *irgendwann* das Beste geworden, und als ein solches von der nothwendigen Ursache gebilligt und hervorgebracht worden sein' ('Morgenstunden', Band I, p. 386).
53. Wolff, *Vernünftige Gedanken,* p. 610, § 988.
54. Leibniz, 'From a letter to Des Bosses (1711)', in *Selections,* p. 95.
55. Gottsched, *Erste Gründe,* Band I, p. 132, § 249.
56. Ibid., p. 573, § 1140. Cf. also Hermann Samuel Reimarus' treatment of God's intentions in creating the world: *Abhandlungen von den vornehmsten Wahrheiten der natürlichen Religion,* 5th ed. (1781), pp. 217—299 and 541—572. Reimarus writes: 'Wir setzen hiebey die Absicht der Schöpfung voraus, daß nämlich die Welt zum Wohl aller möglichen Lebendigen hervorgebracht sey' (p. 546).
57. Ibid., p. 586, § 1164.
58. Ibid., pp. 586—587, § 1165. It is obvious from the above presentation that

Enlightenment speculations upon the destiny of man entail a philosophico-theological theodicy.

Mendelssohn, for one, writes: 'Ohne Gott, Vorsehung und Unsterblichkeit haben alle Güter des Lebens in meinen Augen einen verächtlichen Werth, scheint mir das Leben hienieden, um mich eines bekannten und oft gemissbrauchten Gleichnisses zu bedienen, wie eine Wanderschaft in Wind und Wetter, ohne den Trost, Abends in einer Herberge Schirm und Obdach zu finden . . .' ('Morgenstunden,' Band I, p. 358).

Reimarus writes: 'Man kann also die göttliche Vorsehung nicht läugnen, ohne das Dasein Gottes, und seiner Vollkommenheiten, nebst der Schöpfung, aufzugeben' (*Abhandlungen*, p. 542).

The young Lessing writes in 'Aus einem Gedichte über die menschliche Glückseligkeit': 'Beklagenswürdige Welt, wenn dir ein Schöpfer fehlt, Des Weisheit nur das Wohl zum Zweck der Taten wählt! . . . Ein Weiser schätzt kein Spiel, wo nur der Fall regieret, Und Klugheit nichts gewinnt, und Dummheit nichts verlieret. Verlust ohn' meine Schuld ist ein zu bittres Gift. Und Glück ergötzt mich nicht, das auch die Narren trifft. Stirb, und verlaß die Welt, das Urbild solcher Spiele. Wo ich Pein ohne Schuld, und Lust mit Ekel fühle. Doch warum eifr' ich so? Gott ist, mein Glück steht fest, Das Wechsel, Schmerz und Zeit mir schmackhaft werden läßt' (Band I, p. 185).

For some secondary sources concerning the problem of theodicy in the eighteenth century see: Richard A. Brooks, *Voltaire and Leibniz* (1964); John Hick, *Evil and the God of Love* (1966), pp. 151–174; Joseph Kremer, *Das Problem der Theodicee in der Philosophie und Literatur des 18. Jahrhunderts mit besonderer Rücksicht auf Kant und Schiller* (1909); Otto Lemp, *Das Problem der Theodicee in der Philosophie und Literatur des 18. Jahrhunderts bis auf Kant und Schiller* (1910), and Arthur O. Lovejoy, 'The Principle of Plentitude and Eighteenth Century Optimism', in *The Great Chain of Being: A Study of the History of an Idea* (1960), pp. 208–226.

59. Ibid., p. 587, § 1166.
60. Ibid., Band II, p. 34, § 50.

E. Reason and the critique of Christianity

61. Besides Aner's work (cited above) see Henry F. Allison's presentation of the English, French, and German Enlightenment as a background to Lessing's theology: *Lessing and the Enlightenment: His Philosophy of Religion and Its Relation to Eighteenth-Century Thought* (1966), pp. 1–49.
62. At this point I want to acknowledge the difficulty entailed in attempting to subsume 18th-century theology under the designation of *Aufklärung*. Wolfgang Philipp has sought to revise the 'usual' interpretation of the *Aufklärung* (e.g., that of Aner's). See his 'Einleitung', in *Das Zeitalter der Aufklärung* (1963), pp. xiii–civ. Philipp's position differs from the usual position in two basic ways.
   First, Philipp distinguishes three basic movements in the theology of the *Aufklärung*: (1) 'die Physikotheologie', (2) 'die Neologie', and (3) 'der Rationalismus'. But of more importance is Philipp's contention that these

movements did not so much replace each other chronologically as they coexisted and mutually influenced one another. What Philipp has designated as 'Rationalismus' is in effect the theological position I will now analyze. This is not to deny, however, that the rationalistic paradigm was active in the other positions.

Secondly, Philipp contends that the term *Aufklärung* refers to the biblical *claritas claritatum,* i.e., the light of divine glory as manifested to man through creation. There is no point in quarreling over terminology. Certainly what Philipp defines as *Aufklärung* can be encountered in the so-called 'Rationalismus' (cf. Reimarus for one). However, Philipp's use of the term is not the normal use (which refers to accepting as true only what reason certifies). Cf. Cassirer, *The Philosophy of the Enlightenment* (trans. 1951), pp. 3—36, and Gerhard Funke, 'Einleitung', in *Die Aufklärung in ausgewählten Texten dargestellt* (1963), pp. 1—12.

The term *'Aufklärung'* as used by thinkers such as Bahrdt, Kant, and Mendelssohn refers to the pursuit of truth based upon the exegencies of reason. At the beginning of the eighteenth century the moderate *Aufklärer,* J. Salat, when he thought he discovered some dangers in the *Aufklärung,* did not conceive of the term in the way Philipp does, rather as used by Cassirer and Funke; cf. his *Auch die Aufklärung hat ihre Gefahren* (1804). Insofar as the term *'Aufklärung'* has been used not only by historians but also by eighteenth-century contemporaries to refer to rationally grounded truth, it would seem that an analysis of the paradigm of reason and its application to theology could appropriately be designated an analysis of the theology of the *Aufklärung.*

In this sense the term *'Aufklärung'* is not simply to be identified with the eighteenth century *per se* (something Philipp does) but with a certain way of theologizing, namely theological thinking based upon 'der cartesianische Ansatz' (cf. Thielicke's analysis of such a theological model). For a balanced history of eighteenth-century theology which, while not losing sight of Philipp's contentions, nevertheless pays adequate attention to the rationalistic trends, see Friedrich Wilhelm Katzenbach, *Protestantisches Christentum im Zeitalter der Aufklärung* (1965), particularly pp. 22—30.

63. Mendelssohn, 'Sendschreiben an den Herrn Magister Lessing in Leipzig,' in *Schriften,* Band II, p. 337.

64. Leibniz, 'The Monadology', in *Selections,* p. 550, § 84.

65. 'The Principles of Nature and Grace Based on Reason', in *Selections,* p. 530.

66. Ibid., pp. 530—531.

67. Mendelssohn, *'Was heißt Aufklären?',* in *Schriften,* Band II, p. 247.

68. *Über Aufklärung und die Beförderungsmittel derselben* (1789), reprinted in part in *Die Aufklärung* (ed. by Gerhard Funke), pp. 98—99.
    The concept of human autonomy grounded upon man's rationality underlies Bahrdt's defense of freedom of thought. Cf. *Ueber Preßfreyheit und deren Gränzen* (1787), pp. 1—31. Bahrdt writes: 'Ich will euch überzeugen, daß Freiheit zu denken und zu urtheilen, daß der Gebrauch euer eigenen Vernunft, euer höchstes Kleinod und — die wichtigste Grundlage euer Glückseligkeit ist. . . . Freiheit zu denken und zu urtheilen ist die einzige wahre Quelle aller menschlichen Aufklärung. . . . Aufklärung ist der wesent-

liche Grund aller menschlichen Glückseligkeit' (pp. 4—5). Similarly new
members of the order (or lodge) of the *Illuminati* were advised: 'Wer hat
den Menschen . . . zur ewigen Knechtschaft verdammt: Warum soll es unmöglich sein, daß das menschliche Geschlecht zur höchsten Vollkommen-.
heit, zur Fähigkeit, sich selbst zu leiten gelangen können? Warum soll der
ewig geführt werden, der sich selbst zu führen versteht' (*Anrede an die neu
aufzunehmenden Illuminatos dirigentes,* in *Die Aufklärung im deutschen
Schrifttum* [ed. by Ulrich Haacke], p. 9). The manuscripts for the *Anrede*
were found in 1786 and printed 1787. When Friedrich Schiller had his
Marquis Posa in *Don Carlos* half demand and half ask for 'Gedankenfreiheit'
from the King of Spain, Schiller was but echoing the demand of the
Aufklärung for autonomy.

69. *The Formula of Concord. Thorough Declaration II: Of Free Will,* in *Triglot
Concordia.* The Symbolic Books of the Ev. Lutheran Church (1921), p. 883.
70. Ibid., p. 787.
71. Ibid., p. 861.
72. Ibid.
73. Ibid., p. 863. Concerning the Lutheran notion of 'sin' see Werner Ebert, *Die
Morphologie des Luthertums,* Band II, pp. 15—52.
74. Cf. Aner, *Die Theologie der Lessingzeit,* pp. 158ff and 297ff, and Martens,
*Die Botschaft der Tugend: Die Aufklärung im Spiegel der deutschen mora-
lischen Wochenschriften,* pp. 172—217.
    Summarizing the results of his intensive and comprehensive research Wolf-
gang Martens writes: 'Von der Erbsünde, von Gnade und Prädestination, der
Heiligen Dreieinigkeit, der Satisfaktion durch den Opfertod Christi, von
Christi Gottessohnschaft, von Höllenfahrt und Auferstehung, von Wundern,
Engeln und Teufeln ist in den vernünftigen Betrachtungen der Wochen-
schriften nicht — oder nur ganz beiläufig in herkömmlichen Formeln — die
Rede. Gott erscheint nicht mehr als der Gott Abrahams, Isaacs und Jacobs,
sondern in allgemeinen Wendungen als die Allmacht, der Urheber alles
Guten, der große Gesetzgeber, die ewige Weisheit, die göttliche Vorsehung,
das höchste Wesen. Er ist nicht mehr der Verborgene, und Unbegreifliche,
sondern der — wenn auch nur in beschränktem Umfang — Begreifliche und
Beweisbare. Das Tremendum weicht philosophischem Respekt und vernünftiger Ehrerbietung. . . . Das Mysterium des Glaubens ist aufgelöst in die
Klarheit vernünftiger Erkenntnis. Ein Credo quia absurdum kann nicht den
Erwartungen Gottes entsprechen, der dem Menschen das Licht der Natur
verliehen hat' (p. 205). However it must be noted that the overthrow of the
doctrine of 'spiritual death' of man was a gradual process. Hans M. Wolff has
described this process in: *Die Weltanschauung der deutschen Aufklärung in
geschichtlicher Entwicklung* (1949), pp. 27—152. Compare also Cassirer's
discussion of the rejection of the doctrine of 'original sin' in: *The Philosophy of the Enlightenment,* pp. 137—160.
75. 'Der Prediger Andreas Riem über Aufklärung und Gewissensfreiheit' (1792),
in: *Bibliothek der Deutschen Aufklärer des achtzehnten Jahrhunderts,* ed.
by Martin von Geismar), Band II, pp. 319—320.
76. Christian Wolff, *Vernünftige Gedanken,* p. 665, § 1076. Concerning the role
of Wolff's attempts to justify the 'health' of human reason in spiritual

matters see Hans Wolff, *Weltanschauung der deutschen Aufklärung*, pp. 109—116. Hans Wolff writes: 'Dieses unbegrenzte Vertrauen zur Vernunft führt nun Wolff . . . zu derselben optimistischen Auffassung vom Menschen, die der gelehrten Philosophie zugrunde gelegen hatte. . . . [D] er Unterschied zwischen [Gott und Mensch] liegt weniger in ihrer Natur als im Grade der Vollkommenheit. . . . Der lutherische Deus absconditus ist durch den vernünftig-begreiflichen Gott ersetzt, daher besteht Hoffnung auf vernünftige Lösung aller Welträtsel, denn da Gottes Geist dem der Menschen altverwandt ist, so muß Gott auch als Weltschöpfer nach ähnlichen Prinzipien handeln, wie der schöpferisch tätige Mensch. [Der Mensch] ist keiner gottgleichen Erkenntnis fähig, wohl aber einer gottähnlichen, so daß von einem geistigen Unvermögen des Menschen keine Rede sein kann' (p. 113).

77. Leibniz, 'The Principles of Nature', in *Selections*, p. 530.
78. Gottsched, *Erste Gründe*, Vol. I, p. 319, § 654.
79. 'Über Aufklärung und Gewissensfreiheit', Band II, p. 332.
80. Gottsched, *Erste Gründe*, Band II, p. 23, § 31.
81. Ibid., p. 26, § 37.
82. Ibid., p. 25, § 35.
83. Quoted by Martens, *Botschaft der Tugend*, p. 321.
   Critically evaluating the *Aufklärung* Johann Heinrich Jung (genannt Stilling) writes: 'Der Grundsatz der Aufklärung aber ist nun folgender: Die ganze Schöpfung ist ein zusammenhängendes Ganze, welchem der Schöpfer seine geistigen und physischen Kräfte angeschaffen und ihnen ihre ewige und unveränderliche Gesetze gegeben hat, nach welchen sie unaufhaltbar wirken; so daß also nun keine göttliche Einwirkung mehr nötig ist; folglich geht alles in der ganzen Schöpfung einen unabänderlichen notwendigen Gang, der das allgemeine Beste aller Wesen zum Zweck hat. Die Menschenklasse ist ein Teil dieses Ganzen, und die ewigen Gesetze der Natur wirken so, daß der freie Wille jedes Menschen bei jeder Handlung so gelenkt wird, daß er das tut, was er tut. Die Sittenlehre enthält die Gesetze, nach denen der freie Wille geleitet werden muß. Dieser Grundsatz ist der eigentliche Determinismus, und man mag sich verstecken und verwahren, wie man will, bei allen, auch den gemäßigsten Neologen ist er mehr oder weniger, offener oder versteckter, die Grundidee von allem.' (*Rückblick auf Stillings bisherige Lebensgeschichte* [1804], in *Jung-Stillings Lebensgeschichte* [ed. by Karl Otto Conrady], p. 240).
84. Nicolai, *Das Leben und die Meinungen das Herrn Magister Sebaldus Nothanker* (Ed. 1938), p. 119.
85. Aner, *Die Theologie der Lessingszeit*, pp. 163—164.

F. Criticism of the Bible as a medium of revelation

86. Mendelssohn, 'Brief an den Erbprinzen von Braunschweig-Wolfenbüttel' (1770), in *Schriften*, Band II, p. 556.
87. *Works of Spinoza* (trans. 1951), Vol. I, p. 63.
88. Ibid., p. 61.
89. *Brief über die Bibel im Volkston* (1782), reprinted in part in *Das Zeitalter*

der Aufklärung (ed. by Wolfgang Philipp), p. 210.

90. *Brief über den Rationalismus* (1813), reprinted in part in *Das Zeitalter der Aufklärung*, p. 224.

91. Toulmin and Goodfield, *The Discovery of Time*, p. 101.

CHAPTER 3: THE COGNITIVE CRISIS OF THE ENLIGHTENMENT

1. Wundt, *Die deutsche Schulphilosophie im Zeitalter der Aufklärung* (Ed. 1964), pp. 122—124.

2. Ibid., p. 265 ff.

3. Cf. Cassirer, *The Philosophy of the Enlightenment* (trans. 1951), pp. 93—133.

4. For secondary sources dealing with the German Enlightenment and its development including for the most part the pre-critical Kant see Lewis White Beck, *Early German Philosophy: Kant and His Predecessors* (1969), pp. 243—501; Frederick Copleston, S. J., *A History of Philosophy*, Vol. 6: *Modern Philosophy*, Part I: *The French Enlightenment to Kant* (1964), pp. 121—172; Emerich Coreth, *Einführung in die Philosophie der Neuzeit*, Band I: *Rationalismus, Empirismus, Aufklärung* (1972), pp. 136—150; Kuno Fischer, *Geschichte*, Band II: *Leibniz und seine Schule*, 2nd ed. (1867), pp. 743—884; M. Kronenberg, *Geschichte des Deutschen Idealismus* (1909), Band I, pp. 180—234, 338—374; John Herman Randall, Jr., *The Career of Philosophy*, Vol. 2: *From the Enlightenment to the Age of Darwin* (1970), pp. 50—127; Heinrich Straubinger, *Die Religion und ihre Grundwahrheiten in der deutschen Philosophie seit Leibniz* (1919), pp. 6—39; Wundt, *Die Schulphilosophie im Zeitalter der Aufklärung* (Ed. 1964), pp. 122—341; and Eduard Zeller, *Geschichte der deutschen Philosophie seit Leibniz* (1873), pp. 211—421.

For a penetrating analysis of the epistemological crisis of the eighteenth century and its meaning for ontology see Ernst Cassirer, *Das Erkenntnisproblem in der Philosophie und Wissenschaft der neueren Zeit* (1922), Band II, pp. 521—557, 567—647.

For the ramification of such a crisis in this area of aesthetics (which at the same time includes the realm of logic) see Alfred Baeumler, *Das Irrationalitätsproblem in der Ästhetik und Logik des 18. Jahrhunderts bis zur Kritik der Urteilskraft* (1967), particularly pages 170—352.

Finally, for a partially historical and partially theoretical discussion of the cognitive crisis involved in eighteenth and nineteenth century physics see Giorgio de Santillana and Edgar Zilsel, *The Development of Rationalism and Empiricism* (1970). Also to be noted for the philosophy of the period is Heinz Heimsoeth, *Metaphysik der Neuzeit* (1967), pp. 79—98.

5. Cassirer, *Philosophy of the Enlightenment*, pp. 192—196.

A. The anomaly of existence and the rise of empiricism

6. Mendelssohn, 'Über die Evidenz', in *Schriften,* Band I, p. 82.

7. Ibid., p. 79.

8. Immanuel Kant, *Frühschriften* (Ed. 1961), Band II, pp. 23—134.

9. Ibid., p. 36.

10. Ibid., pp. 31—32.

11. Ibid., p. 31.

12. Concerning the role played by the discovery of existence in the destruction of Kant's belief in all rationalistic metaphysics see Etienne Gilson, *Being and Some Philosophers*, 2nd ed. (1952), pp. 119—128.

13. Concerning the hotly debated question of the validity of the mathematical method in the eighteenth century see Giorgio Tonelli, 'Der Streit über die mathematische Methode in der Philosophie in der ersten Hälfte des 18. Jahrhunderts und die Entstehung von Kants Schrift über die "Deutlichkeit",' *Archiv für Philosophie* 9 (1959), pp. 37—66.

14. Concerning the scepticism implicit in the empiricism of Locke, Berkeley, and Hume see Harry Prosch, 'The Yawning Chasm of Scepticism', *The Genesis of Twentieth-Century Philosophy* (1966), Chap. 4, pp. 83—112. Also concerning Hume's role in eighteenth-century England see Basil Willey, *The Eighteenth-Century Background* (1961), pp. 110—119.

15. 'A Treatise of Human Nature' (1739), in David Hume, *Selections* (Ed. 1955), p. 104.

16. 'An Enquiry Concerning Human Understanding,' in David Hume, *Selections*, p. 116.

17. 'A Treatise of Human Nature', in David Hume, *Selections*, p. 40.

18. Ibid., p. 49.

B. Empiricism in Germany

19. Beck, *Early German Philosophy*, p. 396.

20. For an interpretation of Crusius' philosophy see Heinz Heimsoeth, *Metaphysik und Kritik bei Chr. A. Crusius: Ein Beitrag zur ontologischen Vorgeschichte der Kritik der reinen Vernunft im 18. Jahrhundert* (1926).

21. Crusius, *Entwurf der Notwendigen Vernunftwahrheiten, wiefern sie den zufälligen entgegengesetzet werden*, § 8.

22. Randall, *Career of Philosophy*, Vol. II, 64.

23. Crusius, *Der Weg zur Gewißheit und Zuverlässigkeit der menschlichen Erkenntnis*, § 260.

24. Kant, 'Versuch, den Begriff der negativen Größen in die Weltweisheit einzuführen' in *Frühschriften*, Band II, p. 206.

25. Béguelin, *Mémoires sur les premiers principe de la Métaphysique*, § 17.

26. Kaestner, *Anfangsgründe der höheren Mechanik*, III. Theil, § 196.

27. *Lettres de Maupertuis* L. IV. *œuvres*, Tome II, p. 202, quoted in Cassirer, *Das Erkenntnisproblem*, Band II, p. 427.

28. Lossius, *Physische Ursachen der Wahrheit*, p. 58.

29. Meier, *Vernunftlehre*, § 30.

30. 'O Nacht! O Quelle meiner Trauerlieder!' (1752) reprinted in *Deutsche Dichtung im 18. Jahrhundert*, p. 234.

31. 'Versuch über die Seele' (1753/1754) reprinted in part in *Deutsche Dichtung im 18. Jahrhundert*, p. 237.

C. *The cognitive crisis of the Aufklärung*

32. Whether or not Leibniz' *New Essays* directly influenced Kant is not universally agreed upon. I follow Randall in making the assertion; cf. *Career of Philosophy*, Vol. II, pp. 117—118.
33. For the importance of Leibniz for the development of German epistemology see Cassirer, *Philosophy of the Enlightenment*, pp. 120—133.
34. Tetens, *Philosophische Versuche über die menschliche Natur und ihre Entwicklung* (1777), Band I, pp. 24—25, reprinted in *Neudrucke seltener phüosophischer Werke* (1913), Band IV.
35. Ibid., p. 320.
36. Cassirer, *Philosophy of the Enlightenment*, pp. 124—125.
37. Randall, *Career of Philosophy*, Vol. II, pp. 76—77.
38. Ibid., p. 77.
39. Benno Erdmann, *Reflexionen Kants zur kritischen Philosophie* (1884), Band II, Reflexion 513, cited in Cassirer, *Das Erkenntnisproblem*, Band II, p. 622.
40. 'Letter to Marcus Herz', Feb. 21, 1772, cited and translated by Randall, Vol. II, p. 124.
41. Mendelssohn, 'Über die Evidenz', in *Schriften*, Band I, p. 47.
42. *Summarium oder Menschen-Katechismus in kurzen Sätzen nebst einer Vorrede* (Schleswig, 1796), reprinted in part in *Das Zeitalter der Aufklärung* (ed. 1963), p. 300, § 21.
43. Ibid., p. 301, § 22.
44. The interpretation of Enlightenment thought in the terms of generative paradigms rather than in the terms of a specific philosopher enables the investigator to avoid all sorts of difficulties, particularly those of oversimplification. Gerhard Funke attempts to typify the *Aufklärung* in the terms of Leibniz' philosophy. Funke writes: 'Denn Leibniz war kein Leibnizianer — er war nicht Empirist, nicht Rationalist, nicht Kritizist, er war Aufklärer' ('Einleitung', in *Die Aufklärung in ausgewählten Texten dargestellt*, p. 45). Funke's attempt to describe the complexities of Enlightenment thought as the function of the philosophy of Leibniz — the non-Leibnizian — causes Funke to oversimplify and to misconstrue the essentially crisis nature of the period, even though much of what Funke has to say is in accord with the ensuing brief description of the *Aufklärung* to be given in the text. As a general methodological principle it is not possible, in my judgment, to describe the complexities, divergencies, and even contradictions of an age solely in the terms of the concepts of one thinker. Such a description is only possible in terms of 'generative paradigms'. A paradigm allows for diversity in conclusions, while only demanding unity in the basic approach to problems. Therefore, the unity of an age is the unity of its questions and approaches to problems based on a shared set of generative paradigms.
45. See Wundt, *Die deutsche Schulphilosophie*, pp. 265—341.
46. The use of practicality as a standard was not only applied as a criterion of truth but also as a justification for religion. Indeed, it became the 'Aufgabe' of the theology of the *Aufklärung* to prove religion valid, particularly

Christianity, because of the practical effects of religion. Klaus Scholder writes: 'Diese Aufgabe aber hieß: einer Zeit, die an der Existenzberechtigung des Christentums überhaupt zu zweifeln begann, den Sinn und die Notwendigkeit der christlichen Religion zu beweisen. Der Weg, den die Neologie zur Lösung dieser Frage beschritt, war überall und einhellig derselbe. Er lautete, auf eine kurze Formel gebracht: den Beweis für Sinn und Notwendigkeit der christlichen Religion kann nicht die Lehre, sondern nur das Leben, nicht die theologische Reflexion, sondern nur die Praxis pietatis, nicht der Glaube, sondern nur die Heiligung erbringen' ('Grundzüge der theologischen Aufklärung in Deutschland', in *Evangelischer Glaube im Wandel der Zeit*, p. 72).

47. Wundt, *Die deutsche Schulphilosophie*, p. 314.
48. The discovery of the self was also the discovery that the psychology of the self is not a function of pure reason, but of emotions, passions, etc. The turn towards a psychological self-analysis in which the irrational and emotional sides of the self are investigated is typical for the Enlightenment throughout Europe. For a brief description of the discovery of the irrational in the self see Peter Gay, *The Enlightenment: An Interpretation*, Vol. II: *The Science of Freedom*, pp. 187—207.

CHAPTER 4: THE CRISIS IN LESSING'S THINKING

A. The problem of approaching Lessing

1. To date the most subtle and comprehensive discussion of the problem of interpreting Lessing has been carried out by Helmut Thielicke. See *Offenbarung, Vernunft und Existenz* (3rd ed., 1957), pp. 36—57.
2. Plavius, 'Revision des Humanismus: Die Wandlungen im Lessing-Bild der westdeutschen Reaktion', *Neue Deutsche Literatur* 12 (1964), p. 98.
3. Plavius contends that Lessing's writings on theological matters 'eine ganze bestimmte Funktion in Lessings Kampf um Aufklärung und bürgerliches Selbstbewußtsein spielten, daß ihr wesentlicher Gehalt somit nicht auf dem Felde der Theologie, Religionsgeschichte usw., sondern auf dem der Philosophie und Politik lag' (Ibid., pp. 96—97).
4. Plavius, for instance, quotes Lessing's letter of March 20, 1777 to his brother Karl as the primary proof of Lessing's rejection of 'religion' in favor of philosophy (presumably a proto-atheistic kind). The letter reads in part: '. . . weil es im Grunde allerdings wahr ist, daß es mir bei meinen theologischen . . . Neckereien oder Stänkereien, mehr um den gesunden Menschenverstand, als um die Theologie zu tun ist, und ich nur darum die alte orthodoxe (im Grunde *tolerante*) Theologie der neuern (im Grunde *intoleranten*) vorziehe, weil jene mit dem gesunden Menschenverstande offenbar streitet, und diese ihn lieber bestechen möchte' (IX, 729). Plavius' argument is: Lessing prefers orthodoxy (which rejects the role of reason in religion) to neology (which seeks to support religion with reason) and then rejects orthodoxy in the name of 'der gesunde Menschenverstand', i.e., pure 'scientific' reason. Plavius writes: '[Lessing] betrat einen Weg, der zur immer

stärkeren und souveräneren Geltung des wissenschaftlich-vernünftigen Denkens führte' (p. 103). If Plavius were correct in his interpretation of Lessing's 'true' esoterism, then one would have to conclude that Lessing dissimulated (if not showed himself to be an out and out hypocrite) in every published work on religion including the *Erziehung*. There is no writing in which Lessing explicitly contrasts reason with religion as an irreconcilable antithesis. Every piece of evidence indicates that religious truth (e.g., God, providence, morality) represents the sort of conclusion that 'der gesunde Menschenverstand' should make. The problem in comprehending Lessing revolves around the relationship between theological truths of reason and those of revelation. Plavius also overlooks the fact that 'das wissenschaftlich-vernünftige Denken' of Lessing's time was undergoing a paradigm crisis and, as will be shown, this crisis is at the basis of Lessing's preference for orthodoxy over neology and for his sincere attempt to find 'einen erträg-lichen Sinn' in traditional Christianity.

5. Moses Mendelssohn, *Gesammelte Schriften*, Band V, pp. 702, 698 as quoted by Ingrid Strohschneider-Kohrs, *Vom Prinzip des Maßes in Lessings Kritik* (1969), p. 9.

6. The problem of determining the 'pure' content of Lessing's alleged esoterism is a major obstacle for those who wish to contrast Lessing's alleged esoteric rationalism with any possible belief in Christianity. Friedrich Loofs is driven to admit: 'Eine "Theologie" Lessings geben zu wollen, wäre deshalb ein Unding. Denn Lessings exoterisch geäußerte theologische Gedanken liegen zum Teil auf *einer* Ebene, und seine esote-rische Meinung kennen wir viel zu wenig' ('Lessing's Stellung zum Christen-tum', *Theologische Studien und Kritiken* [1913], p. 63). Although Loofs cannot ascertain the content of Lessing's esoterism, he is certain that Lessing had such a position! Loofs is certain, moreover, that Lessing categorically rejected orthodoxy and neology (p. 52) and therefore 'alles, was in den theologischen Streitschriften und in der "Erziehung des Menschengeschlechts" dem [i.e., Lessing's supposed rejection of revelation] widerspricht, gehört nur. dem "exoterischen Vortrage" an' (p. 58). Loofs argumentation in favor of this position is circular. Loofs (a) assumes that Lessing's esoterism and exoterism exist upon two different and exclusive plains, (b) he accepts Lessing's 'anti-supernaturalistic' statements at face value, (c) concludes therefore that Lessing's pro-Christian statements are 'merely' exoteric and (d) yet Loofs cannot give any real positive content to Lessing's 'pure' esoteric position. Without being able to determine the positive content of Lessing's esoterism, an interpreter has no real means to justify his categorical rejection of a whole class of Lessing's statements as somehow not Lessing's true opinion. Such a methodology cannot but lead to little or no results (which is precisely the result of Loofs' endeavors). Indeed, because Lessing speaks so often in an exoteric manner, Loofs must grudgingly admit that there is some substance to the charge that Lessing was not always honest (cf. p. 59).

7. Cf. Thielicke, *Offenbarung, Vernunft und Existenz*, pp. 41—44.

8. Thielicke writes: 'Das letzte Ziel unserer Frage kann somit gar nicht der esoterische Kern des Lessingschen Denkens sein, sondern die Art der unlös-

baren Verwobenheit von exoterischer and esoterischer Denkweise, hinter die
nicht zurückgegangen werden kann, weil sie im Wahrheits — "Dogma" selber
und keinesweges in seiner Verkündigungsart begründet liegt' (*Ibid., p. 45*).

9. Concerning the tentativeness of Lessing's thinking Oelmüller has written:
'Lessing entwickelt von der Subjektivität und Geschichte aus Denkmodelle,
die Plausibles und Verbindliches für die in seiner Zeit ungelösten Spannung
zwischen dem Christentum und der Moderne entfalten sollen. Denkmodelle
beanspruchen keine Totallösungen . . ., sie sind Lösungsversuche für bestimmte geschichtliche Situationen' (*Die unbefriedigte Aufklärung*,
pp. 101–102).

10. Thielicke contends that the exoteric peculiarity of Lessing's theological
speculations are 'aus dem Ansatz des Lessingschen Denkens selber zu verstehen' (*Offenbarung, Vernunft und Existenz*, p. 45). Thielicke further
contends that the 'Ansatz' of Lessing's thinking derives from the fact that
Lessing remained 'ein ständig Fragender' (p. 46). Thielicke has not, in my
judgment, sufficiently explained the theoretical and historical reason why
Lessing remained 'ein ständig Fragender'. Thielicke slips all too easily into
speculations about, history, knowledge, etc. indicating an existentialistic
orientation on his part. Hence his comparison of Lessing with Kierkegaard.
Lessing remained a questioner because he was a victim of the eighteenth-
century cognitive crisis and therefore the 'Ansatz des Lessingschen Denkens'
is precisely this crisis.

B. The rationalistic paradigm

11. Peter Heller is correct in suggesting that Lessing's reference to Erysichthon
is perhaps indicative of a lack of satisfaction with the various alternative
answers (the spiritual food) given during his life time. Cf. *Dialectics and
Nihilism: Essay on Lessing, Nietzsche, Mann and Kafta* (1966), pp. 59–68.
Heller's thesis is substantiated by the comments made in the *Bibliolatrie*
directly following the quotation just given above.
'So blieb es auch eine geraume Zeit. Ich ward von einer Seite zur andern
gerissen: keine befriedigte mich ganz. Die eine sowohl als die andere ließ
mich nur mit dem festen Vorsatze von sich, die Sache nicht eher abzu-
urteiln, "quam utrinque plenius fuerit peroratum [als bis sie von beiden
Seiten ausführlicher durchgesprochen wäre]' . . .
'Je zusetzender die Schriftsteller von beiden Teilen wurden . . . desto mehr
glaubte ich zu empfinden, daß die Wirkung, die ein jeder auf mich machte,
diejenige gar nicht sei, die er eigentlich nach seiner Art hätte machen
müssen. . . . Je bündiger mir der eine das Christentum erweisen wollte, desto
zweifelhafter ward ich. Je mutwilliger und triumphierender mir es der
andere ganz zu Boden treten wollte: desto geneigter fühlte ich mich, es
wenigstens in meinem Herzen aufrecht zu erhalten' (*B., VIII, 488–489*).
This quotation can also be viewed as a preliminary piece of evidence
indicating a state of crisis in Lessing's theological reflections. Otto Man has
succinctly formulated the starting point of Lessing's speculations. '[Lessings]
Grunderfahrung ist nicht Gott, sondern der Mensch, und nicht der Mensch,

der im schönen Glanze der Religion und Vernunft lebt, sondern der Mensch als das grundsätzlich und unaufhebbar problematische Wesen' (*Lessing: Sein und Leistung,* 2nd ed., p. 57).

12. Although the *Erziehung* has often been discussed and — also paragraphs 93—100 as a unity (though less frequently), § 100 itself has received scant attention.

   Martha Waller, one of the few interpreters to quote § 100, has correctly noted that the function of § § 93—100 are theodicean, i.e., they serve the function of solving the problem of evil relative to the individual's ultimate fulfillment. Cf. *Lessings Erziehung der Menschengeschlechts. Interpretation und Darstellung ihres rationalen und irrationalen Gehalts. Eine Auseinandersetzung mit der Lessingforschung* (1935), pp. 109ff.

   Gottfried Fittbogen has interpreted the 'Ewigkeit' of § 100 as essentially constituting an 'infinite' succession of 'nows'. Cf. *Die Religion Lessings* (1923), pp. 302—305.

   Surprisingly Oelmüller and Thielicke, both of whom interpret Lessing as somehow 'Christian', simply do not mention, let alone discuss § 100 (or § § 93—100). This they should have done as § 100 is not easily reconcilable with the doctrines of traditional Christianity.

   Otto Mann refers briefly to the paragraphs (cf. *Lessing,* pp. 347—350) and interprets them as showing that for Lessing man finds his fulfillment in the absolute being of God.

   Harold Schultz briefly interprets § § 94—100 as showing Lessing's eschatological belief, according to which man, proceeding from a mysterious identity with God, shall gradually approach an infinite goal. Cf. *Lessings Toleranzbegriff: Eine theologische Studie* (1969), p. 105, footnote 84.

   For an interpretation of § 100 as containing proto-atheistic implications (albeit implications Lessing would not have wanted to draw) see Leonard P. Wessell, Jr. 'Lessing's Eschatology and the Death of God', *Lessing Yearbook VI* (1974), pp. 59—82.

13. For an outstanding analysis of the principles involved in Lessing's style of criticism (or, perhaps more accurately, his critical style) see Ingrid Strohschneider-Kohrs, *Vom Prinzip des Maßes in Lessings Kritik.*

14. Indeed, Christian Wolff defines eternity as necessity: 'Was nothwendig ist ist auch *ewig* / das ist / kan weder Anfang noch Ende haben' (*Vernünftige Gedancken von Gott* [1729], p. 21, § 39).

15. For example, Alexander Gottlieb Baumgarten writes: '*Necessarium* est, cuius oppositum est impossible, non necessarium est *contingens*' (*Metaphysica,* 7th ed. [Halle, 1779], p. 28, § 101). In the German version of the *Metaphysica* the term *contingens* is translated as *zufällig,* cf. *Metaphysik* (Halle, 1766), p. 30, § 80.

16. Richard Campbell considers that Lessing along with Kierkegaard have by their analyses of the relationship between historical investigations and the construction of theological doctrine set the tone of subsequent discussion to this day, cf. 'Lessing's Problem and Kierkegaard's Answer', *Scottish Journal of Theology,* 19 (1966), pp. 35—54. Campbell further contends that Lessing's identification of valid theological truth with necessary and eternal truth is one of the sources for the 'great gulf . . . between biblical scholarship and

dogmatics' (p. 44), i.e., the purely historical is seen as irrelevant to authentic religious experience and any 'dogmatic' explanation of such experience based upon history. Campell has adequately grasped the effects of the rationalistic paradigm in Lessing's theological speculations, but has totally overlooked the effects of the empiricistic paradigm and the resultant crisis in Lessing's thinking. As a result Campell simply identifies Lessing's theology with eighteenth-century rationalism and its supra-historical concept of reason (cf. p. 45f). But, as will be shown, Lessing, on account of the crisis in the rationalistic paradigm, came to accept history not only as a means for gaining eternal truths, but also as a necessary means. Therefore, Lessing's problem is not really the problem to which Kierkegaard suggested an answer. For Kierkegaard, religious 'truth' is mediated to man independent of history in a moment of pure inwardness. For Lessing the problem is how 'truth' can be given in and through history. Cf. Oelmüller, *Die unbefriedigte Aufklärung,* p. 99f. Oelmüller in his analysis of the historical in Lessing's thinking has overlooked the influence of rationalism in Lessing's speculations and thereby misses the contradictions in Lessing's thinking or, more accurately, that Lessing's thinking is contradictory (cf. p. 297, footnote 54). Lessing's distinction between accidental and necessary truth (discussed above in the text) amply testifies to Lessing's acceptance of the rationalistic paradigm.

17. The degree to which Lessing has subordinated God to the rational becomes strikingly clear when his statements are compared with Luther's. For instance, Luther writes: 'Denn wenn es für Gottes Willen irgendeine Richtschnur und Maß gäbe oder eine Ursache oder einen Grund, so könnte er bereits nicht mehr Gottes Wille sein. Denn nicht deswegen, weil es ihm ziemt oder ziemte so zu wollen, ist richtig, was er will, sondern im Gegenteil: weil er selbst so will, deswegen muß recht sein, was geschieht. Dem Willen des Geschöpfes wird Ursache und Grund vorgeschrieben, aber nicht dem Willen des Schöpfers, es sein denn, daß Du ihm einen anderen Schöpfer vorziehen willst.' (*Vom unfreien Willen* [1525] in *Luther Deutsch: Die Werke Martin Luthers,* ed. Kurt Aland [1961], Band III, pp. 280—281).

18. Maurice Colleville designates the *C.V.* chronologically as the point where Lessing becomes open to rationalistic arguments, cf. 'L'évolution religieuse der Lessing', *Études Germaniques,* 19 (1964), p. 15.

19. Thielicke has sought to show that a fragment such as *Ü.E.G.R.* cannot be used to prove the 'systematic core' of Lessing's theological speculations to be rationalistic or 'immanental' because it breaks off exactly at the point that the content of the rational religion should be described. Therefore, according to Thielicke, the ultimate meaning of *Ü.E.G.R.* is its uncertain and questioning attitude towards what is maintained in the fragment up to the point where it ends, cf. *Offenbarung, Vernunft und Existenz,* pp. 48—49. Whereas I agree with Thielicke that the fragments such as the *Ü.E.G.R.* end in scepticism (or frustration), nevertheless, they can be used to illustrate that and how Lessing utilized the rationalistic paradigm. In my opinion, the *Ü.E.G.R.* and *C.V.* end as fragments because they also exhibit the influence of the empiricistic paradigm which is not reconciled with the rationalistic paradigm. Lessing breaks off the works precisely because of the crisis in his thinking.

20 My contention, if correct, invalidates Otto Mann's thesis: '[Lessing] hält vielmehr, gegenüber der Aufklärung, die alte Religion, die Theologie fest' (*Lessing,* p. 61).

C. *The empiricistic paradigm and the crisis in Lessing's thinking*

21. Thus Emanuel Hirsch writes: 'Die letzte Gesinnung Lessings kann in die allgemeine Formel gefaßt werden: das *Positive,* d.h. das über die Natürliche-Vernünftige Hinausgehende am Christentum wie an jeder andern geschichtlichen Religion fällt unter den Begriff des *Vorurteils* oder *Wahns,* von dem frei zu werden Bestimmung des Menschen ist' (*Geschichte der neuern evangelischen Theologie im Zusammenhang mit den allgemeinen Bewegungen des europäischen Denkens* [1952], Band IV, p. 133).

22. Although differing in particulars, the immanental interpretation of Lessing is common to the following interpreters, to name a few: Henry E. Allison, *Lessing and the Enlightenment: His Philosophy of Religion and Its Relation to Eighteenth-Century Thought* (1966), pp. 150—151; Arthur von Arx, *Lessing und die geschichtliche Welt* (1944), pp. 125—139; Martin Haug, *Entwicklung und Offenbarung bei Lessing* (1928), pp. 79—80; Wilm Pelters, *Lessings Standort: Sinndeutung der Geschichte als Kern seines Denkens* (1972), pp. 47—48; Ferdinand Josef Schneider, *Lessing und die monistische Weltanschauung* (1929), pp. 11—12; Heinrich Scholz, ed. *Die Hauptschriften zum Pantheismusstreit zwischen Jacobi und Mendelssohn* (1916), p. xixff.; and Benno von Wiese, *Lessing: Dichtung, Aesthetik, Philosophie* (1931), pp. 155—158.

23. Moses Mendelssohn, *Schriften zur Philosophie, Aesthetik und Apologetik,* ed. Mortiz Brasch (1968), Band II, p. 555.

24. 'The Treatise of Human Nature' in Hume: *Selections* (ed. Charles W. Hendel, Jr., 1955), p. 93.

25. For a penetrating analysis of the inconsistencies and difficulties entailed in Lessing's twofold analysis of the problem of historical truths see Friedrich Traub, 'Geschichtswahrheiten und Vernunftwahrheiten bei Lessing', *Zeitschrift für Theologie und Kirche,* 28 (1921), pp. 193—207. Traub's analysis of the curious inconsistency in Lessing's thought has substantially influenced my own interpretation. Traub fails to see, however, that the inconsistency contained in Lessing's analysis is due to the crisis nature of Lessing's thought. The failure to perceive the influence of the empiricistic paradigm in *Ü.B.G.K.* has led Gottfried Fittbogen to conclude that Lessing totally rejects any relationship between history and religious truth, cf. 'Die Grundlagen von Lessings Religion', *Preußische Jahrbücher,* 170 (1917), pp. 333—339. As a result of his one-sided view of Lessing, Fittbogen remains almost totally oblivious of the crisis nature of Lessing's anthropological conception of man.

26. Christoph Schrempf also discovered a contradiction at this point in Lessing's argumentation. Schrempf writes: 'Denn [Lessing] lehnt es als eine *metábasis eis allo génos* ab, daß er nach den Wundern, die er nicht leugnet, seinen Gottesbegrif umbilde und eben dadurch anerkennt er, daß sie diese Wunder

allerdings eine Umbildung seiner Grundidee von dem Wesen der Gottheit notwendig machen würden' (*Lessing als Philosoph* pp. 157—158). Cf. also Traub, 'Geschichtswahrheiten und Vernunftwahrheiten bei Lessing', p. 202.

27. Rationality entailed for eighteenth-century rationalists the principle of sufficient reason which, when applied to an interpretation of reality, yielded the concept of order as a key structural element of being. For instance, Christian Wolff distinguishes between dream and reality in the following manner: 'Da nun dergleichen Ordnung sich im Traume nicht befindet / als wo vermöge der Erfahrung kein Grund anzuzeigen / warum die Dinge bey einander sind und so neben einander stehen / auch ihre Veränderungen auf einander erfolgen; so erkennet man hieraus deutlich / daß die Wahrheit von dem Traume durch die Ordnung unterschieden sey. Und ist demnach die Wahrheit nichts anders als die Ordnung in den Veränderungen der Dinge: hingegen der Traum ist Unordnung in den Veränderungen der Dinge. . . . Wer dieses wohl erweget / der wird zur Genüge erkennen / daß ohne den Staz des zureichenden Grundes keine Wahrheit seyn kann' (*Vernünftige Gedanken,* pp. 74, 76, § § 142, 144). Cf. also Johann Christoph Gottsched, *Erste Gründe der gesamten Weltweisheit* (1733) Band I, p. 119, § 218. See also Cassirer's comments on Wolff's concept of truth and the difficulties it entails: *Das Erkenntnisproblem in der Philosophie und Wissenschaft der neueren Zeit,* Band II, p. 521ff.

D. *The effects of the empiricistic paradigm on Lessing's anthropology*

28. Kant, for instance, in his *Träume eines Geistersehers, erläutert durch Träume der Metaphysik* (1766) criticized the Wolffian belief in formal order and freedom from contradiction as a criterion for distinguishing between dreams and reality. A dream, according to Kant, can be just as ordered as reality and therefore the ontological and systematic constructions of the rationalists may be no more than the 'dreams of metaphysicians'. In other words, the norms of mathematical metaphysics are not necessarily valid for reality. For a brief analysis of the *Träume* see Cassirer, *Erkenntnisproblem,* Band II, p. 601ff.

29. Concerning the crisis in the life of the young Lessing see F. J. Schmitz, *The Problem of Individualism and the Crisis in the Lives of Lessing and Hamann* (1944), pp. 125—148.

30. Concerning the young Lessing's basic religious question Mann writes: 'Der Ansatz für die echte religöse Frage setzt [für Lessing] das Negativsein des Menschen voraus' (*Lessing,* p. 60). However, Mann concludes too much from this fact when he asserts (p. 61) that, according to Lessing, not reason rather the Judaic-Christian tradition *alone* can show man the way out of his imperfect condition. For a more balanced and cautious analysis of what conclusions can be drawn from *R.* see J. C. Schneider, *Lessings Stellung zur Theologie vor der Herausgabe der Wolfenbüttler Fragmente,* pp. 54—58.

31. Cf. Lovejoy, 'The Parallel of Deism and Classicism', *Essays in the History of Ideas* (1960), p. 80.

32. Ibid., p. 86.

33. Lessing clearly used the paradigm of 'rationalistic primitivism' in his rhetorical justification of the metempsychosis hypothesis at the end of the *Erziehung*. Lessing writes: 'Ist diese Hypothese darum so lächerlich, weil sie die älteste ist? weil der menschliche Verstand, ehe ihn die Sophisterei der Schule zerstreut und geschwächt hatte, sogleich darauf verfiel?' (*Erziehung*, VIII, 614, § 95).
34. Lovejoy, 'The Parallel', p. 80.
35. Cf. Leisegang, *Lessings Weltanschauung*, pp. 101—102.
36. Baumgarten, *Metaphysik* (Halle, 176), p. 164, § 383.
37. Ibid., p. 235, § 499.
38. Concerning the influence of Leibnizian-Wolffian concepts (primarily those of Baumgarten) on Lessing's philosophical reflection (albeit primarily in the area of aesthetics) see Victor Anthony Rudowski, *Lessing's Aesthetica in NUCE: An Analysis of the May 26, 1769 Letter to Nicolae* (1971), pp. 23—33.
39. In the *Erziehung* Lessing explicitly uses the words 'sinnliche Vorstellungen' to refer to the concept of Jehova that the Jews slowly transcended under the influence of the Persians, cf. VIII, 601, § 39.
40. Why Lessing broke off the *C.V.* when he did, is, of course, conjectural. J. Schneider contends that Lessing stopped at the point where he should explain the origin and essence of evil (i.e., 'Unvollkommenheiten') and this he could not accomplish given his thesis that each grade of being is a 'Vollkommenheit' (*Lessings Stellung*, pp. 115—116). Schneider is correct as far as he goes, but he overlooks an essential fact. Lessing has speculatively constructed the world according to a *static* concept of the 'chain of being'. Lessing postulates a grade of being is not fully self-conscious (and this grade is occupied by man). Lessing was therefore making man's cognitive and moral imperfection (i.e., man's empirical consciousness) into a metaphysical and hence rational necessity. Within the static framework of rationalism, Lessing was being faced with an empirical anamoly (i.e., man's limited consciousness) which was hopelessly insolvable. Lessing discontinued the fragment because he did not yet have the conceptual means with which to maintain the rationality of the world and yet accept man's *de facto* irrationality. Thielicke has also convincingly shown that such an imperfect consciousness makes the reality of revelation useful for man, cf. *Offenbarung, Vernunft und Existenz*, pp. 51—52.

E. The structure of Lessing's cognitive crisis

41. Care must be exercised however not to *over*interpret *Nathan der Weise* in a rationalistic fashion, i.e., as manifesting solely the rationalistic paradigm. Recently Ruth K. Angress has made evident the subrational if not irrational elements within the play (or in my terms, the influence of the empiricistic paradigm), cf. ' "Dreams that Were More Than Dreams" in Lessing's *Nathan'*, *Lessing Yearbook III* (1971), pp. 108—127.
42. Cf. Thielicke, 'Vernunft und Existenz bei Lessing: Das Unbedingte in der Geschichte', in *Lessing und die Zeit der Aufklärung* (1968).
43. Cassirer, *The Philosophy of the Enlightenment* (trans. 1951), p. 195.

CHAPTER 5: LESSING'S ATTEMPTED THEOLOGICAL SYNTHESIS

A. Lessing's relationship to Christianity

1. The integration of the temporal with the metaphysical or, indeed, the mere conceptualization and analysis of 'time' was not just a peculiar difficulty facing Lessing, rather a general problem that brought about a major revolution in thought throughout the latter part of the 18th century. For an analysis of the break through of time into theories of history, cosmic evolution, development of nature, and geological changes in the eighteenth century see Stephen Toulmin and June Goodfield, *The Discovery of Time* (1966), pp. 125—170. For a description of the role time came to assume in eighteenth-century biological theory see Arthur O. Lovejoy, *The Great Chain of Being: A Study of the History of an Idea* (1960), pp. 227—241. For an analysis of the temporalization of the most important paradigm of eighteenth-century thought, namely the principle of plenitude, see Lovejoy, 'The Temporalization of the Chain of Being', *The Great Chain of Being,* pp. 242—287. Finally, for an analysis of 'progressive' thinking in eighteenth-century theological speculations in England see Ernest Lee Tuveson, *Millenium and Utopia: A Study in the Background of the Idea of Progress* (1964), especially pp. 153—206.

2. It is important to recognize that Lessing analyzed the problem of the relationship between the empirico-historical and the absolute (i.e., the metaphysical) within the framework of the rationalistic and empiricistic paradigms (i.e., within the framework of eighteenth-century thought) and that, therefore, his attempted solution falls within the parameters of such paradigms. The failure to do so has led Helmut Thielicke to formulate Lessing's problem with the terminology (and hence paradigms) of Kierkegaardian thought. Therefore, Thielicke 'squeezes' out of Lessing's speculations an alleged commitment by Lessing to an 'existentialistic subjectivity' free from all claims of history relative to grasping the divine, cf. 'Vernunft und Existenz bei Lessing: Das Unbedingte in der Geschichte', *Lessing und die Zeit der Aufklärung* (1968), pp. 100—115. Thus Thielicke comes to the odd conclusion concerning the nature of Lessing's thinking: 'Ist es nicht, − wenn wir ihm aus *dieser* Richtung des Denkens und Befragens nahen − ein ganz anderer Lessing, der uns hier anblickt, einer, der wenigstens in bestimmten Augenblicken seines Denkens, die Aufklärung hinter sich gelassen hat, einer, den man mit deistischen Kategorien überhaupt nicht mehr angemessen versteht, sondern den man von Kierkegaard aus interpretieren müßte?' (p. 114). Such an a-historical approach reveals more about Thielicke's own theological existentialism than about Lessing's and constitutes, in my judgment, a gross methodological error. An investigator can, indeed, compare Lessing's thought with Kierkegaard's, but first an investigator must determine what Lessing did think and that means first analyzing the paradigms underlying his thinking. In the above cited article Thielicke has failed to accomplish such a task. For a more balanced interpretation of Lessing's historical analysis and paradigms see Mattijs Jolles, 'Lessing's Conception of History', *Modern Philogy,* 43 (1946), pp. 175—191.

3. For a comprehensive and detailed analysis of this passage see Edward S. Flajole, S. J., 'Lessing's Retrieval of Lost Truths', *P.M.L.A.*, 74 (1959), pp. 52—66.

4. Ibid., p. 57. However penetrating Flajole's analysis of Lessing's theology is, he nevertheless misses the crisis nature of Lessing's thinking and thereby mistakenly identifies Lessing's religion with a Spinozistic theology.

5. It is precisely Ernst Walter Zeeden's contention that Lessing's assertions concerning his own alleged Lutheranism and his refutation of Reimarus constitute a dissimulating tactic on Lessing's part in order to be able to continue unmolested by censorship his attacks upon the traditional concept of revelation, cf. *The Legacy of Luther: Martin Luther and the Reformation in the Estimation of the German Lutherans from Luther's Death to the Beginning of the Age of Goethe* (trans. 1954), pp. 141—150. Zeeden's contention saves him the task of examining Lessing's 'refutations' of Reimarus and thus of finding his own interpretation of Lessing to be tenuous.

6. Heinrich Schneider quotes from reports of a trip made through Germany by a Dane, Andreas Christian Hviid. Hviid had a conversation with Lessing on September 12, 1777. Hviid writes: 'Als [Lessing] erfuhr, daß ich Theologie studiere, sagte er, daß die Theologen eine Menschenklasse seien, mit denen er in der Welt am allerwenigsten hätte übereinkommen können, sie schlössen in einem ewigen Zirkel. Ich brauche nur die Bücher zu lesen, die deren Widerlegung (Refutationes) enthielten, um mich davon zu überzeugen. Ich antwortete darauf, indem ich Reimarus, Jerusalem und Leß lobte: darauf antwortete er nicht, sondern fragte, ob ich weiter als nach Deutschland reisen wollte.' Cf. Schneider, *Lessing: Zwölf biographische Studien* (1951), p. 51.

7. Martin Rade was correct when he summarized Lessing's relationship to Christianity (at least as accurately as an interpreter can determine): 'Wir sind keine Herzenkündiger und wissen nicht, ob Lessing ein Christ war; aber was sich feststellen läßt, ist, daß Lessing ein Christ sein, als Christ anerkannt werden wollte' ('Lessing als Theolog', *Jahrbuch des Freien Deutschen Hochstifts*, p. 16).

8. Rohrmoser, 'Lessing und die religionsphilosophische Fragestellung der Aufklärung', *Lessing und die Zeit der Aufklärung* (1968).

B. Lessing's principle of reconciliation

9. Despite the rich possibilities that Lessing's dramaturgical speculations (which were completed before his major theological efforts) offer for comprehending Lessing's theological interpretations of history, there has been surprisingly little attention paid to Lessing's dramaturgy in such a context. One major exception is Arthur von Arx, *Lessing und die geschichtliche Welt* (1944), pp. 36—38. For an interpretation of Lessing's dramaturgy from the standpoint of the crisis in his *ars cogitandi* (particularly as manifested in his theological speculations) see Leonard P. Wessell, Jr., *'Geist* and *Buchstabe* as Creative Principles in Lessing's Dramaturgy', in *Lessing Yearbook V* (1973), pp. 107—146.

10. Seldom has sufficient emphasis been placed upon the function of the 'present' in Lessing's dramaturgy. Concerning this function see Hans Herrmann, *Der Gegenwärtigkeitsgedanke in der theoretischen Behandlung des dramatischen Kunstwerks bei Lessing, A. W. Schlegel und Hegel* (1934), pp. 1—27.

11. The concept of *telos* as the key conceptual element in Lessing's reconciliation of the historical and the metaphysical has been discussed by Georg Eichholz, *Die Geschichte als theologisches Problem bei Lessing* (1933), pp. 15—19.

12. Cf. *Science and the Modern World* (1960), p. 57. Lovejoy has emphasized the fact that one of the sources leading to the temporalization of the chain of being in the eighteenth century was the theodicean problems arising from the rationalistic doctrine of 'the best of all possible worlds' (*The Great Chain of Being*, p. 244ff.). Lessing's problem was by no means unique, rather a manifestation of the crisis in the *Aufklärung*.

13. The concept of progressivity was not, of course, foreign to Lessing. In a letter (Jan. 21, 1756) to Mendelssohn, Lessing writes:
'Ich glaube, der Schöpfer mußte alles, was er erschuf, fähig machen, vollkommner zu werden, wenn es in der Vollkommenheit, in welcher er es erschuf, bleiben sollte. Der Wilde, zum Exampel, würde, ohne die Perfektibilität, nicht lange ein Wilder bleiben, sondern gar bald nichts besser als irgend ein unvernünftiges Tier werden; er erhielt also die Perfektibilität nicht deswegen, um nichts Geringeres zu werden' (IX, 63). Nevertheless, there is no surviving evidence that Lessing ever analyzed philosophically to any comprehensive degree the notion of perfectibility, particularly as an explanatory principle for interpreting history.

C. The rationality of the empirico-historical life of man

14. Cf. Durzak, 'Vernunft und Offenbarung im Denken Lessings', *Poesie und Ratio: Vier Lessing-Studien* (1970), pp. 105—139.

15. Ibid., pp. 130, 133. Durzak's line of argumentation is in effect the same as used by Arthur von Arx to come to similar conclusions. See *Lessing und die geschichtliche Welt*, p. 125f.

16. The contradiction between § 4 and § 77 has caused a great amount of difficulty for interpreters and has provoked various dialetical subtleties in this attempt to reconcile the two paragraphs.
Henry Allison contends that § 4 refers to the 'logical structure' of religious truth and § 77 to the 'psychological conditions necessary for their apprehension'. Just as the slave boy of the Platonic dialogues would never have recognized geometrical truth without the prodding of Socrates, so would the human race perhaps not have recognized rational truths of religion without the occasion of the obscure teachings of alleged revelation. Cf. *Lessing and the Enlightenment: His Philosophy and Its Relation to Eighteenth-Century Thought* (1966), pp. 158—159.
Martha Waller conceives § 77 essentially as an exoteric expression not rendering Lessing's 'true' position. The inclusion of § 77 was allegedly a

prudent tactic of Lessing's to conceal somewhat his attack upon the orthodox conception of revelation (seen in § 4). Cf. *Lessings Erziehung des Menschengeschlechts: Interpretationen und Darstellung ihres rationalen und irrationalen Gehaltes* (1935), pp. 16—37, 93.

Martin Haug contends that § 77 is only one of those hypotheses Lessing makes in order later to have the pleasure of tearing it down. Basically § 77 is but a tactic by Lessing, i.e., Lessing talks in the terminology of his opponents in order to bring them over to his way of thinking. At any rate, the people referred to in § 77 are the slow developing nations that need the help of the advanced and more intelligent peoples (those referred to in § 4). See *Entwicklung und Offenbarung bei Lessing* (1928), pp. 61—64.

Henry Chadwick grants that there is a contradiction between the two paragraphs but draws no conclusions from this fact nor explains why it occurs. For Chadwick § 4 totally renders the existence of a transcendent revelation (implied in § 77) meaningless. Cf. 'Introduction', *Lessing's Theological Writings* (1967). p. 39f.

Helmut Thielicke has a much more subtle and penetrating analysis. Thielicke sees in § 4 a reference to the pure rational power to grasp truths of reason whereas § 77 refers to an 'empirische *ratio*' which, because man's historical existence must and does remain unfathomable to it, is equivalent to an '*ir-ratio*'. There is according to Lessing, claims Thielicke, no such thing as 'eine sich überlassene Vernunft', at least at the beginning of history, and therefore, revelation conceived as a transcendent act of divine education has the task of developing man's empirical reason to the level of 'transcendental reason'. Cf. *Offenbarung, Vernunft und Existenz: Studien zur Religionsphilosophie Lessings* (3rd ed., 1957), pp. 128—139.

Whereas my own position concerning the function of 'transcendent' revelation is similar to Thielicke's, I see no reason to invent adjectives such as 'transcendental' and 'empirical' to qualify respectively Lessing's use of the term 'Vernunft' in § § 4 and 77 in order to reconcile the two paragraphs. In my judgment the term 'Vernunft' has an analytical or rationalistic meaning and that, therefore, there is a real contradiction. The problem is not to interpret away the contradiction but to explain it, i.e., why it occurs. As long as the contradictoriness of Lessing's thinking is not acknowledged, interpreters will continue to invent ever new and ever more ingenious ways of reconciling the irreconcilable.

17. The notion that the ameliorative evolution of man has been brought about by an act of a transcendent God (i.e., by a source distinct from the immanental powers of the human mind) does not seem to be the sole peculiarity of Lessing. For instance, the theologian J. D. Salzmann, friend and confidant of Goethe's during his Straßbourg period, seems to have maintained a similar notion. Salzmann writes: 'Da die wahre und höhere Glückseligkeit des Menschen sich auf richtige Begriffe, wahre und verhältnißmäßige Empfindung gründet, und diese nur die Früchten von unzählig vielen gesammelten Kenntnissen und Erfahrungrn seyn konnten, so hatte er Anstalten von nöten, welche seinem eigenen Vermögen zuvorlaufen, und ihn unter währendem jugendlichen Alter der Menschheit auf den rechten Weg der moralischen Erkenntniß einleiten mußten. Weilen er Verhältnisse, Ur-

sachen und Folgen noch nicht deutlich einsehen konnte, so mußten all diese Begriffe in sinnliche Vorstellungen eingekleidet werden: Ursachen und Verhältnisse mußten Vorschriften und Gesetze heißen, und die guten oder übeln Folgen jeder selbständigen Handlung mußten in dem Begriff Kindmenschen Belohnungen oder Strafen seyn. Die ersten Verfügungen dazu konnte er sich nicht selbst machen; denn wo hätte er sie hernehmen sollen: sondern es mußte eine höhere und befördernde Macht den Schwung und die Anleitung dazu geben. Der Anfang der Gesetzgebung mußte also der Menschheit von aussen her und ohne ihr Zuthun überliefert werden, und zwar mußte sie ganz einfach, sinnlich, und den kindischen Begriffen des Menschen angemessen seyn; sonst wäre sie gar nicht verstanden worden, und hätte also ihre Wirkung verfehlt. . . .' (*Kurze Abhandlungen über einige wichtige Gegenstände aus der Religions- und Sittenlehre* [Frankfurt/M., 1776; reprinted Stuttgart, 1966], pp. 141—142). For a discussion of a similar interpretation of revelation as a necessary means for educating man in the thought of Johann Fr. Wilh. Jerusalem see Karl Aner, *Die Theologie der Lessingzeit* (1929), pp. 182—186. Aner, of course, believes that Lessing renounced such a conception of the relationship between revelation and reason in his mature final years.

18. Those interpreters who claim that man's development for Lessing was purely immanental and natural must and do seek to show that the concept of 'Offenbarung' and even that of 'Erziehung' are 'nothing but' exoteric trappings and therefore, the structure of the 'exoteric' argument must (1) be ignored as not reflecting Lessing's 'true' position, or (2) reduced and transformed into immanental and evolutionary concepts.

For example, Gottfried Fittbogen maintains that Lessing continually used the technique of 'dressing up' his immanental and naturalistic opinions in the garb of traditional Christian terminology in order to entice the orthodox into entering into a different pattern of thought. Cf. *Die Religion Lessings* (1923), pp. 183—185.

Martha Waller even goes further and maintains that the concept of 'Erziehung' is not to be taken seriously on its own right, but to be viewed as an "exoteric" shorthand for the immanental self-development of human reason. Cf. *Lessings Erziehung des Menschengeschlechts* (1935), pp. 23ff. Cf. also Aner, *Theologie der Lessingzeit*, p. 356. Insofar as the notion of 'Erziehung' is retained, it is equated in a semi-Hegelian fashion with an imminent and indwelling divine *telos* monistically active in the world and in human history. Cf. Allison, *Lessing and the Enlightenment* (1966), pp. 150—151. In short, such interpreters, by interpreting Lessing's alleged 'exoteric' and 'esoteric' thinking as two mutually exclusive bodies of thought and by assuming that Lessing's 'true' esoteric position is purely immanental, have invented a way simple to ignore the logic of Lessing's *actual* (or written) line of argumentation and to translate Lessing's 'exoteric' outer shell into philosophical terminology and concepts he did not use and thereby to conclude that Lessing did not say what he really meant and vice versa. As noted in the last chapter, it is practically impossible to ascertain Lessing's 'esoteric' inner core since he wrote almost exclusively in an exoteric manner. Thielicke has, in my judgment, irrefutably shown that the two ways of thinking are not to be contrasted with each other, but are integrally related. Cf. *Offenbarung, Vernunft und Existenz,* pp. 27—57. For a further defense of Lessing's positive evaluation of revelation see Rudolf Hermann, 'Zu Lessings religionsphilosophischer und theologischer Problematik', *Zeitschrift für systematische Theologie,* 22 (1953), pp. 127—148. In my opinion the structure of Lessing's alleged 'exoteric' argumentations must be analyzed, not ignored if the nature and problematic of Lessing's theological speculations are to be grasped.

19. Haug concludes that Lessing's 'idealistischer teleologischer Entwicklungsgedanke' saved 'alle geoffenbarten Religionen' (*Entwicklung und Offenbarung,* p. 80). But Lessing in the *Erziehung* makes no reference to Islam (to name a major 'revealed' religion), to say nothing of the myriads of man's minor religions. On the contrary, Lessing explicitly contrasts Judaism (and derivatively Christianity) with all other religions as the chosen means of divine education. Lessing writes: 'Da [Gott] aber einem jeden *einzeln Menschen* sich nicht mehr offenbaren konnte, noch wollte: so wählte er sich ein *einzelnes Volk* zu besonderen Erziehung . . .' (VIII, 592, § 8) and that whereas 'die anderen Völker des Erdbodens' developed 'bei dem Lichte der Vernunft', God led 'sein erwähltes Volk durch all Staffeln einer kindischen Erziehung' (VIII, 595, § 20). Of course, if one assumes that Lessing's 'exoteric' language is 'nothing but' external dressing, then it is no problem to conclude that Lessing saved all revealed religions (or none, if one's assumed esoteric essence of Lessing's theology should demand it).

20. Cf. Haug, *Ibid.,* p. 89. Haug contends that the divine education of man is actually just the education of the less developed part of humanity by the more developed part. This position, however, contradicts the explicit, albeit 'exoteric', meaning of § 21. How 'das ungeschliffenste, das verwilderste [Volk]' (VIII, 592, § 8) could by its own natural power intellectually outstrip the intellectually more gifted peoples is a mystery that Haug does not solve, let alone mention. Furthermore, Lessing explicitly states that the existence of such advanced peoples proves 'nichts gegen den Nutzen und die Notwendigkeit der Erziehung' (VIII, 595, § 21), which certainly suggests that 'Erziehung' is something more than the mere immanental and natural unfolding of man's intellect.

21. *Offenbarung, Vernunft und Existenz,* pp. 91—92.

22. All the sources cited that interpret thinking monistically or at least as an immanental process make such an equation to one degree or another.

23. Cf. *Lessing and the Enlightenment,* p. 151. Cf. also Ferdinand Josef Schneider, *Lessing und die monistische Weltanschauung* (1929), p. 13.

24. Flajole, S. J., in my judgment, mistakenly contends that Lessing means by his neighbor the Neologians and Unitarians of the time, cf. 'Lessing's Attitude in the Lavater-Mendelssohn Controversy', *P.M.L.A.,* 73 (1958), p. 212. But clearly, from the context of the letter, Lessing was referring to the house of his neighbor — the orthodox Lutheran. Hermann is of the same opinion, cf. 'Zu Lessings religions-philosophischer und theologischer Problematik', p. 13.

25. For an excellent presentation of Lessing's rationalization of such Christian doctrines as original sin and justification (i.e. § § 72—76 of the *Erziehung*)

see Thielicke, *Offenbarung, Vernunft und Existenz*, pp. 120—123.

26. Cf. Willie Oelmüller, *Die unbefriedigte Aufklärung: Beiträge zu einer Theorie der Moderne von Lessing, Kant und Hegel* (1969)' pp. 82—83 for a similar interpretation.

27. In a very interesting article Stuart Atkins has contended that Lessing had Nathan avoid answering Saladin's question concerning the 'Gründe' for Nathan's religious belief. This indicates to Atkins that Lessing, writing on the eve of Kant's first *Kritik*, was actually doubtful of the validity of the rationalistic and humanistic Deism in which Nathan was expressing his religious belief, cf. 'The Parable of the Rings in Lessing's *Nathan der Weise*', *Germanic Review*, 26 (1951), pp. 259—267 (particularly p. 266). Atkins has in effect inchoately stumbled upon the crisis nature of Lessing's theological thinking.

28. In a very penetrating article Michael J. Böhler has shown how Lessing answers Saladin's request for the 'Grund' for Nathan's beliefs. Saladin understood by *Grund* a *Woher* of belief (i.e., in effect, he was looking for an objective grounding of faith) whereas Nathan's answer gives a *Warum* as the *Grund*, i.e., religious belief should have as its *causa finalis* the moral perfection of the believer. For Böhler this is indicative that Lessing was shifting from an analytical to a synthetic concept of reason, cf. 'Lessings *Nathan der Weise* als Spiel vom Grunde,' *Lessing Yearbook III* (1971), pp. 128—150. Thielicke has also contended that historical religion in the ring-parable is for Lessing an *Aufgabe* rather than a *Gabe*, cf. *Offenbarung, Vernunft und Existenz*, pp. 126—127.

29. Oelmüller makes the same distinction concerning the ultimate purpose of the two endeavors by Lessing without apparently seeing any contradiction being involved, cf. *Die unbefriedigte Aufklärung*, p. 79.

30. *The Spirit of Medieval Philosophy* (1940), p. 61.

31. Peter Heller has focused his attention upon this endlessly dynamic aspect of Lessing's thinking and has interpreted Lessing as a ceaselessly active 'dialectician' concerning whom Heller writes: 'The dialectician is a "naked man", a *gymnastikos*. He owns nothing. Or he owns what he owns but to give it away. He knows that since his essential task, and the law of human existence, is the transcending movement, he owns no truth. He knows that he is ignorant, that his nakedness is his only advantage. He knows that he knows nothing . . . And if he is but the protagonist of a movement, and if this movement is all-pervasive, his only true distinction is that he is aware of this movement, that he affirms it in his conscious intellectual life and, ideally, in his entire existence. He is not merely the object of a universal law but, being in its movement, he affirms the movement. He affirms the law' (*Dialectics and Nihilism: Essays on Lessing, Nietzsche, Mann and Kafka* [1966], p. 50). Concerning Lessing's immanental eschatology see Hans Urs von Balthasar, *Prometheus: Studien zur Geschichte des deutschen Idealismus* (1947), pp. 45—52.

32. Karl Schmid refers to the just cited passage from Lessing and the very next one which reads: 'Wenn Gott in seiner Rechten alle Wahrheit, und in seiner Linken den einzigen immer regen Trieb nach Wahrheit, obschon mit dem Zusatze, mich immer und ewig zur irren, verschlossen hielte, und spräche zu

mir: wähle! Ich fiele ihm mit Demut in seine Linke, und sagte: Vater gib! die reine Wahrheit is ja doch nur für dich allein!' (*D.*, VIII, 27). Schmid writes: 'Wo Gottes Hand so sehr und für immer die Wahrheit verschlossen halten muß — was liegt da näher, als das *'Streben'* absolut zu setzen?' ('Lessings Religiösität', *Zeitspuren: Aufsätze und Reden* [1967], p. 153). Although Schmid is correct in placing emphasis upon the subjective, personal, and dynamic element in Lessing's thinking, he is wrong when he contends: 'Lessing "besaß" keine Theologie. Er hatte nur Frömmigkeit' (p. 141). It is true that Lessing had no worked out, systematic, and comprehensive theology. But the *telos* underlying his life-long theological speculating was the desire to develop a theology that would adequately express, explain, and justify his 'Frömmigkeit'. He could not reach this goal because of the crisis nature of his thinking.

33. Cf. *Vom Prinzip des Maßes in Lessings Kritik* (1969), p. 29.
34. Concerning Lessing's application of principles of *Geist* and *Buchstabe* to the realm of dramaturgy see my article cited in note 9.
35. Cf. 'Lessing and Religion', *Germanic Review*, 43 (1968), p. 251.

D. Excursus: Lessing's concept of God

36. *Philosophia prima sive Ontologia*, pp. 137—138, § 169.
37. Cf. *Philosophers Speak of God* (1963), pp. 1—2.
38. The term 'panentheistic' is used in the sense defined by Hawthorne and Reese, cf. ibid., pp. 1—25.
39. Lessing's conversation with Jacobi has been the source of endless quarrels amongst scholars since Jacobi had the conversation published. A full and critical evaluation of the secondary literature would demand a monograph in itself. It will suffice to say that I agree with Alexander Altmann (whose essay is perhaps the most recent and most comprehensive study of the problem) that Lessing's statements to Jacobi, especially when viewed in the light of statements in other works, are to be interpreted monistically. Cf. 'Lessing und Jacobi: Das Gespräch über den Spinozismus', *Lessing Yearbook III* (1971), pp. 25—71. For contrary opinions see Schultze, *Lessings Toleranzbegriff: Eine theologische Studie* (1969), pp. 107—110, and Thielicke, *Offenbarung, Vernunft und Existenz*, pp. 93—114. Whereas I agree with Schultze and Thielicke that Lessing's speculations about God are not Spinozistic (in a strict sense), it does not follow that they are not monistic, specifically panentheistic.
40. Cf. *Being and Some Philosophers*, 2nd ed. (Toronto: Europe Printing, 1951), pp. 109—110.
41. Letter, August 1641, quoted by Gilson, ibid., p. 110.
42. Cf. *Geschichte des Deutschen Idealismus* (München: C. H. Beck'sche Verlagsbuchhandlung, 1909), I, 105—106.
43. *Offenbarung, Vernunft und Existenz*, pp. 48—49.
44. In the concluding remarks to his reported conversation with Lessing Jacobi writes concerning § 73 of the *Erziehung*: 'Ich möchte wissen, ob sich

jemand diese Stelle anders, als nach spinozistischen Ideen deutlich machen kann?' (VIII, 633). In my judgment, at no point is Lessing's trinitarian speculation closer to traditional Christianity than at this point. Hans Leisegang contends that Lessing's trinitarian speculations in § 73 are very close to no less an 'orthodox' thinker than Melanchthon. Cf. *Lessings Weltanschauung* (Leipzig: Felix Meiner Verlag, 1931), p. 81.

CHAPTER 6. SUMMARY AND CONCLUSIONS

1. Hermann Kesten sees Lessing's commitment to the moral education of mankind as the thread that weaves itself through the various endeavors Lessing undertook during his life. Cf. 'Lessing, ein deutscher Moralist.' *Gotthold Ephraim Lessing. Werke,* ed. Hermann Kesten. (Köln/Berlin: Kiepenheuer & Witsch, n.d.), II, 873—891.

Bibliography

A. PRIMARY SOURCES

Die Aufklärung in ausgewählten Texten dargestellt. Ed. Gerhard Funke. Stuttgart: K. F. Koehler Verlag, 1963.

Die Aufklärung im deutschen Schriftum. Ed. Ulrich Haacke. Bielefeld/Leipzig: Velhagen & Klasing, 1931.

Bahrdt, Karl Friedrich. *Ueber Preßfreyheit und deren Gränzen.* Züllichan: 1787.

Baumgarten, Alexander Gottlieb. *Metaphysica.* 7th ed. Halle: 1779 (reprinted Hildesheim: Georg Olms Verlag, 1963).

— *Metaphysik.* Halle: 1776.

Béguelin. *Mémoires sur les premiers principes de la Metáphysique.* Berliner Akademie, 1755.

Bibliothek der deutschen Aufklärer des achtzehnten Jahrhunderts. Ed. Martin von Geismar. 2 vols. Leipzig: Otto Wigand, 1847.

Crusius, Christian August. *Der Weg zur Gewißheit und Zuverlässigkeit der menschlichen Erkenntnis.* Leipzig: 1747.

— *Entwurf der Notwendigen Vernunftwahrheiten, wie fern sie den zufälligen entgegengesetzt werden.* 3rd ed., Leipzig: 1766 (Originally 1745).

Descartes, René. 'Rules for the Direction of Mind' (1628), in *The Philosophical Works.* Trans. S. Haldane and G. R. T. Ross. 2 vols. Cambridge: Cambridge University Press, 1968.

Deutsche Dichtung im 18. Jahrhundert. Ed. Adalbert Elschenbroich. München: Carl Hanser Verlag, 1960.

The Formula of Concord. Thorough Declaration II: Of Free Will, in *Triglot Concordia: The Symbolic Books of the Ev. Lutheran Church.* St. Louis: Concordia, 1921.

Gottsched, Johann Christoph. *Erste Gründe der gesamten Weltweisheit, darin alle philosophische Wissenschaften in ihrer natürlichen Verknüpfung abgehandelt werden. Erster, Theoretischer Theil; Anderer, Practischer Theil.* 2 vols., Leipzig: Bernhard Christoph Breitkopfen, 1733–1744.

Hume, David. *Hume Selections.* Ed. Charles W. Hendel, Jr. New York: C. Scribner's Sons, 1955.

Jung-Stilling, Johann Heinrich. *Jung-Stillings Lebensgeschichte.* Ed. Karl Otto Conrady. Leck/Schleswig: Rowohlt, 1969.

Kant, Immanuel. *Frühschriften.* Ed. Georg Klaus. 2 vols. Berlin: Akademie-Verlag, 1961.

Kaestner, A. G. *Anfangsgründe der höheren Mechanik.* Göttingen: 1766.

Leibniz, Gottfried Wilhelm. *Philosophical Papers and Letters.* Ed. Leroy E. Loemker. 2 vols., Chicago: 1956.

— 'On Wisdom', in *Leibniz Selections.* Ed. Philip P. Wiener. New York: C. Scribner's Sons, 1951.

Lessing, Gotthold Ephraim. *Gesammelte Werke.* Ed. Paul Rilla. 10 vols. Berlin: Aufbau Verlag, 1954—1958.
All references will be made in the text according to volume and page number.

Lossius, Johann Christian. *Physische Ursachen der Wahrheit.* Gotha: 1755.

Luther, Martin. *Luther Deutsch: Die Werke Martin Luthers.* Ed. Kurt Aland. Stuttgart: Ehrenfried Klotz Verlag, 1961, Band III.

Meier, Georg Friedrich. *Vernunftlehre.* Halle: 1752.

Mendelssohn, Moses. *Gesammelte Schriften.* Ed. C. B. Mendelssohn. Leipzig, 1844.

— 'Morgenstunden, oder Vorlesungen über das Dasein Gottes' (1785), in *Schriften zur Philosophie, Aestetik und Apologetik.* Ed. Mortiz Brasch. Leipzig: 1880 (photographically reprinted Hildesheim: Georg Olms Verlag, 1968), Band I.

— 'Über die Evidenz in Metaphysischen Wissenschaften' (1763), in *Ibid.* Vol. 1.

Nicolai, Friedrich. *Das Leben und die Meinungen des Herrn Magister Nothanker* (1775). Ed. Fritz Brüggemann. Leipzig: Reclam Verlag, 1938.

Reimarus, Hermann Samuel. *Die Vernunftlehre, als eine Anweisung zum richtigen Gebrauche der Vernunft in dem Erkenntniß der Wahrheit aus zwoen ganz natürlichen Regeln der Einstimmung und der Widerspruches hergeleitet.* 5th ed. Hamburg/Kiel: Carl Ernst Bohn, 1781.

— *Abhandlungen von den vornehmsten Wahrheiten der natürlichen Religion.* 5th ed. Hamburg/Kiel. Carl Ernst Bohn, 1781.

Salat, J. *Auch die Aufklärung hat ihre Gefahren.* München: Joseph Lundauer, 1804.

Salzmann, J. D. *Kurze Abhandlungen über einige wichtige Gegenstände aus der Religions- und Sittenlehre.* Frankfurt/M.: 1776 (reprinted Stuttgart: J. B. Metzlersche Verlagsbuchhandlung, 1966).

Spinoza, Baruch. *Works of Spinoza.* Trans. R. H. M. Elwes. 2 vols. New York: Dover Publications, Inc., 1951.

Tetens, Johann Nicolas. *Philosophische Versuche über die menschliche Natur und ihre Entwicklung.* Leipzig: M. G. Weidmanns Erben & Reich, 1777, (reprinted in *Neudrucke seltener philosophischer Werke,* Ed. Kantgesellschaft. Berlin: Reuther & Reichard Verlag, 1913. Band IV).

Wolff, Christian. *Philosophia prima sive Ontologia: Methodo scientifica pertractata, qua omnis cognitionis humanae principia continentur.* Frankfurt/Leipzig: 1736 (reprinted Hildesheim: George Olms Verlag, 1962).

— *Preliminary Discourse on Philosophy in General* [1728]. Trans. Richard J. Blackwell. Indianapolis: Bobbs-Merrill, 1963.

— *Vernünftige Gedanken von Gott, der Welt und der Seele des Menschen, und allen Dingen überhaupt den Liebhabern der Wahrheit mitgetheilt.* Frankfort/Leipzig: 1729.

Das Zeitalter der Aufklärung. Ed. Wolfgang Philipp. Bremen: Carl Schönemann Verlag, 1963.

B. GENERAL SECONDARY SOURCES

Baeumler, Alfred. *Das Irrationalitätsproblem in der Ästhetik und Logik des 18. Jahrhunderts bis zur Kritik der Urteilskraft.* Darmstadt: Wissenschaftliche Buchgesellschaft, 1967.

Beck, Lewis White. *Early German Philosophy: Kant and His Predecessors.* Cambridge: Harvard University Press, 1969.

Bissinger, Anton. *Die Struktur der Gotteserkenntnis: Studien zur Philosophie Christian Wolffs.* Bonn: Bouvier & Co., 1970.

Blackwell, Richard J. 'Christian Wolff's Doctrine of the Soul', *Journal of the History of Ideas* 22 (1961), 339–354.

– 'The Structure of Wolffian Philosophy', *The Modern Schoolman*, 37 (1961), 203–218.

Brooks, Richard A. *Voltaire and Leibniz.* Geneva, Droz, 1964.

Burtt, E. A. *The Metaphysical Foundations of Modern Science.* Garden City: Doubleday, 1955.

Caird, Edward. *Essays on Literature and Philosophy.* 2 vols. New York: Macmillan & Co., 1892.

Cassirer, Ernst. *Das Erkenntnisproblem in der Philosophie und Wissenschaft der neueren Zeit.* Berlin: Verlag Bruno Cassirer, 1922. Band II.

– *The Philosophy of the Enlightenement.* Trans. Fritz C. A. Koelln and James P. Pettegrove. Boston: Beacon Press, 1951.

Cohn, Felix. 'What is a Question?', *The Mind*, 39 (1929), 350–364.

Collins, James. *God in Modern Philosophy.* Chicago: Henry Regnery Co., 1959.

Coplestone, S. J., Frederick *A History of Modern Philosophy.* Garden City: Image Books.

Vol. 4: *Modern Philosophy: Decartes to Leibniz* (1963).

Vol. 6: *Modern Philosophy,* Part One: *The French Enlightenment to Kant* (1964).

Coreth, Emerich. *Einführung in die Philosophie der Neuzeit.* Band I: *Rationalismus, Empirismus, Aufklärung.* Freiburg, Verlag Rombach, 1972.

Ebert Werner. *Die Morphologie des Luthertums.* 2 vols. München: C. H. Beck'sche Verlagsbuchhandlung, 1958.

Fischer, Kuno. *Geschichte.* Band II: *Leibniz und seine Schule.* 2nd ed. Heidelberg: Friedrich Bassermann, 1867.

Funke Gerhard. 'Einleitung', in: *Die Aufklärung in ausgewählten Texten dargestellt.* Stuttgart: K. F. Koehler Verlag, 1963. Pp. 1–92.

Gay, Peter. *The Enlightenment: An Interpretation.* Vol. II: *The Science of Freedom.* New York. Alfred A. Knopf, 1969.

Gilson, Etienne. *Being and Some Philosophers.* 2nd ed. Toronto: Europe Printing, 1952.

– *The Spirit of Medieval Philosophy.* New York: C. Scribner's Sons, 1940.

– *The Unity of Philosophical Experience.* New York: C. Scribner's Sons, 1937.

Hawthorne, Charles, and William L. Reese. 'Introduction', in *Philosophers Speak of God*. Chicago/London: The University of Chicago Press, 1963. Pp. 1–25.

Hazard, Paul. *European Thought in the Eighteenth Century*. Trans. J. Lewis May. Middlesex: Penguin Books, 1954. (Originally published in 1946.)

Heidegger, Martin. *What is a Thing?* Trans. W. B. Barton, Jr., and Vera Deutsch. Chicago: Henry Regnery Co., 1967.

Heimsoeth, Heinz. *Metaphysik der Neuzeit*. München: R. Oldenbourg, 1967.

– *Metaphysik und Kritik bei Chr. A. Crusius: Ein Beitrag zur ontologischen Vorgeschichte der Kritik der reinen Vernunft im 18. Jahrhundert*. Berlin: Deutsche Verlagsgesellschaft für Politik und Geschichte, 1926.

Heiss, Robert. *Der Gang des Geistes: Eine Geschichte des neuzeitlichen Denkens*. Bern/München: Francke Verlag, 1959.

Hick, John. *Evil and the God of Love*. New York: Harper & Row, 1966.

Hirsch, Emanuel. *Geschichte der neuern evangelischen Theologie im Zusammenhang mit den allgemeinen Bewegungen des europäischen Denkens*. Gütersloh: Carl Bertelsmann Verlag, 1952, Band IV.

Hulme, T. E. 'Humanism and the Religious Attitude', in *Speculations*. Ed. Herbert Read. New York: Harcourt, Brace & Co., n.d. Pp. 64–71. (First published in 1924.)

Katzenbach, Friedrich Wilhelm. *Protestantisches Christentum im Zeitalter der Aufklärung*. Gütersloh: Gerd Mohn, 1965.

Kremer, Joseph. *Das Problem der Theodicee in der Philosophie und Literatur des 18. Jahrhunderts mit besonderer Rücksicht auf Kant und Schiller*. Berlin: 1909.

Kronenberg, M. *Geschichte des Deutschen Idealismus*. München: C. H. Beck'sche Verlagsbuchhandlung, 1909. Band I.

Kuhn, Thomas. *The Structure of Scientific Revolutions*. 2nd ed. Chicago: University of Chicago Press, 1970.

Langer, Susan. *Philosophy in a New Key: A Study in the Symbolism of Reason, Rite, and Art*. New York: Mentor Books, 1961.

Lemp, Otto. *Das Problem der Theodicee in der Philosophie und Literatur des 18. Jahrhundert bis auf Kant und Schiller*. Leipzig: 1910.

Lovejoy, Arthur O. *Essays in the History of Ideas*. New York: G. P. Putnam's, Sons, 1960, p. 80.

– *The Great Chain of Being: A Study of the History of an Idea*. New York: Harper & Row, 1960.

Lüthje, Hans. 'Christian Wolff's Philosophiebegriff', *Kant Studien*, 30 (1925), 39–66.

Luijpen, W. A. M. *Existential Phenomenology*. Pittsburgh: Duquesne University Press, 1965.

Martens, Wolfgang. *Die Botschaft der Tugend: Die Aufklärung im Spiegel der deutschen moralischen Wochenschriften*. Stuttgart: J. B. Metzlersche Verlagsbuchhandlung, 1971.

Pepper, Stephen C. *World Hypotheses: A Study in Evidence*. Berkeley/Los Angeles: University of California Press, 1961.

Pferderer, Otto. *Geschichte der Religionsphilosophie von Spinoza bis auf die Gegenwart*. 3rd ed. Berlin: Georg Riemer, 1893.

Philipp, Wolfgang. 'Einleitung', in: *Das Zeitalter der Aufklärung*. Ed. W. Philipp. Bremen: Carl Schönemann, 1963. Pp. XIII–CIV.

Prosch, Harry. *The Genesis of Twentieth-Century Philosophy: The Evolution of Thought from Copernicus to the Present*. Garden City: Anchor Books, 1966.

Randall, Jr. John Herman. *The Career of Philosophy*. 2 vols. New York/London: Columbia University Press, 1970.

Reichmann, Eberhard. *Die Herrschaft den Zahl: Quantitatives Denken in der deutschen Aufklärung*. Stuttgart: J. B. Metzlersche Verlagsbuchhandlung, 1968.

Röd, Wolfgang. *Descartes: Die innere Genesis des cartesianischen Systems*. München/Basel: Ernst Reinhardt Verlag, 1964.

Sentilliana, Giorgio de, and Edgar Zilsel. *The Development of Rationalism and Empiricism*. Chicago/London: University of Chicago Press, 1970.

Scholder, Klaus. 'Grundzüge der theologischen Aufklärung in Deutschland', in: *Evangelischer Glaube im Wandel der Zeit*. Ed. Theodor Braun. Stuttgart: J. F. Steinkopf Verlag, 1967, Pp. 68–100.

Scholz, Heinrich, D. 'Einleitung', in: *Die Hauptschriften zum Pantheismusstreit zwischen Jacobi und Mendelssohn*. Berlin: Reuther & Reinhard Verlag.

Smith, Norman Kemp. *New Studies in the Philosophy of Descartes*. London/New York: Russell & Russell, 1952.

Sorokin, Pitirim A. *Social and Cultural Dynamics. Vol. I: Fluctuations of Forms of Art*. New York: The Bedminster Press, 1962.

Straubinger, Heinrich. *Die Religion und ihre Grundwahrheiten in der deutschen Philosophie seit Leibniz*. Freiburg im Breisgau: Herder'sche Verlagsbuchhandlung, 1919.

Thielicke, Helmut. *Der evangelische Glaube: Grundzüge der Dogmatik*. Band I: *Prolegomena. Die Beziehung der Theologie zu den Denkformen der Neuzeit*. Tübingen: J. C. B. Mohr, 1968.

Tonelli, Giorgio. 'Der Streit über die mathematische Methode in der Philosophie in der ersten Hälfte des 18. Jahrhunderts und die Entstehung von Kants Schrift über die "Deutlichkeit" ', *Archiv für Philosophie*, 9 (1959), 37–66.

Toulmin, Stephen and June Goodfield. *The Discovery of Time*. New York: Harper & Row, 1966.

Tuveson, Ernest Lee. *Millenium and Utopia: A Study in the Background of the Idea of Progress*. New York: Harper & Row, 1944.

Unger, Rudolf. *Hamann und die Aufklärung*. 2nd ed., Halle/Saale: Max Niemeyer Verlag, 1925.

Whitehead, Alfred North. *Science and the Modern World*. New York: Mentor Books, 1960.

Wilhelmsen, Frederick D. *Man's Knowledge of Reality: An Introduction to Thomistic Epistemology*. Englewood Cliffs: Prentice-Hall, Inc., 1958.

Willey, Basil. *The Eighteenth-Century Background: Studies on the Idea of Nature in the Thought of the Period*. Boston: Beacon Press, 1961.

Wolff, Hans, *Die Weltanschauung der deutschen Aufklärung in geschichtlicher Entwicklung*. Bern: A. Francke Verlag, 1949.

Wundt, Max. *Die deutsche Schulphilosophie im Zeitalter der Aufklärung*. 1945 (reprinted Hildesheim: Georg Olms Verlag, 1964).

Zeeden, Ernst Walter. *The Legacy of Luther: Martin Luther and the Reformation in the Estimation of the German Lutherans from Luther's Death to the Beginning of the Age of Goethe.* Trans. Ruth Mary Bethell. Westminister: Newman Press, 1954.

Zeller, Eduard. *Geschichte der deutschen Philosophie seit Leibniz.* München: R. Oldenbourg, 1873.

C. SECONDARY SOURCES ON LESSING

Allison, Henry. *Lessing and the Enlightenment: His Philosophy of Religion and Its Relation to Eighteenth-Century Thought.* Ann Arbor: University of Michigan Press, 1966.

Altmann, Alexander. 'Lessing und Jacobi: Das Gespräch über den Spinozismus', *Lessing Yearbook III* (1971), Pp. 25—71.

Aner, Karl. *Die Theologie der Lessingzeit.* Halle/Saale: Max Niemeyer Verlag, 1929.

Angress, Ruth K. ' "Dreams that were more than dreams" in Lessing's *Nathan*', *Lessings Yearbook III* (1971), pp. 108—127.

Arx, Arthur von. *Lessing und die geschichtliche Welt.* Frauenfeld/Leipzig: Hubert & Co., 1944.

Atkins, Stuart. 'The Parable of the Rings in Lessing's *Nathan der Weise*', *Germanic Review*, 26 (1951), 259—267.

Balthasar, Hans Urs von. *Prometheus. Studien zur Geschichte des deutschen Idealismus.* Heidelberg: F. H. Kerle Verlag, 1947. Pp. 45—52.

Barth, Karl. 'Lessing', in: *Protestant Thought from Rousseau to Ritschl.* Trans. H. H. Hartwell. New York: Harper & Row, 1959. Pp. 118—149. (Originally: Lectures, given in 1932—1933.)

Baumgarten, S. J. Alexander. *Lessing's religiöser Entwicklungsgang.* Freiburg im Breisgau: Herder'sche Verlagsbuchhandlung, 1879.

Berger, Arnold E. *Lessings geistesgeschichtliche Stellung.* Darmstadt/Leipzig: Hofmann & Co., 1929.

Böhler, Michael J. 'Lessings *Nathan der Weise* als Spiel vom Grunde', *Lessing Yearbook III* (1971), 128—150.

Brown, F. Andrew. *Gotthold Ephraim Lessing.* New York: Twayne Publishers, Inc., 1971.

Brüggemann, Fritz. 'Lessings Bürgerdramen und der Subjektivismus als Problem', *Jahrbuch des Freien Deutschen Hochstifts* (1936), 69—110.

Campbell, Richard. 'Lessing's Problem and Kierkegaarde's Answer', *Scottish Journal of Theology*, 19 (1966), 35—54.

Chadwick, Henry. 'Introduction' in: *Lessing's Theological Writings.* Stanford: Stanford University Press, 1957. Pp. 9—49.

Colleville, Maurice. 'L'évolution religieuse de Lessing', *Études Germaniques* 19 (1964), 9—22.

Durzak, Manfred. 'Vernunft und Offenbarung im Denken Lessings' in: *Poesie und Ratio: Vier Lessing Studien.* Bad Homburg: Athenäum Verlag, 1970. Pp. 105—139.

Eichholz, Georg. *Die Geschichte als theologisches Problem bei Lessing.* Bonn: n. publ., 1933.

Fittbogen, Gottfried. 'Die Grundlagen von Lessings Religion', *Preußische Jahrbücher*, 170 (1917), 329—344.

Fittbogen, Gottfried. *Die Religion Lessings*. Leipzig: Mayer & Müller, 1923.

Flajole, S. J., Edward S. 'Lessings Attitude in the Lavater — Mendelssohn Controversy', *P.M.L.A.*, 73 (1958), 201—213.

— 'Lessing's Retrieval of Lost Truths', *P.M.L.A.*, 74 (1959), 52—66.

Guthke, Karl S. *Der Stand der Lessing Forschung: Ein Bericht über die Literatur von 1932—1967.* Stuttgart: J. B. Metzlersche Verlagsbuchhandlung, 1965.

Haug, Martin. *Entwicklung und Offenbarung bei Lessing.* Gütersloh: Bertelsmann Verlag, 1928.

Heller, Peter. *Dialectics and Nihilism: Essays on Lessing, Nietzsche, Mann, and Kafka.* Amherst: University of Massachusettes Press, 1966. Pp. 3—68.

Hermann, Hans. *Der Gegenwärtigkeitsgedanke in der theoretischen Behandlung des dramatischen Kunstwerkes bei Lessing, A. W. Schlegel, und Hegel.* Breslau: Verlag Priebatsch's Buchhandlung, 1934. Pp. 1—27.

Hermann, Rudolf. 'Zu Lessings religionsphilosophischer und theologischer Problematik', *Zeitschrift für systematische Theologie*, 22 (1953), 127—148.

Jolles, Mattijs. 'Lessing's Conception of History', *Modern Philology*, 43 (1946), 175—191.

Kesten, Hermann. 'Lessing, ein deutscher Moralist', in *Gottfried Ephraim Lessing: Werke*. Köln/Berlin: Kiepenheuer & Witsch, n.d., Band II, pp. 873—891.

Koch, Franz. 'Lessing und der Irrationalismus,' *Deutsche Vierteljahrschrift für Literaturwissenschaft und Geistesgeschichte*, 6 (1928), 114—143.

Kretzschmar, Ernst. *Lessing und die Aufklärung.* Leipzig: Bernhard Richter's Buchhandlung, 1905.

Leisegang, Hans. *Lessings Weltanschauung.* Leipzig: Felix Meiner Verlag, 1931.

Lessing Yearbook. Ed. Jerry Glenn, American Lessing Society, University of Cincinnati, Cincinnati, Ohio. München: Max Hueber Verlag, 1969—1974.

Loofs, Friedrich. 'Lessings Stellung zum Christentum', *Theologische Studien und Kritiken* (1913), 31—64.

Mann, Otto. *Lessing: Sein und Leistung.* Hamburg: Marion von Schröder Verlag, 1948; 2nd ed. Berlin: Walther de Gruyter & Co., 1961.

Moor, Leonard de. 'The Problem of Revelation in Eighteenth-Century Germany: With Particular Reference to Lessing', *Evangelical Quarterly*, 39 (1967), 66—74, 139—151, 205—215.

Oelmüller, Willi. *Die unbefriedigte Aufklärung: Beiträge zu einer Theorie der Moderne von Lessing, Kant und Hegel.* Frankfurt/M.: Suhrkamp Verlag, 1969.

Pelters, Wilm. *Lessings Standort: Sinndeutung der Geschichte als Kern seines Denkens.* Heidelberg: Lothar Stiehm Verlag, 1972.

Plavius, Heinz. 'Revision des Humanismus: Die Wandlungen im Lessing-Bild der westdeutschen Reaktion', *Neue Deutsche Literatur*, 12 (1964), 98.

Pons, Georges. *Gotthold Ephraim Lessing et le Christianisme.* Paris: Marcel Didier, 1964.

Rade, Martin. 'Lessing als Theolog', *Jahrbuch des Freien Deutschen Hochstifts (Frankfurt/M)*, (1906), 3—19.

Ritzel, Wolfgang. *Gotthold Ephraim Lessings.* Stuttgart: W. Kohlhammer Verlag, 1966.

Ritzel, Wolfgang. 'Lessings Denkformen', *Kant Studien,* 57 (1966), 155—166.

Rohrmoser, Günther. 'Lessing und die religionsphilosophische Fragestellung der Aufklärung', in: *Lessing und die Zeit der Aufklärung.* Göttingen: Die Jungius-Gesellschaft der Wissenschaften/Vandenhoeck & Ruprecht, 1968.

Rudowski, Victor Anthony. *Lessing's Aesthetica in N.U.C.E.: An Analysis of the May 26, 1769 Letter to Nicolae.* Chapel Hill: University of North Carolina Press, 1971.

Schmid, Karl. 'Lessings Religiosität', in: *Zeitspuren: Aufsätze und Reden.* Zürich/Stuttgart: Artemis Verlag, 1967. Pp. 132—154.

Schmitz, Friedrich Joseph. *Lessings Stellung in der Entfaltung des Individualismus.* Berkeley: University of California Press (Series 'Modern Philology', Nr. 23), 1941.

— *The Problem of Individualism and the Crisis in the Lives of Lessing and Hamann.* Berkeley, University of California Press Series 'Modern Philology', n. 27), 1944. Pp. 125—148.

Schneider, Ferdinand Josef. *Lessing und die monistische Weltanschauung.* Halle/Saale: Max Niemeyer Verlag, 1929.

Schneider, Heinrich. *Lessing: Zwölf biographische Studien.* Bern: A. Francke Verlag, 1951.

Schneider, J. *Lessings Stellung zur Theologie vor der Herausgabe der Wolfenbüttler Fragmente.* Diss. Amsterdam, 1953. 's-Gravenhage: Excelsior, n.d.

Scholz, Heinrich. 'Einleitung', in: *Die Hauptschriften zum Pantheismusstreit zwischen Jacobi und Mendelssohn.* Berlin: Reuther & Reichard Verlag, 1916. Pp. XI-LXXV.

Schrempf, Christof. *Lessing als Philosoph.* Stuttgart: Chr. Belserische Buchdruckerei, 1921. Pp. 157—158.

Schultz, Harold. *Lessings Toleranzbegriff: Eine theologische Studie.* Göttingen: Vandenhoeck & Ruprecht, 1969.

Stamm, Israel. 'Lessing and Religion', *Germanic Review,* 43 (1968), 239—257.

Strohschneider-Kohrs, Ingrid. *Vom Prinzip des Maßes in Lessings Kritik.* Stuttgart: J. B. Metzlersche Verlagsbuchhandlung, 1969.

Traub, Friedrich. 'Geschichtswahrheiten und Vernunftwahrheiten bei Lessing', *Zeitschrift für Theologie und Kirche,* 28 (1921), 193—207.

Thielicke, Helmut. *Offenbarung, Vernunft und Existenz: Studien zur Religionsphilosophie Lessings.* 3rd ed. Gütersloh: Carl Bertelmann Verlag, 1957.

— 'Vernunft und Existenz bei Lessing: Das Unbedingte in der Geschichte' in *Lessing und die Zeit der Aufklärung.* Göttingen: Die Jungius-Gesellschaft der Wissenschaften/Vandenhoeck & Ruprecht, 1968. Pp. 100—115.

Waller, Martha. *Lessings Erziehung des Menschengeschlechts: Interpretationen und Darstellung ihres rationalen und irrationalen Gehaltes. Eine Auseinandersetzung mit der Lessingforschung.* Berlin: Verlag Dr. Emil Ebering, 1935.

Wessell, Jr., Leonard Paul. 'Geist and Buchstabe as Creative Principles in Lessing's Dramaturgy', *Lessing Yearbook V* (1973), 107—146.

— 'Lessing's Eschatology and the Death of God', *Lessing Yearbook VI* (1974), 59—82.

– 'The Problem of Lessing's Theology: A Prolegomenon to a New Approach', *Lessing Yearbook IV* (1972), 94–121.

Wiese, Benno von. *Lessing: Dichtung, Ästhetik, Philosophie.* Leipzig: Verlag Quelle & Mayer, 1931.

Wölfel, Kurt. 'Einleitung', in: *Lessings Werke.* Ed. Kurt Wölfel. Frankfurt/M., Insel Verlag, 1967. Band II.

Zscharnack, Leopold. 'Einleitung des Herausgebers', in *Lessings Werke.* General eds. Julius Petersen and Waldemar Ohshausen. Berlin/Leipzig: Deutsches Verlagshaus Bong Co., 1925–1935. Band XX, Pp. 9–96.

Index of selected authors